WHAT'S LEFT NOW?

'The future of social democracy depends on better understanding its past. Andy Hindmoor provides a clear-headed rather than optimistic assessment, backed by convincing evidence and careful analysis. His commentary will help a great deal in the process of rediscovering what is the social democratic project and how it could be delivered.'

Gerry Stoker, University of Southampton and University of Canberra

'The Left prides itself on its intellectual optimism but Andrew Hindmoor shows convincingly that the opposite is the case. This important book isolates the tendency of the political Left to regard its own nation with pessimism.'

Phil Collins, *The Times*

WHAT'S LEFT NOW?

THE HISTORY AND FUTURE OF SOCIAL DEMOCRACY

ANDREW HINDMOOR

OXFORD
UNIVERSITY PRESS

OXFORD
UNIVERSITY PRESS

Great Clarendon Street, Oxford, OX2 6DP,
United Kingdom

Oxford University Press is a department of the University of Oxford.
It furthers the University's objective of excellence in research, scholarship,
and education by publishing worldwide. Oxford is a registered trade mark of
Oxford University Press in the UK and in certain other countries

First edition published in 2018

Impression: 1

Published in the United States of America by Oxford University Press
198 Madison Avenue, New York, NY 10016, United States of America

British Library Cataloguing in Publication Data
Data available

Library of Congress Control Number: 2017939217

ISBN 978–0–19–880599–1

Printed in Great Britain by
Clays Ltd, St Ives plc

Jane, Jordan, and Asha

Preface

I remember first writing the outline of this book in 2013. At the time, I was convinced it would take about a year to write. I hope there are no other mistakes as egregious as that in what follows. As it has worked out, it has taken me three years to finish as I have struggled to incorporate new bits of academic research; new data; and, above all, an onslaught of unexpected circumstances: most notably the rise, near-fall, and (at the time of writing) rise again of Jeremy Corbyn; the rise, fall, and disappearance of David Cameron and large swathes of the government he appointed in 2015; and, above all, the results of the EU referendum and the 2017 general election.

Along the way, I have discussed my ideas and argued my case with several friends and colleagues: many of whom have taken the time to comment on draft chapters. So, my sincere thanks go to Steve and Jo Bell, David Blunkett, Jim Colvin, Matthew Cotton, Kate Dommett, Tim Dunne, Mihaela Gruia, Iain Hampsher-Monk (whose pointed 'do you really think that?' on a long car journey back from Scotland served as a constant reminder that many people whose judgment I trust don't think that), John Hobson, Tom Hunt, Mike Kenny, Luciana O'Flaherty, Perri 6, Gerry Stoker, Liam Stanley, Shashi van de Graaf, and Keith Zimmerman.

Along the way, I have uploaded data sets, short essays on some of the big issues I touch upon in the chapters but do not pursue in enough detail, a few readings, references, and other bits and pieces connected to the book on a dedicated website. This can be accessed via: http://www.sheffield.ac.uk/politics/people/academic/andrew-hindmoor/whatsleftnow

Contents

List of Illustrations

I

Introduction

I

At 9.59 pm on the 8 June almost everyone expected the Conservatives to have comfortably won that day's general election. Most polls indicated that the Conservatives had a six to eight-point lead over Labour: enough for a majority of anything up to a hundred seats. At 10pm when the polling stations closed and the exit poll results were revealed, it became clear that the world was a very different place. Theresa May, whose public pronouncements during the election had been so stilted they would probably have failed the Turing test for artificial intelligence, had done disastrously and Jeremy Corbyn had performed far better than anyone had expected.

For those on the left there was a sudden rush of joy. The Labour Party had not been crushed and in Jeremy Corbyn it had found a new hero. But, over the next few hours and days, joy gave way to a sense of despair and anger. The Conservatives had not only scraped over the line but were set to join forces with the Democratic Unionists. Austerity, growing inequality, welfare cuts, and Brexit were still going to happen. The NHS was still going to be privatized and dismantled. A week later, the horrific Grenfell Tower fire, in which at least eighty people died, further demonstrated, in many people's minds, the social costs of spending cuts, deregulation, and inequality.[1]

What made things worse was the sense of *déjà vu*. 2017 was so painful for many on the left because it was one more nail in the coffin: one more confirmation that, over ten, twenty, thirty years or more Britain has changed and changed for the worse. Margaret Thatcher in the 1980s; the 'Prince of Greyness' John Major in the 1990s; America's Poodle, aka Teflon Tony, for far too long in the 2000s; Dodgy Dave, Calamity Clegg, and never-ending austerity; all washed down with Nigel Farage, and the imploding 'strong and stable' leadership of Theresa May and Brexit.

II

Our sense of history shapes how we think about who we are.[2] One of the distinguishing features of the left in Britain is that it holds to a remorselessly bleak and miserabilist view of our recent political history—one in which Margaret Thatcher's election in 1979 marked the start of a still-continuing fall from political grace made evident by the triumph of a free market get-what-you-can neoliberal ideology, dizzying levels of inequality, social decay, rampant individualism, state authoritarianism, and political corruption. The left does not like what has happened to us and it does not like what we have become.

I am going to argue that this history is wrong and self-harming. It is wrong because Britain has in many (although certainly not all) respects become a more politically attractive and—much as I cringe whenever I hear this term—progressive country over the last few decades. It is self-harming because this bleak history undermines faith in politics. I offer an alternative and more optimistic and balanced history of modern Britain. Britain is not a social democratic paradise. But it is a long way from being a poster child for neoliberalism. Left-wing ideas and arguments have shaped and continue to shape our politics. To answer the question that I pose in the title of the book, there is still plenty left now. Over the last year or so, my optimism has been tested by Iceland's footballers, Brexit, the backlash against immigration, the foreign policy failure and humanitarian disaster that is Syria, and, perhaps above all, by President Donald Trump. But if these events present huge challenges for the left, they also serve as a stark reminder of the limits of the reach of neoliberalism. Neoliberals support greater European economic integration and a free market in the movement of labour and view Trump's commitment to greater infrastructure spending and apparent indifference to the size of the budget deficit with horror.

What do I mean by neoliberalism? The essence of the neoliberal philosophy is perhaps best captured in Ronald Reagan's quip—during his Inaugural Address as President in January 1981—that 'government is not the solution to our problem; government is the problem'.[3] Neoliberals are 'market fundamentalists' or, alternatively, 'market imperialists' who believe the public is best served when competitive markets are rolled forward and the state and democratic and collective decision-making is rolled back.[4] I will say a great deal more about the nature and history of neoliberalism at the start of the next chapter. Before then, I will say something about 'the left' and about the term 'progressive' in this chapter and then, later, about the extent to which arguments between the left and right have been eclipsed by a now more salient cleavage between liberals who support globalization and welcome immigration, and authoritarians who worry about national sovereignty and see globalization as more trouble than it is worth. But, before all that, I want to introduce some of the other arguments I am going to develop. When the left looks back at the 1960s and 1970s—the age Before Thatcher—it does so with an unjustified degree of nostalgia. The Britain I grew up in was one of ingrained inequalities, shoddy public services, entrenched racism, and casual sexism. Britain is not a neoliberal country in which the frontiers of the state have been rolled back. Many industries have been privatized and some new markets have been created. But we are a long way from being a laissez-faire economy, let alone a laissez-faire society. Britain has not become a mini-me version of the USA. New Labour ended badly. But it is cutting history horribly short to reduce Blair's legacy to imbecilic wars and the 2008 financial crisis.

Britain has not become an atomized 'society of strangers' consumed by self-interest and mutual indifference.[5] We have become a more individualistic society. But we have not become an obviously more selfish one. Public opinion has not become markedly more right-wing. Attitudes toward public expenditure, inequality, and government have ebbed and flowed but, looked at over the long haul, they have pretty much ended up where they started thirty or more years ago. We now spend far more money (both in absolute terms and as a share of GDP) on health, education, and welfare than we did in the halcyon days of the post-war consensus. There was a 40 per cent increase in real (that is inflation-adjusted) public expenditure during the 2000s. In 2010, the Coalition pledged itself to cutting public expenditure and shrinking the deficit. In fact, real public expenditure rose slightly between 2009/10 and 2016/17. The NHS has not been privatized by stealth. In 2015/16, around 7.5 per cent of the NHS England budget was spent on private contractors or charities (up from around 4.4 per cent in 2009/10 and 6 per cent in 2014/15).[6] Meanwhile, the number of people opting out of the public sector and paying for a private education or private health care has fallen.

Britain is a markedly unequal country. But over the last few decades, inequality has moved in different directions. Judged in terms of wealth and the income of the richest 1 per cent, inequality has increased. But judged in terms of the ratio of the market income (before taxes and government spending and transfers) of the richest 10 per cent of households compared with that of the poorest 10 per cent of households, inequality is now 22 per cent *lower* than it was in 1979 and 45 per cent *lower* than it was in 1999. Britain is still a country in which there is a considerable redistribution of income. The final income of the poorest 10 per cent of households (after taxes and government spending and transfers) is three times greater than their market income. Redistribution reduces the income inequality between the richest and poorest 10 per cent of households by around 75 per cent. The recession which was triggered by the 2008 financial crisis was severe but its costs have not been loaded disproportionately on to the poorest households. By 2015/16, the real (inflation-adjusted) income of the poorest 5 per cent of households was 110 per cent of the level it had been in 2007/8. The real income of the richest 5 per cent of households, on the other hand, was the same as it had been in 2007/8. Our democratic system is flawed but it is not broken. Voting makes a difference. Political parties are not all the same. They make different promises and, by and large, they keep those promises. Government is responsive to changes in public opinion and, when it is not, the party in government tends to lose. Big business does not get to decide what really happens in the country (if it did, we would not be poised on the edge of Brexit and a new runway would have been built at Heathrow a few decades ago). Very few politicians are corrupt. *The Thick of It* is not a documentary.

The left in general and the Labour Party in particular has taken some real hits over the years. The Conservatives have, at the time of writing, emerged as the largest party in seven of the last ten general elections. The unions have been largely destroyed as an effective political force. Large swathes of once nationalized and publicly owned industries have been privatized. The New Labour brand has been discredited. Keynesian economics has been publicly repudiated in favour of belt-and-braces austerity economics. But the left has not been left behind. There are more than enough good news stories to discredit the miserabilist history of Britain.

In a collection of short essays and reminiscences, *From the Diary of a Snail*, the novelist Günter Grass documents Willy Brandt's 1969 campaign to become Chancellor of Germany as leader of the Social Democratic Party.[7] In describing Brandt's faith in social democrat reformism over revolutionary politics, Grass invokes the image of a snail's slow progress. The snail, he writes, 'seldom wins and then by the skin of its teeth. It crawls, it goes into hiding but keeps on, putting down its quickly drying track on the historical landscape.' The snail's slow doggedness is unheroic but it makes a difference. The left's progress in Britain has been snail-like. Yes, there have been plenty of setbacks and long periods in which left-wing ideas appear to have been marginalized. But there have also been some notable victories and, looked at over the long haul, the track of left-wing ideas is nevertheless not only visible but impressive.

One obvious problem with challenging the left's miserabilist history is that you risk appearing to be, at best, stupidly naive and, at worst, a Conservative apologist. So, just for the record, I'm not a Tory and I don't think everything is just fine and dandy in Britain today. Indeed, at various points in what follows I pause to lament the policy failures which have resulted in an acute and accelerating housing crisis; an increasingly regressive tax system; high levels of corporate tax avoidance; stagnating business investment and truly awful levels of productivity; a bloated, fragile, and often socially parasitic banking sector; and low wages. Many things can and should be changed in Britain. And there are a lot of things I would change in our political system. But I don't think it is reasonable to believe that everything which could have gone wrong over the last few decades has gone wrong. That is my argument.

III

So, who believes in the history of Britain I am challenging? Well, at the very least, I did. I grew up in the 1980s in a union-belonging and Labour-voting family in a city, Sheffield, which regarded the result of the 1979 election as a declaration of war upon the North. Without really thinking about it, I listened to Billy Bragg and read *The Road to Wigan Pier* when I was a teenager. I instinctively felt Margaret Thatcher was more than a little mad and that the closure of the steel mills in Sheffield and the pits in the towns surrounding it was unnecessary and vindictive. And from what I can remember, everyone else at my school and on the telly seemed to think the same thing. There was a strong sense that anyone who cared about the world around them and had a sense of social justice and wanted to be a basically decent human being ought not to be voting Conservative. Having turned 18 in 1987, I voted Labour in that year's election and when Labour lost, I felt an ever-so-prim sense of disappointment at the rest of the country. What were people thinking? Was everyone really that selfish? Who were these people voting Conservative? How could anyone think Margaret Thatcher was preferable to Neil Kinnock and why-oh-why did people believe what *The Sun* told them to believe?

By 1990, I was studying politics at university and when Margaret Thatcher was toppled, I remember the lecturer walking in to the classroom and dancing with glee—safe in the knowledge that we, a bunch of long-haired lefties, would join in. For a while, it looked like the Conservatives were finished; that Thatcherism would be undone; and everything would be OK after all. So, when Neil Kinnock somehow conspired to pull defeat from the jaws of victory in 1992 (and a political rally in Sheffield somehow ended up being blamed for what had happened), many people concluded that Britain had become a one-party state and that Labour would never win again. Many concluded that politics was pointless and stopped caring.[8]

By 1993, I was a postgraduate student at the London School of Economics. One of my tutors, the late Brian Barry, an eminent political philosopher, used to regularly fulminate against social injustice and the idiocies of Conservative ministers. In one of his final and most powerful books, *Why Social Justice Matters*, he vented his intense irritation at the world in which he had found himself. 'To the best of my ability, I have aimed to reinforce the convictions of those who think things are bad and getting worse.'[9] These words were written in 2005 but they capture what Brian and the rest of the left were already thinking in the early 1990s: that the long social democratic boom was over; that neoliberalism was in the ascendant; and that the post-war consensus was gone for good. But, suddenly, and for a short while at least, things began to look up. Having won the 1992 election, the Conservatives fell apart over the issue of Europe. Tony Blair became leader of the Labour Party and the electoral landscape started to change. By 1997, I had my first proper job (at least sort of a proper job) as a lecturer at the University of Exeter and was canvassing door-to-door for Ben Bradshaw, the Labour candidate. And long before polling day it was clear that the Tories were doomed.

New Labour's campaign song was by D-Ream: *Things Can Only Get Better* (with a young Professor Brian Cox playing keyboards on live performances). At the time, it seemed to fit. There was a strong sense that New Labour was offering a fresh start and the prospect of better things to come. But the fear of betrayal runs deep within the left and more than a few Labour Party members were, right from the start, convinced that New Labour was basically neoliberalism with a better marketing strategy; that Tony Blair was, deep down, a Tory; and that the things which were meant to get better probably weren't going to change. Within a few years, cynicism about New Labour had become a commonplace. Benefit cuts for lone parents, dodgy-looking deals with Formula One tycoons, and yet more attacks on the trade union movement began to look like a high price to pay for one night of electoral euphoria. And then in the second term there was Iraq and the alliance with George 'Dubya' Bush. Britain, it seemed, had devolved its foreign-policy and political judgement to Washington and the left held its collective head in its hands.

At this point, I moved to Australia and for a while lost interest in British politics. Filling in the gaps, the next part of the story goes like this. After scraping home in an election in 2005 which was most noteworthy for the fact that so few people voted in it, New Labour's bubble finally burst in 2008 when the banks New Labour had assiduously courted and deregulated went bust and had to be bailed out. And then things got really bad. Having previously presented a not-at-all-nasty new face to the world, the Conservatives, with just 36 per cent of the popular vote, reverted to type and used the recession as a pretext to slash-and-burn the public sector and demonize anyone claiming welfare benefits. Having somehow co-opted the hapless Liberal Democrats to their Coalition cause, the Conservatives returned to power.

In 2013, I moved back home to work at the University of Sheffield. Politics was not pretty. Russell Brand told Jeremy Paxman of the 'absolute indifference and weariness and exhaustion' he felt when listening to the 'lies, treachery and deceit of the political class' who were 'destroying the planet', creating 'massive economic disparity', and 'ignoring the needs of the people'.[10] Not voting and saying (repeatedly) that you were not going to vote became quite fashionable. And then there was the 2015 election, which proved, if nothing else, that virtue-signalling on Twitter and Facebook and signing on-line petitions about spending cuts is not in itself enough to win an election.

At this moment, I expected many people on the left would, once again, and as had happened in 1992, just give in and walk away. But I was completely wrong. Jeremy Corbyn managed to get enough nominations to stand as leader and secured nearly 60 per cent of the vote (a massive 40 percentage points more than his nearest rival). Having endured an overwhelming vote of no confidence from the Parliamentary Labour Party, Corbyn was then re-elected in September 2016 with almost the same share of the vote. Corbynism is, in some respects, soaked in political optimism. Corbynites believe that, if only they can win the next general election, the country can be transformed. More than that, Corbyn's supporters believe there are obvious and quite simple solutions to some apparently profound policy problems facing the country. At the same time, Corbynism is a textbook example of miserabilism. Corbynites are Corbynites because they think that almost everything that has happened since Margaret Thatcher arrived in Downing Street in 1979 has been a disaster and that, under New Labour, things, far from getting better, predictably got a lot worse.

In this respect, the EU referendum result showed that large swathes of the country are at one with the Corbynites. The referendum was not simply about the merits of European integration or even about immigration. It was a referendum about the state of the country and the track record of its political establishment and, understood in this way, the result was, as David Cameron himself argued in a speech he gave to American college students in late 2016, a mass demonstration of miserabilism.[11] There is, in this regard, a neat anecdote in Nick Clegg's anguished political reflections about the state of public opinion in Britain today. Following UKIP's near-triumph in a 2013 by-election, the Liberal Democrats convened a focus group with a dozen voters who had previously voted for them but had switched to UKIP. When asked for their views, the members of the focus group expressed their unease with various aspects of life in modern Britain: ranging from TV programmes to aggressive drivers and loud music in supermarkets.

> Towards the end of the session one of the somewhat exasperated Lib Dem researchers asked the group: 'Can anyone perhaps tell me of one thing they actually like in modern Britain?' A long silence ensued. And then a man raised his hand and said: 'Yes, I know. The past.'[12]

This miserabilism is, I want to suggest, misplaced.

IV

Having introduced some of my basic arguments, it is time for a brief statement of some terms and conditions.

Let's start with an obvious question. What do I mean when I talk about the left? What does it mean to say that left-wing ideas and arguments have shaped and continue to shape our politics? The left might, most obviously, be defined in terms of its beliefs: what it is against and what it is for. The left is against a lot of things. Anti-Conservative—obviously. But also, anti-New Labour; anti-austerity; anti-neoliberal; anti-globalization; anti-corporations; anti-consumerism; anti-privatization; anti-imperialism; and, at times, anti-capitalism. What is the left in favour of? To be on the left is to be politically progressive: a term the *Guardian*'s political columnist Polly Toynbee defines as involving a presumption in favour of the underdog; a trust in reason; a preference for higher taxes to fund higher public expenditure; a keen sense of social justice; a belief not only in greater equality of opportunity but greater equality; and an unyielding faith in human diversity and tolerance for almost everything except intolerance.[13] This is, I think, a good list. I would only add that being on the left also means believing that people are inherently social creatures who thrive in strong communities, as well as that competitive markets can sometimes fail, and that when they fail, the state can and should do something to correct those failures. When I say that left-wing ideas and arguments have shaped and continue to shape our politics, what I intend to show is that these values are embedded within public policy.

I will say more about the values of the left and the ways in which these values translate into support for policies later. But for the moment, I want to suggest that there are other ways in which we might think about what it means to be on the left. One simple but fun alternative is to define the left in terms of choice of hate figures. To be on the left is to shudder publicly and visibly at the mention of the *Daily Mail*, Boris Johnson, Rupert Murdoch, Margaret Thatcher, and of course Jeremy Clarkson and Katie Hopkins. Increasingly, being on the left also means absolutely hating Tony Blair: in part for force-feeding the Labour Party a diet of neoliberalism; in part for starting what most people on the left now regard as an illegal war; and in part for making millions of pounds since leaving office.[14] Or, alternatively, we might define the left—at least the middle-class progressive left—in terms of its habits: reading and generally agreeing with the editorial line in the *Guardian* or the *Independent*; practising ethical consumerism and decrying shallow materialism. Understood in this way, being on the left can get quite personal. In 2015, the *Guardian*'s Rhiannon Cosslett entertainingly pondered the cultural significance of 'never kissed a Tory' T-shirts, badges, and mugs. In passing, incidentally, she describes the Tories in question as 'these NHS-destroying proponents of austerity, privatisation, political isolationism and environmental destruction', which does not make them sound very attractive.[15] Finally, I also want to suggest that, over the last few decades, the left can also be defined in terms of its basic sympathy with the kind of history I have outlined here. To be on the left is, in this sense, to believe the 1979 election was a turning point from which the country has never recovered; that New Labour was a pale imitation of the Conservatives; that the Coalition was a disaster; and that austerity is unnecessary and unfair.

Next, I want to draw an important boundary line around the argument. This book is primarily about left-wing miserabilism in Britain. It is important to say this because the British left does not have a monopoly on miserabilism. Members and supporters of left-wing parties like Syriza in Greece and Podemos in Spain also believe that everything is going or has gone to the dogs; that the democratic status quo is failing; that neoliberalism is triumphant; and that the rich are getting richer while the poor are getting poorer. Bernie Sanders's very nearly successful run for the Democrats' 2015 Presidential nomination was sustained by the conviction of hundreds of thousands of young activists that the United States is politically and economically fractured and that electing a mainstream politician like Hillary Clinton would not make any real difference.

I also entirely accept that caring deeply about what happens in other parts of the world is an important part of what it means to be on the left. There is nothing new in this. In the nineteenth century, the left railed against nationalism and rallied to the cause of socialist international solidarity. In the 1930s, several thousand left-wing Britons travelled to Spain to fight fascism. Yet, in recent decades, my sense is that the left has become, if anything, more internationalized. This is, no doubt, partly because it is now much easier than it once was to learn about and travel to other parts of the world. But it is also because the left recognizes that its arch-opponent, neoliberalism, is a globalizing ideology: the horrific impacts of which can be felt not only in Britain but in other European countries where the European Central Bank has imposed growth-destroying fiscal austerity as the price of a single currency; in the rust-belt cities of the United States where manufacturing jobs have evaporated; in sub-Saharan Africa where the IMF continues to impose fiscal stabilization policies; and in the dormitory factories in Chinese cities which make expensive computers.

Given that the left increasingly thinks in global terms, it might seem quite perverse to want to narrow the scope of this book down to British politics. But it is important to note that, in this respect, the left's arguments about the impact and costs of neoliberalism are inexorably bound up with an argument about what has happened to Britain over the last three or more decades. The left does not argue that things are kind of all right here, all things considered, but that we need to remember just how awful things are in other places. It argues that there is an even spread of awfulness. Things are awful and getting worse here and they are awful and getting worse everywhere else as well. It is this argument that I want to challenge. To be clear, I am not making any claims about whether this argument is or is not mistaken when it comes to global politics or the state of politics in the United States, Europe, South America, Asia, or Australasia. For what it is worth, I suspect it is not misplaced when it comes to the United States and that it may well not be misplaced in parts of Europe. But this is not an argument I am going to pursue. This is a book about left-wing miserabilism in Britain.

A second reason for saying that this is primarily a book about *left-wing* miserabilism in Britain is that the right also does its own nice line in despondency. *Daily Mail* journalists, UKIP activists, and those parts of the Conservative Party which despaired of David Cameron's social liberalism and Europhilia are equally sure Britain is going to the dogs. In 2016, with Jeremy Corbyn missing in action, UKIP managed to frame the EU referendum debate as a question about whether the present was better than the past and whether the future was likely to be even worse than the present. The left and the right disagree about what has gone wrong in Britain and they disagree about when it went wrong. The right finds its scapegoats in left-wing teachers, BBC bureaucrats, Eurocrats, overpaid footballers, welfare scroungers, Brexit saboteurs, teenage yobs, and endless lorry-loads of East European migrants. It looks back to an imagined age in the 1950s when people did not lock their doors when they went out at night and we were a world power which had no truck with silly ideas about ever closer European Union. The left, for its part, finds its preferred hate-figures in millionaire bankers, tabloid journalists, and tax-avoiding businessmen, as well as in Margaret Thatcher, Tony Blair, and Top Gear. It looks back to the golden age of the post-war Attlee government and the establishment of a benign post-war consensus. Yet whatever the differences, it is interesting that the left and right offer a similar story of decline and fall.

It is perhaps tempting to try to account for the shared miserabilism of the left and right in terms of our underlying national identity and our Olympian-level commitment to low-level moaning about the world around us and the inconsiderate people in it. In her excellent book *The English,* the anthropologist Kate Fox observes that whenever she makes a critical comment about English culture or behaviour, people nod in agreement but that when she offers praise, however mild and qualified, people accuse her of wearing rose-tinted spectacles and of not seeing things as they really are.[16] To be English is, on this reading, to believe that things—pubs, football, manners, music, art, TV sitcoms, the railways, Jonathan Ross, the weather, and the state of society in general—are not as good as they once were and that something should be done about it, although it is all probably too late do so. Cecil Rhodes (not necessarily the left's favourite racist imperialist) once wrote that to be born English was to have won first prize in the lottery of life.[17] Those days seem long gone. The British today are far more likely to describe their homeland in terms like those employed by Emma Thompson during a press conference in Berlin at the start of the EU referendum campaign: a 'tiny little cloud-bolted, rainy corner of sort-of Europe, a cake-filled, misery-laden, grey old island'.[18] I don't want to get too carried away here. I don't, ultimately, think that our national character explains everything. The left in Britain has not always been steeped in miserabilism and the fact that the left in other parts of the world are now also highly miserable suggests that there is no straight causal link to be uncovered here. Nevertheless, I think the fact that so many on the right as well as left are so negative ought to give the left pause for thought. Can things really be so bad if the *Daily Mail* thinks things really are so bad?

One further bit of housekeeping. Most of the time in what follows I talk about Britain: meaning the nations of England, Scotland, and Wales. When I was studying politics as an undergraduate in the late 1980s, the textbooks I read often started with a disclaimer to the effect that they were going to say next to nothing about Northern Ireland. This was pretty annoying at the time because it seemed obvious that Northern Ireland was one of the most interesting things about UK politics. There was, after all, a civil war going on there in which, on average, nearly a hundred people a year were being killed. Not talking about Northern Ireland seemed perverse in these circumstances. In the context of a more general discussion of the nature and value of politics as an activity, I talk about the Northern Ireland peace process in a later chapter. But, by and large, and just like those textbooks which used to annoy me so much, I don't say a great deal about Northern Ireland because my sense is that it is still sufficiently distinctive in political terms to make it difficult to export my argument across the Irish Sea. Hence, in most of what follows I talk about Britain rather than the UK.

I have at times also wondered whether this book is really (or at least mostly) about the left in England and whether Scotland and Wales are now also fundamentally different. It is obvious that politics in Scotland and, to a lesser but still significant extent, Wales, is very different to politics in England and that it has been both enlivened and complicated by devolution and, in Scotland, by the campaign for independence. In England, the Conservatives won 55 per cent of the available seats at the 2017 general election. In Scotland, they won 22 per cent and in Wales they won 20 per cent. The Scottish and Welsh governments have, in large part, opted out of English health and education policy. All of this suggests that I may well be better off talking about the downward trajectory of English politics over the last few decades rather than British politics. But at the same time, the left in Scotland and Wales (whether it is voting Labour, Green, SNP, or Plaid Cymru) seems, by and large, to share the same basic conviction as the left in England that things have gone horribly wrong over the last thirty or so years; that the 1979 election was a disaster; and that New Labour was a failure. So, in this sense at least, I think it makes sense to take Britain rather than England as the standard point of reference and to say so explicitly when this sometimes changes: as it does when, for example, I cite statistics which refer to the whole of the UK or to England, Scotland, or Wales separately.

V

Who is this book written for? I have, first and foremost, written it for me: to help settle a long-running argument I have had in my head about how I feel about the state of the country I am, once again, living in. I hope the book will appeal to people who are interested in British politics; who feel many of the debates between left and right have acquired a slightly sterile

Groundhog Day feel; and who feel, instinctively, that they belong to the left but who feel a mismatch between some of the things the left says and their own experiences and who find themselves uncomfortable with many of the things Jeremy Corbyn and his supporters say.

There is, however, another question here which is always worth asking. Why does it matter? Why invest time in reading a book challenging the left's version of our miserable recent history? (a meta-moan in so far as it might be interpreted as a moan about other people moaning).

The simplest answer to this question is that history matters and bad history is always worth arguing with.

The second and more complex answer is that the left's bleak history is in several different ways self-harming. The first sense in which it is self-harming is that it is too easy to dismiss. If the left is constantly arguing that the NHS is being privatized and on the edge of collapse; that a 'chainsaw massacre' of the welfare state is taking place (to quote Polly Toynbee[19]); that Conservative ministers exclusively and cruelly blame the poor for their poverty; that the banks have got away with it and escaped without punishment or reform; that David Cameron and Theresa May are no different from (and may even be worse) than Thatcher; and that Britain is now a more unequal society than it was in the nineteenth century, the left risks being ignored by large parts of the electorate.

There is a case to be made for rhetorical exaggeration when it comes to conducting and trying to win political arguments. This case was most poetically outlined by Leon Trotsky: 'The awareness of relative truths never gives one the courage to use force and spill blood.'[20] If the left is to mobilize support, this argument might run, it needs to generate a sense of outrage and if this means cutting a few corners and over-egging things now and again, so be it. But as well as alienating voters who consider the claims being made by the left to be implausible, an overly bleak history risks demoralizing potential voters and supporters by encouraging them to conclude, erroneously, that it is all too late; that too much of what is worth fighting for has been lost; and that, in the end and no matter what they say, Labour governments end up doing the same things as Conservative governments because the exercise of power is inherently oppressive and corrupting. Besides, I don't think the Corbyn-led left is simply engaging in rhetorical exaggeration. It really does believe in what it says about what has happened.

Politics is an inherently messy and often disappointing business. Politics is about setting inspiring goals; challenging power; and transforming people's lives. But on a day-to-day basis it is also about concessions and compromises; tactical alliances; arguments and betrayals; U-turns and hypocrisies.[21] Politics is, as the German sociologist Max Weber once observed, the slow boring of hard boards.[22] It takes time and is not always very pleasant to do on a Saturday afternoon. There is a chasm between the promise of what politics can sometimes achieve and the reality of what it involves. This chasm arises because we live in a country in which people disagree about who we are and what we ought to be doing. Democratic politics is therefore always going to involve compromises and it is always going to be a laborious process involving innumerable setbacks. The danger in painting our recent political history as one avoidable disaster followed by another is that it risks leaving people with unrealistic expectations about what can be done if, at the next election, a left-wing populist like Jeremy Corbyn is elected.

The left's bleak history is also self-harming because it risks undermining faith in government and the left needs to believe government can work if it is going to change things. A recurring theme within the left's history is that politicians in general and government ministers in particular only care about getting re-elected, keeping their chauffeur-driven cars, and making sure that they have a nice private sector job to fall back on when it all goes wrong. Politicians are out of touch and often quite dim. The Civil Service is there to neuter radical ideas. Behind the pantomime of Prime Minister's Questions, the real levers of power are held by multinational businesses which contribute just enough to party funds to make sure they get the policies they want. If power corrupts and absolute power corrupts absolutely, then what is needed, many on the left argue, is an alternative kind of politics and an alternative way of getting things done. So, politics needs to become less about getting elected and more about participation, consciousness-raising, and direct action.[23]

There is a certain sense to right-wing economists and bloggers peddling arguments of this kind. The neoliberal right, after all, believes that the competitive market is good and that the state is bad and that we need more of the former and less of the latter, and that it is all that simple. It makes sense for them to argue that elected politicians are entirely self-interested and invariably incompetent because they want more markets and less government.

But it is troubling to see a similar-sounding set of arguments about the failings of government being articulated by the left. The kind of things the left believes in—greater equality, social mobility, regulation of markets for the collective good, and the universal provision of public services—don't happen by accident. They happen because governments do things out of a conviction that some key decisions about how we organize our lives ought to be decided collectively and democratically. Politics is often shambolic and governments do sometimes stuff things up badly. And politicians, being human, do sometimes have one eye on their own interests. But the left also needs to recognize that government does sometimes work; that policies are sometimes effectively implemented; that business interests do not always get their wicked way; and that politicians do sometimes put the public interest ahead of their own electoral interests and are not, by and large, thieves and liars. And this may sometimes mean saying governments have, over the last few decades, got some things right.

Here, I want to say something more about Corbynism and the schisms within the Labour Party. The left—in Britain and beyond—has, of course, always been riven by disputes between gradual reformers and radical revolutionaries. In the late 1890s, the German left split between a reformist wing led by Eduard Bernstein, who became a leading figure in the German Social Democratic Party, and fundamentalists like Karl Kautsky and Rosa Luxemburg. In more recent times, similar battle lines have been drawn within the Labour Party during the 1981 deputy leadership contest between Dennis Healey and Tony Benn; during the 1992 leadership contest between Bryan Gould and John Smith; and, up to a point, during the contest between Ed and David Miliband in 2010. The only thing that is, in this respect, obviously distinctive about Jeremy Corbyn's triumph in 2015 is that it was so convincing. Jeremy Corbyn won by a landslide because he found himself pushing at what had suddenly become a wide open door of a argument that the neoliberal Conservatives were destroying the country and that New Labour had achieved next to nothing of lasting value.

One of the most distinctive things about Corbyn's supporters is that, by and large, a significant minority of them don't seem to mind that much whether Labour can win the next election with Corbyn as leader. During the 2015 leadership campaign, only 10 per cent of Corbyn's supporters thought it important that Labour's leader 'understands what it takes to win an election'.[24] During his 2016 re-election campaign, a YouGov poll found that 40 per cent of those who planned to vote for Corbyn did not believe he was competent and that 44 per cent believed he was unlikely to lead Labour to victory at the next general election.[25] Supporting Corbyn is, in many respects, a form of emotional declamation. 'This far and no further.' It is also about rejecting a form of politics which is about compromise and give-and-take. Compromising to win power is not only faintly immoral (politics is about having principles and sticking to them) but ineffective. After all, and as the miserabilist can acidly observe, Labour Party members bit their collective tongues in 1994 when they elected Tony Blair and all they got for their troubles was a decade of neoliberalism and a lost decade of austerity.

I think this position is doubly wrong. It is wrong because compromise is an essential, unavoidable, and attractive feature about politics. In the 2017 election, Corbyn's Labour performed far better than most people—including its supporters–expected'. One reason why Labour performed so well was that it offered such an uncompromising and principled opposition to austerity and to the Conservatives. Labour was able to promise to be all things to all people: to abolish tuition fees but to adequately fund higher education; to reduce inequality but to maintain the 'triple lock' on pensions; to oppose the government on Brexit but to not actually oppose leaving the European Union. But if Labour was elected, it would, like any government, need to cut deals, make trade-offs, and accept compromises. This is no bad thing. In a democratic system, compromise is how we all just about manage to rub along together. It is also wrong because the history of the last few decades in general and of New Labour in particular is not one of endless political retreat and failure. The left-wing snail has won some battles and lost some others but has progressed.

VI

The alternative history of Britain which follows does not, for the most part, take a chronological form. In the following chapter, I describe in more detail the miserabilist history I am challenging. Whilst doing this, I sketch a timeline running from the end of the Second World War through to today. But for the most part, the argument is organized around themes and subject areas: public opinion and attitudes in the third chapter; the role and reach of the state in the fourth chapter; the state of the NHS and our state education system in the fifth chapter; equality and inequality in the sixth chapter;

economic growth and austerity in the seventh chapter; and democracy in the eighth chapter.

At the start of each of these chapters, I sketch the basic terms of the miserabilist argument as it relates to that issue: that the electorate has rolled to the neoliberal right; that the frontiers of the state have been rolled back; that inequality is accelerating; that the benefits of economic growth have not trickled down; that the poorest and most vulnerable have been left paying the price of austerity; and that democracy is not working and that there is no point voting. I then set out to show that these arguments are exaggerated, one-sided, and incomplete or just plain wrong. The *Daily Mail* and others on the right are wrong about Britain being an awful and broken post-apocalyptic place in which gangs of left-wing social workers and BBC journalists have been left to roam free. But left-wing miserabilism is equally problematic.

2

Enter neoliberalism . . . and it all went horribly wrong

I

In horror films and hospital dramas you know something bad is going to happen when things start with a family or group of friends hanging out together without an apparent care in the world. So be warned. This is going to be a horror story of a chapter. I'm going to relate a history of Britain which starts with the left in the ascendancy in the 1940s but then takes a horrible turn for the worse in the 1980s.

I have three main aims in writing the chapter. The first is to put more flesh on the skeleton of the miserabilist history I outlined before. I want to show in more detail what the left thinks has gone wrong in Britain, why it thinks it went wrong, and when it thinks it went wrong. In doing this, I want to set the scene for some of the more specific arguments about public attitudes, the role of the state, equality, and austerity to follow. Second, I want to show beyond any reasonable doubt that I am not setting up a straw man of an argument. I want to show that there really are lots of people on the left—academics, journalists, and activists amongst others—who subscribe to the terms of this miserabilist history. Finally, I want to put the concept of neoliberalism at the front and centre of this history and, in doing so, provide an overview of some arguments about what neoliberalism is and what kind of an impact it has had. I do this by tying together the history of neoliberalism with that of Thatcherism.

II

Friedrich Hayek (1899–1992) was an Austrian economist and philosopher who won the Nobel Prize for economics in 1974. Hayek can make a strong claim to being the founding figure of neoliberalism. Having studied and worked at the University of Vienna, Hayek moved to the London School of Economics in 1931, where his strident criticisms of John Maynard Keynes's path-breaking work on the causes of and best policy response to the depression attracted a measure of public recognition.[1] In March 1944, Hayek published his most famous and accessible book, *The Road to Serfdom*.[2] In it he argued that the Western democracies were in danger of abandoning market individualism in favour of state collectivism and political tyranny. Whereas Keynes argued a 'third way' between 1930s-style economic liberalism and communism was possible, Hayek maintained that even limited attempts at government planning and economic coordination would lead to economic and political disaster.

The Road to Serfdom was an ode to freedom and competitive free markets at a time when socialism was in the ascendancy. In July 1945, the Labour Party won a landslide general election victory and, with this, a mandate to create a social security system, nationalize large swathes of industry, establish a national health service, and pursue a Keynesian economic strategy. Two years later, with the Cold War starting and the Soviet Union offering an apparently workable example of socialism-in-action, Hayek, undeterred, invited thirty-six like-minded economists, philosophers, and historians to meet in the Swiss holiday resort of Mont Pelerin, near Montreux, Switzerland, to discuss how to begin the ideological fightback. The subsequent establishment of the Mont Pelerin Society constitutes the ground zero of neoliberalism and the agreed statement of the Society's aims (below) shows the influence of Hayek's urgent arguments about the dangers posed by democratically elected governments.

> The central values of civilization are in danger. Over large stretches of the Earth's surface the essential conditions of human dignity and freedom have already disappeared. In others, they are under constant menace from the development of current tendencies of policy. The position of the individual and the voluntary group are progressively undermined by extensions of arbitrary power.[3]

The Mont Pelerin Society does not knowingly do understatement.

Putting things crudely, neoliberals believed then and believe now that competitive markets are good and that government and populist forms of democracy in which politicians are constantly pandering to voters by seeking to interfere with the market and plan things in the name of the public interest are bad. There is nothing particularly new in this argument. In the eighteenth century, Adam Smith had offered a clear statement of the virtues of the market and the inequities of government. In the nineteenth century, 'Manchester' liberals led by Richard Cobden provided a trenchant defence of free trade and, more generally, of laissez-faire economics. Neoliberalism was, in this respect, simply a restatement of classical economic liberalism for a new and more socialist age in which government and the state had been rolled dangerously forward.

Markets are good because they promote choice, freedom, and individual autonomy; utilize the dispersed and often tacit knowledge of millions of ordinary consumers and producers about what people want and how much it will cost; create incentives for entrepreneurs to identify new and better ways of making use of scarce resources; all whilst rewarding hard work, clear thinking, and creativity. Markets are not perfect. They often fail. But a market system gives consumers and producers alike the opportunity and an incentive to learn from their mistakes. Above all, markets act as both a bulwark for and an expression of individual freedom.[4] Markets predictably generate inequalities. But inequality is not evidence of injustice. Indeed, neoliberals are wary of the concept of social injustice in so far as it suggests the existence of an independent metric for establishing the 'right' distribution of wealth, income, and resources against which the results of millions of voluntary market-based transactions can be judged and found wanting.[5] What matters is not equality of outcome but equality of opportunity. The great virtue of free markets is that they give everyone the chance to choose what to do and how to live and, in doing so, generate growth which trickles down and benefits all. What counts is not the relative gap between the rich and the poor today but how much money the poorest have. The problem with the left is, as Margaret Thatcher once observed, that it would 'rather that the poor were poorer, provided that the rich were less rich'.[6]

Governments, on the other hand, are clumsy, aggressive, and duplicitous. They are clumsy because they lack the knowledge needed to understand what people want and how best to go about providing it. No matter how well intentioned they may be, government intervention predictably generates unpredictable and perverse consequences. Hospital targets encourage bureaucrats to discharge patients when they are still sick. Welfare policies create long-term poverty traps. Forcing people to wear seatbelts encourages them to drive faster, so leading to more accidents. And so on. Governments are aggressive. In the name of social justice, they trample their opponents and restrict free choice. To correct perceived injustices or inefficiencies, they constantly demand new powers limiting individual freedom. Finally, governments are duplicitous. Politicians promise to be guided by the public interest. But, in practice, they are, like everyone else, resolutely self-interested. This is the argument a group of so-called public choice economists based in the United States in the 1970s contributed to the intellectual development of neoliberalism. Politicians may promise to protect the public interest but they are out to maximize their own chances of re-election and their own perks and privileges. Government fails because politicians can be relied upon to inflate long-term public debt to secure an immediate election victory, sell policy favours to business and other special interests, and practise pork-barrel politics (I'll vote for your bridge to nowhere if you vote to keep open my army base).[7]

Neoliberals are, as I said at the start of the opening chapter, 'market fundamentalists' or, alternatively, 'market imperialists' who believe the public is best served when competitive markets are rolled forward and the state and democratic and collective decision-making is rolled back.[8] According to the senior sociologist and political scientist Colin Crouch, neoliberalism is a free-market ideology, 'the essence' of which is its 'preference for the market over the state as a means of resolving problems'.[9] According to the geographer David Harvey, who has written extensively about its nature and impact, neoliberalism 'seeks to bring all human action into the domain of the market'.[10] The French sociologist and public intellectual Pierre Bourdieu describes neoliberalism as a 'programme for destroying collective structures which impede the market logic'.[11] In policy terms, this faith in free markets translates into a commitment to privatization and deregulation; lower taxes to create incentives for wealth creation; free trade, free exchange rates, and the promotion of economic and financial globalization; the prioritization of low and stable inflation; spending cuts and a balanced budget; strict limits on welfare spending and a preference for means-testing over the provision of universal services; the establishment of 'internal markets' within public services and the contracting out of those services to private firms; strict controls on trade unions; and the creation of unelected arms-length government bodies staffed by technocrats and businessmen who, free from the meddling interference of elected politicians out to feather their own nests, can best take whatever decisions cannot be left to the free market.

Neoliberals disagree, within limits, about how far the state should be pruned back. Hayek, although a zealous defender of the free market, recognized that markets do not 'bring about any close correspondence between subjective merit or individual need and reward' (i.e. that hard work does not always pay) and argued the case for an 'extensive system of social services'.[12] So-called Ordoliberals argue that a strong state is needed to police competition rules and ensure business plays fairly by free-market rules, and that a strong state is also needed to reduce market inequalities through employment insurance, free education, and wealth taxes.[13] In Britain and the United States, this kind of progressive state-centric neoliberalism, with its focus upon the 'social market' economy, has been largely marginalized. In Germany and—by extension, the European Union—Ordoliberalism remains influential.[14]

On the other hand, so-called Paleoliberals associated with the Chicago School of Economics argue that everything the state touches is likely to turn to dust and that government should restrict itself to the 'nightwatchman' functions of providing internal law and order and external defence. On the more extreme libertarian end of the debate, the American economist Murray Rothbard exhibits, in his own words, a 'deep and pervasive hatred of the state and all of its works, based on the conviction that the State is the enemy of mankind'.[15] These differences are real and important and, at one point, threatened to split the Mont Pelerin society apart. Yet, over the years, a middle-ground position has emerged. Its spirit is perhaps best captured by one of its former Presidents, the public choice theorist James Buchanan. On the one hand, Buchanan argues that 'social order without a state is not readily imagined'. Strike one for the Ordoliberals. On the other hand, he argues that 'it is critically and vitally important to recognise that ten per cent slavery is different from fifty per cent slavery'.[16] Government is, at best, in other words, a necessary evil. The kind of extreme libertarian views expressed by Murray Rothbard might not be feasible but the growth-reducing and liberty-crushing state which emerged in the post-war years must be radically rolled back.

III

Neoliberal ideas burnt on a slow fuse. In the 1950s and 1960s, Hayek, who had left Britain to work at the University of Chicago and then at the University of Freiburg in West Germany, was a largely marginal figure within economic theory. The Keynesians appeared to have won the argument about the need for government intervention to manage the economy and Hayek's arguments about a slippery slope toward tyranny began to look a bit silly. In 1945, Churchill—echoing Hayek's arguments in *The Road to Serfdom*—had warned that the implementation of Labour's statist programme would require 'some form of Gestapo'.[17] He was widely ridiculed and the Conservatives lost. In 1951, they returned to power but did so under the banner of a 'one nation' brand of Conservatism signalling an acceptance of Keynesian economics and state planning, the welfare state, and a close working relationship with the trade union movement. Thus was born the post-war consensus and the apparent burial of classical liberalism and its neoliberal offspring.[18]

In *The Future of Socialism*, published in 1956, the future Cabinet Minister Tony Crosland confidently predicted that any liberal-inspired 'wholesale counter-revolution' was extremely unlikely because public opinion would not tolerate 'any government which tampered seriously with the basic structure of the full employment welfare state'.[19] In 1970, Edward Heath briefly promised to reverse Labour's diet of 'more taxes, more blanket subsidies, more state ownership, more civil servants and more government interference'.[20] To the purist's eye, Heath, however, was a fraud and a failure who, in office, introduced price controls and a state-sponsored incomes policy.

It was only when Heath was deposed by Margaret Thatcher in 1975 that the neoliberal free-market ideology began to really gain ground. Thatcher had read Hayek's *Road to Serfdom* as an undergraduate at Oxford: she later said that it was 'the most powerful critique of socialist planning and the socialist state which I read at this time . . . and [one] to which I have returned so often since'.[21] With the global economy crumbling and the post-war consensus visibly fraying, Margaret Thatcher pledged to end what she saw as her party's tacit acceptance of state socialism and to strike out in a new policy direction. The Conservatives' 1979 manifesto could not have been clearer. 'The state takes too much of the nation's income; its share must be steadily reduced.'[22] When she won the election and entered Downing Street, Hayek, by then 80 years old, described it as the best birthday present 'anyone could have given me'.[23]

In May 1979, the Conservatives secured 44 per cent of the vote (compared with Labour's 37 per cent). By December 1981, the Conservatives were down to 27 per cent in the opinion polls.[24] For a time, it appeared almost certain that Margaret Thatcher would not last: that she would be removed from office either by her own Cabinet—in which the non-Thatcherite 'wets' were, on paper at least, in a majority—or by a vengeful electorate unwilling to tolerate mass unemployment, inner-city riots, and growing inequality. So poor was the government's position that the *Guardian*'s political commentator, Peter Jenkins, published a short obituary of Thatcherism.[25] When, eighteen months later, the Conservatives won the 1983 election, it was therefore tempting for everyone on the left to conclude that Margaret Thatcher had been hugely lucky: lucky to have inherited the financial elixir of North Sea oil; lucky to have faced a political opposition split between Labour and the Liberal–SDP Alliance; and, during the Falklands War, lucky to have had a military opponent as unpalatable and as incompetent as General Galtieri.

It seemed certain that Thatcher's luck would eventually run out. But it never quite happened. The Conservatives fought and beat the National Union of Mineworkers; the economy boomed; the 1987 election was won; and the left could apparently do little more than seethe in righteous anger. The *Guardian*'s Polly Toynbee suggests that 'where once we stood within a recognisable postwar social democratic European tradition, after Thatcher the country had rowed halfway across the Atlantic, psychologically imbued with US neoliberal individualism'.[26] Some of the sense of anger and hopelessness the left felt at that time was captured, nearly two decades later, by the comedian Alexei Sayle in an interview on *Channel 4 News* the day Margaret Thatcher died:

> I think of her as the first modern personality disorder politician . . . she was just bonkers. I mean she seemed completely nuts . . . This woman is completely crazy and false . . . this woman has a messy and extensive sense of her own rightness . . . This is just a string of clichés and prejudices strung together.

When then asked rather mercilessly by the presenter, Jon Snow, whether she could, nonetheless, be said to have won, Sayle replied:

> what we had was a disaffected minority . . . you could sit in a club and some nights if you didn't feel like doing your material you could just shout 'Thatcher's a bastard' for twenty minutes.[27]

Which was pretty much like saying . . . yes, she had.

By the time she was, finally, removed from office by her own party in November 1990, Margaret Thatcher had changed everything—the economy and geography of the country; people's sense of social obligation to each other; the homes they lived in; and their expectations of what the state could and should do. The last point is perhaps the most important. As she herself boasted during a speech delivered at the College of Europe in Bruges in 1988 made famous by its strident denunciations of the European Commission and its ambitions for ever more European integration, Thatcherism had resulted in a 'rolling back of the frontiers of the state'.[28] Thatcherism marked the political triumph of neoliberalism in Britain.

So, what was the alternative? In the end, there was—as Margaret Thatcher had herself once assured everyone—no alternative. In the early 1980s, Labour swung to the left under Michael Foot and lost. Neil Kinnock then pulled Labour back toward the centre ground but lost in 1987 and lost again in 1992. After the tragic death of John Smith, Labour elected Tony Blair in the hope, finally, of regaining power. For a while, the hope was that Blair was saying Thatcher-like things in order to get Labour elected. It soon became clear that he was, in fact, a true believer who regarded Margaret Thatcher as a fellow radical.[29] New Labour was not about the reinvention of social democracy. It was, the miserabilist argues, all about its repudiation. As Tony Blair put it a decade later in his political autobiography, New Labour meant 'no return to old union laws; no renationalisation of the privatised utilities; no raising the top rate of tax'.[30] Blair accepted the argument that Britain had to cut costs and shed jobs to compete in global markets and did not care about how unequal Britain was becoming. Indeed, New Labour was, in the words of one of its architects, Peter Mandelson, 'intensely relaxed' about people getting 'filthy rich'.[31] When it came to taxes, welfare reform, redistribution, and the public services, Blair wanted, once again in his own words, to 'preserve' the essential Thatcher 'legacy'.[32] No wonder Margaret Thatcher, for her part, viewed Blair and New Labour as 'her greatest achievement'.[33] Lacking any philosophical objections to free-market capitalism, the New Labour 'project' boiled down to the hope that a debt-fuelled economy would keep growing; that international banks would relocate to London in order to take advantage of New Labour's 'light-touch' regulation; and that the resulting tax revenues would be enough to secure another election victory.

New Labour was a continuation and extension of neoliberalism. Bob Jessop, a sociologist at Lancaster University, suggests New Labour became the 'emperor of European neoliberalism'.[34] The geographer Danny Dorling observes: 'Thatcherism continued after New Labour came to power, that is part of what made it new.'[35] The former *Financial Times* journalist Robert Taylor suggests that New Labour 'embraced the neoliberal capitalist order, not in a defensively apologetic way but with a real sense of pride and swagger'.[36]

The columnist Simon Jenkins argues that Blair and his Chancellor were 'prisoners of a revolution affected by Margaret Thatcher in the 1980s'.[37] The writer and former *Observer* editor Will Hutton suggests that Blair and the rest of the Labour leadership came to believe that the pro-market Conservatives had been right all along. New Labour offered, at most, 'a gentler, more public-spirited custodian of the Thatcherite settlement'.[38] Armando Iannucci, co-creator of *The Thick of It*, describes New Labour as being 'in the pockets of media barons' and run by 'flash southern bastards who'll privatise anything that moves'.[39] In 2009, Sheffield-born Jarvis Cocker, whilst reaffirming his steadfast opposition to the Conservatives, nevertheless suggests in an interview with *GQ Magazine* that New Labour had failed and that the Conservatives were left standing as the only political alternative.[40]

IV

New Labour's bubble burst in 2008 when a banking system built upon debt and the pursuit of short-term profits collapsed, leading to a credit crunch and a deep recession. For a short while, it appeared that the implosion of the global financial system and the self-evident failure of free markets had discredited neoliberalism and that a political tipping point had been reached. If played as a *Star Wars* movie, with neoliberalism as the Empire, the financial crisis looked like it was going to be that Luke Skywalker moment when the Death Star is, against all the odds, destroyed. The Nobel-Prize-winning economist Joseph Stiglitz predicted that the collapse of Lehman Brothers investment bank would be to market fundamentalism what the fall of the Berlin Wall had been for Communism.[41] For a short while, Keynesian economics and financial re-regulation were indeed the order of the day. Gordon Brown—who had replaced Tony Blair in June 2007—chaired the G20 summit in London in April 2009 and led the calls for governments across the world to boost public spending and run short-term fiscal deficits to stave off a global depression.

In the end, however, nothing really changed. *The Empire Struck Back*. As Boris Johnson observed in the 2013 Margaret Thatcher Memorial Lecture:

> We all waited for the paradigm shift, after the crash of 2008. The left was ushered centre stage, and missed their cue; political history reached a turning point, and failed to turn. Almost a quarter of a century after the collapse of Soviet and European communism—a transformation that Mrs Thatcher did so much

> to bring about—there has been no intellectual revival of her foes, whose precepts are now conserved only by weird cults in south London.[42]

Gordon Brown repudiated the name of New Labour but struggled to find an alternative to it. As the economy shrank and the deficit grew, it became clear that Labour was going to lose the next election. In the end, it was perhaps fitting that, just as Gordon Brown's premiership was grinding to an awful final halt, Maggie's nightclub was opening in Chelsea. It features a wall of photos of Thatcher and Ronald Reagan and toilets which are wired to play excerpts from the audiobook of her diaries. As described in a review in the *Guardian*, the results are surreal.

> This is uncanny. I'm washing my hands in a toilet in Chelsea and Margaret Thatcher is lecturing me. At least, I think it's her. I can't see her face, but her shrill voice echoes eerily around the urinals. 'We also had to deal,' she harangues me as I turn the tap, 'with the problem of trade union power, made worse by successive Labour governments and exploited by the confidence of militants who had risen to key positions in the trade union movement. Positions which they ruthlessly exploited'.[43]

As Leader of the Opposition, Cameron had worked hard to correct the Conservatives' image as the 'nasty party' (© Theresa May). Cameron had spoken about gay marriage, the environment, and the need to rejuvenate civil society and had promised to protect the NHS. The philosopher Phillip Blond—who, for a time, was identified as a key intellectual influence upon Cameron—promoted a 'Red Toryism' founded upon a distrust of free markets and a commitment to local communities.[44] Yet, once the Coalition had assumed power, the Conservatives reverted to type: using the recession, the deficit, and the imagined threat of a Greek-style default to pursue a neoliberal austerity agenda with the support of the Liberal Democrats. Cameron's views on government were like Ronald Reagan's (quoted previously). In 2009, he told the Conservative Party Conference: 'Labour say that to solve the country's problems, we need more government. Don't they see? It is more government that got us into this mess.'[45]

Between 2010 and 2015, Polly Toynbee argues that Cameron set out to 'abolish the post-war welfare state'.[46] Public expenditure was slashed at the same time as the top rate of tax was cut. Tuition fees were raised and the student loan book privatized; benefits were frozen; child benefit withdrawn from higher-income earners as a part of what Suzanne Moore describes as a 'war on women';[47] new and demeaning tests introduced requiring disabled people to demonstrate that they were incapable of work; a cap on welfare expenditure introduced; the bedroom tax invented; welfare sanctioning accelerated; housing benefit cut; and welfare claimants publicly taunted.[48] The journalist Owen Jones argues that Margaret Thatcher's dream of privatizing the NHS was 'turned into a reality' via the Health and Social Care Act which opens up all NHS services to private sector competition.[49] According to Kailesh Chand, Deputy Chair of the British Medical Association, the NHS has been turned into a 'repository of privateers with the mindset of venture capitalists'.[50]

When the Conservatives were given their unexpected majority in 2015 and so freed from whatever restraints the Coalition with the Liberal Democrats had entailed, they returned to office promising never-ending austerity; new restrictions on trade unions; the neutering of the BBC; the redefinition of poverty;[51] the decimation of tax credits; and legally enshrined budget rules to prevent any future government from running a budget deficit. In 2016, the Chancellor cut benefits for the disabled at the same time as he cut capital gains tax for the very richest. Even the Thatcherite Iain Duncan-Smith was left feeling that he had no alternative but to resign, asking, plaintively, whether 'enough has been done to ensure that we are all in this together'.[52]

In the end, Cameron was of course undone by the EU referendum (the 'greatest blunder ever made by a British Prime Minister', according to Michael Portillo).[53] Brexit may well prove to be Cameron's lasting legacy but his time in office was marked, above all, by austerity. One of the readers of the *Guardian*, Stephen Nulty, when invited to reflect upon Cameron's time in office, had this to say:

> He came to office with the narrow-minded belief that everything must rotate around reducing the deficit. This has led to terrible consequences for the poor, for working families and for the public sector and public spending. His inability and unwillingness to deviate, even when his deficit-reducing policies and austerity measures were failing makes him one of the worst Prime Ministers this country has ever seen.[54]

Cameron's replacement, Theresa May, was chosen by a small cabal of Conservative MPs. In her first major speech, at the 2016 Conservative Party conference, she argued that the EU referendum result reflected a 'sense—deep, profound and let's face it often justified—that many people have today that the world works well for a privileged few, but not for them'.[55] During her first year in office, May promised to focus her attention on those on lower incomes who were 'just about managing'. In her speech to the 2016 Conservative Party conference, she also promised to intervene to fix dysfunctional markets and reminded her audience of the 'good that government can do'. This was powerful stuff from a Conservative leader. But, in practice, and as ITV's political editor, Robert Peston, observed, whilst 'her rhetoric is more left-wing than Cameron's was, her cabinet is more right-wing than his was'.[56] To nobody's great surprise, the new Prime Minister found a way of talking about genuine equality of opportunity whilst also promoting grammar schools, cutting public spending, and promising yet more crackdowns on immigration. In the 2017 election, May ran on a manifesto which, according to Polly Toynbee offered 'austerity forever: that's no exaggeration. Her budget planned to shrink the state permanently to a size so small it would change the nature of Britain'.[57] Meanwhile, the Institute of Fiscal Studies predicts that Brexit, combined with planned spending cuts, will mean that average real wages in 2021 will be no higher than they were in 2008.[58]

The post-war consensus lasted, give or take, for nearly thirty years from 1950 to 1979. The Thatcherite consensus has now lasted longer—for nearly forty years and counting. The 2017 election shook that consensus but, in the end, changed very little. As the *Guardian* columnist Jonathan Freedland observes, we live in a land Maggie built.[59]

V

Where are we now? The ideology of neoliberalism has not only survived the financial crisis, it has thrived.[60] George Monbiot suggests that neoliberalism has become so pervasive that 'we seldom even recognise it as an ideology'.[61] My colleague at the University of Sheffield, Andrew Gamble, proposes that neoliberal ideas about the virtues of markets and the failings of government have become the 'dominant common sense' of our age.[62] According to the commentator and academic Philip Mirowski, we now live in a 'quintessentially neoliberal age'.[63] David Harvey argues that neoliberalism 'dominates the political horizon'.[64] Owen Jones suggests neoliberalism has become the 'shared ideology of the modern establishment'.[65] No less a body than the IMF has concluded that the economic benefits of neoliberalism have been oversold.[66] Yet this seems to make no difference. The 'fantastic suppositions' of neoliberal ideology have 'become part of the air we breathe, elements of our most fundamental assumptions about how the world works'.[67] Martin Jacques, who in the 1980s edited the journal *Marxism Today* (and did so in a way which did not make the title appear oxymoronic), argues that 'it is puzzling, shocking even' that politicians have largely ignored the problem of growing inequality and then explains this puzzle by saying that 'the explanation can only lie in the sheer extent of the hegemony of neoliberalism and its values'.[68]

Neoliberalism has entered people's souls. Markets have been created. But, more than this, people have been reshaped over the last few decades as self-disciplined, competitive, and enterprising subjects fit to operate within a cut-throat market environment. Markets have cut us apart from our communities, families, and friends. We have been conditioned to assume entrepreneurial responsibility for our own futures; to reinvent ourselves, take risks, and accept failures and injustices as somehow inevitable. Philip Mirowski talks about how we now live in a society of 'everyday sadism', in which people have been 'galvanised to find within themselves a kind of guilty pleasure in the thousand unkind cuts administered by the enforcers of trickle-down austerity'.[69] Public opinion has been dragged to the right and rendered fit for neoliberalism.

Neoliberalism has of course suffered setbacks along the way. In the immediate aftermath of the financial crisis, the British government was forced to nationalize Lloyds and the Royal Bank of Scotland and to disburse over £134bn in public funds to prop up the rest of the financial sector.[70] More recently, the Conservatives have put aside their reservations about the awfulness of government intervention to subsidize the savings of pensioners and first-time house buyers (pp. 81–2). The academic Jamie Peck argues that there is a pattern here. Over the years, neoliberalism has been subject to what he calls both 'roll-out' and 'roll-back'.[71] This process begins when, in a fit of ideological pique, neoliberal policies intended to roll back the frontiers of the state are introduced. When these policies predictably fail, the state then comes under intense pressure to intervene in some shape or form to mop up the pieces and, in doing so, to protect business interests and its own election chances. Government is, as he neatly puts it, afflicted by 'irritable intervention syndrome'.[72] The Paleoliberal ideal—the one in which there is only a nightwatchman state doing as little as it can to interfere with free markets—is a utopian ideal.[73] On the ground, in the real world, to quote Jamie Peck again, 'in fact, [neoliberalism] has only ever existed in a range of partial and impure forms and messy hybrids'.

The fact that neoliberal-inspired governments have fallen far short of their free-market ideals has, however, provided ideologues with the impetus they need to push their ideas further and harder.[74] When an inveterate leftie like Joseph Stiglitz argues that the banking crisis conclusively demonstrates the folly of neoliberalism, neoliberals can argue in response that the banking crisis was in fact caused by too *much* government intervention: by silly regulations in the United States designed by Congress to encourage wider homeownership; by the imposition of minimal capital buffers; and, above all, the government-backed edict that some banks were 'too big to fail' and would always be rescued no matter what stupid risks they took.[75] What is therefore needed, the neoliberal can conclude, is not less of the market but more. In this way, whenever neoliberalism is required to take one step backwards, the opportunity is always created for neoliberals to then argue the case for taking two steps forward. The end result is an endless process of what Peck calls 'neoliberalisation', in which there is roll-out and roll-back but an 'overall tendency' for strategic selection in favour of 'market-orientated, relatively privatized . . . and corporate-friendly approaches'.[76]

VI

What have we become? How has this horror story ended? At the heart of the post-war consensus was a commitment to the state as a guardian of the public interest over the antagonistic competitive market. Perhaps the simplest way of describing the impact neoliberalism has had on Britain is to say that it has resulted in the privatization of the economy and of society, and of democracy itself.

The state has been rolled back. Industries have been privatized and handed over to private companies who have exploited their market power to jack up prices in the pursuit of shareholder dividends and corporate bonuses.[77] Infrastructure investment has been privatized through successive iterations of New Labour's private finance initiative. To raise funds and further eviscerate the state, the Conservatives have pledged to re-privatize Lloyds and the Royal Bank of Scotland and sell its remaining holdings in the Royal Mail. Markets have been deregulated in the name of flexibility, job creation, and consumer choice. The trade union movement has been destroyed, with total membership falling from over 13 million in 1980 to 6.2 million today.[78] As a result, wage bargaining has been privatized. Regulations which once held the power of business in check have been removed. Companies like Sports Direct have been allowed to treat their workers like 'disposable kit' in a workplace regime where an unduly long trip to the toilet can lead to disciplinary action and where the dead time required for searches at the end of shifts means that workers have been paid less than the minimum wage.[79]

The NHS and the state education system have been starved of funds in the quest for endless efficiency savings (code for lower wages and poorer terms and conditions). Those working in the public sector have been routinely denigrated. Profit-maximizing firms like ATOS, Capita, G4S, and Serco have been awarded contracts to run state schools, hospitals, the probation service, and children's homes.[80] What is left of the state sector has been re-engineered by way of internal markets and profit targets to look, sound, and behave like the private sector on the explicit understanding that only the private sector can do things properly and that competition is always and everywhere an economic and human virtue. There is, in this respect, a noteworthy difference between the classical liberalism of Adam Smith and contemporary neoliberalism. Classical liberals argued the case for more markets and less government. Neoliberals have gone further, arguing that competitive free-market solutions can be applied *to* and *within* the state.[81] In the name of a ridiculously narrow and politically loaded concept of 'efficiency', economists and politicians have championed the causes of self-interest and competition within the public sector. Nothing is off-reach for the free market.[82]

The economy has been globalized through the elimination of capital controls, tariffs, and managed exchange rates. Globalization has offered companies new sources of profit and it has given governments the opportunity to argue that, in a highly competitive global economy, the only way that a country can prosper is by cutting taxes, regulations, and wages. In September 2014, for example, George Osborne told delegates to the Conservative Party conference that 'in a modern global economy—where people can move their investment from one country to another at the touch of a button and companies can relocate jobs overnight—the economics of high taxation are a thing of the past'.[83] In a post-Brexit British economy, the Conservatives are likely to double down on this kind of argument. Withdrawing from the European Union offers Britain the opportunity to forge new global trading relationships . . . but only if the economy is deregulated and made lean and mean. The economy has also been financialized. The pro-City lobby group CityUK estimates that banking and finance and related professional services employ 7 per cent of the UK workforce and account for 10 per cent of total national output.[84] The manufacturing sector has been destroyed. Firms now hold over 50 per cent of their retained profits in the form of financial assets.[85] Ordinary workers have been encouraged to compensate for the piecemeal destruction of the welfare state by accumulating financial assets: most notably private pension schemes and housing equity, to protect them in their retirement. Society has been commodified—that is, made subject to the logic of prices, competition, and demand and supply. Things which would once have been free at the point-of-use must now be paid for. Hospitals charge exorbitant sums to park. Courts levy a criminal courts surcharge. The Home Office charges £2,141 to process a dependency visa.[86] Universities charge tuition fees and use this money to open new business centres.[87] Airports charge people for express check-in services.[88] Once-free music festivals have become a £1.6bn business.[89] We pay people to care for our elderly relatives, entertain our children at parties, and counsel us during moments of depression.

Public space has been privatized. As city centres have been redeveloped, land has been handed over to developers. The result has been a 'creeping privatisation of public space', with the owners of developments like London's Canary Wharf and Olympic Park, Birmingham's Bull Ring, and Manchester's MediaCity given the authority to decide who to admit and what they are allowed to wear.[90] Will Hutton observes that the 'upper middle class increasingly live in gated communities' protected by high walls, CCTV, and a sense of social superiority.[91] Luxury flats have been built with inch-high metal studs in their entrances to deter the homeless from sleeping there.[92] Suburbs have been gentrified and socially cleansed. One of the greatest achievements of the post-war Labour Government, the Green Belt, has been slowly but steadily eroded in the pursuit of suburban housing development (as John Prescott once famously said when Secretary of State for the Environment, 'the green belt is a Labour achievement and we mean to build on it').[93]

People's lives have been privatized. Trapped by poverty and economic insecurity, most people no longer have the time to volunteer in their local communities or even to socialize with friends and family. Dazzled by a market-based logic which sanctifies the pursuit of self-interest, people have become less trusting and warier of others. Neoliberalism has dissolved the bonds between people, 'removing individuals from broader social obligations' by promoting a form of individualism which is, according to the writer Henry Giroux, 'almost pathological in its disdain for public goods, community, social provisions and public values'.[94] In one of a series of articles on the future of the left (a series on the future of the left is never a great sign for the left), John Harris observes that 'people who work . . . are no longer part of a monolithic mass: many increasingly think of themselves as lone agents, competing with others in much the same way that companies and corporations do'.[95] In *Bowling Alone: The Collapse and Revival of American Community,* the American sociologist Robert Putnam documents a precipitous fall in levels of social trust, volunteering, political participation, formal and informal socializing, and community engagement in the United States since the late 1960s.[96] My colleague Colin Hay neatly summarizes Putnam's argument as follows:

> A society which once bowled together in extensive networks of community now bowls alone if it can summon the energy to put down the remote control and lift its bloated carcass from the sofa. Social capital, civic engagement, political participation are now all largely gone, victims of the persuasive atomism that comes with the disintegration of community.[97]

Large swathes of the electorate have been dragged to the right and led to believe that government is wasteful, that lower taxes are always preferable to higher public expenditure, and that redistribution is a political sin.

No wonder so many people used the EU referendum as an opportunity to have a say about the state of the country and the track record of its political establishment. Theresa May has made this connection. But so, too, have Jeremy Corbyn's supporters. Diane Abbott has argued that 'for decades now, there has been disquiet among most Britons that our economic system is designed for the benefit of the few over the many'. It was this sentiment, she continues, that prompted a No vote that tells us as much about the way in which the Conservatives have 'valued profit over people . . . slashing public services and widening inequality under the dubious banner of austerity' as it does about how the public feel about migration and sovereignty.[98]

Finally, the democratic process itself has been privatized. A £2bn lobbying industry has been allowed to contaminate the policy process.[99] The largest political parties have become increasingly dependent upon the largesse of a small number of corporate donors who have been able to evade fig-leaf legislative controls by declaring their support as loans rather than donations.[100] As company executives and management consultants have been imported to run what is left of the public sector, public servants and ministers have departed to take positions on the boards of the firms they once regulated. Owen Jones argues that, as a result, the 'borders between the political and business elite are now so porous it is increasingly difficult to treat them as separate worlds'.[101] Colin Crouch similarly concludes that, behind the sound and fury of party politics, 'politics is really shaped in private by the interaction between elected governments and elites that overwhelmingly represent business interests'.[102] Business—which can threaten to move abroad, cut investment, or withdraw party funding—can put issues on to the policy agenda and veto policy proposals it does not approve of. An official report by the Cabinet Secretary, Gus O'Donnell, concluded that lobbying by BP to protect its commercial interests in Libya had 'played a part' in the British government's decision to release the convicted terrorist Abdelbaset al-Megrahi.[103] Will Hutton argues that despite the huge costs of the financial crash, 'big finance had—and still has—the politicians in its pockets'.[104]

In so far as political institutions have been left with any real power, they have been shielded from the control of elected politicians and ordinary voters. Public bodies like the Bank of England, NHS England, the Education Funding Agency, and the Low Pay Commission have been set free of ministerial control and handed over to independent boards on which business is liberally represented and on which neoliberal economists' views about the virtues of competition are treated as sacrosanct. The preparation of budget forecasts has been delegated to the Office for Budget Responsibility. Infrastructure planning has been delegated to a National Infrastructure Commission. Democracy has been intentionally bypassed as a part of a project to neuter democracy.[105]

MPs, the supposed guardians of our public interest, have been corrupted by the neoliberal creed that greed is good. In 2006, the senior Labour fundraiser and envoy to the Middle East, Michael Levy, was arrested in relation to allegations that political honours were being sold in return for party donations. He was not charged but he did subsequently say that: 'very few of the businessmen who gave large-scale donations to any of the parties did so without at least the vague hope that they might get some honour in return'.[106] In 2009, dozens of MPs were shown to have been fiddling their expenses. In 2010, two former New Labour ministers, Geoff Hoon and Stephen Byers, were accused of hawking their services to a fake public relations firm.[107] Meanwhile, business executives and lobbyists can reportedly pay £2,500 to sit next to a minister during lunch at the Conservative Party conference.[108] It came as no great surprise when

David Cameron—who benefited from an offshore trust in Panama established by his father—rewarded donors and political advisors in his resignation honours list.[109]

In this political environment, it is hardly surprising that just 16 per cent of people trust politicians to tell the truth;[110] that 46 per cent agree that politicians are in it only for what they can get out of it personally;[111] that 62 per cent believe corruption is a major/widespread problem in British public life;[112] that turnout in general elections has slumped; and that so many people feel that voting changes nothing. Politics has been privatized and it has been broken.

All the while, inequality is spiralling out of control. The TUC's General Secretary, Frances O'Grady, argues that Britain is becoming a 'Downton Abbey-style society in which the living standards of the vast majority are being sacrificed to protect the high living of the well-to-do'.[113] Will Hutton argues that Britain has arrived at a 'tipping-point' where 'unchecked inequality of both income and wealth, is about to metastasise in to serious economic and social cancer'.[114] Economic growth has stalled. The benefits of that growth have not trickled down. The costs of austerity have been loaded on to the poorest households. As Jeremy Corbyn maintains,

> It's not about me of course, or unique to Britain but across Europe, North America and elsewhere, people are fed up with a so-called free market system, that has produced grotesque inequality, stagnating living standards for the many, calamitous foreign wars without end and a political stitch-up which leaves the vast majority of people shut out of power.[115]

VII

I have, so far, equated neoliberalism and Thatcherism with the rolling back of the frontiers of the state and the rolling forward of the market. But there is an interesting puzzle here in so far as Thatcherism also, simultaneously, resulted in a strengthening of the British state. During the 1980s, defence expenditure was ramped up to fight and win a new round of the Cold War and the Falklands War. Mass peace protests at US Air Force bases and the Faslane nuclear submarine base were brushed aside. New laws regulating and stifling trade unionism were approved. Police forces were given new recruits, new powers, and a green light to take on and defeat the miners and the print workers at Wapping. The Greater London Council was abolished and other local authorities politically neutered through rate-capping. A national curriculum was imposed and control over the NHS was centralized. Government departments and recalcitrant ministers were bypassed. The Cabinet was 'handbagged' and power was transferred to Number 10.[116] Margaret Thatcher's own leadership style became first Presidential and then maniacal. Ministers and advisors who questioned her judgements were brushed aside.

So how are we to account for this apparent paradox?[117] Why did Thatcherism result in a free economy but a strong state?[118] One option here is to say that Thatcherism was an ideological hybrid. On economic issues Margaret Thatcher was a neoliberal who believed in free markets but on social issues she was a Conservative with a Victorian sense of morality and on political issues she was a Unionist and a defender of Parliamentary sovereignty. Thus, and as the politically smitten former editor of the *Sunday Telegraph* Peregrine Worsthorne put it, Thatcherism meant 'bitter-tasting market economics sweetened and rendered palatable by great creamy dollops of nationalistic custard'; and, it might be added, the smack of strong leadership from a conviction politician.[119]

Yet the politics of the free economy and the strong state outlasted Thatcher. Under New Labour, political authority was further centralized within 10 Downing Street and the Treasury. Around 3,000 new criminal offences were created.[120] A government which, according to the Director of the privacy campaign group *Big Brother Watch*, Nick Pickles, seemed to believe Orwell's '1984 was an instruction manual' subsidized the mass installation of surveillance cameras.[121] Hospitals and schools were subject to a never-ending raft of costly and counterproductive targets and inspections. Following the 9/11 attacks, the intelligence agencies were given new legal powers and enhanced budgets. Weapons of mass destruction were invented and countries were invaded. Then, under Cameron, the state was further strengthened via new surveillance powers, legal requirements upon universities to monitor extremism, and new limitations on the right to strike. In January 2016, Bob Kerslake, the former Head of the Civil Service, pointed to David Cameron's 'worryingly authoritarian streak', manifest in proposals to reduce the Labour Party's funding and to water down the Freedom of Information Act.[122] In 2016 the Investigatory Powers Act was passed. This introduced new powers allowing UK intelligence agencies and other law enforcement bodies to carry out targeted interception of communications, bulk collection of communications data, and bulk interception of communications whilst requiring communication service providers to retain UK internet users' connection records. Theresa May, for her part, has promised, at various times, to withdraw from the European Court of Human Rights and, in the aftermath of the 2017 terrorist attacks, pledged that 'enough is enough' and said that tough new anti-terrorism measures are essential.

None of this has happened by accident. Rather than viewing the combination of the free market and the strong state as either a contradictory paradox or as the manifestation of Margaret Thatcher's unique personality, they may simply be complementary and equally important parts of the ideology and practice of neoliberalism.[123] Neoliberalism came of age in an era of state collectivism. What this means is that neoliberals must—whether they like it or not—use the state to establish and protect free markets and to defeat vested interests in the trade union movement, local government, and civil service who oppose them. As Philip Mirowski observes, 'neoliberalism turned out to be very nearly the polar opposite of libertarian anarchism' in the sense that it seeks to 'infuse, take over, and transform the strong state, *in order to impose* the ideal form of society'.[124] A strong state is needed to protect the winners of the free market game from the economic losers. As the broadcaster and journalist Paul Mason observes, neoliberalism is a 'doctrine of uncontrolled markets' which 'says that the state should be small (except for its riot squad and secret police)' and, it might be added, its armed forces, court system, police force, and prisons.[125] In an American context, the academic Loic Wacquant writes, similarly, about neoliberalism's 'carceral state' founded upon the extension of the police and prison system.[126] Similarly, and with at least one eye on Britain, William Davies talks of a new incarnation of neoliberalism 'organised around an ethos of punishment', in which government sanctions welfare claimants and economic losers for the moralizing sake of punishing them.[127] The point here is that neoliberals are not against the state per se—only against the idea of the state doing certain things: protecting the poor, redistributing income, chasing corporate tax avoiders, or providing high-quality public services.

VIII

There we have it: the worst of all possible worlds for the left. A horror story. Market liberalism combined with state authoritarianism.

At some point between the disintegration of the post-war consensus in the 1970s and the Conservatives' fourth consecutive election victory in

1992, the British left embraced miserabilism as a vaccination against the endless disappointments of the world. To be on the left is to know with a grim sense of certainty that no matter how apparently close the election may appear, the Conservatives always win on penalties. More than that, to be on the left is to know that during the 1990s and 2000s it did not really matter which party won the elections because Labour was no different to the Conservatives. Tony Blair was a con artist under whose Third Way banner socialism was buried. The Corbynite left has of course been energized by the election of Jeremy Corbyn. But its sense of joy was always tempered by its sure knowledge that the political establishment—including the tattered remnants of New Labour—would do everything it could to discredit and destabilize his efforts to develop a meaningful political alternative. The left knows that social inequality is accelerating and social mobility is declining. But it also knows that large swathes of a tabloid-soaked electorate are only likely to get excited by titbits of stories about East European immigrants, welfare scroungers, and petrol price rises. Above all, the left knows that we live in an age in which ideas about the virtues of free markets and the economic follies of government have somehow acquired the status of a simple common sense to which there is no alternative. Far from inducing a political sea change in attitudes and values, the 2008 financial crisis and the recession and self-induced austerity which followed has—incredibly—strengthened the grip of the iron cage of neoliberalism. Writing perhaps in anticipation of the 2016 Conservative leadership contest and Boris Johnson's elevation to the position of Foreign Secretary, John Milton got the tone of things on the left just about right nearly four hundred years ago in the fourth book of *Paradise Lost*.

> Me miserable! Which way shall I fly
> Infinite wrath and infinite despair?
> Which way I fly is hell; myself am hell;
> And in the lowest deep a lower deep,
> Still threat'ning to devour me, opens wide,
> To which the hell I suffer seems a heaven.

This is the history I am going to challenge in the rest of this book. Britain has (of course) changed in countless ways since the early 1980s. Industries have been privatized. The service sector has grown and banking and finance have exploded. The contracting out of services has become a day-to-day part of life in the public sector. Tuition fees have been introduced. The trade union movement has been marginalized. Other pillars of traditionally male working-class culture have been destroyed. Working men's clubs have closed. Football has been commercialized and corporatized, with season tickets priced at well over £1,000 at some clubs. It would be pointless to argue that nothing has changed in Britain. What I am going to object to, however, is the idea contained within this history that everything has changed for the worse and that the only direction of political travel has been to the right and toward neoliberalism. I am going to start in the next chapter by examining changes in public attitudes and by arguing that neoliberalism has had a surprisingly limited impact on our collective understandings of the world around us. In the fourth chapter, I am then going to question the idea that the state has been rolled back before turning to the issue of inequality.

3

Bad attitude? Public opinion, the left, and neoliberalism

I

What lessons ought to be drawn from the 2017 general election? The upbeat, optimistic, one-more-heave argument is that Labour only narrowly lost the election and is well-placed to win its eventual re-run. After all, the left-of-centre parties—Labour, the SNP, Plaid Cymru, the Liberal Democrats, and the Greens—collectively secured 52 per cent of the vote: far more than the Conservatives and UKIP combined. Jeremy Corbyn showed that it is possible to mobilize electoral support without having to move toward a bland political centre-ground. He showed, against expectations, that it is possible to energize young voters and to build a coalition of the poor and dispossessed, the young, and the socially progressive middle class. Corbyn took Labour to above 40 per cent of the vote for only the third time in the last twelve general elections and did so despite the fierce opposition of the Conservative tabloid press. Labour got more votes than the Conservatives amongst those in work. The retired were the only social group Labour failed to win. With the Conservatives hugely divided over Brexit and just about every other policy issue, reduced to a tiny majority and left facing a choice between a failed leader and a divisive leadership contest, Labour is ideally placed to sustain its political momentum. In an age of entrenched anti-political sentiment, Corbyn has shown that anti-austerity left-wing populism is not only viable but hugely attractive to tens of millions of voters. Furthermore, there is now an ever-larger number of voters, particularly young voters, who, whilst they may not always vote Labour, have clearly decided that they will never, under any circumstances, vote Conservative.

The alternative and more pessimistic view is that the result in 2017 is not as good as it first appeared and is unlikely to be repeated. Labour increased its share of the vote by nearly 10 percentage points. But the Conservatives increased theirs by 5 per cent fielding an awful leader who ran a truly awful campaign. Labour increased its share of the vote at the expense of the Liberal Democrats and UKIP. The swing from Conservatives to Labour was only 2 per cent. In 1997, the swing from Conservatives to Labour was 10 per cent. In 2010, the swing from Labour to the Conservatives was 5 per cent.[1] Labour did spectacularly well in London and, famously, in university towns like Canterbury, but in its traditional working-class strongholds its vote continued to decline. The Conservatives gained Mansfield with an 18 per cent increase in their share of the vote. Furthermore, in Scotland, Labour remained moribund increasing its share of the vote by less than 3 percentage points and being beaten into third place by the Conservatives (who increased their share by nearly 14 points). 2017 was not only an unexpected election result, it was an unexpected, bizarre and unlikely-to-be-repeated campaign. Theresa May ditched the Conservative Central Office script and campaigned on her own leadership style whilst apparently launching policy initiatives like the 'dementia tax' without bothering to consult with her colleagues. Two of the issues on which Labour has, over the last decade, struggled, immigration and the economy, became side issues. In 2015 YouGov found that when it asked people what the most important issues in the election were, 52 per cent said immigration, 47 per cent said the economy and 43 per cent mentioned health. In 2017 63 per cent said leaving the EU, 49 per cent said health, and only 35 per cent said the economy.[2] One so-far-unanswered question for Labour is whether, with Jeremy Corbyn as leader, it can win a future election in which the economy is, once again, a major issue. Another question is whether it can win an election in which voters think it might be able to win an election. In 2017 voters punished Theresa May for calling an early election and sought to deny her a landslide victory. Many people voted Labour because they expected Labour to lose badly: as it had done as recently as the May 2017 local elections when the Conservatives had gained over 500 council seats and Labour had received a projected 27 per cent of the national vote. In the end, 2017 was a triumph relative to expectations. It was not a triumph. As the electoral commentator John Curtice observed in the immediate aftermath of the election result:

> There is a risk that, because the election result is being greeted through the prism of the widespread expectation that Labour would lose badly, it is forgotten that not only did Labour lose, but it did so almost as badly as in 2010, when Gordon Brown's administration was ejected from power. Corbyn might

> have succeeded in persuading many voters that he was an effective party leader after all, but he has still not demonstrated that he can persuade enough to do so to be able to take his party to victory.[3]

How does miserabilism come into this debate? Most obviously, a sense of political and economic despondency drove many voters to the polls to enthusiastically endorse Jeremy Corbyn's take-no-prisoners condemnation of the Conservatives and of New Labour's muddled compromises and concessions to the centre. But there is also a miserabilist explanation of why, despite the massive and manifest failings of the Conservative Party and the immense economic and social costs of austerity, Labour still lost.

Decades of neoliberal government have rewired Britain and pushed the electorate to the right. Too many people have been persuaded that greed is good and that the public sector is inherently inefficient, and they will not now vote for a party which makes the principled case for raising taxes to fund public services. Too many people have accepted the quasi-religious argument that wealth is a sign of economic virtue. After years in which the Conservatives and New Labour have scapegoated welfare claimants and asylum-seekers, too many people are, as the European Union referendum definitively demonstrated, now susceptible to dog-whistle authoritarian-populism. After decades in which the aggressive rolling out of markets has led to the disintegration of social capital, people no longer know or trust each other and no longer feel a sense of social solidarity.

What holds for the electorate in general holds doubly for the cohort of voters raised under neoliberalism. A new generation of voters—variously described as 'Thatcher's children', 'generation right', or the 'Boris generation'—will push the country even further to the right in the years to come.[4] In short, the left lost in 2010, 2015, and 2017 and may well lose again next time because the electorate has been remade in a neoliberal image. There are of course millions of people who recognize the follies of neoliberalism and campaign against it. Yet, the miserabilists will maintain, they are performing the electoral equivalent of pushing a very large rock up a very steep mountain. Arguments may be won and converts secured but large parts of the electorate are slipping out of the left's reach into a hermetically sealed world.

In this chapter, I am going to ask whether this story stacks up and examine whether and to what extent the electorate has been converted to neoliberalism. My basic argument is that the miserabilist argument is exaggerated and that the electorate has not been transformed. There have certainly been some dramatic shifts in public opinion over the last few decades. We have become much less deferential toward and less trusting of politicians and other authority figures. Our attitudes toward gender, race, and sexuality have become far more liberal and tolerant. Yet our collective attitudes towards issues like public expenditure, inequality, and the role of government have remained surprisingly stable and are a long way from being anything which could reasonably be described as neoliberal. To this extent, the 2017 election did not mark a moment of political conversion. Voters had never been firmly on the right. When it comes to immigration and welfare, public opinion is, it is true, well to the right of centre. But on these issues public opinion has always been well to the right. There was no great turning point in public opinion in the late 1970s. Britain has not been rewired.

I don't want to be thought to be arguing that, beneath the surface, we are a nation of socialist revolutionaries. Public attitudes are nothing if not confusing. On some issues, the balance of opinion is to the left. On others, it is to the right. And, as we will see in a moment, most people—in so far as they think in terms of left and right—think of themselves as being somewhere in the centre. But the important take-home message is that the electorate is a long way from being neoliberal. The left needs to work hard to persuade swathes of the electorate of the merits of its views and the credibility of its policies. But, however depressing the results of recent elections may have been, and however hopeless its chances of winning the next general election may sometimes appear to its critics, its position is reasonably strong.

II

Before looking at some of the nitty-gritty of surveys and polls, I want to first take a quick step back in order to look again at the terms 'left' and 'right'. These two words have of course become a standard part of our political vocabulary. Journalists and others routinely describe people, policies, and political parties as being on the left, on the right, or at the centre. I previously equated being on the left with a set of 'progressive' political values; a shared set of political hate figures and habits; and, above all, with the endorsement of a miserabilist history of modern Britain. I have also equated the right with the ideology of Thatcherism and neoliberalism. There is, however, a broader history here, which it is worth briefly relating if only to understand how arbitrary our use of left and right as terms of political description is.

The application of the terms left and right in politics is conventionally dated back to the moment when, at the start of the French Revolution, delegates to the Estates-General broke away to form a National Assembly. Since voting within this Assembly was conducted by physically standing at required moments, representatives started to sit themselves next to like-minded colleagues on, literally, the left- and right-hand sides of the Assembly floor. Assembly rules prevented representatives from describing each other as belonging to named political factions such as the Girondists. Therefore, left and right came to be used as terms of description and abuse. Out of this simple and exclusive contrast between left and right, there soon developed a conception of political space as a continuum with a centre, centre-left, centre-right, and so on. Propelled first by the Revolutionary and then Napoleonic wars, the use of the spatial metaphor spread first to Scandinavia and the Low Countries, then to Southern Europe, and, eventually, to Britain.[5]

Over time, left-wing and right-wing have become associated with sets of policies. The left is equated with higher taxes and higher public spending; generous welfare services; a greater emphasis upon reducing income inequalities; historically with support for the trade union movement; and, above all, with a belief in the need for an active state willing to challenge and constrain the market. The right is, by contrast, associated with lower taxes and lower public spending; a fear of welfare dependency; an emphasis upon equality of opportunity; opposition to trade unions; a commitment to low inflation and a balanced budget; and a faith in the virtues of free markets.

As a first cut at saying something about British political attitudes, how left-wing or right-wing are the electorate? The polling company YouGov regularly asks people about their underlying political positions. Figure 3.1 shows how, in February 2017, prior to the start of the general election campaign, people positioned themselves. 46 per cent of people described themselves as being at the centre or slightly to the right or left of centre. Only 6 per cent said they were very right-wing or very left-wing.[6]

The fact that so many people regard themselves as being at the centre of the political spectrum is important because there is strong pressure on parties to move to and to be seen to move to the centre-ground to get elected. To secure enough votes to have a realistic prospect of forming a government, parties must present themselves as being moderate, sensible, and in touch with mainstream public opinion, and their opponents as benighted

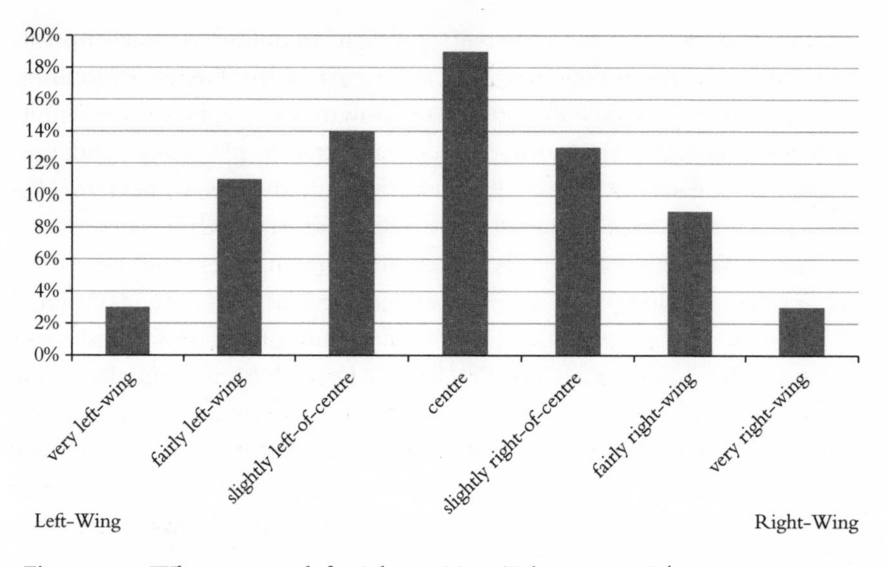

Figure 3.1. Where we are: left–right position (February 2017).[1]

Question: Some people talk about 'left', 'right' and 'centre' to describe parties and politicians. With this in mind, where would you place .... Yourself?

extremists who have vacated the political centre-ground. In recent times, Blair and Cameron have quite explicitly described their political strategy as being one of colonizing the centre-ground of politics, and in her speech to the 2016 Conservative conference, Theresa May also made a claim to the political centre.[7] The 2017 election showed that it is not an iron-law of politics that parties position themselves at the centre-ground. Labour, under Corbyn, did well despite positioning itself well to the left. But Labour lost in 2017 and it lost despite the Conservatives running an awful campaign in which they refused to give any ground to a centre-ground position on Brexit and threatened to increase the taxes and reduce the benefits of their core retired voting constituency.

My argument, so far, has two parts. First, most voters see themselves as being at the centre rather than on the neoliberal right. Second, parties need to appeal to voters at the centre if they are to have a good chance of winning an election. There is, however, a one-word objection to each of these claims: Thatcher. Margaret Thatcher was not a centrist politician. Far from it. Yet she won three consecutive general elections. More than that, in winning these elections, she changed the country. Voters may think of themselves as being centrist and moderate. But that centre, the miserabilist will argue, is now a neoliberal one forged by Margaret Thatcher and New

Labour. Through the promotion of never-ending austerity requiring tax cuts for the richest and welfare cuts for the poorest and most vulnerable, Britain has been shifted and is still being shifted to the right.[8] The fact that most voters still tell pollsters that they see themselves as being at the political centre is therefore neither here nor there. By the time of the next election, once moderate left-of-centre policies and politicians will be regarded as hopelessly naive and dangerously extremist.

III

We have reached a bit of a deadlock here. We know that people think of themselves as being at the centre but we don't know whether the centre has changed. So, we need to dig a bit deeper by looking at how people's answers to recurring questions about political issues have changed over time. If the miserabilist history is correct, what we ought to find is that people's average views have become much more right-wing and neoliberal.

Let's start with a classic issue which divides left and right. Should we increase taxes in order to spend more on health, education, and social services? Or cut taxes and expenditure? Or leave things as they are? Neoliberals—it ought to be clear—want a smaller state. They favour cutting taxes and expenditure. What does public opinion look like on this issue? Figure 3.2 is drawn from NatCen British Social Attitudes survey data and shows per cent support for each of these options between 1983 (the date of the first survey) and 2016. Support for increasing taxes and public expenditure rose steadily during the 1980s; stabilized at a high level during the 1990s; fell steadily in the 2000s (to a low of 32 per cent in 2010); rose once again following the Conservatives' election in 2010; and climbed to 37 per cent in 2014 before jumping quite dramatically to 48 per cent in 2016. Support for cutting taxes and spending flatlines its way through the 1990s and 2000s at below 10 per cent and fell to just 4 per cent in 2016. All in all, it is difficult to see in these shifts in public opinion clear evidence of the electorate being gradually converted to neoliberalism.

The discussion of attitudes toward taxation and expenditure leads us on neatly to the issue of austerity. The Conservatives have made a political virtue of their determination to cut the deficit by cutting public expenditure. How popular is this position? The evidence here is a bit mixed. In the aftermath of the 2010 election, public opinion split on the question of whether, as the

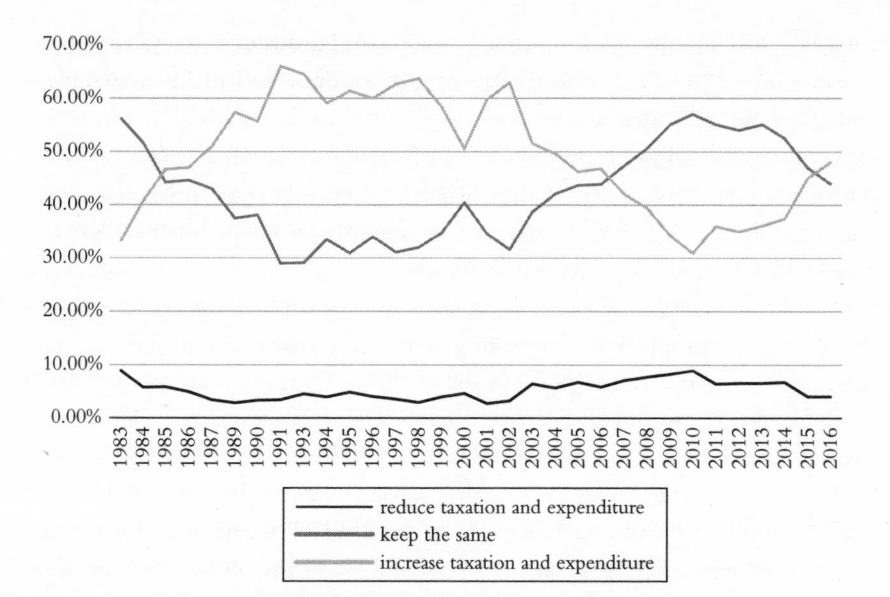

Figure 3.2. Attitudes toward public expenditure and taxation.[2]

Question: Which of these three options do you think the government should choose? Reduce taxes and spend less on health, education, and social benefits, OR keep taxes and spending on these services at the same level as now, OR increase taxes and spend more on health, education, and social benefits?

Conservatives argued, the deficit had been caused by excessive government spending. 37 per cent agreed and 36 per cent disagreed with this view and 27 per cent did not know. Yet, at the same time, and whatever they may have thought about the causes of the deficit, 47 per cent agreed and only 30 per cent disagreed with the proposition that spending cuts were 'essential for the long-term health of the economy'.[9] Over the next few years, the public continued to support the idea that cutting spending in order to reduce the deficit was essential, whilst slowly coming round to the view that the Coalition was cutting spending by too much and too quickly.[10] A poll on the eve of the 2015 election nevertheless showed that 46 per cent agreed with the view that 'the national economy is not yet fully fixed, so we will need to continue with austerity and cuts in government spending over the next five years' (30 per cent agreed that 'while a period of austerity was needed to fix the national economy, we don't need another five years of cuts in government spending').[11] Subsequent polling has shown that, at the time of the 2015 election, 25 per cent blamed the Conservatives for the size of the public debt; 39 per cent blamed global financial institutions; 55 per cent blamed the British banks; and 60 per cent blamed the previous Labour government.[12] The mood on austerity began quite dramatically in the aftermath of the 2015 election.

I previously said that the best way of finding out about changes in public attitudes is to look at the results of answers to recurring questions about underlying issues. There is, however, an obvious catch here. Social scientists and pollsters may ask people the same question year after year but the world in which they are asking those questions is constantly changing. It is hardly surprising that support for increasing taxes and public expenditure rose during the 1980s and early 1990s, given just how savagely public expenditure was being cut during this period. It is certainly true that public opinion about policy reacts to changes in policy. The American political scientist Christopher Wlezien has shown that, across a range of different kinds of issues, public opinion reacts as if it were set on a thermostat.[13] When the public believes that spending is being cut, it tends to favour increasing spending and taxes. When the public believes that spending is being increased, support for raising taxes and spending further tends to fall. Looking back at Figure 3.1, this makes intuitive sense. Support for higher public spending increases during the 1980s when the public believes that spending is being cut; falls steadily between 2000 and 2010 when the public believes that spending is being increased; and rises again from 2010 onwards when the public believes that spending is being cut. Labour governments tend to lose elections because they spend too much. Conservative governments tend to lose because they spend too little. In 2017 the Conservatives came within a whisker of losing because the public came to believe that austerity had gone too far.

This, however, raises another question. Do the public get it right? Are their views on issues like public expenditure grounded in reality? There is a long tradition in the social sciences of arguing that public opinion is spectacularly ill-informed and fickle. A lot of people don't know some fairly basic things about politics.[14] A survey by the Hansard Society in 2013 showed, for example, that only 22 per cent of people knew the name of their MP; that a majority of people did not know that Members of the European Parliament are directly elected; and that 33 per cent wrongly believed that peers in the House of Lords are elected.[15] It is also true that, in the case of two specific issues I will discuss presently, immigration and welfare, the public routinely believe a number of things to be true which are just not true. In the case of public expenditure, however, the public's thermostat does appear to be working. Measured as a share of national income, public expenditure did fall in the 1980s and early 1990s and did then increase in the 2000s, ending up after three decades pretty much where it had started. So, the miserabilist is, in this case at least, wrong. Public support for increasing spending cannot simply be explained as a reaction to ongoing cuts in public expenditure over the last few decades.

IV

Let's continue to look at some other measures of public opinion. Neoliberals want a smaller state which does fewer things. The basic role of government and the state is to create the conditions in which markets can flourish.[16] There are important differences between different branches of neoliberalism but neoliberals would generally be hostile to claims that the government ought to reduce income differences between rich and poor; ought to provide jobs for everyone who wants one; ought to provide decent housing for those who can't afford it; ought to provide health care for the sick; and ought to provide a decent standard of living for the old. I will say a great deal more about what the government does and does not do in relation to each of these issues later. For the moment, I just want to focus on what the public thinks about the government's responsibilities in relation to these issues and how what it thinks has changed over time.

The most recent data we have comes from the 2017 British Social Attitudes Survey.[17]

- 65 per cent believed government has a responsibility to reduce income differences between rich and poor (down slightly from 69 per cent in 1985).
- 48 per cent believed government has a responsibility to provide a job for everyone who wants one (down from 68 per cent in 1985).
- 79 per cent believed government has a responsibility to provide decent housing for those who can't afford it (down from 90 per cent in 1990—the first time this question was asked).
- 96 per cent believed government has a responsibility to provide health care for the sick (down from 98 per cent in 1985).
- 93 per cent believed government has a responsibility to provide a decent standard of living for the old (down from 97 per cent in 1985).

- 83 per cent believed government should support industry to develop new products and technology (down from 86 per cent in 1996). The same number believe that government should finance projects to create new jobs (unchanged since 1996).

What lessons can be drawn from these numbers? On the one hand, the number of people who think government should be doing the things listed here has generally fallen. Over time, we have moved closer to a neoliberal position. On the other hand, it is striking that clear majorities of people continue to believe that the government should be doing things neoliberals do not believe government should be doing. Public opinion may have moved slightly toward a neoliberal position but it is has not moved very far.

Next, we come to inequality. What matters for neoliberals is not equality of outcome but equality of opportunity. As we will see presently, levels of income inequality have waxed and waned over previous decades. The public's attitudes to inequality have, however, remained relatively stable. The British Social Attitudes survey asks people whether they think the 'income gap in Britain is too large'. Figure 3.3 shows that in 1983 74 per cent agreed it was. By 1995, this had risen to 89 per cent. Once the Conservatives were ejected from office in 1997, concern about inequality fell slightly. By 2004, 75 per cent thought that the income gap was too large. By 2013 (the latest available figure), the Conservatives had returned to power, inequality had, once again, become a headline agenda item, and the number who thought the income gap was too large had risen again to 81 per cent.

It is difficult to square these numbers with the idea that, over the last few decades, people have internalized nostrums about the economic benefits and moral virtues of inequality. A clear majority of voters believe that income differences are too large. There are, however, two important caveats here. The first is that lots of people who think incomes are too unequal are nevertheless opposed to income redistribution. In 2016, only 42 per cent agreed or strongly agreed that government should redistribute income from the better off to the less well off (up from 30 per cent in 2014).[18] This is startling. The question people are being asked here is not whether government should redistribute *more* income. Read literally, it is about whether the government ought to redistribute *any* income. So how should we interpret this finding? We might see it as offering clear-cut support for miserabilism. People say that they think income differences are too large but when push

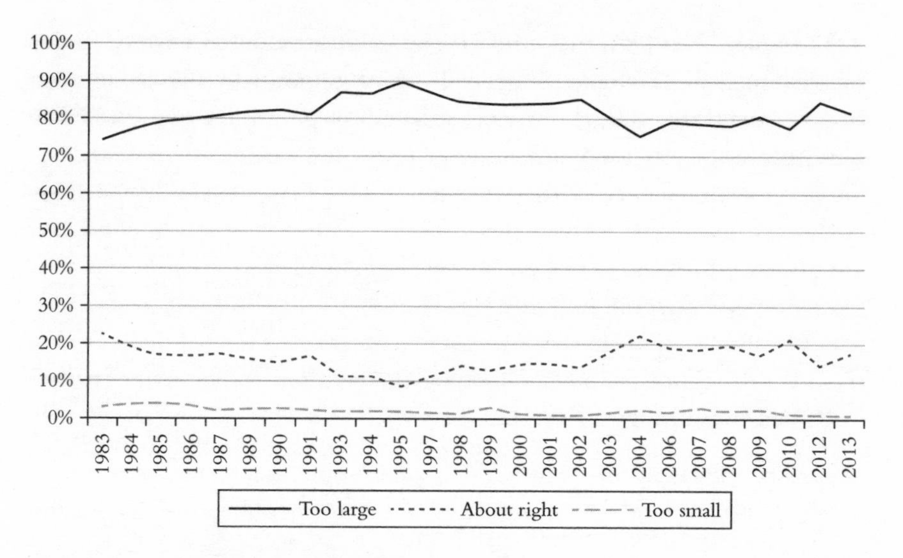

Figure 3.3. Income and inequality.[3]

Question: Would you say that the gap between those with high incomes and those with low incomes is too large, about right, or too small?

comes to shove, they are not prepared to do anything about it. This, however, does not make sense. We already know from Figure 3.2 that there is strong public support for raising taxes and increasing public expenditure and very little support for cutting taxes and cutting public expenditure. Opinion polls also reveal strong public support for other policies which have clear redistributive effects: such as raising the top rate of taxation and introducing a living wage.

So, what is going on here? People support policies which have redistributive effects but it would appear that there is something about the word redistribution itself which seems to raise people's hackles by conjuring up images of punitive taxation.[19] We may regard this as evidence for the triumph of neoliberalism. In the United States, Republicans appear to have successfully rendered the 'l-word' (liberalism) politically toxic by associating it with big government and a non-judgemental 'anything goes' moral relativism.[20] Any mainstream politician who describes themselves as being a liberal is now taking a major political risk. In Britain, it may be that redistribution is now also beyond the pale. This is, however, a rather limited victory. The bottom line is that most people still think that income inequality is too high and that the government ought to do something about it, which is not consistent with the basic terms of the miserabilist argument.

The second caveat is that when it comes to attitudes to poverty (rather than inequality per se), people generally think of poverty in absolute rather than relative terms. People think of somebody as poor if they can't afford to buy necessities like food and heating. They don't think of somebody as being poor simply because they have less money than somebody else. Only 20 per cent of people endorse this kind of a relative conception of poverty (a number which has remained largely unchanged since data on this issue were first directly collected in the mid-1980s).[21] The brilliant writer John Lanchester notes that, if we think of someone as being poor if they earn less than 60 per cent of the median income, then around 20 per cent of people in Britain today are poor, but that

> many people simply don't believe it. They don't think that what is called poverty constitutes *actual* poverty. They don't think it is true to say that 13 million UK citizens are poor. Beveridge defined want as the lack of 'what is necessary for subsistence', a much stricter criterion than the one that defines modern British poverty. Plenty of people agree with him. It is a secret thought, not much expressed in public, but...this is one of those ideas that run strongly through modern Britain, without being as forcefully expressed as it is felt.[22]

Lanchester argues that the left needs to recognize this problem and talk about inequality rather than poverty if it is going to engage with the public. I am minded to agree. It is, however, worth noting that David Cameron, at least the version of David Cameron that was Opposition Leader, had a different view. In a speech he gave in 2006 to mark the 25th anniversary of the publication of the Scarman Report into the 1981 Brixton riots, he argued that 'in the past we used to think of poverty in absolute terms—meaning straightforward material deprivation...that's not enough. We need to think about poverty in relative terms—the fact that some people lack those things which others in society take for granted.'[23]

V

I have so far focused on the results of surveys and polls relating to issues. John Bartle of the University of Essex has, however, developed a far more general measure of the 'policy mood' in Britain going back to the 1960s.[24] To do this, he has aggregated lots of individual bits of data about people's attitudes towards issues revealed in hundreds of surveys and opinion polls. The policy mood is not—I should emphasize—recycling the kind of data

I looked at in Figure 3.1 in relation to people's own sense of where they fall in terms of a left–right spectrum. Rather, the policy mood is telling us about people's underlying attitudes toward all kinds of different policy issues, including taxation, equality, trade unions, and unemployment. When people's views on these issues change, the policy mood changes and it does so regardless of whether people see themselves as having moved to the right. Bartle measures the policy mood on a scale running from 0 (consistently and absolutely right-wing) to 100 (consistently and absolutely left-wing). Figure 3.4 shows how the policy mood has changed. The first point to note here is that the policy mood in Britain is relatively moderate: rarely moving above 55 per cent or below 45 per cent. The second point to note is that it consistently swings against the incumbent party in a thermostat-like fashion. When Labour was in power in the 1970s, the policy mood moved to the right, reaching nearly 45 in 1980. When the Conservatives were in power in the 1980s and early 1990s, it moved to the left, reaching 56 in 1997. When New Labour was in office, it moved back to the right, reaching 47 in 2010. Since then, it has moved to the left again, hovering at just under 50 in 2014. The net result is that after fifty years of political change, we have ended up almost exactly where we started in the early 1960s, with a political mood that is neither left-wing or right-wing but resolutely centrist.

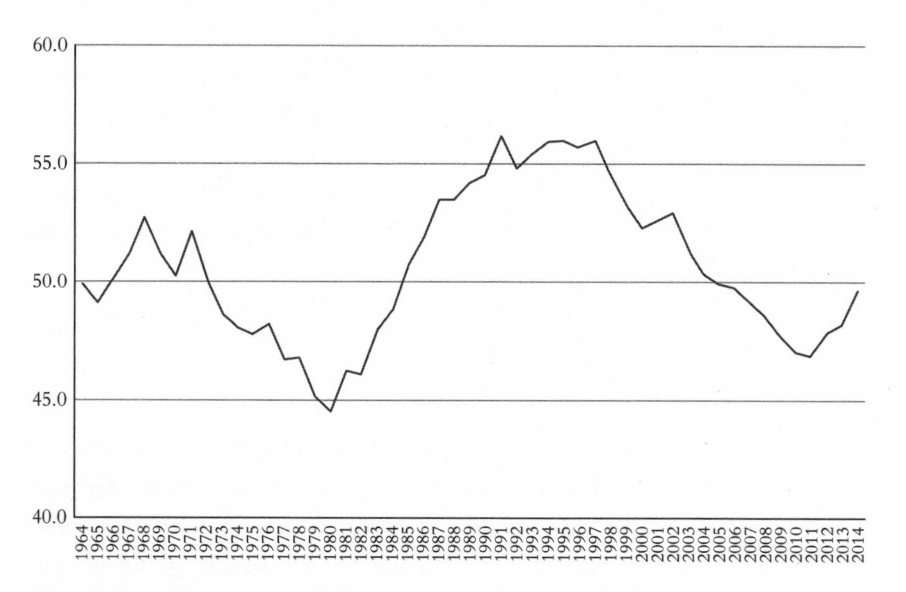

Figure 3.4. The policy mood in Britain, 1964–2014.
Courtesy of: John Bartle, University of Essex and NatCen Social Research.

VI

The interesting thing about the public's views on tax and spending, the responsibility of government to do things, and inequality is not how much they have changed but how little they have changed. There is, however, one clear exception to this general rule. Attitudes toward sexuality, race, and gender have changed beyond recognition.

In 1983, only 17 per cent of people said that sexual relations between two adults of the same sex were 'not wrong at all'. In 2016, 64 per cent thought homosexuality was not wrong at all.[25] In 2015, more UKIP voters supported gay marriage than opposed it.[26] Support for a woman's right to choose whether to have an abortion has risen from 37 per cent in 1983 to 62 per cent in 2012.[27] In 1983, 50 per cent of people were opposed to mixed-race marriages. By 2012, this number had fallen to 15 per cent.[28] Since the 1960s, each generation has become more liberal as it has grown older. Each new generation has, in turn, been more liberal than its predecessors. In 2012, only 4 per cent of those aged between 18 and 25 believed that 'it is a man's job to earn money and a woman's job to stay at home', compared to 28 per cent of those aged over 66.[29] In 2016, 73 per cent of those born in the 1980s believed that same-sex relationships are not wrong at all, compared with 41 per cent of those born in the 1940s.[30] 25 per cent of those born in the 1940s say they would be uncomfortable about their child or grandchild marrying someone from a different race. Only 5 per cent of those born since the mid-1980s feel the same.[31]

In *The Future of Socialism,* the future Labour Cabinet Minister Tony Crosland outlined a political agenda for the left at a time (the mid-1950s) when, in Crosland's eyes, full employment and the establishment of the welfare state had transformed Britain. Crosland's arguments about nationalization, comprehensive schooling, and inequality attracted a great deal of attention at the time. Tucked away toward the end of his book, however, was a little-noticed plea to the British left to widen its horizons, shake off its traditional social authoritarianism, and campaign for women's rights, reform of the divorce laws, abolition of capital punishment, and the legalization of homosexuality. Crosland argued that socialists should always have a 'trace of the anarchist and the libertarian [about them], and not too much of the prig and the prude'.[32] Crosland's reform agenda was taken up by a Labour Home Secretary, Roy Jenkins, in the 1960s and then, later, in the late 1970s and 1980s by campaign groups such as Stonewall, Labour-controlled local authorities, and parts of the trade union movement. At the time, each one of these groups was branded as belonging to the 'loony left'. Their arguments are, however, now regarded as being largely conventional. I don't think that the left in Britain can take sole political credit for shifting people's attitudes on social issues. *The Economist* has consistently supported gay marriage. Socially liberal Conservatives can point to the fact that it was David Cameron who legalized gay marriage. The campaign for greater sexual, racial, and gender equality and tolerance has, however, been led first and foremost by the left and, judged simply in terms of changes in public attitudes, has been one of its great success stories. It is of course the case that there is more to be done here in terms of changing attitudes. And yes, it is the case that changes in attitudes have not always translated into changes in behaviour. The left can and should continue to campaign on these issues. It can, however, do so from a position of strength.

VII

I have, so far in this chapter, been shovelling on the good news stories with a thick trowel. I now want to make things a bit more challenging. Notwithstanding what I have just said, the big shift in British politics in recent years, it might be argued, is one away from liberalism and toward social authoritarianism. The argument between the left and right is increasingly unimportant. Indeed, to quote Nick Clegg, this argument increasingly sounds like a 'distant echo from a bygone age'.[33] The big bang moment here came of course with the EU referendum, which split the left and right and pitted young voters against old voters; voters in London, Scotland, and the major metropolitan cities against voters in rural and small-town England; and voters with degrees against those with few qualifications.[34] The problem here comes not just with Europe. It comes with immigration and welfare. John Harris, whose work on the future of the left I quoted previously, characterizes the problem as follows:

> The rising inequality fostered by globalisation and free-market economics manifests itself in a cultural gap that is tearing the left's traditional constituency in two. Once, social democracy—or, if you prefer, democratic socialism—was built on the support of both the progressive middle class and the parts of the working class who were represented by the unions. Now, a comfortable, culturally confident constituency seems to stare in bafflement at an increasingly resentful part of the traditionally Labour-supporting working class.[35]

Let's start by looking at some of the evidence in relation to immigration. Since at least the mid-1990s, the left has recoiled in horror at the promises made by New Labour, Coalition, and now Conservative ministers to reduce immigration, cut the number of asylum-seekers, and get tough on welfare claimants. To rub salt in this wound, the public supports even tougher controls on immigration and welfare. In 2015, 76 per cent of people believed that too many immigrants had been let into this country.[36] In 2013, 77 per cent wanted immigration reduced 'a little' or 'a lot', with 56 per cent wanting a large reduction.[37] 80 per cent supported David Cameron's pledge to reduce net immigration to the tens of thousands.[38] Moreover, and since around 2010, people have come to regard immigration as a more important policy issue than poverty, pensions, low pay, or housing.[39] Are people more sympathetic to the plight of refugees? The answer is that they are probably not. At the height of the refugee crisis in 2015, newspapers published pictures of a 3-year-old boy, Alan Kurdi, who had drowned and been washed up on a Turkish beach. Just a few days later, YouGov asked people whether Britain should accept more Syrian refugees. 36 per cent said yes, 13 per cent said Britain should reduce the number it takes, and 14 per cent said it should not accept any at all.[40]

What about attitudes toward welfare? As we have already seen, the public believes that the income gap between the rich and poor is too large. But they don't like the idea of redistribution and, increasingly, they are suspicious of anyone claiming welfare. Drawing, once again, upon the results of the 2015 British Election Study, 62 per cent agree that 'if welfare payments weren't so generous, people would learn to stand on their own two feet' and 61 per cent agree that 'people could get a job if they really wanted one' (up from 41 per cent in 1987).[41] 69 per cent agreed 'our welfare system has created a culture of dependency'.[42] Unsurprisingly, given these numbers, the public has expressed consistent support for Conservative proposals to cut welfare expenditure. 74 per cent supported the introduction of a total benefit cap. 76 per cent supported measures to stop the benefits of people who refuse offers of employment.[43] New Labour's constant drip-talk about benefit fraud and welfare dependency seems to have undermined the faith of even natural Labour supporters. In 1995, 18 per cent of self-declared Labour identifiers believed 'benefits for the unemployed are too high and discourage them from finding jobs'. By 2014, this had risen to 38 per cent.[44]

VIII

So, have we now reached an unavoidable miserabilist moment? Up to a point... perhaps. But a lot of the debate about social issues, when it comes to immigration and welfare, is, like the noise at a swimming pool, concentrated largely at the shallow end.

The first point to make is that, when it comes to social authoritarianism or liberalism, the public's views are all over the place (as they are when it comes to left versus right). Bleeding-heart liberalism is a minority taste in the case of immigration and welfare. But when it comes to social issues like abortion and attitudes toward homosexuality, gender, and race, people are now much more liberal than they once were. Here are some other very quick and illustrative data. 64 per cent of people agree that 'young people today don't have enough respect for traditional values' and 63 per cent agree that 'censorship of films and magazines is necessary to uphold moral standards'. But 63 per cent also agree that 'people in Britain should be more tolerant of those who lead unconventional lives'; 82 per cent describe themselves as 'not prejudiced at all' against people who are transgender and 87 per cent agree that 'people should be allowed to organise public meetings to protest against the government'. At the same time, 80 per cent think the government definitely or probably should have the right to keep people under video surveillance in public areas, while 50 per cent think they should have the right to monitor emails and other information exchanged on the internet.[45]

The second point to make is that, in so far as issues like Europe, immigration, censorship, and respect for traditional values split the left, they also split the right into a liberal camp and a hang-them-and-flog-them old-school conservative camp. So, the left (meaning, in terms of parties, Labour, the Liberal Democrats, the SNP, and the Greens) has an opportunity here to build cross-cutting coalitions on a range of issues with liberal Conservatives.[46]

Turning now to the specific issues of immigration and welfare, the third point to make is that there never was a golden progressive age which we have lost. Quite the opposite in fact. In 1966, 85 per cent of people thought that too many immigrants had 'been let into Britain'. In 1974, 36 per cent supported 'sending coloured immigrants' back to their own country. In 1978, 52 per cent agreed that 'coloured people not born here should be sent back to their own country'.[47] As for welfare, by the late 1960s, only 22 per cent of voters favoured increasing welfare spending if this meant higher taxes.[48] Around a third of people at this time thought that the reason people were poor was because they did not make enough effort (a further third thought that the problem was both a lack of effort and circumstances).[49] In the 1970s, the media was awash with stories about welfare scroungers. The trial of 42-year-old Liverpudlian Derek Deevy on welfare fraud charges made headline news when it was revealed that the perpetually unemployed 'King Con' had spent upwards of £25 a week on luxury cigars whilst claiming over £35,000 in benefits.[50] A survey at the time found that 60 per cent agreed with the view that 'the trouble with welfare benefits is it's too easy to get them' and that 30 per cent estimated at least 25 per cent of the welfare budget was being claimed fraudulently.[51] The idea that public hysteria about immigration and welfare fraud is a modern neoliberal-induced invention is simply not true.

The fourth point to make is that when it comes to immigration and welfare, the news is not all bad. The number of people who believe that migration is good or very good for the economy has increased from 26 per cent in 2002 to 42 per cent in 2015 (up from 31 per cent in 2014). It is also worth noting that, when it comes to attitudes toward immigration, there is a strong generational gap. Whereas only 29 per cent of those aged 70 or over and only 37 per cent of those aged between 60 and 69 believe that immigration has been good for the economy, the equivalent figures for those aged between 18 and 29 and 30–9 are 47 per cent and 50 per cent respectively.[52] The same is also true, up to a point, for Euro-scepticism. Polling suggests that 73 per cent of those aged 18–24 and 62 per cent of those aged 25–34 voted to remain in the EU in June 2016 but only 43 per cent of those aged 55–64 and only 40 per cent of those aged 65 or above.[53] I am not sure whether anyone has run the actuarial numbers but it would appear pretty likely that, even if nobody changes their mind on the issue, there will be a majority in favour of staying in the EU by 2019 at the outside. When it comes to welfare, it is also worth remembering that only 32 per cent of people agree that 'many people who get social security don't really deserve help' (up only slightly from 31 per cent in 1987 when this question was first asked) and that there is strong public support for government spending on the sick and disabled (75 per cent in favour), parents who work on low incomes (61 per cent), and disabled people who cannot work (61 per cent) and only minuscule support for cutting benefits for those groups. There is also strong support for topping up wages for working couples with children (55 per cent) and lone parents (66 per cent).[54]

A fifth point to make is that often-harsh attitudes towards immigration and welfare, far from being expressions of neoliberal 'everyday sadism', are underpinned by a collectivist ethos in which notions of fairness loom large.[55] People are not simply worried that immigrants will take *their* jobs or their children's jobs. They are worried that immigrants are going to take the jobs of people in their communities and destroy our culture. People are worried that the country is full, immigrants are getting unfair priority access to social housing and the best schools, and that people claiming asylum are just economic migrants pretending to be something else. These attitudes might be both unpleasant and wrong but they are not neoliberal. They imply a sense of shared commitment to and concern about the nation and local communities which cannot simply be reduced to a calculation of self-interest. The same is broadly true of welfare policy. In some way, people have quite left-wing views on welfare. The Director of the Centre for Analysis of Social Exclusion at the LSE, John Hills, observes that there is a higher level of support in Britain for a progressive tax system, whereby the richest pay a higher rate of tax than the poor, and for the payment of flat-rate universal benefits over either earnings-related benefits or means-tested benefits than there is in most other European countries.[56] But it is equally clear that people are absolutely intolerant of even the faintest whiff of others unfairly abusing the system. People care about whether the welfare system is fair and whether others are treating it fairly.

The final and perhaps most important point to make is that, in so far as the left does find itself out of kilter with public opinion, it can and should do something about it. Doing something means, in part, arguing its case. When it comes to immigration, this means pointing out that the public (egged on by tabloid editors) massively overestimates the level of immigration. In 2013, King's College London and the Royal Statistical Society asked people questions about a range of factual policy issues.[57] What proportion of the population are immigrants? The public's average estimate was 31 per cent. It is something like 13 per cent. It also needs to keep saying that, on balance, migrants make a net contribution to the public finances; that inward migration accounts for as much as half of recent economic growth; that inward migration is balanced by an outward flow of British citizens; and that there is, at most, limited evidence that immigration has had any impact upon unemployment.[58] When it comes to welfare, this means pointing out that the public massively overestimates the extent of welfare fraud. The King's College survey asked people to estimate how much welfare money is claimed fraudulently each year. The average estimate was £24 out of every £100 spent. Most official estimates suggest that the actual figure is around 70 pence out of every £100.[59] Is more public money spent on pensions or on jobseeker's allowance? 29 per cent think that we spend more on jobseeker's allowance. In fact, we spend fifteen times more on pensions. It also means pointing out that, over the course of their life, most people go through stages of being net contributors to and net recipients of government transfers[60] and that, for all the fears about welfare dependency, only around 10 per cent of people with incomes amongst the lowest 10 per cent of incomes in 2000 still had amongst the lowest 10 per cent of incomes in each of the following eight years.

Doing something on these issues will also mean making policy decisions. Some of this will be relatively painless for the left. So, for example, faced with (contested) evidence that inward migration has put a downward pressure on wages at the lower end of the income scale and pockets of intense pressure upon health and education services in areas of high immigration, the left can stay within its comfort zone in calling for higher public expenditure via the Migrant Impact Fund; a higher living wage; new regulatory and legal powers to punish employers who recruit illegal workers; and, via the tax system, more redistribution to ensure that the key winners from migration (employers and those on higher incomes) compensate the losers.[61] But, like it or not, the left may also need to accept the post-Brexit case for at least a temporary brake on some forms of migration in a context in which there was a 35 per cent increase in the annual level of immigration to the UK between 2012 and 2016 and in which 81 per cent think it is important that people coming here to live have skills that Britain needs. There may, like it or not, also be a case for a renewed focus on social integration given that 87 per cent think it important that immigrants speak English and 84 per cent that they be 'committed to the way of life in Britain' (by comparison, only 19 per cent think it important that someone come from a Christian background and only 11 per cent that they be white).[62] The possible good news here is that, in the years to come, the debate about immigration may begin to move. Following the EU referendum net migration fell to its lowest level in thirty years. In March 2017, it was reported that the number of EU nurses registering to work in the UK had fallen from an average of 797 per month in late 2015 to just 194 a month. In a situation in which there are 24,000 unfilled nursing jobs, any sustained fall in the number of nurses arriving to work in the UK is likely to put a severe strain upon the NHS and shift the tone of the debate about immigration.[63]

When it comes to welfare, there is a case for arguing that the current system is fundamentally broken. Beveridge conceived of a flat-rate and universal social security system which would—when needed—pay people enough to live.[64] Yet once the welfare state was run through the Treasury's austerity mangle in the 1940s, it soon became clear that social security payments would not be enough and so, over the years, additional and means-tested supplementary benefits were introduced. Around two-thirds of welfare spending on working age benefits is now means-tested.[65] One obvious problem here is that the ongoing shift from universal to means-tested benefits has fuelled public mistrust in welfare spending. Means-testing is appealing to politicians because it promises to save money and, simultaneously, to ensure public money is being spent on those most in need. One problem with means-testing, however, is that it encourages people to distinguish between the deserving and the undeserving poor not simply in terms of their prior income (they don't deserve support because they already have enough to be able to afford to buy a new car and go on a foreign holiday each year) but in terms of whether they are doing enough to help themselves or are spending their money responsibly (they don't deserve support because they spend a lot of their money on booze and cigarettes and they are faking their disability). Politicians have sought to reassure the public that their money is not being wasted by launching new programmes to name, shame, and prosecute benefit cheats and to sanction those who are not doing enough to look for a job. The publicity given to these new initiatives may have had the opposite effect of persuading more people that there *is* a major problem with welfare fraud.

Over the years, the administrative and political costs of means-testing have just about persuaded me of the case for introducing a universal basic income. I know the objection here: that a basic income means paying people regardless of whether they work. But the current social security system has created a world in which large numbers of people are convinced that other people are not working anyway and in which support for the welfare system is ebbing away. The decision of Swiss voters to overwhelmingly reject the introduction of a universal basic income in a referendum held in June 2016 is a salutary political lesson.[66] The think tank Compass has, however, shown how a basic income might be introduced in the UK in stages and, at least initially, at a relatively low cost of around £8bn a year (equivalent to around 0.5 per cent of GDP).[67] Politically, I suspect that it may be tough to sell the case for a basic income if it is to be paid for through income tax. It may make more sense to offset the cost of a basic income through the introduction of a highly progressive annual wealth tax. Is talk of a basic income simply a left-wing pipe dream? Perhaps, but it should be remembered that no less a hardcore socialist than Friedrich Hayek was a supporter:

> The assurance of a certain minimum income for everyone, or a sort of floor below which nobody need fall even when he is unable to provide for himself, appears not only to be a wholly legitimate protection against a risk common to all, but a necessary part of the Great Society in which the individual no longer has specific claims on the members of the particular small group into which he was born.[68]

IX

What of the argument that the real impact of neoliberalism can best be seen in the attitudes of 'generation right': those born in the 1990s and 2000s? There is certainly plenty of evidence that young voters think differently to older people when it comes to politics. As we have seen, young voters have much more liberal and tolerant views when it comes to race, gender, sexuality, and migration. On a number of socio-economic issues, younger voters do, however, seem to be to the right of their elders. In 2012, 76 per cent of people aged between 18 and 34 thought the income gap between the rich and the poor to be too large. By comparison, 86 per cent of those aged over 55 thought the gap was too large. There is also some evidence that young voters today have more right-wing views than previous generations of voters. In the mid-1980s, 51 per cent of voters aged between 18 and 34 thought that the government should redistribute income and 48 per cent thought that the government should spend more money on the welfare state. By 2012, only 41 per cent of those aged 18–34 supported redistribution and only 28 per cent favoured spending more money on welfare.[69]

It may be tempting for anyone on the left over a certain age to roll their eyes at this point and start muttering about a Selfie-Stick generation. There are, however, good reasons to be cautious. In many cases, younger voters are to the right of where their parents once were but still, nevertheless, hold recognizably left-wing views. The fact that 76 per cent of people aged 18 to 34 still think that the income gap between the rich and the poor is too large is not the kind of politics we might expect from 'generation right'. It is also worth adding that we simply don't know how young voters' attitudes will change. The generational norm here is that people tend to become more right-wing as they grow older. Is this as inevitable a feature of ageing as listening to Radio 2 and wearing slippers? Churchill's line about anyone who is not a socialist at 25 having no heart and anyone who is not a conservative by 35 having no brain comes to mind. If today's young voters keep moving to the right, it is possible they will end up somewhere south of Sarah Palin. But it may be that today's young voters—raised during the long economic boom—have got their political realism in early and will not now drift further to the right.

It is also worth noting that, whatever the differences in their attitudes, young voters have become *less* likely, not more likely, to vote Conservative. Figure 3.5 shows the gap between the Conservatives' share of the *national* vote in general elections between 1979 and 2017 and their share of the vote among young people aged 18–24. In 1979, the Conservatives secured 45 per cent of the national vote and 42 per cent of the vote of young people: a 3 per cent gap. By 1992, that gap had grown to 8 per cent. It then fell to 5 per cent in 2005 before growing to 7 per cent in 2010 and 11 per cent in 2015. In 2017 the gap rose to nearly 23 per cent. Whereas 43 per cent of the

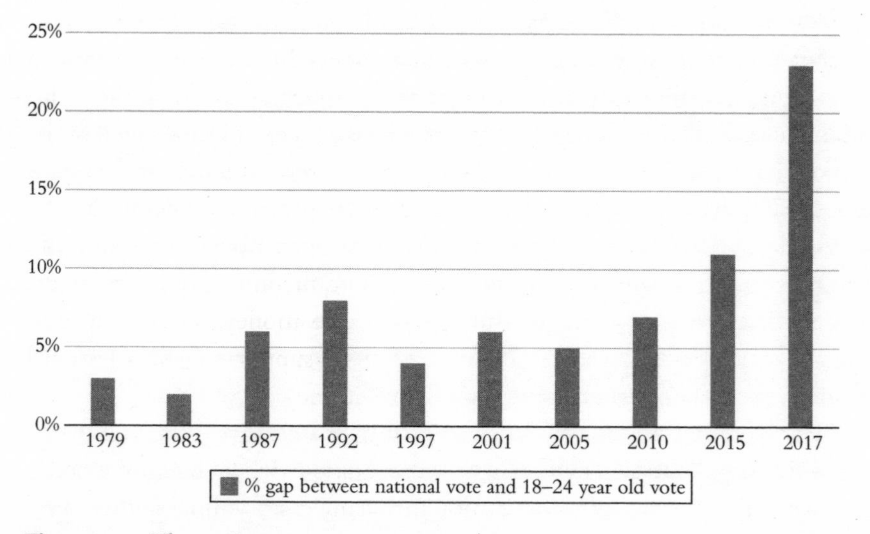

Figure 3.5. The voting-age gap, 1979–2017.[4]

country voted Conservative: less than 23 per cent of those aged 18–24 did so. At the same time, the number of younger people voting jumped dramatically from 43 per cent in the 2015 general election to 58 per cent in 2017 (although, at the same time, it is worth recalling that 84 per cent of those aged over 70 voted and that 77 per cent of those aged 60–69 voted).

X

Up until this point, I have focused the argument upon attitudes toward social and political issues. There is, however, a further argument to briefly consider here which I introduced previously. Has neoliberalism atomized society and destroyed social capital (the links, shared values, and understandings in society that enable individuals and groups to trust each other and so work together)? Robert Putnam's arguments about the decline of social capital in his evocatively titled *Bowling Alone* attracted a great deal of interest from politicians on both sides of the Atlantic. For a while, Putnam became Tony Blair's 'favourite guru'.[70] There is, however, an obvious question here. Putnam showed that there has been a significant fall in overall levels of social capital in the United States. Has the same thing happened in Britain? The data we have on changing levels of social capital are not strong enough to provide a clear-cut answer to this question. However, the balance of the available evidence suggests that it has not.

One key measure of social capital is trust. There is some evidence that overall levels of trust declined in the 1960s and 1970s. In 1959, 56 per cent of people thought 'in general, you can trust other people'. By 1981, this number had fallen to 43 per cent (before rising again to 44 per cent by 1990).[71] What has happened since then? Using a 10-point scale, the European Social Survey asks people across Europe whether 'most people can be trusted or you can't be too careful'. Between 2002 (the first survey) and 2012 (the most recent survey), the number of British people giving high-trust answers (points 7–10 on the scale) increased from 29 per cent to 34 per cent, whilst the number giving low-trust answers (points 1–4) fell from 24 per cent to 19 per cent.[72]

How engaged are people in their local communities? This is another key measure of social capital. 12 per cent of people belong to and actively participate in voluntary associations. 26 per cent belong to and actively participate in a sports, leisure, or cultural group.[73] These numbers have not changed significantly since the early 2000s. The number of people who feel a very strong sense of attachment to their neighbourhood has increased slightly from 21 per cent in 2000 to 25 per cent. 70 per cent of people agree or strongly agree that the friendships and associations they have with people in their neighbourhood mean a lot to them. The left has expressed considerable concern about the rise of gated communities. But gated communities are quite rare in Britain. In the United States, around 10 million homes are located within gated communities.[74] There are no precise figures for Britain. In the early 2000s, it was estimated there were something like 1,000 gated communities in England.[75] Since then, new planning restrictions have been introduced which make it harder to build gated communities in urban areas.[76] Moving on, the National Council for Voluntary Organizations reports that there has been a large increase in the size of the largest charitable organizations since the early 1970s, with, for example, the membership of the Ramblers Association rising from 22,000 to 130,000. The Council also finds that whilst there has been a slight fall in the percentage of people donating to charity each month, Britain has one of the highest rates of volunteering in Europe and the highest percentage of its population donating to charity each month in the world.[77] In 1980, the BBC's annual Children in Need appeal raised £1m in donations (when adjusted for inflation, a sum that is equivalent to around £4.5m today). In 2000, it raised £20m (around £31m today). In 2010, it raised £36m (£43m). In 2016, it raised £46m.

Britain has not, it would appear, been turned into a socially atomized, low-trust society in which people have been re-engineered as paragons of self-disciplined, competitive, and self-interested subjects.

XI

General elections are focal points through which we view our modern history. The Labour Party's history is littered with disappointing election nights. In 1951, Labour lost the election despite winning a larger share of the vote than the Conservatives. In 1959, Labour's great social democratic reformist, Hugh Gaitskell, was crushed by Harold Macmillan. In 1970, the polls suggested Harold Wilson was going to comfortably beat Edward Heath. He lost. In 1992, Neil Kinnock somehow lost an election that seemed to be his to win. In 2015 there was a sense of crushing disappointment on the left when the Conservatives gained an overall majority. In 2017 there was a sense of profound loss when the Conservatives just about held on to a majority. In the aftermath of the 1959 and 1992 losses, parts of the left publicly wondered whether Labour was doomed to a state of permanent opposition. In 1959, the social scientist and pollster Mark Abrams published an influential book asking whether *Labour Must Lose*.[78] In 1994, the academic book analysing the results of the British Election Survey was called *Labour's Last Chance?*[79] Yet, after losing in 1959, Labour won four of the next five general elections. After losing in 1992, Labour won the next three general elections.

Can a left-wing party or coalition of parties now win a general election? The key argument to be taken from this chapter is that the electorate has not been rewired. Indeed, on a range of issues it is startling just how non-neoliberal the electorate is. Let's look back, quickly, at some of the key findings. In doing so, I want to utilize once more the idea of a left–right spectrum of attitudes running from nought to ten. At the right-hand end, we can put Margaret Thatcher. To her left we can put John Major. Somewhere in the centre we can put Paddy Ashdown. To his left, we can place Ed Miliband. Finally, on the far left we can imagine a joyous combination of Tony Benn Jeremy Corbyn.

Where would we place average public opinion across each of the issues we have examined (figure 3.6)? This is obviously a subjective judgement, but given just how few people support cutting taxes and spending, I would describe public opinion on this issue as being to the left of centre at point 3. On attitudes to the responsibilities of the state, I would put the public further to the left at point 2. On attitudes toward inequality, the public is also to the left of centre at point 3 (although, as we have seen, when it comes to redistribution, things look a little different). When it comes to immigration and welfare, the public are well to the right: somewhere around point 8. At the risk of repeating myself, however, I would say that public opinion on these issues has always been well to the right of centre. Finally, and judging in terms of their reluctance to vote for the Conservatives, young voters can still be placed to the left of centre at point 4.

There is nothing in the overall balance of public opinion which would suggest that it is impossible for a left-of-centre party or coalition of parties to win future elections. Indeed, in 2015, a poll published in *Prospect* found majority public support for the nationalization of the rail and energy companies, higher corporation tax, greater regulation of low pay and rents, and

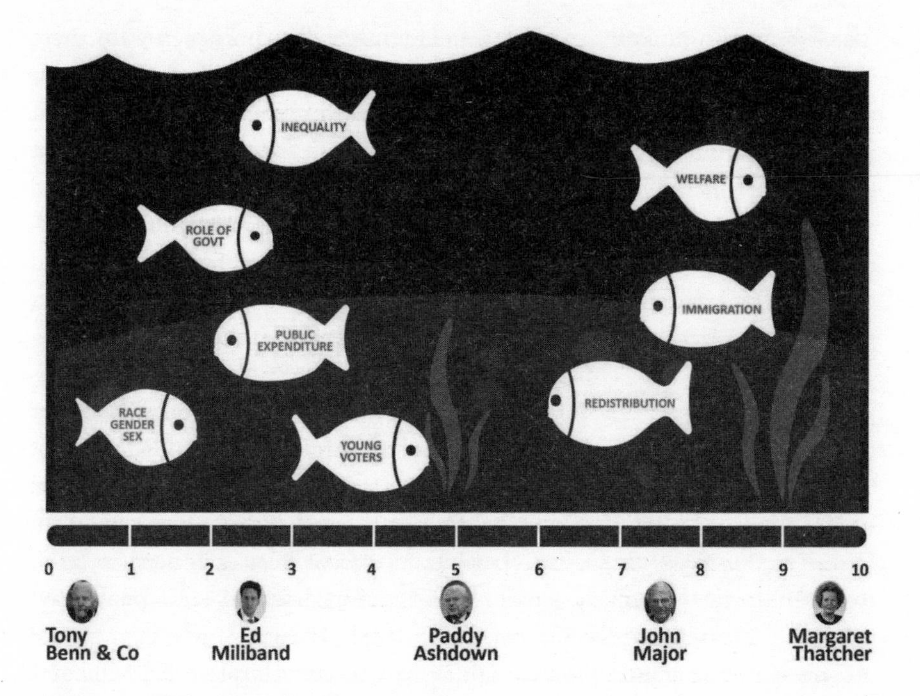

Figure 3.6. The state of public opinion.

local authority control of all schools (all policies Jeremy Corbyn is closely associated with).[80] In 2015, 78 per cent of people agreed that big business in this country has too much power. 68 per cent disagreed with the statement that there is no need for strong trade unions to protect employees' working conditions and wages. 48 per cent agreed that major public services ought to be in state ownership (28 per cent disagree). Only 32 per cent supported the idea of restricting free health care to those on lower incomes.[81] Looking back to the 2013 NatCen British Social Attitudes Survey, only 18 per cent of people supported the idea of private companies running state schools.[82] Only 19 per cent supported private companies or businesses running NHS hospitals.[83] 60 per cent support raising the top rate of tax to 50p. 40 per cent would support this even if doing so did not actually raise any extra revenue.[84] Only 24 per cent agree with the 'trickle-down' argument that cutting taxes for entrepreneurs and the wealthy can stimulate the economy, leading to economic growth and greater wealth for all.[85] 63 per cent agree with the moral argument that 'people have a duty to contribute money to public services' and only 23 per cent with the proposition that 'people have a right to keep the money they earn'. In the United States, 37 per cent endorse the 'contribution' argument and 57 per cent the 'right to keep' argument.[86] When Theresa May can say that most people in the country have a 'deep, profound' and 'often justified' belief that the world works well for a privileged few but not for them, it is clear the country has not shifted irrevocably to the right.[87]

It should not therefore come as a surprise that Jeremy Corbyn did so well in 2017. There is—and for some time has been—an appetite for left-wing policies. The question, looking ahead, is whether, by the time of the next general election, Labour can further improve its share of the vote and acquire enough seats to win. Labour's strategy, when the next election comes, will presumably be to see if can further increase turnout among younger voters; further squeeze the Liberal Democrat vote; and attract more ex-UKIP voters by promising to honour the result of the 2016 referendum whilst, at the same time, appealing to younger and metropolitan-based voters who remain in favour of European Union membership. All the while, it will need to hold together the Parliamentary Labour Party: most of whom have previously expressed no confidence in Corbyn.

This is not an impossible task. The 2016 referendum result and the 2017 election result showed that British politics is sufficiently febrile to make describing any future result as impossibly foolhardy. But it will be a difficult task. 2017 was, in some respects, and as the former Shadow Chancellor Chris Leslie has argued, 'an open goal'.[88] Next time round, Labour may face a more competent Conservative leader than Theresa May; a campaign focused upon economic credibility; and 'remain' voters who are more reluctant to vote Labour if Labour is signed-up to leave. The Labour campaign did an amazing job of mobilizing younger voters who had previously shunned polling stations. But this strategy is likely to be subject to diminishing marginal returns. Turnout has now risen from a low of 59 per cent in the 2001 election to 65 per cent in 2010, 66 per cent in 2015, and just short of 69 per cent in 2017. But on one account, Labour would need to raise overall turnout to something like 78 per cent in order to secure a mandate unless it can start to persuade people who voted Conservative in 2017 to vote Labour.[89]

In the past—in 1964, 1974, and 1997—Labour has regained power when it has been perceived to have captured the centre-ground and has been able to attract Conservative voters. In 1997 Labour captured five seats in Hertfordshire. In 2017, it did not win one. It may be that this conventional wisdom no longer holds and that Labour can stitch together a winning coalition without appealing to the centre and without attracting a reasonable number of the current 13.6 million Conservative voters (42.4 per cent of the electorate) to vote for them. But given that most voters are at the centre and that no party has lost an election with less than 40 per cent of the vote since 1970 this is going to be a hard ask.

XII

There is little evidence that the British public have or are on the way to acquiring neoliberal attitudes and values. On some issues, the public has quite left-wing views. On other issues, the public has for some time had broadly right-wing views. People have become much more liberal in their attitudes toward race, gender, and sexuality but they are a long way from being neoliberal.

All of which begs an obvious question. If the electorate are not neoliberal, why have they voted for a succession of neoliberal governments? After the obvious failures of the financial crisis and austerity economics, why has neoliberalism not 'merely survived but thrived'?[90] There are several plausible stand-by stories here which the left can fall back on. The public, although decent at heart, have been hoodwinked by a right-wing sensationalist media which sets out to deliberately destroy the credibility of left-wing leaders. Neoliberals have been extraordinarily effective at raising the salience of issues like immigration and welfare fraud on which the left is at a disadvantage. Neoliberal ideas have become so institutionalized within organizations like the IMF and the Treasury that sane alternatives to them are immediately dismissed as crazy.

As for the Labour Party, Gordon Brown and Ed Miliband failed to offer a clear and convincing policy alternative or a charismatic and engaging style of leadership. In 2010 and 2015, Labour offered 'austerity light' and was punished for its lack of conviction. In 2017, Labour came close but was, in the end, defeated not only by the electorate but by a rabid tabloid press and a political establishment which was all-too-ready to proclaim Corbyn as being beyond the political pale. Meanwhile, real-deal neoliberals have perversely but successfully been able to blame the economic crisis upon a lack of commitment to markets and fiscal responsibility. Government has somehow been left carrying the can for a crisis which financial markets created. The problem the left faces here is that there is an appealing simplicity to neoliberal ideas about austerity, the need to maintain balanced budgets, and the lazy inefficiencies of the public sector. It is nonsense to argue that because households must balance their budgets, states must obviously do the same thing.[91] But these arguments are not easily dislodged.

There is, I think, some mileage in some of these arguments. Much of the print media is openly hostile to the left.[92] In 2014/15, the Conservatives were ruthlessly efficient at focusing their campaign upon a small number of issues on which they had the beating of Labour. But notice how the phrasing of the question being asked here—'if the electorate are not neoliberal, why have they voted for a succession of neoliberal government?'—takes it for granted that successive governments *have* pursued a steadfastly neoliberal agenda. Similarly, the question which is often asked by political economists about why the 2008 crisis and recession have not led to a roll-back of neoliberalism assumes that Britain *was*, prior to the onset of the crisis, the 'emperor of neoliberalism'.[93] Viewing the 2017 election as marking the moment of a heroic but, in the end, futile protest against neoliberalism assumes that the Conservative Party which won these elections *is* unambiguously the political incarnation of neoliberalism. But once we go beyond public attitudes and look at what has actually happened in Britain over the last few decades, does this make sense? I will argue that it does not.

4

Alive and kicking

What the state does and why it has not been rolled back

I

In 1979, Margaret Thatcher entered Downing Street armed with the conviction that government is not the solution to problems but is the problem. By 1988, she had, in her own words, 'rolled back the frontiers of the state'.[1] We know from the history I outlined previously what happened next. New Labour picked up and ran with her agenda. In the immediate aftermath of the 2008 financial crisis, it looked for a moment as if neoliberalism had been fatally wounded and that the state was on its way back. But the turning point failed to arrive and, somehow or other, we still live in a political age in which markets are venerated and privatization extolled. The American philosopher Michael Sandel argues that, as a result, we have gone from having a market economy to living in a market society in which 'almost everything can be bought and sold'.[2] We now know from the polling data discussed in the previous chapter that most of the public continues to believe in an activist state which takes responsibility for the provision of housing, jobs, pensions, and healthcare. On this issue, as on so many others, the miserabilist argues that the public has been ignored.

There is no single metric we can use to measure the size, reach, and significance of the state; no single figure on a scale running from nought to ten which summarizes what the state once did and what it does today. What I want to argue, however, is that this history of the state is horribly one-sided and incomplete. In some ways, the frontiers of the state have been rolled back over the last few decades. In other respects, they have been rolled forward. The state has been prodded and poked but it is very much still alive and kicking.

I don't usually like introductory paragraphs which tell me what I am going to read before I read it. I am nevertheless going to include such a paragraph here because the rest of the chapter jumps from one place to another. I develop six arguments. First, in drawing such starkly clear lines between the post-war activist state and the post-1979 neoliberal state, the left forgets just how limited the reach of that post-war state often was. Second, when highlighting the scale and impact of post-1979 privatization, the left ignores or downplays the significance of those occasions since then when markets have failed and the frontiers of the state have been rolled forward. Third, and relatedly, whilst rightly emphasizing the fact that the state now owns fewer things, the left tends to ignore the fact that the state now regulates many more things. We are a long way from being a laissez-faire economy: let alone a laissez-faire society.

Fourth, when measured in terms of its overall contribution to national income, the state has not been downsized. Public expenditure as a share of GDP has risen and fallen over the last thirty or so years but has not changed that much overall. Is this because state expenditure has been shifted away from nice things like health and education to nasty things like policing and defence? I previously quoted Paul Mason's view that neoliberalism is a 'doctrine of uncontrolled markets' which 'says that the state should be small (except for its riot squad and secret police)'.[3] My fifth claim is that this argument about authoritarian neoliberalism does not stack up. The state now spends proportionately *less,* not more, of its money on things like defence and law and order. Is the state now being slashed and burned because of spending cuts? This question takes us to the heart of the left's arguments about austerity. My sixth argument is that when it comes to spending cuts, we need to distinguish between the Conservatives' words and their deeds. Since 2010, there have been plenty of announcements of spending cuts. Some of these cuts have been implemented. Quite a few have not. The Conservatives have not been free-spending hippies. But, equally, the state has not been radically downsized. Finally, I look at the issue of contracting out (or, as it is also often called, outsourcing). On this issue, I feel quite torn. My reading of the available evidence suggests that contracting out services often creates as many problems as it solves and rarely delivers genuine efficiency savings. On the other hand, I think the idea that contracting out can be easily equated with the rolling back of the frontiers of the state is too simple.

I should offer one brief point of clarification before I start. This is a chapter about the state. At various times, however, I talk about the government. The government refers to the group of ministers who are appointed to serve for a particular period. The state is a broader entity constituted by the many and varied kinds of departments, agencies, and other organizations which take their ultimate direction from and are in some shape or form accountable to the government. Governments may come and go. The state is the thing which endures.

II

When the left looks back to the 1960s and 1970s, the era of the post-war consensus, it often does so with an unjustified degree of nostalgia. In its rush to condemn everything which has happened since the election of Margaret Thatcher in 1979, the left remembers all the good things which once happened, whilst forgetting or putting to the back of its mind all the setbacks and disappointments.

I want to preface some of my other arguments by suggesting that there was no golden post-war age in which the state was rolled forward to right any wrongs and take on all comers. Yes, industries were nationalized and the NHS was established. Tens of thousands of council homes were built and planning regulations were established. Keynes was lionized and, for a time, Hayek was quietly forgotten. But there is another side to this story. Industries were nationalized but for the most part the directors who had been allowed to run them into the ground in the 1930s were allowed to run them again in the post-war years. There was very little in the way of strategic planning for these industries and almost nothing in the way of Parliamentary accountability.[4] So long as the nationalized firms kept their prices tolerably low, their managers were, for the most part, largely left alone.

When it came to economic policy, ministers talked the language of Keynesianism and planning but the Treasury remained unconvinced and made the defence of Sterling the cornerstone of its economic policy. Throughout the 1950s and 1960s, interest rates, taxes, and credit controls were raised and lowered not to flatten out the economic cycle as the Keynesians wanted but to provide a line of defence for the pound.[5] The Bank of England was nationalized in 1946 but this was a largely symbolic affair.[6] The Bank was, in reality, allowed to run its own affairs and the Bank, for its part, decided to allow the commercial banks to self-regulate theirs. In *Treasure Islands*, a history of the creation of offshore tax havens and banking, Nicholas Shaxson shows that the Bank of England did just what it wanted to do when it wanted to do it in relation to the establishment of the Eurodollar market and other unregulated offshore financial centres.[7] As for the commitment to planning, ministers ducked a commitment in the late 1940s to create a National Investment Board to set overall investment levels for the economy. In the 1960s, Labour promised a comprehensive national economic plan to be overseen by a new Department for Economic Affairs. But when it was eventually established, the department was effectively neutered by the Treasury and the national plan was ignored.[8] Whatever the rhetorical commitment to state intervention may have been, there were large swathes of economic and social life into which the state did not intrude during the post-war years. Financial markets, the legal and medical professions, the police, and the universities were allowed to organize and regulate themselves. Issues like workplace safety, food hygiene, gender and racial equality, bullying in schools and workplaces, and university access were largely excluded from the policy agenda and from political debate.[9]

III

In the 1970s, neoliberals argued that nationalized industries were failing because they were being run to benefit their owners, the state, rather than their customers. Once Margaret Thatcher had been elected, privatization became the tool through which the boundaries of the public and private sectors were redrawn. British Aerospace, British Gas, Rolls Royce, British Leyland, British Steel, and the water companies were privatized in the 1980s. British Coal, the electricity companies, and British Rail were privatized in the 1990s by John Major. British Nuclear Fuels and the National Air Traffic Service were privatized by New Labour. The Royal Mail, the Defence Support Group, Eurostar International, and the Tote have been privatized since. In each case, the government argued that public ownership had failed; that consumers would benefit from privatization through better service and lower prices; and that the privatized companies would be better able to raise investment funds.

Privatization is not, however, the end of the story. Markets also fail, and when they fail, politicians can come under immense pressure to intervene to protect customers and maintain services. Whilst rhetorically paying homage to the market, governments continue, in practice, to suffer from what I previously described as 'irritable intervention syndrome'.[10] Since the 1980s, the frontiers of the state have been subject to both 'roll-out' and 'roll-back'.

When British Rail was privatized in 1994, responsibility for the operation and maintenance of 15,000 km of track, signalling, bridges, and stations was transferred to a privately owned and, for a short time, extremely profitable private company, Railtrack. Critics argued that privatization was a mess and that Railtrack would struggle to attract enough capital to modernize Britain's dilapidated rail system. They were right. In 2000, the Hatfield rail accident killed four people and exposed the often diabolical quality of track and signalling. Railtrack—which was already struggling to meet the spiralling costs of modernizing the West Coast mainline—was left with a £600m bill for emergency repairs. Haemorrhaging money, it was placed into administration in October 2001. When no private buyers came forward, its assets were transferred to the state-owned and non-profit company Network Rail. Franchises to run passenger services are of course still contracted out to private companies (including, ironically enough, state-owned European railway companies like Nederlandse Sporwegen, Deutsche Bahn, and SNCF). To keep fares down and some of the rail franchises in profit, Network Rail charges ludicrously low prices for maintenance and track investment. As a result, it now carries over £30bn in debt and spends as much money servicing this debt as it spends on track investment.[11] The total level of public subsidy for the rail industry has increased from £0.7bn a year in 1994/5 to over £3bn today.[12] British Rail is long gone. But it has been replaced by a rather bizarre-looking public–private hybrid. What is unclear, at the time of writing, is whether the plans announced by the Transport Secretary, Chris Grayling, in late 2016, to require new franchise operators to establish 'integrated operating teams' combining Network Rail and operator staff will, in practice, result in the complete emasculation of Network Rail and, in effect, and as critics have argued, the re-privatization of the rail network.[13]

A similar story has been played out on the London tube. After years of extremely costly contract negotiations, responsibility for the maintenance of the tube system was awarded to a private company, Metronet Rail, in 2003. At the time, New Labour hailed the deal as living proof of the virtues of private enterprise and promised a rush of new investment. It all went horribly wrong. Having failed to meet its targets to refurbish stations or buy new train carriages, Metronet was blamed for a train derailment at White City in 2004. Losing money and facing a series of court cases, it was placed in administration in 2007 and its assets were transferred back into public ownership via Transport for London in 2008. It has been estimated that the failure cost the taxpayer anywhere between £2.5bn and £30bn.[14]

The semi-privatization of the pension system has created a similar dynamic in which the roll-back of the state created the conditions for its subsequent roll-forward. In the 1980s, the Conservatives part-privatized the pension system by offering people generous incentives to opt out of the state system. The number of people with a personal private pension increased from 1.2 million in 1988 to 4.3 million in 1994. What slowly became clear was that many of these pensions generated huge commissions for providers but minimal and uncertain returns for investors. Eventually, the Financial Services Authority, which, in a portent of the financial crisis to come, had been widely criticized for its 'light-touch' regulatory approach, stepped in and issued £12bn worth of fines for the mis-selling of pensions.[15] Amidst fears of a looming pension 'time bomb' for an ageing and under-provisioned population, New Labour eventually established a new state pension scheme and imposed a new legal obligation upon firms to provide a low-cost workplace pension scheme to their employees in which people are automatically enrolled.[16] At the same time, a new public pension provider—the National Employment Savings Trust—was established to provide an alternative to occupational pensions. Total public expenditure on pensions, it is worth recording, has risen from around 3 per cent of GDP in 1960 and 4.6 per cent of GDP in 1980 to over 8 per cent today.[17]

Then we come to the banks. In the 1986 'Big Bang', the City of London was deregulated. Under New Labour, the virtue of a light-touch regulatory approach was lauded as being necessary to attract the business and taxes of overseas (particularly American) banks. Peter Gowan argues that, during this period, London became to New York something akin to what Guantanamo Bay would become to Washington: the place where you could do abroad what you would not be allowed to do at home.[18] In June 2007, Gordon Brown lauded a 'new golden age for the City of London' (David Cameron responded by arguing, at the time, that there was 'too much regulation').[19] Two months later, the Northern Rock failed and had to be saved by the Bank of England. When no buyer was forthcoming, it was nationalized. Then, in September 2008, the global financial system melted. The Royal Bank of Scotland, HBOS, and Bradford and Bingley failed and were nationalized.[20]

As the economy slipped into recession, New Labour—which was widely held to have renounced Keynesianism—adopted a classic Keynesian response: cutting taxes, increasing spending, and running a budget deficit. Between 2007/8 and 2009/10, the annual budget deficit rose from £40bn a year to £154bn a year: an eye-watering 10 per cent of GDP. By 2010, twenty-five pence in every pound being spent by the government was being borrowed.[21]

What caused the deficit? I find it quite amazing that this is still the subject of political dispute. The right argues that the deficit was ultimately caused by New Labour spending too much. In 2005/6, the annual borrowing deficit was 2.6 per cent (up from −1.6 per cent in 2000/1). Total public sector debt at this time was 36 per cent of GDP (up from 29 per cent in 2001). The fact that New Labour had been running an annual deficit since 2001/2 made the fiscal situation worse when the financial crisis happened. It is, however, only a relatively small part of the public debt which was subsequently accumulated. The left argues that the deficit was due to the bank bail-outs. This is closer to the truth but we must be careful when it comes to what we mean by the bail-out. Over £134bn of public money was spent propping up the financial sector. This amounts to something like 1.3 per cent of GDP. But the annual public sector deficit as a share of GDP soared from 2.9 per cent of GDP in 2007 to 11.3 per cent by 2013. The real cause of the deficit was increased government welfare spending in the aftermath of the financial crisis and a huge fall in tax revenues as the economy fell into recession.

The rolling forward of the state to save the banks and to protect the broader economy may now look like ancient history. The Conservative-led Coalition, it might be argued, (re)abandoned Keynesianism in favour of a masochistic philosophy of deficit reduction, austerity, and an ever-smaller state. I will examine the Coalition's record on cutting public expenditure and reducing the deficit shortly. For the moment, I simply want to note that however apparently reluctant the Coalition may have been to use fiscal policy—that is, overall rates of public spending and taxation—to reflate the economy, it has promoted a wildly interventionist monetary policy through a £375bn quantitative easing programme. Quantitative easing is an unconventional form of monetary policy whereby the state (or, more precisely, the Bank of England) creates new money electronically to buy financial assets like government bonds. Quantitative easing has the effect of lowering interest rates and raising asset prices. It lowers interest rates because with the government creating money to buy its own bonds, the amount private investors can charge the government to borrow money (the interest rate) is lower. It raises asset prices because with less money to be made from lending money to the government, investors tend to spend more of their money buying other assets—such as shares, houses, or fine wines—which pushes up their prices.[22]

The Bank of England estimates that quantitative easing added 1.5 per cent to GDP and as much as £600bn to household wealth. This windfall has, however, disproportionately benefited a minority of wealthy households for the simple reason that household wealth itself is unequally distributed. The Office for National Statistics estimates that the wealthiest 10 per cent of households own 45 per cent of total aggregate household wealth (composed of property wealth, financial wealth, physical wealth, and private pension wealth) and that the least wealthy half of households own less than 10 per cent of total aggregate household wealth.[23] So the left has good reason to be wary of quantitative easing as it is currently practised. The Labour Party has, at times, spoken about pursuing a more radical and egalitarian form of quantitative easing whereby the Bank of England would purchase bonds issued by a National Investment Bank to fund large-scale housing, energy and transport projects.[24] But, to return to the issue at hand, quantitative easing is most certainly not an expression of laissez-faire economics. Indeed, right-wing commentators in the US have denounced the Federal Reserve's own quantitative easing programme as a socialist conspiracy to debase the currency and fuel inflation.[25]

IV

How can we best describe what has happened to the state in Britain over the last few decades? It does not seem particularly satisfactory to simply say that at certain times and in certain ways the state has been rolled back and at other times and in other ways it has been rolled forward. What is the alternative? One headline story here is the growth of the regulatory state.[26] Governments are now far less likely than they once were to directly own and control assets. Instead, they increasingly govern at a distance, relying upon rules and oversight. To use an oft-quoted metaphor, states increasingly seek to steer rather than row.[27]

The miserabilist history of modern Britain presents New Labour as a cheerleader for neoliberalism. It is certainly true that, during its time in office, more industries were privatized. Yet, in regulatory terms, New Labour unambiguously rolled forward the frontiers of the state. New Labour banned smoking in pubs and restaurants and the direct or indirect advertising of cigarettes. It passed legislation requiring charities—including fee-paying schools—to demonstrate a public benefit. It set new standards for nursery education and nursing homes. It criminalized the payment of bribes by British companies competing overseas. It passed right-to-roam legislation giving people access to 3 million acres of land in England and Wales. It criminalized speech or behaviour intended to generate religious hatred and made it a criminal offence to commit a sexual offence against a child overseas or to pay for the services of a prostitute subject to force. It subsidized savings within low income families via Children's Trust Funds. It established a minimum wage, a right to paid holidays, a plethora of tax credit schemes, a right to take paternity leave, and legislated to ensure workers' employment rights were guaranteed when a company was taken over. The Gangmasters Licensing Authority was established in 2006. Minimal standards for the quality of school meals were introduced and in 2008 the UK became the first country in the world to set a legally binding target to reduce carbon emissions (by at least 8 per cent of 1990 levels by 2050).

Throughout the 2000s, the Conservatives attacked what they characterized as New Labour's regulatory excesses and the creation of an all-intrusive 'nanny state'. Yet, during its time in office, the Coalition passed legislation requiring standardized cigarette packet advertising; extended provision for free nursery care and free school meals for primary school children; and, following a report by the Commission on Funding of Care and Support, imposed a cap on the maximum cost of residential care (but then delayed its introduction to 2020). Building on work undertaken by Britain's first female Home Secretary, Labour's Jacqui Smith, the Coalition also prioritized violence against women; legislating to make stalking a specific offence; enacting the EU Commission's anti-trafficking directive; developing the Modern Slavery Bill; criminalizing forced marriage; and launching an action plan to address female genital mutilation.[28] The Coalition also promoted 'help-to-buy' schemes which provided interest-free loans to cover 20 per cent of the cost of a new-build home and a state-backed guarantee on mortgage loans which has the effect of allowing people to take out larger loans relative to their income (a policy that was immediately abolished by Theresa May). It followed this up by launching 'pensioner bonds' which guarantee an above-market rate of interest for elderly savers. In their 2015 election manifesto, the Conservatives promised to build 200,000 state-subsidized starter homes; double the free childcare allowance; and cap increases in rail prices. In July 2015, the Conservatives announced that they were introducing a 'living wage' and a compulsory 'apprenticeship levy' on business. In March 2016, it was announced that a new 'fat tax' on sugary drinks was going to be introduced. In the Queen's Speech in May 2016, the government unveiled legislation to establish a legal right to a fast broadband connection; new measures to encourage investment in driverless cars; and new pension regulations to cap exit fees.[29] For her part, Theresa May has signalled the need for government to 'step up' to protect taxpayers (from tax-avoiding businesses), workers (from unscrupulous bosses), and householders (from exploitative utility companies).[30] In his 2016 Autumn Statement, the Chancellor unveiled a ban on letting agencies charging fees to renters; a proposal to ban businesses from cold calling people about their pension; a new National Productivity Investment Fund; a new Housing Infrastructure Fund; and new penalties for those helping someone use a tax avoidance scheme. In a significant legal ruling in October 2016 with important implications for other parts of the 'gig economy' characterized by the employment of independent workers for short-term periods, a London employment tribunal ruled that Uber drivers must be classified as workers rather than as being self-employed, giving them a practical entitlement to holiday pay, paid rest breaks, and the national minimum wage.[31] None of this looks like a programme of neoliberalism in action. Finally, in their 2017 manifesto, the Conservatives promised a cap on energy prices, new legal requirements around executive pay and new protections for workers on zero-hour contracts. Norman Tebbit and Nigel Lawson fulminated, during the campaign, about the way in which May had, in their view, abandoned Thatcherism.

What about financial regulation? It is often argued that the Conservatives have protected their friends and supporters in the City; that nothing has changed since the financial crisis; and that the banks are now 'the masters again'.[32] It is certainly true that Conservative ministers have not wavered in their commitment to the future of the City of London as a global trading hub. It is also true that the Bank of England and the government have steadfastly opposed the introduction of a European-level cap on bonuses and financial transactions tax. The idea that, a decade on from the financial crisis, nothing has changed and that an ethos of light-touch regulation survives intact is, however, just not true. The investment and commercial divisions of the largest banks are being ring-fenced in a way which will, in future, prevent banks from using deposits within the commercial (business and customer account) divisions of a bank to cover losses incurred within an investment banking division.[33] Since 2011, the Bank of England's Financial Policy Committee has assumed overall responsibility for the stability of the financial system. It explicitly operates on the assumption that markets are not always efficient; that banks are not always able or willing to identify sources of 'systemic' risk; and that the financial system is inherently prone to patterns of boom and bust.[34] Against sustained objections from the banking sector, the Financial Policy Committee has increased minimal capital buffers by a factor of ten and imposed an overall leverage ratio capping the value of a bank's assets to its capital.[35] It has also intervened in the housing market to limit the number of high loan-to-income mortgages banks are able to make. These reforms look (and up to a point are) dull. Criminal sentences for rogue traders, caps on bank bonuses, and the stripping of knighthoods make for better headlines. But they are nevertheless important reforms which amount to a significant rolling forward of the regulatory state.[36]

V

I now want to say something about globalization. Writing in the 1850s, Karl Marx spoke about the way in which 'capital, by its nature drives beyond every spatial barrier' and of how advances in communication and transport were resulting in the 'annihilation of space by time'.[37] The term globalization itself was coined by a Harvard Business School professor, Theodore Levitt, in the early 1980s.[38] He argued that companies like Coca-Cola and McDonalds were increasingly operating on a global scale without reference to differences in national or regional customs or tastes. Neoliberals—who seek to promote globalization through trade deals and capital liberalization—argue that globalization encourages trade and generates wealth. They also argue that globalization is politically attractive in so far as it leaves states with little alternative but to control inflation and reduce taxation and regulation if they are to attract inward investment and maintain the competitiveness of their exports. The American journalist Thomas Friedman argues that globalization is, in this sense, a 'golden straightjacket' which shrinks politics and grows economies.[39]

The left has, traditionally, viewed economic globalization with a mixture of trepidation and some horror. It argues that economic globalization, as it has currently been practised, leads to greater inequality and environmental degradation.[40] It points to the way in which financial globalization has made it easier for wealthy individuals to shelter their wealth offshore and for companies like Google and Starbucks to minimize their tax liabilities.[41] The left also worries that globalization might indeed be a straightjacket which leads to a regulatory race-to-the-bottom.

The impact of globalization on the states is not, however, clear-cut. Globalization has been promoted by states through trade deals and generous taxation rules. Globalization can also be managed by states. In recent years, the intergovernmental think tank the OECD—sometimes aided and sometimes abetted by the United States—has, for example, promoted greater tax disclosure through threats of financial sanctions.[42] Before, during, and particularly after the publication of the so-called Panama Papers, 11 million leaked documents providing details about hundreds of thousands of offshore trusts and other entities created by the Panamanian law firm Mossack Fonseca, governments have pledged to crack down further on tax havens and corporate tax avoidance.[43] Furthermore, various academic studies have actually found that there is a *positive* association between state expenditure and the degree of globalization on the one hand and the level of business regulation and inward investment on the other.[44] This is exactly the opposite of what we might expect if there was indeed a globalizing race-to-the-bottom.

Why do we see this? One argument here is that business is more likely to want to invest in economies with a skilled workforce, a strong university sector, good vocational training programmes, and strong transport infrastructure. Globalization does not lead to a minimal state. It creates the conditions for an interventionist 'competition state' in which governments take a lead role in ensuring that businesses can effectively compete in a global market.[45] Governments can play a key role in promoting commercial innovation. Technologies such as touch screens, lithium-based batteries, the internet, and GPS positioning were initially developed through state-sponsored and often state-run research and development programmes.[46] David Cameron, for his part, repeatedly argued that Britain is in a 'global race' and that winning this race requires government to 'have a proper industrial strategy to get behind the growth engines of the future'.[47] On this basis, the Coalition actively promoted the establishment of a Business Bank to stimulate lending to small and medium-sized enterprises; launched a Green Investment Bank; and invested public money in 'catapult' technology and innovation centres (to promote commercial research into cell therapy, digital technology, high-value manufacturing, offshore renewable energy, and precision medicine).[48] Theresa May has promised to 'rebalance the economy' and to develop an industrial strategy that will identify 'the industries that are of strategic value to our economy and support them through policies on trade, tax, infrastructure, skills, training and research and development'.[49]

There is a great deal to be done here. The basic argument for free trade is that it is a positive-sum game from which all gain. More recent research suggests that free trade agreements have had damaging and lasting effects on employment and household income in geographically specific areas of manufacturing industry and that the key to offsetting these effects is an active state-led labour market policy to retrain and relocate workers.[50] The OECD estimates that, on average, countries spend around 0.6 per cent of their GDP on such policies. In the United States—where public support for free trade has plummeted in the 2000s—federal and state governments spend just 0.1 per cent of GDP on active labour market policies. What about Britain? Following a freedom of information request, *The Economist* reported in 2016 that the Rapid Response Service—which provides financial support in the event of mass redundancies—had a budget of just £2.5m (less than 1 per cent of the value of United States expenditure).[51]

On occasions, ministers have presented Brexit as an opportunity to further globalize the UK economy and to achieve greater deregulation. In a speech in October 2016, Boris Johnson said that Brexit was about 'taking the machete of freedom to the brambles of European Union regulation'. (He also promised to make a 'titanic success' of Brexit: prompting George Osborne, who was standing next to him at the time, to remind him that the *Titanic* sank.)[52] Yet it seems equally likely that the rolling back of the frontiers of the European state following Brexit will result in the further rolling forward of the British state. The template here was set by the negotiations between the government and the Japanese car company Nissan. There were fears that Nissan was going to halt investment at its Sunderland plant over concerns that it might lose access to the single market. In October 2016, Nissan announced that it was going to go ahead with this investment. It is still not entirely clear what happened here. The government publicly promised funding for training and future investment in research and transport infrastructure. It was also widely reported that the government had promised to compensate Nissan for any losses it would incur if Britain did leave the single market without a free-trade agreement in place: a potentially huge liability.[53] Assuming that Brexit happens and really does mean Brexit, the government is going to come under pressure to negotiate new subsidies and support for farmers, the fishing industry, and universities. It is also going to have to put in place new regulatory regimes for issues as varied as product standards, drug approval, copyright, data protection, food inspection in third countries, and competition policy in relation to state aid as a replacement for European regulations. In their 2017 manifesto, the Conservatives, for example, promised to continue paying farmers the £2.5bn pounds they currently receive under the terms of the Common Agricultural Policy plus the further £0.8bn they get from European environmental conservation and rural development projects until 2022. The government is also going to need to develop a new migration regime for EU citizens. This is why, in late 2016, it was reported that Brexit negotiations would require over 500 separate legal and administrative project streams demanding the attention of up to 30,000 extra civil servants.[54]

VI

In the immediate aftermath of the First World War, the Hungarian Finance Minister, Rudolf Goldscheid, remarked that 'the budget is the skeleton of the state, stripped of all misleading ideologies'.[55] I like the simplicity of this observation. Politicians may talk about rolling forward or rolling back the frontiers of the state. The state's budget tells us what they have done. Figure 4.1 shows total public expenditure (central and local government spending) as a share of GDP between 1920 and 2016/17. What does it show? Between 1920 and 1938, public expenditure averaged just over 25 per cent of GDP. It is obvious that the Second World War then changed everything. By 1944/5, public expenditure accounted for over 60 per cent of GDP. In the aftermath of the war, public expenditure fell but did not fall back to anything like the levels it had been in the 1930s. During the years of the post-war consensus, public expenditure steadily grew from around 40 per cent to around 45 per cent of GDP. In the twenty-nine years between 1950 and 1979, public expenditure averaged just over 40 per cent of GDP.

I previously quoted the Conservatives' 1979 manifesto as an emblematic statement of the neoliberal philosophy. 'The state takes too much of the nation's income: its share must be steadily reduced.' What happened when Margaret Thatcher entered office? Between 1979 and 1990, public

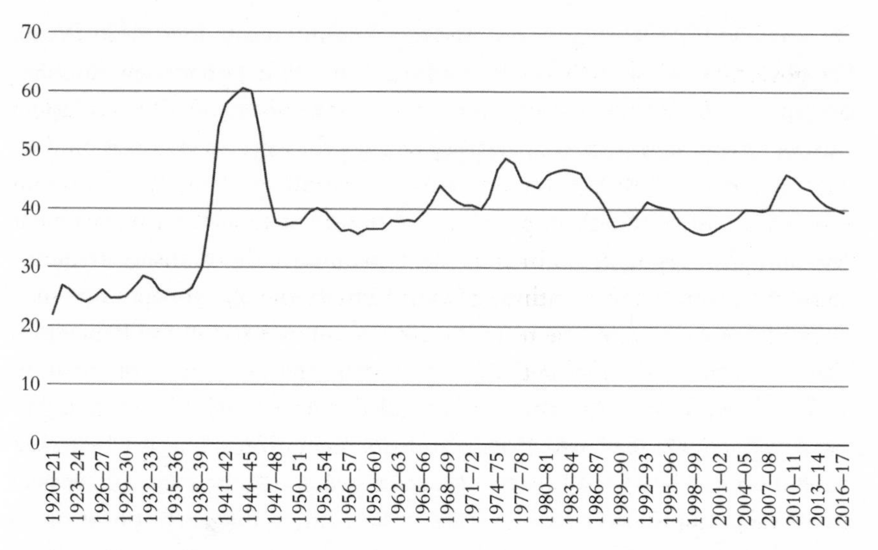

Figure 4.1. Total public sector managed expenditure as % of GDP, 1920/1–2016/17.[1]

expenditure fell from 43 per cent of GDP to just over 37 per cent of GDP. This is a significant although hardly earth-shattering change. Margaret Thatcher stopped the state growing. She did not, however, manage to roll it right back. Between 1990 and 1999, public expenditure then pretty much flat-lined. It was 37 per cent of GDP in 1991 and 36 per cent of GDP in 1999. Towards the end of its first term in office, New Labour then started to spend. Between 1999 and 2007/8, public expenditure rose from 36 per cent to 40 per cent of GDP. At the start of the recession, public expenditure then jumped to 46 per cent of GDP (the highest level it had been at for thirty years). Labour then lost the general election and between 2010 and 2016/17 public expenditure fell once again to 40.5 per cent of GDP. This is a significant fall over a relatively short period but it is not incontrovertible evidence of a neoliberal assault and a smoking-gun piece of evidence for miserabilism. Public expenditure as a share of GDP increased dramatically during the recession because welfare expenditure was increasing at the same time as the private sector was shrinking. This is what always happens during a recession. When the economy slowly began to recover in 2011/12, public expenditure as a share of GDP was always likely to fall. The important point to note here is that by 2016/17, public expenditure as a share of GDP had effectively reverted to the level it had been in 2007/8 prior to the financial crisis, at a point at which public expenditure had been rising for seven years.

I said previously that during the years of the post-war consensus between 1950 and 1979 public expenditure averaged just over 40 per cent of GDP. Between 1980 and 2015—the years in which the orthodox history maintains Britain swung decisively in a neoliberal direction—public expenditure waxes and wanes but averages 41 per cent of GDP.

If we turn from a historical to a cross-country comparison, Britain's public expenditure looks quite unexceptional. Using the most recently available OECD figures from 2015, public expenditure ranged from lows of 29.4 per cent in Ireland, 33.9 per cent in Switzerland, and 37.7 per cent in the USA to highs of 57 per cent in Finland, 56.6 per cent in France and 55.4 per cent in Greece. British public expenditure was slightly below the OECD average—just over 1 per cent lower than Germany.[56]

There is one further and important continuity here in public spending. Public expenditure is incredibly centralized. For all the talk—from both Labour and Conservative ministers—in recent decades of empowering local government, only 25 per cent of public expenditure is delivered at a local government level (down from 27 per cent in 1990). By comparison, 62 per cent of public expenditure in Denmark; 48 per cent of public expenditure in Sweden, and 33 per cent of public expenditure in Norway is delivered locally. In federal systems, 47 per cent of public expenditure in the United States is delivered through the states. In Canada, 69 per cent of public expenditure is delivered at either state or local level and in Germany the equivalent figure is 40 per cent.[57]

VII

So, if the state has not been shrunk, what has happened? One possible answer to this question is that it has been re-engineered. Recall here the argument that neoliberalism is, simultaneously, an ideology of the free economy and the strong state. Neoliberalism came of age in an era of state collectivism and has learnt to use the coercive power of the state to establish markets and to protect the winners of the free-market game from the economic losers. The fact that the state continues to grab a large share of the national income is, on this reading, unsurprising. The neoliberal state has had to recruit more police, build more prisons, and beef up its defence expenditure to prosecute imperial wars in faraway places.

I find this argument unconvincing. It is true that the state spends billions of pounds on policing and defence and is set to spend tens of billions of pounds more building new submarines to carry new nuclear missiles. It is also true that the prison population in the UK has nearly doubled from 42,000 in 1980 to around 86,000 today.[58] England and Wales now imprison around 148 people per 100,000 of their population and Scotland around 134 per 100,000. This is compared with 94 per 100,000 in Germany, 85 in France, and 82 in Sweden . . . but a staggering 737 in the USA.[59] It is also true that from the Falklands through to Sierra Leone, Kosovo, Iraq (twice), Afghanistan, and Libya, Britain has deployed troops to fight a succession of wars, very few of which are likely to receive nominations in a future United Nation's 'most effective exercise in state-building' award ceremony. Political miserabilism on the left is driven on by a cast-iron conviction that Blair was a war criminal who lied about weapons of mass destruction to justify an oil-grabbing invasion in Iraq.

The overall balance of public expenditure is not, however, consistent with arguments about neoliberal authoritarianism. In 2017/18, total public sector spending on public order and safety (including fire services as well as police, courts, and prisons) was £34bn and total spending on defence was £48bn. Total spending on social protection (welfare state cash benefits and in-kind provision) was £245bn. A further £32bn was spent on personal social services, £149bn on health, £37bn on transport, £102bn on education, £23bn on industry, agriculture, and employment, and £36bn on housing and the environment.[60] Using government figures, the website *Public Spending UK* estimates that total public expenditure on social protection fell fractionally from 1.61 per cent of GDP in 1980 to 1.5 per cent of GDP in 2017 and that defence expenditure fell from 5.4 per cent to 2.3 per cent of GDP over the same period. By contrast, public expenditure on health rose from 4 per cent to 7.2 per cent of GDP, whilst expenditure on welfare and pensions rose from 9.2 per cent to 13.75 per cent of GDP.[61]

The size of the armed forces has been cut quite dramatically from 320,000 in 1980 to 156,000 in 2017.[62] The number of police officers in the UK increased year-on-year from 110,000 in 1979 to 155,000 in 2003 and 171,600 in 2010. As of March 2016, there were a total of 151,000 police officers operating within the UK (a decrease of 11.7 per cent since 2010).[63] Around 6,000 of these officers are authorized to carry guns. In the year ending March 2016 there were just seven incidents in which the police discharged a firearm.[64] In the United States, around four people are killed each day by the police.[65]

I want to make one final but very brief point. I previously noted the statistic that New Labour created almost 3,000 new criminal offences during its time in office. This number is often cited in evidence of the claim that New Labour was an authoritarian party and recalls the endless iterations of ASBOs (antisocial behaviour orders) and detention orders during this period. But the existence of so many new criminal offences was, in other respects, the necessary legislative outcome of a rolling forward of a state which was doing things the left has always wanted the state to do. To put the point bluntly, it is not possible to create a minimum wage without making it a criminal offence for employers not to pay that wage.

VIII

In 2010, the Conservatives and the Liberal Democrats signed a Coalition Agreement setting out what they wanted to do in office. The key line in this long document was a quite simple one: 'the deficit reduction programme takes precedence over any of the other measures in this agreement'.[66] Spending cuts and austerity became the order of the day. Coalition ministers argued the case for what has become known as a 'contractionary fiscal expansion'. Keynesians argue that the government can generate confidence, consumer demand, and economic growth during a recession by increasing government spending. The theory of the contractionary fiscal expansion holds that the opposite can also be true. Higher deficits lead to higher interest rates because government has got to fund its debt. So, the argument goes, if governments cut spending in the here and now, business and consumers will conclude that, in the future, interest rates are going to fall and this will generate more business investment and consumer confidence.[67]

During its self-styled 'emergency' budget of July 2010, the Coalition announced £82bn in spending cuts to be phased in over four years. When the economy threatened to tip back into recession in 2012 and the rest of the world was calling upon the British government to abandon austerity and increase spending, the Chancellor assured everyone that there was no 'plan B' and carried on cutting. When the economy started to recover in 2013, the Chancellor then moved the goalposts: outlining a plan to permanently reduce the size of the state not simply as a means of reducing the deficit but as an end in its own right.[68] Put back in office following the 2015 election, the Chancellor, sure enough, announced plans to reduce departmental expenditure limits by an average of a further 1.6 per cent a year between 2015 and 2020.

Austerity in general and spending cuts have become the flashpoint of political protest. The left argues that spending cuts are not an economic necessity but a political choice and that spending cuts damage the economy and have been targeted on the poorest and most vulnerable. The Conservatives argue that spending cuts have been painful but unavoidable and that everyone has had to share in the pain. In other words, whilst the left and the right disagree about whether the cuts have been justifiable, they agree that they have occurred and that they have been dramatic.

I am not so sure that I agree with this argument about the impact of austerity. From what I can see, the Conservatives' attitude towards spending cuts bears a certain resemblance to that of St Augustine towards chastity (i.e. not quite yet). Let's go back over our recent spending history a second time. In 2010, the Coalition announced a dramatic £82bn package of spending cuts at a politically expedient time when, having just entered office, it was possible to blame New Labour for pretty much everything which had gone wrong in Britain since Bucks Fizz won the Eurovision Song Contest in 1981. Labour's outgoing Chief Secretary, Liam Byrne, had written a note telling his successor that there was no money left and the Conservatives persuaded most people that there was no alternative to spending cuts.[69] But as the economy faltered and the prospects of a double-dip recession increased, the threat of further cuts slowly receded. The 2011, 2012, 2013, and 2014 budgets *together* only resulted in a further £8bn in cuts.[70] Furthermore, in late 2012, and whilst swearing blind there was no 'plan B', the Chancellor announced he was delaying a tranche of the spending cuts announced in the 2010 budget.[71] As a result, departmental expenditure actually rose in real (inflation-adjusted) terms in 2013/14.[72]

In 2015, the left-of-centre American economist Paul Krugman published a mocking indictment of austerity economics in the *Guardian*.[73] One part of his argument involved an intellectual demolition of the economic theory of a contractionary fiscal expansion. The evidence that cuts can stimulate the economy was, he argued, pretty much non-existent. Others had already made the same point. Indeed, in a stunning and generally under-reported indictment of government policy, the Head of the Office for Budgetary Responsibility, Robert Chote, had written to David Cameron in March 2013 to say that, far from boosting the economy as he, Cameron, had claimed in his speeches, spending cuts had resulted in a 1.5 per cent further reduction in GDP.[74] The second part of Krugman's analysis was, however, just as interesting. By 2015, the British economy was, once again, growing. The Conservatives were arguing that this vindicated their strategy of spending cuts and deficit-cutting. Krugman argued otherwise:

> The key point to understand about fiscal policy under Cameron and Osborne is that British austerity, while very real and quite severe, was mostly imposed during the coalition's first two years in power... a return to growth after austerity has been put on hold is not at all surprising. As I pointed out recently: 'If this counts as a policy success, why not try repeatedly hitting yourself in the face for a few minutes?' After all, it will feel great when you then stop.

The economy did not grow because of spending cuts. The economy grew because austerity was parked.

During the 2015 election, the Conservatives played up the extent of the cuts they had made and promised the country a lot more face-slapping. Yet in his July 2015 budget, the Chancellor unexpectedly announced an additional £83bn in spending over the lifetime of the 2015–20 Parliament in order to reduce the extent of the cuts in departmental expenditure limits.[75] Then, in November 2015, when changes to the economic forecasting model employed by the Office for Budget Responsibility generated significantly improved fiscal forecasts for the 2015–20 Parliament, the Chancellor chose not to maintain the planned pace of deficit reduction but, instead, to further delay the application of welfare and departmental spending cuts. In a staggering but politically clever U-turn, the Chancellor also announced at this moment that he was abandoning plans to slash expenditure on tax credits prior to the introduction of his self-styled living wage. In February 2016, the economic skies suddenly darkened and the Office for Budget Responsibility revised its growth forecast downwards.[76] Shortly after, the Chancellor announced that spending on Personal Independence Payments for the disabled was going to be cut, only to abandon that plan following the resignation of the Secretary of State for Work and Pensions, Iain Duncan Smith. By October 2016, with a new Chancellor and Prime Minister in place, growth forecasts had been cut further but the Autumn Statement was used to unveil a set of new spending decisions adding around a total of £38bn to public sector net borrowing between 2016/17 and 2021/22.[77]

Between 2000/01 and 2009/10, public sector current expenditure measured in real (inflation-adjusted) terms at 2016/17 prices rose from £477bn to £680bn (a 42 per cent increase). Between 2009/10 and 2016/17, real public sector current expenditure rose from £680bn to

£691bn (a 1.6 per cent increase).[78] Spending on health and social protection also grew in real terms.[79]

What has happened to the deficit? In 2009/10, the annual deficit was £151.7bn (or 9.9 per cent of GDP) and total public sector debt was £1,010bn (or 64.8 per cent of GDP). The Coalition promised to work towards eliminating the deficit and significantly cutting the overall public debt. This has not quite worked out. By 2015/16, the annual deficit (excluding public sector banks) was still £72.2bn (3.8 per cent of GDP) and by 2017 total public sector debt had risen to £1,727bn (or 86.5 per cent of GDP).[80] In the first six months of 2016, the Office for Budget Responsibility was estimating that there was just over a 50 per cent chance that the government would be running a small budget surplus by 2019/20—fully thirteen years after the start of the financial crisis and after what is forecast at that point to have been eight years of continuous growth.[81] Then, in October 2016, citing the new economic challenges posed by Brexit, the Chancellor formally abandoned any target of returning the budget to surplus and announced an additional £122bn in borrowing over five years.[82]

During the 2017 election, Theresa May focused her campaign on Brexit and her own leadership qualities and generally downplayed debt and the deficit. In the immediate aftermath of the election she then told Conservative MPs that austerity was being reviewed and perhaps parked. The deficit has remained stubbornly high partly because economic growth has been consistently lower than expected. As a result, tax revenues have been lower than initially forecast, meaning that the deficit has not fallen. But the deficit has also remained stubbornly high because government spending has not been cut by nearly as much as the Conservatives and Labour and the left imply.

I don't want to overstate my case here. There have been cuts and some of these cuts have been severe. Overall public expenditure may have risen between 2009/10 and 2016/17 but there were real (inflation-adjusted) cuts to spending on education, economic affairs, and two totems of neoliberal authoritarianism: defence (a 12 per cent real cut) and public order and safety (a 20 per cent real cut).[83] Local government budgets have been cut and social care provision has been hammered.[84] Public sector wage increases have been capped at 1 per cent and, since 2014 at the latest, have fallen behind private sector wage growth. Public sector investment has also been cut dramatically. Between 2000/01 and 2009/10, public sector net investment, the amount of money invested by government on new infrastructure, in inflation-adjusted 2016/17 prices rose from £8.8bn a year to £58bn (a staggering 559 per cent increase). Between 2009/10 and 2016/17, public sector net investment then fell from £58bn to £38bn (a 34 per cent decrease).[85] This is an incredibly depressing figure. What makes it even more depressing is that the deficit and the debt are still very much with us and are likely to be exacerbated further by Brexit, which is expected to lead to a reduction in inward migration and so a fall in tax revenues.[86] In a generally gloomy report published in July 2017, the Office for Budget Responsibility noted that:

> A decade after the outbreak of the financial crisis and recession, net borrowing is well down from its peak. But the budget is still in deficit by 2 to 3 per cent of GDP—as it was on the eve of the crisis—and net debt is more than double its pre-crisis share of GDP and not yet falling. As a result, the public finances are much more sensitive to interest rate and inflation surprises than they were. In terms of the political backdrop, the previous Government had to abandon a number of measures to increase taxes and cut welfare spending, the new Government has just agreed a 'confidence and supply' arrangement that increases public spending significantly in Northern Ireland and the Chancellor of the Exchequer notes of austerity that 'people are weary of the long slog'.[87]

Unless Britain defaults on its debts (which would seem unlikely) or intentionally or unintentionally allows inflation to rise to such an extent that it significantly reduces its real value, the debt is not going to go away. £1,904bn (the Office for Budget Responsibility's forecast total public sector debt in 2021/22 as of March 2017) is a lot of money and, sooner or later, it is going to have to be repaid (with interest). In 2017/18, £46bn was already being spent on debt interest: more than on public order and safety, housing and the environment, or transport and nearly as much as on defence. Over the last five or six years, the left and the right have fought something of a phoney war on austerity. Sooner or later, it may get a whole lot more serious.

IX

In this final section of the chapter, I want to consider an objection to my argument that the state is alive and kicking. I have so far focused on the relative balance between and the size of the public and private sectors. The objection to this is that it misses the way in which the state has in recent decades been transformed and re-created in the image of the private sector. One key argument here relates to the extent and impact of contracting out.

The government now spends around £90bn each year buying goods and services from the private sector and has contracted out a further £90bn of activities to the private sector.[88] This amounts to around 25 per cent of total public expenditure. ATOS, a French IT and business processing service, earns around £0.7bn a year in revenue from the public sector; Capita around £1.1bn; G4S £0.7bn; and Serco £1.8bn.[89] Central government departments spend around £1bn a year on management consultancy services and the NHS spends a further £640m.[90] Within local government, a number of councils have moved from contracting out individual services to signing contracts in which a private firm agrees to deliver a bundle of very different services.[91] In the case of the Grenfell Tower disaster, it became clear that at least eight contractors and sub-contractors, led by the construction firm Rydon, were involved in separate elements of the refurbishment of the tower or the provision of materials used for the work.[92]

The first point I want to make here is that services have been contracted out to charities and local voluntary groups as well as to profit-making firms. In the 1990s, the provision of drug treatment programmes within prisons was hugely improved as a result of the contracting out of services to locally based drug charities with a background in harm minimization programmes and strong contacts in local communities.[93] More recently, the government has issued a Social Impact Bond through which seventeen charitable foundations fund a £5m investment to work with prisoners at Peterborough prison to cut reoffending rates.[94] As part of the contracting out of probation services, community rehabilitation companies have been established to provide joined-up housing and employment services and to reduce reoffending rates amongst, in particular, young offenders. Profit-making companies like Sedox have been awarded contracts but are doing so in partnership with local authorities and charities like NARCO, Adaction, and Shelter.[95]

Contracting out is often described as a form of privatization.[96] This is particularly the case when it comes to the contracting out of NHS services (something I discuss in more detail in the next chapter). I can see why the term privatization is, in some respects, a useful one. Wages and terms and conditions of workers are often cut and pension entitlements and contractual obligations relating to minimum periods of notice for redundancy offered to public sector workers are sometimes withdrawn when services are contracted out.[97] Yet, at the same time, if this is privatization, it is a partial kind of privatization. In the 1980s and 1990s, nationalized industries were sold to private firms who then acquired ownership rights. Contracting out does not entail the privatization of ownership. The government gets to decide which services to contract out, on what terms, and for how long. It gets to set the objectives contractors must meet; how performance is to be measured and at what intervals; and what happens when contractors fail to meet their obligations. These are, in short, highly managed markets in which government retains overall responsibility for the provision of services.[98]

Contracting out, like regulation, blurs the lines between public and private. This is not simply a matter of making the public sector more like the private sector. In entering contracts with government, private companies are also subject to a reverse process of what might be called 'publicization'. To survive and thrive, companies like Serco must acquire new contracts and to acquire new contracts, they must demonstrate that they are meeting the terms of their existing contracts. This, clearly, does not always happen. There is no shortage of horror stories attached to the contracting out of private services. In 2012, G4S was widely criticized for its failure to recruit or train enough staff to provide security at the London Olympics. The following year, G4S guards were charged with manslaughter following the death in custody of a deportee, Jimmy Mubenga. Serco was fined for overcharging on a contract it held with the Ministry of Justice to electronically tag prisoners. Capita was widely criticized for failings in a contract it held to provide court interpreters. ATOS was attacked for the inhumane and often inaccurate way it conducted tests to determine whether people were eligible to claim Employment and Support Allowance (formerly Incapacity Benefit). These were all very public failures which were widely reported upon and resulted in a fall in the company's share price and a turnover in its senior management.

The important point here is that government has the opportunity, if it wants, to impose fines upon failing firms and withhold future contracts from them unless and until they have changed their management team or business practices. The government may not always choose to exercise this option and it is true that parts of the contracting-out market are dominated by a small number of large firms. Yet in many respects, the effect of contracting out services has been to politicize the provision of public services and enhance levels of accountability as much as it has been to privatize it.

There are also some real success stories here. Residential children's care is now dominated by the private sector and in 2016 Sir Martin Narey issued an overwhelmingly positive report about the quality of care being provided across the sector in England.[99]

It is not just private firms engaged in contracting out which have been subject to a process of steady politicization. To a degree which would have seemed quite extraordinary just a few decades ago, publicly listed profit-making firms are now subject to a sometimes intense pressure from politicians, the media, and campaign groups to maintain their 'social licence' by accounting for and, on occasions, changing their policies in relation to wages and labour conditions (including those of subsidiary firms or contractors); the number of women appointed to senior positions; their environmental record; bonus payments; the treatment of suppliers (particularly in the case of supermarket chains, which have been accused of squeezing the profits of, in particular, farmers); and, in the case of large firms like Google, paying their fair share of taxes.[100] I am mindful here of not wanting to appear to be arguing that the glass is always half-full but it is striking that, in recent years, corporate practices at firms like Sports Direct, Wonga, and BHS have attracted sustained political attention and public opprobrium. Business is not simply allowed to get on with doing whatever it wants to do without anyone bothering it.[101]

X

There are some things the state used to do which it no longer does. Food rationing was ended in 1954. The obligation to undertake National Service was phased out in the early 1960s. The last people to be executed by the state in Britain, Peter Allen and Gwynne Owen Evans, were hanged in August 1964. Incomes policies (state-directed attempts to agree wage and productivity deals with unions and employers) ran aground in the 1970s. In 1979, most forms of exchange controls limiting the amount of money which could be taken out of the country were abolished. Maintenance grants are no longer paid to university students.[102] There are plenty of things the left argues the state should do which it currently does not do. At the time of writing, this list would include the imposition of a Tobin tax on financial transactions (a small tax levied on short-term transactions, principally, as it was initially conceived, spot conversions of one currency into another, to discourage financial speculation); the introduction of a carbon tax to mitigate environmental damage; the full nationalization of the railways; a ban on the advertising of junk food to children;[103] fully state-subsidized university education; tougher action on corporate tax avoidance; more effective regulation of private company pensions; and a far more aggressive programme of state-led housebuilding.

Being on the left, I would endorse most of the items on this list. What I don't, however, buy is the idea that the frontiers of the state have been rolled back under the onslaught of neoliberalism. The state still plays a central role in all our lives. It employs over five million of us.[104] It collects around seven hundred billion pounds in taxes each year from us. It houses more than six million of us.[105] It tells us at what age we can drink alcohol, have sex, leave school, drive, smoke cigarettes, and retire. It tells us what we can watch on TV and tries to regulate what we can see on the internet and, through hate speech legislation, what we can say in public. It sets rules for developers about where they can build houses and tells us what we can and cannot do if we want to build an extension or convert a loft. The state decides whether and for how long animals must be kept in quarantine. It decides who gets to visit the country and in what circumstances they can stay. It registers births and deaths. It determines who can marry and what has to happen in order for a marriage to end. It subsidizes rail tickets, the installation of solar electricity panels, and the cost of nursing homes. Within the terms of the European Emissions Trading Scheme, governments set the overall level of permitted emissions and the terms under which carbon permits can be bought and sold. It sets rules about the maximum amount universities can charge for tuition fees; determines at what point former students must start to repay their tuition fees (currently £21,000 a year at a 3 per cent interest rate); and after how many years this debt is wiped out.

The state has ruled that there can be no market in surrogacy, organ donation, or votes. The state determines where roads are built and how they are paid for (although congestion charging has been introduced in London, there are only a couple of toll roads and around half-a-dozen toll bridges in Britain[106]). The state tries to persuade us to drink less alcohol, eat more vegetables, do more exercise, quit smoking, save more for our pensions, have safer sex, undertake voluntary work, drive more carefully, sleep more at night, buy British goods, waste less food, and use less energy. It starts and ends wars and signs treaties and now and again makes apologies for things it has done in the past. The state has educated my children and cared for them when they were sick. The idea that the state has been rolled back does not tally.

5

Public services

Health and education

I

I have, so far, looked at the role of the state in quite general terms. I now want to look at two public services, health and education, that are particularly close to the left's heart but which are also the stuff of day-to-day politics. The aim is, once again, to think through how much has changed over the last few decades; how strong the grip of neoliberalism has become; and how tenable a miserabilist history is.

The left believes passionately in the public provision of high-quality health and education services free at the point of delivery. The health care and education you receive ought not to depend upon your ability to pay or where you live but upon your medical need and, in the case of education, beyond a high basic minimum, on academic ability. Public services bring out the best in us. Markets in health care and education risk reduce us to profit-and-loss numbers. They divide us and bring out the worst in us.

When the left starts to get misty-eyed about social solidarity and equality, neoliberals, for their part, want to ask some difficult questions about efficiency and incentives. Removing health and education from the disciplining effects of competitive markets may sound like a good idea but doing this has predictably come at the expense of higher costs and poorer services. Health and education are bloated bureaucracies in which the interests of producers are routinely put ahead of those of patients and pupils and in which doctors and teachers find it too easy to blame any failings on a lack of resources. What should be done? We already know the answer to this question. The state must be rolled back and the competitive market rolled forward. Private companies should be set free to compete to provide high-quality and low-cost health and education services with some form of state-subsidized insurance system for the poorest households.

The first and most important thing to say right at the start is that this argument has largely fallen flat. Think tanks like the Institute for Economic Affairs and the Adam Smith Institute still occasionally publish papers extolling the virtues of competitive private health care markets and school voucher systems.[1] There may be some Conservative backbench MPs who, given half a chance, would argue that we can no longer afford to pay for the NHS and that it is time to consider some fully privatized alternative to it. Yet this argument is, for now at least, pretty much out there on the political fringe. The public overwhelmingly think that the state has a responsibility to provide health care. Any Conservative leader who does anything other than promise that the NHS is safe in their hands is, for the foreseeable future, going to come to a sticky electoral end.

It has not always been this way. In the mid-1980s, Margaret Thatcher contemplated dismantling the NHS and replacing it with an insurance-funded health-care system. In the end, she was dissuaded from doing so by, amongst others, her then Secretary of State for Health, Kenneth Clarke.[2] Extremely generous rebates on the cost of private medical insurance were, however, introduced throughout the 1980s. Through the Assisted Places scheme, thousands of children were provided with free or heavily subsidized places at fee-paying independent schools. Yet as time has gone on, the argument for dismantling the NHS and state schools has grown weaker not stronger. The left looks like it has won the argument about the state provision of public services.

Not so quick (I hear many people say). Neoliberals may have lost the argument about health care and education but they have in its place pursued a scorched-earth policy. Funding has been slashed. The fundamental principle that health and education ought to be provided free of charge has, in recent years, been steadily undermined through the introduction of charges for crutches, hospital parking, and even for eating sandwiches in school canteens.[3] Above all, the government has cannibalized state services through successive waves of contracting out. Profit-making companies whose only duty of care is to their shareholders have been awarded juicy contracts on generous terms to run core health services. Dr Youssef El-Gingihy—a GP in East London and author of *How to Dismantle the NHS in 10 Easy Steps*—argues that the NHS is currently on a 'one-way road to privatisation'.[4] Attacks on state schools and the NHS have become a commonplace. David Cameron may have spoken movingly about the treatment his son received within the NHS but he promoted a 'surge in privatisation'.[5] The critic will want to argue that New Labour was not an innocent bystander in all of this. Tony Blair bought the basic argument that public-sector workers needed to be remade in the image of their more attractive and harder-working private-sector cousins. He introduced targets and inspections and promoted the privatization of services. Ken Clarke suggests that Labour ministers 'got away with introducing private sector providers into the NHS on a scale which would have had the Labour Party on the streets in demonstration if a Conservative government had tried it'.[6]

What has been the result of this policy of covert neoliberalization? The answer to this question is a lengthy one. A sense of perpetual crisis. The first national NHS strike (organized by junior doctors). Low staff morale and high staff turnover (20,000 doctors are estimated to have emigrated between 2008 and 2014, whilst the Chief Inspector of Schools in England, Sir Michael Wilshaw, has warned of a 'teacher brain drain' abroad[7]). Escalating waiting lists and a shortage of school places.[8] Rising health and education inequalities.[9] Creeping commercialization. Scandals and disasters in hospitals like Mid-Staffordshire caused by target-chasing and a lack of management accountability.[10] Above all, the result has been a creeping pessimism about the future. Jacky Davis, a consultant radiologist in North London and co-chair of the NHS Consultants' Association, is clear that the NHS is in the process of being 'destroyed'.[11] Most people would be happy to pay more taxes to fund better public services.[12] Yet only 50 per cent of people believe the NHS will be paid for through taxes and be free at the point of delivery in ten years' time.[13] During the EU referendum debate, I lost count of the number of occasions on which people argued that public services were being stretched beyond the breaking point. The left and right agree that there is a crisis in the NHS and in our schools. They just disagree about who caused it and what should be done about it.

Against this, I want to argue that the NHS and state schools are not in that bad a shape. They are not in great shape. The NHS faces huge challenges (and has done since at least the 1960s) to integrate health and social care in a situation in which a lack of funding for the latter is placing additional and partly avoidable strains on the former.[14] The consensus on the need to significantly increase funding on social care now stretches as far as the former Health Secretary, Andrew Lansley, who was reported to be 'disappointed' at the government's failure to increase spending in the 2016 Autumn Statement.[15]

Theresa May's proposal during the 2017 election to fund social care via a 'dementia tax' may have been a political disaster but signalled a further recognition of the need for government action to address this issue. At a time when the number of people attending Accident and Emergency Departments is rocketing, the NHS must also find a way of organizing more health care at a community level through GP surgeries.[16] The education system must find a way—after more than thirty years of trying—of developing an effective vocational training system. It also, increasingly, needs to find a way of attracting more of the best teachers to work in the worst schools in the most socially deprived areas. But the state health and education systems are not teetering on the edge of disaster. We now spend more on health care and education than we used to and in return for this we get better services. Overall satisfaction levels with the NHS have fallen by around 10 percentage points since 2010 but remain reasonably high. Targets have their drawbacks but, overall, they have raised performance levels. The NHS has not been privatized. For all the hullabaloo surrounding the Conservatives' efforts to crack open the NHS to competition from private providers, a relatively small proportion of the NHS budget is spent on private provision.

Pessimism about the current state and prospects for health and education has become a reflexive instinct on the left. This might be thought to be useful. Give the Conservatives an inch and they'll take a yard. Turn your back for a moment and they'll have sold a few hundred NHS hospitals to a venture capital firm in Panama and signed a deal with McDonald's to sponsor the national curriculum. But the risk here is that miserabilism becomes a self-fulfilling prophecy. If the left argues that health and education are on the edge of disaster, the Conservatives might, in the future, persuade more people that the taxpayer-funded and free-at-the-point-of-delivery status quo is no longer viable. The left must tread a delicate line between pointing to problems with existing services and making the case for more public expenditure while, at the same time, celebrating what is being done by the NHS and state schools.

II

Let's start with the resources being invested in health and education. Figure 5.1 shows total public health expenditure as a percentage of GDP between 1940 and 2015. What we see here is a consistent increase in expenditure over time. Between 1940 and the early 1950s, health expenditure more than doubled from 1.4 per cent to 3.3 per cent of GDP in 1951. It then kept climbing to reach a post-war high of 5 per cent in 1980. During Margaret Thatcher's time in office, expenditure then fell to 4.3 per cent of GDP. Over the next decade, health expenditure climbed very slowly back to just over 5 per cent. Something quite dramatic then happened. In January 2000, and without much in the way of a warning to his Cabinet colleagues, Tony Blair promised to increase health-care spending to the European average by 2006. Between 2000/1 and 2009/10, real public health expenditure (adjusted for inflation and at 2016/17 prices) increased by 75 per cent from £74.2bn to £130.5bn and from 5.08 per cent to 7.65 per cent of GDP.[17]

What happened next? Going into the 2010 election, the Conservatives promised to exempt the NHS from spending cuts and to maintain real expenditure. In fact, the Coalition ended up doing more than this. Under intense pressure to be seen to be addressing criticisms from, amongst others, the British Medical Association that it was endangering the 'overall financial viability' of the NHS, new funds were found.[18] Between 2009/10 and 2016/17, overall real (inflation-adjusted) public expenditure on health care in 2016/17 prices increased by 10 per cent from £130.5bn to £144.3bn (although health expenditure as a share of GDP fell over this same period from 7.65 per cent to 7.35 per cent).[19] In their 2017 manifesto, the Conservatives then promised to increase NHS spending by a minimum of £8 billion in real terms over the next five years, delivering an increase in real funding per head of the population for every year of the parliament.[20]

This does not mean that everything is A-OK and that we can simply move on to discuss other things. For one thing, figures on real increases in health spending do not take account of population growth. Between 2009/10 and 2016/17, overall real health expenditure increased by 10 per cent but the UK population grew by 4.6 per cent from 62.7 to 65.6 million people.[21] Furthermore, the demands on the NHS are increasing rapidly as the UK population not only grows but grows older. To take just one example, in 2015 there were estimated to be 14,570 centenarians (people aged 100 or over) living in the UK. This is compared with 3,420 in 1985.[22] The number of people employed within the Department of Work and Pensions who are responsible for ensuring that people receive a congratulatory telegram from the Queen on their one-hundredth birthday has increased from just one to seven.[23] Demand for NHS services is already rising by something like 4 per cent a year.[24] The number of people living with at least one long-term health condition is set to more than double over the next twenty years. The

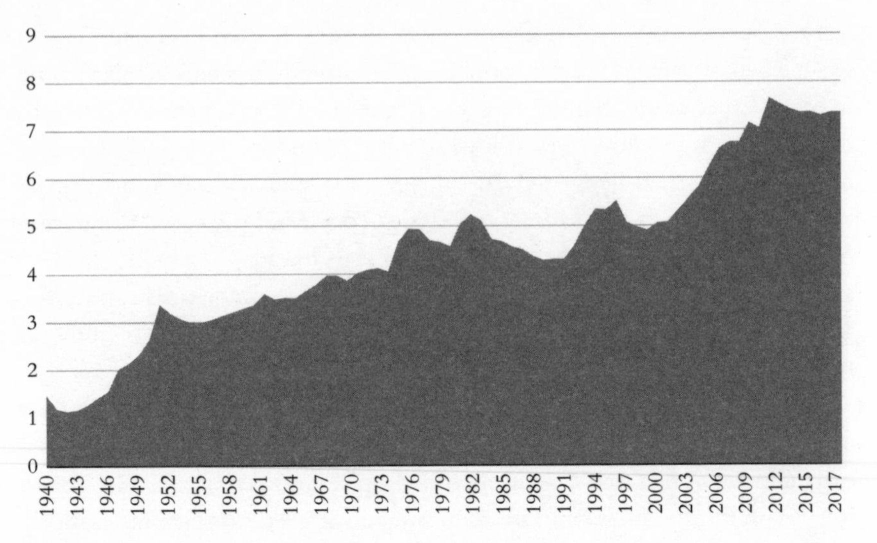

Figure 5.1. Public health care expenditure, % of GDP: 1950–2017.[1]

Coalition dealt with these problems by throwing in some extra money; squeezing 'productivity gains' out of the system via salary freezes and reducing payments to local GPs; and by allowing hospitals to run larger deficits. Theresa May appears, so far, to have adopted a similar strategy.[25] This has bought some time but it does not amount to much of a long-term strategy. Sooner or later, a lot more public money is going to need to be spent on health care and the case for spending that money is going to have to be made all over again.

Figure 5.2 shows total public education expenditure as a percentage of GDP between 1940 and 2015. Public expenditure rose significantly from 2.3 per cent of GDP in 1945 to 4.2 per cent in 1950. Through the 1950s and 1960s, expenditure continued to rise, reaching a post-war high of 6.5 per cent of GDP in the mid-1970s. By 1980, education expenditure had fallen to 5.3 per cent of GDP and by 1990, it had fallen further to 4.3 per cent. There was then a long period in which expenditure levels did not vary greatly. Between 2000/1 and 2009/10, expenditure then rose sharply from 4.37 per cent of GDP to 5.8 per cent and from £62.9bn to £99bn (in 2016/17 prices) (a 57 per cent real-terms increase).[26] The Institute for Fiscal Studies also reports that, during this period, public spending 'increased massively for schools with poorer children relative to schools with children from middle-income or affluent backgrounds'.[27] What happened next? In 2010, there was no firm manifesto commitment to protect education in the same way as there was for the NHS. Following the cuts announced in the 2010 Emergency Budget

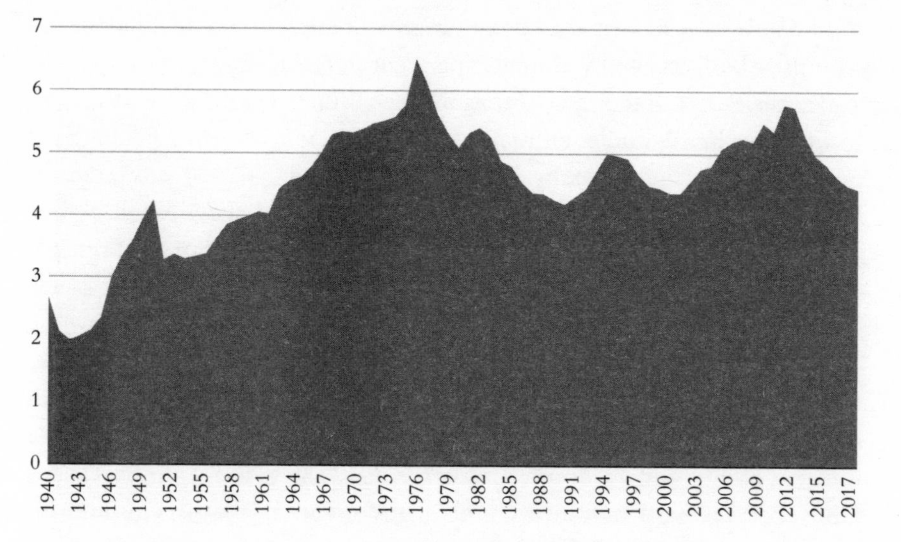

Figure 5.2. Public education expenditure, % of GDP: 1950–2017.[2]

and associated Spending Review, the Institute for Fiscal Studies estimated in 2011 that public spending on education was set to fall by 3.5 per cent a year in real terms between 2010 and 2015.[28] Sure enough, between 2009/10 and 2015/16, public expenditure on education fell from 5.8 per cent of GDP to 4.4 per cent of GDP and from £99bn to £87.2bn (in 2016/17 prices).

This looks like an open-and-shut case for political miserabilism. The Coalition has cut and cut again at education expenditure—with the promise of more to follow.

Some of the numbers here are, however, worth a second look. Between 2010 and 2017, real (inflation-adjusted) expenditure fell. But a large part of these cuts was focused on the further education and higher education budgets (the latter compensating for the introduction of tuition fees[29]). There was in fact a 10 per cent real increase in overall spending on schools in England and a 7.5 per cent increase in school spending per pupil in England between 2010 and 2015.[30] The Coalition also deserves some credit for the introduction of the 'Pupil Premium': a per capita grant given directly to schools for children eligible for free school meals. A lot of the new money being invested in the Pupil Premium was old money recycled from cuts to other programmes. But the Pupil Premium has had a significant redistributive effect on school spending. By 2014, English primary schools in the most prosperous catchment areas with the smallest number of Pupil Premium children had experienced a 1 per cent rise in real budgets. Schools in the most deprived areas with the largest number of Pupil Premium children had seen their budgets rise by around 7 per cent in real terms.[31]

Between 2015 and 2020, education expenditure is forecast to rise. The Institute for Fiscal Studies estimated in 2016 that, in real terms, spending per pupil may nevertheless fall by as much as 7 per cent by 2020 (although the same report also made it clear that in real terms school budgets will, by that stage, still be around 50 per cent higher than they were in 2001).[32] If the UK economy grows at anything like the forecast rate of over 2 per cent a year, this means that education expenditure as a share of GDP will, however, continue to fall. My overall sense here is, in education, as with health care, that we are currently, at best, in a holding pattern. There is a strong case for significantly increasing education expenditure further both to increase social mobility and to boost Britain's long-term growth prospects. The Conservatives have not shown much interest in that case. Funding for the state school sector has not been devastated since 2010. It has, however, been allowed to stagnate.

III

In the following chapter, I am going to spend a great deal of time looking at equality and changes in the relative and absolute gap between the income of the richest and poorest households. As a prelude to this more detailed analysis, I want to quickly emphasize here the redistributive effects of public health and education spending.

Figure 5.3 shows the estimated level of benefit households receive from the provision of free state education and health care. The left-hand side of the chart shows the estimated value of the benefits received by the households with the lowest 10 per cent of incomes and the right-hand side the benefits received by the households with the highest 10 per cent of incomes. As you move from left to right, income increases by 10 per cent deciles. The figures here relate to the 2015/16 period (the latest available figures from the Office for National Statistics at the time of writing).

The median UK household received £6,749 a year in benefits (£2,459 from education and £4,290 from the NHS). The poorest 10 per cent of households received £7,073 in benefits (£2,822 from education and £4,251 from the NHS) and the richest 10 per cent of households £5,092 (£1,325

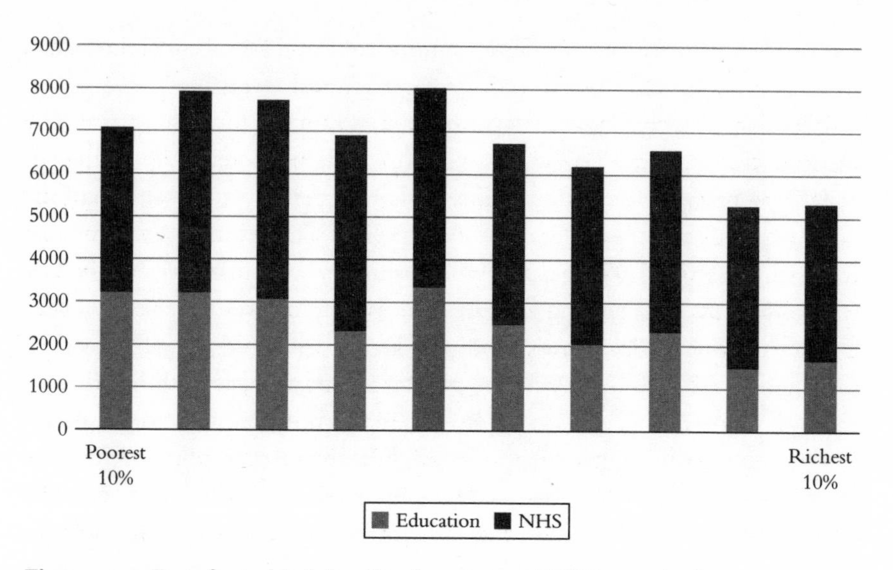

Figure 5.3. Benefits in kind (in £): education and NHS 2015/16.[3]

from education and £3,767 from the NHS). The single largest beneficiaries from state-provided education and the NHS were the households with between the lowest 20–30 per cent of incomes and those with close to the median income. But there is not much in it. Health care and education are provided as universally available services free at the point of delivery and generate universal benefits.

The story here is, so far, that there is not much of a story. Things change, however, when we look at benefits alongside income. Figure 5.4 shows the education and NHS benefits received by each decile of the population as a percentage of that income group's final income in 2015/16. Final income here is the sum left after all direct and indirect taxes, cash benefits from the welfare system, and in-kind benefits from the provision of free government services (including education and the NHS, but also transport and housing subsidies). As we have already seen, the median UK household received £6,749 a year from education and the NHS. The final income of the median household in 2015/16 was £34,605, so benefits from education and the NHS were the equivalent of 19.5 per cent of final income. The benefits received by the poorest 10 per cent of households were the equivalent of 52 per cent of their final income. Those received by the richest 10 per cent of households were the equivalent of just 7 per cent of their final income.

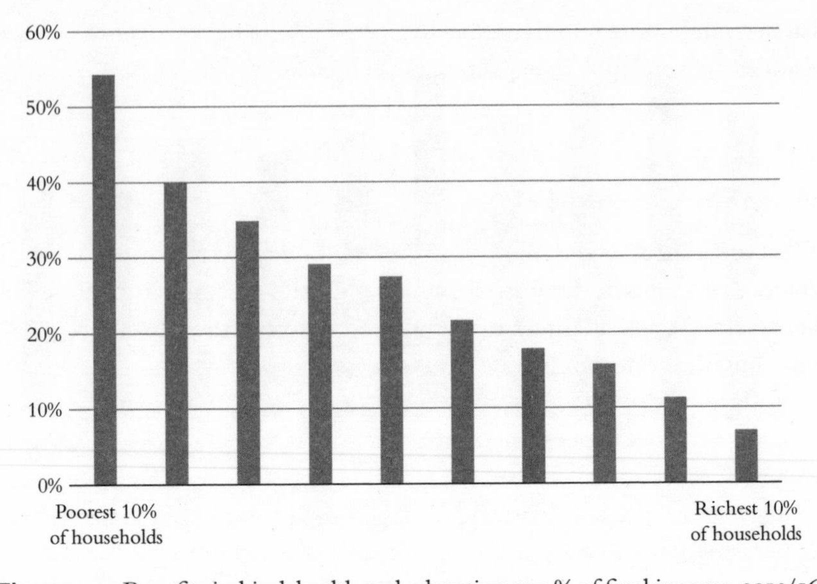

Figure 5.4. Benefits in kind: health and education as a % of final income, 2015/16.[4]

In other words, and when placed in the context of overall income, education and NHS spending is highly redistributive.

Has public spending on health and education become more redistributive over time? In 2015/16, the education and NHS benefits received by the poorest 10 per cent of households were 1.38 times greater than those received by the richest 10 per cent of households. Those benefits, as we have just seen, were equivalent to 52 per cent of the final income of the poorest 10 per cent of households but just 7 per cent of those of the richest 10 per cent of households (a 45 per cent gap).

If we go back to 1980, the benefits received by the poorest 10 per cent of households were 1.49 times greater than those received by the richest 10 per cent of households. In other words, and in this respect, education and NHS spending has become slightly less redistributive over time. On the other hand, in 1980, education and NHS benefits were the equivalent of 38 per cent of the final income of the poorest 10 per cent of households but just 6 per cent of the final income of the richest 10 per cent of households (a 32 per cent gap). It is difficult to read too much into these figures without also looking at changes in wages and taxation over this period. At a first glance, however, these figures suggest that public education and NHS expenditure has become a more important mechanism of redistribution over the last few decades as overall public expenditure has increased.[33]

IV

What difference has the money that New Labour invested made? The right argues that a lot of it was wasted on higher salaries and middle-management bureaucracy. The left argues that a lot of it was wasted on bureaucracy and on filling the coffers of private firms and consultants.

Waiting lists for NHS treatment fell dramatically. The median waiting time for in-patient appointments fell from 15 weeks in 1997 to 4 weeks in 2009.[34] Cancer mortality rates and infant mortality rates also fell significantly. Five-year age-standardized breast cancer survival rates increased from 74 per cent between 1997 and 2002 to 81 per cent between 2008 and 2013.[35] In 2016, Macmillan Cancer Support published a report in which it estimated that, when compared with the 1970s, people are twice as likely to live at least ten years after being diagnosed with cancer. Infant mortality per 1,000 births fell from 5.6 in 2000 to 3.8 in 2013. A large part of this improvement was due to changes in medical technology. But the rates of improvement in health outcomes have, overall, been much higher in the UK than they have in other OECD countries. To take just one example, infant mortality rates fell by 32 per cent in the UK between 2000 and 2012 but by only 25 per cent in the Netherlands; 22 per cent in Germany; 20 per cent in Sweden and France; and just 13 per cent in the United States.[36] Yet it is also worth saying here that improvements in health outcomes in the UK were achieved from a very low base. Most European countries still have significantly lower infant mortality rates and higher cancer survival rates than the UK.

By 2010, 76 per cent of pupils in English schools were achieving five or more GCSEs at grades A–C or equivalent, up from 45 per cent in 1997. The number of pupils achieving expected standards at Key Stage 2 between ages 7 and 11 in Maths rose from 62 per cent to 80 per cent over the same period and in English rose from 61 per cent to 79 per cent. There was also a significant narrowing of the attainment gap between pupils receiving free school meals and other children during this period. Judged in terms of the number receiving five or more GSCEs at grades A–C, the gap fell from around 30 per cent in 2003 (when this measure was initially compiled) to 20 per cent in 2010.[37] Yet there is little if any evidence from the OECD's Program for International Student Assessment (PISA) tests that UK performance has improved. Indeed, on most of the rankings produced from these statistics, the UK fell further down most global league tables in the 2000s.[38]

There are a handful of other statistics which tell us something important about the impact of New Labour's investment. The first relates to overall satisfaction levels with the NHS (there are no equivalent figures for the state education system which I can find). Since the early 1980s, the British Social Attitudes Survey managed through the National Centre for Social Research has asked people the following question: 'All in all, how satisfied or dissatisfied would you say you are with the way in which the National Health Service runs nowadays?' Figure 5.5 shows the numbers who are quite satisfied or very satisfied as against those who are quite dissatisfied or very dissatisfied. Throughout the 1980s and 1990s, there was a rough balance between these camps. Then, in the 2000s, as expenditure rose, satisfaction rates rose dramatically from 42 per cent in 2001 to 70 per cent in 2010. Satisfaction rates then fell quite sharply in the early years of the Coalition to just 58 per cent in 2011, before climbing slowly again to 65 per cent by 2014, before then falling once again to 60 per cent in 2015 before rising to 63 per cent in 2016.[39]

We can also indirectly learn something about the difference that New Labour's investment in the education and health systems made by looking at the changing balance between public and private health care and education

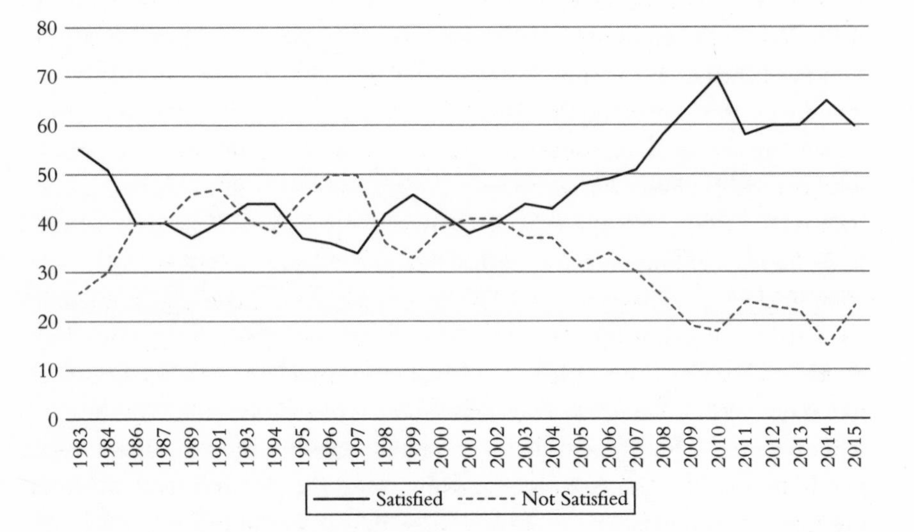

Figure 5.5. Satisfaction with NHS (%).[5]

expenditure during this period. From a neoliberal perspective, health care and education are markets in which people can choose whether to pay for private provision. These markets, the neoliberal argues, are rigged because those who choose to pay for private care still have to pay the same taxes as those who stay in the state system. But there is still a market choice here. So how many people are so dissatisfied with what are effectively free state services that they are willing to pay twice over for their education and health care?

The OECD estimates that private expenditure on health care in the UK in 1980 was equivalent to 0.6 per cent of GDP.[40] This climbed to 0.8 per cent of GDP by 1990 and 1.4 per cent of GDP by 2000. Since then, private expenditure has flatlined at between 1.4 per cent and 1.6 per cent of GDP. By international standards, this is quite low. In the Netherlands, 1.3 per cent of GDP is spent on private health care. In Sweden, the equivalent figure is 1.7 per cent of GDP; in France 2.3 per cent; in Germany 2.6 per cent; in Australia 2.8 per cent; in Canada 3 per cent; and in the United States an eye-watering 8.5 per cent of GDP. Furthermore, between 2000 and 2011, increased public expenditure on the NHS meant that public spending on health as a share of total (public and private sector) spending on health care rose from 79.2 per cent to 82.8 per cent. In 2013, the Institute for Fiscal Studies published a study of the relative balance between public and private expenditure in the 2000s. This was, as we will presently see, a period in which the government was encouraging private health-care firms to deliver routine operations for NHS patients to reduce waiting times. What the study found, however, was that there was something like a 25 per cent fall in the number of *for-fee* hip and knee replacements conducted within the private sector during this period as public provision expanded and waiting times fell.[41] Meanwhile, the number of people with private medical insurance fell from 12.5 per cent in 2006 to 11 per cent by 2013.[42]

As for education, there was a steady rise in the number of UK children attending fee-paying private schools, from 5.1 per cent of all children in 1978 to 7.4 per cent by 1994. During New Labour's time in office, this number fell slightly to 7.2 per cent.[43] Between 2010 and 2015, it fell further to 6.9 per cent.[44] There are a record number of pupils attending fee-paying schools in the UK.[45] However, an increasing number of these are overseas pupils. In 2016, the editor of the *Good Schools Guide*, Ralph Lucas, spoke of the massive improvement in standards in state schools and predicted the closure of a number of fee-paying schools.[46]

Let's put some of these numbers in a broader economic context. Between 2000/1 and 2009/10, median household final income increased by 52 per cent from £20,455 to £31,134. The final income of the richest 10 per cent of households (who we might think would provide the strongest market for private health care and education) rose by 44 per cent from £50,720 to £72,934.[47] Yet the steady growth in the proportion of people exiting the public sector which had occurred in the 1980s and into the early 1990s nevertheless came to an end. This is, I would suggest, good evidence of the difference New Labour's investment in health care and education made.

V

Are the state education and health services slowly being destroyed through a neoliberal reform agenda? Are the distinctive values of the public sector being eroded through commercialization and privatization? In this section, I am going to examine the nature and impact of performance targets upon the NHS and state education systems. I am then going to look at the contracting out of private services within the NHS before, finally, examining the way in which successive governments have sought to simultaneously centralize and decentralize the education system through the promotion of academy schools.

In the early 1990s, John Major overhauled the existing system of locally based school inspection by creating the Office for Standards in Education (OFSTED) and stipulating that their reports be made publicly available. Labour picked up and ran with this system, eventually building a regime that two academics, Gwyn Bevan and Christopher Hood, memorably described as one of 'terror and targets'.[48] Throughout the 2000s, a new and expanded set of targets were introduced for schools—including, eventually, specific targets for children in care and children in receipt of free school meals. Within the NHS, targets were initially set for waiting times. Over time, targets were also set for, among many other things, rates of infection, bed occupancy, mortality rates from various diseases, health inequalities, access to GP services, and patient experience. Meeting targets was a big deal. The careers of a generation of public service managers were made and broken depending upon whether targets were met or missed.

Whilst they were still in opposition, the Conservatives argued that target-setting was causing more problems than it was solving; that there were too many targets; that they had been introduced at the expense of managerial autonomy; and that they were undermining staff morale. Sure enough, once the Coalition entered office, the new Conservative Health Secretary, Andrew Lansley, scrapped a key target: that everyone should be able to see a GP within 48 hours.[49] Yet once Lansley had been reshuffled out of the Department of Health, targets slowly came back into fashion. Indeed, as a part of its response to the Francis Inquiry report into the failure of the Mid-Staffordshire NHS Trust, the government introduced new OFSTED-style ratings for all health and social care providers.[50] The government also introduced a new target under which hospital trusts are now fined for every patient who waits more than a year from referral to treatment.[51] In their 2017 manifesto, the Conservatives promised to retain existing targets in relation to accident and emergency admissions and elective care. In the case of schools, where targets never went out of fashion, the Coalition focused upon reforming the inspection system: scrapping the category of 'satisfactory' in OFSTED inspections in order to create more pressure on schools to raise their standards and introducing more frequent inspections for schools deemed to require improvement.[52]

It would appear that a culture of targets and terror is here to stay. The first question to ask about targets is whether they work (the miserabilist will argue that they do not). The second question is whether they can be connected to and seen as expression of neoliberalism (the miserabilist will argue that they can).

Everyone knows that targets are vulnerable to being gamed and that efforts to meet them can generate perverse and unexpected outcomes. When New Labour first set a target requiring doctors to see patients within 48 hours, many surgeries responded by introducing a rule that patients would not be allowed to book an appointment more than 48 hours in advance.[53] As long ago as 2003, there were reports that hospitals were requiring patients to wait in queues of ambulances outside the front entrance of accident and emergency departments during busy periods in order to help meet targets relating to admission waiting times. In 2016, there were reports that employees working for G4S at an emergency 999 call centre in Lincolnshire were making fake calls during quiet times to increase their chances of meeting a target requiring 92 per cent of calls be answered within ten seconds.[54]

The never-ending pressure to meet targets puts staff under enormous strain and risks eroding morale and the long-term commitment of staff to their jobs. Michael Barber—who served as Chief Advisor to the Education

Secretary in the late 1990s and was head of the Prime Minister's Delivery Unit in the early 2000s—argues that targets are an effective means of improving performance in the short term when there is slack in the system but if used over a longer period, they can be extremely damaging.[55] In the case of the Mid-Staffordshire Trust, there is some evidence that target-chasing became an obsession for senior managers, which sustained a conviction that so long as the hospital was meeting its targets, it must be doing a good job.[56]

Yet, at the same time, target-setting did lead to significant improvements in standards. Following the introduction of a new target in England in 2000, the number of patients waiting more than twelve months for a hospital admission for elective surgery fell from around 5 per cent to less than 1 per cent in the space of little more than a year. In Scotland, where there was no such target, the numbers rose from 2 per cent to nearly 10 per cent over the same period.[57]

One important virtue of targets is that they provide an element of public accountability. Targets may be crude and may be subject to gaming effects but when organizations fail to meet their targets, it is not just the managers of those organizations but politicians who can be held to account. In 2012, Labour argued that the NHS was being starved of funds and that this was leading to deteriorating performance. Coalition ministers initially argued that this was nonsense and that Labour was scaremongering. When it was subsequently revealed that the number of people waiting more than four hours in accident and emergency departments had risen from 2 per cent in 2010 to 6 per cent in 2013, this line of argument became increasingly difficult for ministers to sustain and, shortly after, a new package of hospital funding was announced.

Now, to address the second question, should we see targets as emblematic of the advance of neoliberalism within the public services? There are, it is true, points of similarity here. Neoliberals tend to view the public sector as being inherently inefficient. Targets look like neoliberalism because they also seem to be premised on the assumption that public sector workers will, given half a chance, slack off. A target-setting culture is also suggestive of a certain level of neoliberal state authoritarianism in so far as it has been introduced as one part of a wider managerial revolution through which the once widely held belief that teachers and doctors are the best people to run schools and hospitals has been swept aside.[58] Echoing some of the arguments about the relationship between the free economy and the strong state I outlined previously, the philosopher John Grey argues that targets are, in this respect, an essential part of the 'neoliberal state':

> An increase in state power has always been the inner logic of neoliberalism, because, in order to inject markets into every corner of social life, a government needs to be highly invasive. Health, education and the arts are now more controlled by the state than they were in the era of Labour collectivism. Once-autonomous institutions are entangled in an apparatus of government targets and incentives. The consequence of reshaping society on a market model has been to make the state omnipresent.[59]

The fact that there are points of similarity between managerial-led target-setting and neoliberalism does not, however, mean that the former ought to be seen as an expression of the latter. Neoliberalism, to go back to the discussion in the second chapter, means, above all else, a commitment to rolling back the frontiers of the state and rolling forward competitive markets. One of the things which sets neoliberals apart from classical liberals is their conviction that, when privatization is not an option, attempts at top–down managerial control ought to be eschewed in favour of establishing 'internal markets' which seek to mimic the effects of fully competitive markets. Targets are, in this respect, an inversion of neoliberalism. As Gwyn Bevan and Christopher Hood observe, they are, if anything, more reminiscent of Soviet-style efforts at central planning.[60]

VI

For neoliberals, the main game when it comes to the NHS has always been the introduction of greater competition and, under the guise of choice, more private provision. Having considered and eventually rejected the option of some form of outright privatization, Margaret Thatcher created an 'internal market' in health care in the late 1980s, whereby health authorities and some groups of fundholding GPs were given the authority to sign contracts with hospitals to purchase services for their patients. New Labour, which found itself on to a sure-fire electoral winner with the NHS in the 1990s, argued that the internal market was a form of privatization and proceeded to abolish it. In the late 1990s, Blair, and his new Secretary of State for Health, Alan Milburn, decided that this had been a mistake. In the 2000s, New Labour tried to re-establish a form of internal market by setting national tariff prices for treatments, with the idea that hospitals which could deliver high-quality care at less than this price would be encouraged to take on more patients and that hospitals which could not would be forced to reform or slowly contract. New Labour also introduced new rules allowing locally based Primary Care Trusts to effectively sub-contract NHS work to private health-care providers which met the NHS's cost structures and care standards. By the late 2000s, these Independent Sector Providers were undertaking around 20 per cent of some forms of elective surgery such as hip replacements, a policy which resulted in a sharp fall in waiting lists.[61] One point that Alan Milburn made at the time was that these reforms were introduced in part because it took the NHS several years to build its own capacity once spending had been increased. A second point was that the effect of this policy was to offer patients a greater measure of choice: something which had previously only been available in the private sector.

When he was appointed Secretary of State for Health in 2010, Andrew Lansley planned to significantly increase the role of the private sector within the NHS. The 2012 Health and Social Care Act mandated groups of local GPs to form Clinical Commissioning Groups and to negotiate contracts for their patients with hospitals and other health-care providers. This was, in many ways, back to the future stuff: a rerun of the 1990s internal market. There was, however, a key difference. Clinical Commissioning Groups could choose to award contracts not only to NHS providers but to any clinically approved private or charitable health care group. Indeed, for a while it appeared that Clinical Commissioning Groups would have a legal obligation to open up *all* contracts to competitive tendering. David Cameron argued that 'instead of having to justify why it makes sense to introduce competition . . . the state will have to justify why it makes sense to run a monopoly'.[62] This was, there can be no doubt, radical and very clearly neo-liberal stuff. Management by targets was going to be downplayed in favour of free markets and competition and the miserabilists could nod their heads sagely and say that this is what the Tories had wanted to do all along.

There is an argument to be had about whether, in general, in those cases where private health-care firms have been awarded NHS contracts, standards have risen or fallen. In 2011, Hinchingbrooke Hospital in Cambridgeshire became the first NHS hospital in the country to be run by a private company, Circle. In early 2015, Circle announced that because the hospital was 'no longer viable under current terms' it was exiting from its contract. Shortly afterwards, it emerged that the Care Quality Commission had recommended that the hospital trust be placed into special measures after being found to have offered inadequate levels of care.[63] Another private company, Serco, eventually exited from a contract to provide out-of-hours GP services in Cornwall following the publication of reports by the Care Quality Commission that it had failed to meet quality and safety standards.[64] On the other hand, there are success stories here. Oasis Dental Care has reinvigorated NHS dental care in several areas where dentists had previously stopped treating NHS patients. In other cases, contracts have been used as a way of better integrating community, primary, and secondary health services. The same company which walked away from the Hinchingbrooke contract, Circle, has managed an integrated care contract in Bedfordshire to provide musculoskeletal care services.[65] Opening up public-sector services to tender has often allowed charities and other third-sector bodies to bid to become directly involved in the delivery of services. In 2015, the BBC reported that around 30 per cent of the public money which is spent on public health care by non-NHS providers goes to charities and local government.[66]

There is also an argument to be had about whether the contracting out of NHS services to private companies is, as Jeremy Corbyn argued to great effect during the 2017 election campaign, tantamount to privatization and ought to be opposed regardless of whether it leads to better services. Trade unions representing health-care workers have warned that the 'surge in privatisation' following the implementation of the Health and Social Care Act 'risks creating a system based on ability to pay, rather than need'.[67] Campaign groups like the NHS Support Federation argue that the values of the NHS are undermined when private companies can profit from health care. Against this, it is worth reiterating two very basic points. First, that public health care has always involved a mixture of public and private provision. Most GPs have always worked as independent contractors rather than NHS employees. Second, private companies providing health care on behalf of the NHS must do so free of charge whilst meeting NHS regulatory standards. The implementation of the Health and Social Care Act does not risk creating a system based on ability to pay. It may make it easier to introduce such a system in the future. But this is not the same thing.

In the end, however, I think that the best argument with which to challenge claims about the privatization of the NHS is that the Health and Social Care Act itself is showing signs of being something of a damp squib. After a year of intense opposition from the medical profession and a series of increasingly hostile opinion polls, Andrew Lansley was sacked as Health

Secretary in 2012 and replaced by Jeremy Hunt. Shortly after, it was reported that unnamed 'senior figures' within the government had come to regard the Health and Social Care Act as a huge 'strategic error' (it is unclear whether David Cameron's evident failure to take the time to understand Lansley's proposed reforms before they were published was viewed in similar terms).[68] Hunt himself, it soon became clear, was more interested in promoting quality of care rather than competition, which, in practice, has meant a return to inspection, targets, and new complaint procedures. Responding to this change in the political mood music, the NHS market regulator, Monitor, has indicated, *sotto voce*, that where there is clear evidence that existing service provision is working, Clinical Commissioning Groups can roll over contracts with NHS providers without competitive tendering. It is true that where contracts have been subject to a formal tender, around a third have been awarded to private firms or charities.[69] But most contracts are not being tendered. In 2015/16, only around 7.5 per cent of the NHS England budget was spent on private contractors or charities (up from around 4.4 per cent in 2009/10 and 6 per cent in 2014/15).[70]

VII

Thirty-one pieces of legislation relating to education and education funding were passed between 1990 and 2012.[71] The simplest way in which I have been able to make sense of the many and varied provisions of these bills is that they amount to a sustained assault on the autonomy and role of local education authorities. In the 1980s, LEAs became a favoured target of the right: the very embodiment of the 'loony left'. Rightly or wrongly, they were seen to be too close to the teaching unions; too soft on failing schools; obsessed with political correctness; and just generally not very good. The onslaught against LEAs started in the late 1980s, when the Conservatives introduced a new form of 'grant-maintained' school owned and managed by a board of governors rather than the local authority and funded directly by the Department of Education. By the mid-1990s, around 20 per cent of secondary schools had converted to grant-maintained status. New Labour, when it was elected, abolished grant-maintained schools and replaced them with Foundation schools, which had more autonomy than most state schools had previously had but a closer relationship with local education authorities than grant-maintained schools.

Eventually, New Labour stumbled upon the idea of creating academy schools as an option for failing state schools in socially deprived areas. Academies were meant to attract the philanthropic interest of charities and private firms, with their head teachers being given a licence to run their school as they saw fit. They also came attached with much higher state spending. The Coalition decided that Academies were the best-practice model of the future and gave all state schools—not just the academically struggling ones—strong incentives to convert to academy status. In one of a number of spectacular U-turns which marked the Conservatives' first year in office following the 2015 election, the Education Secretary, Nicky Morgan, then decreed that every school in England would—whether it wanted to or not—be required to become an academy by 2020, only to then announce a few months later that this was not such a good idea after all.[72]

Academies are directly funded by central government. They are established as companies, with a Board of Directors that acts as a Trust who are legally responsible for the operation of the school of which the Trust is a part.[73] Academy schools are subject to inspection by OFSTED; must participate in national key stage tests; are bound by the national admissions code; must establish a Special Education Needs policy; and, although exempt from the national curriculum, must teach certain subjects. They are bound by the same rules as other schools when it comes to the charges that they can levy parents.[74] The key difference is that academies have more freedom than other state schools over their finances, the curriculum they teach, and setting teachers' pay and conditions. Above all, academies can, if they want, operate entirely independently of their LEA.

Personally—and having served as a school governor for a while—I find endless debates about academies to be a bit of a distraction from the day-to-day business of trying to improve school standards. Giving the authority to governing bodies to hire (and potentially fire) head teachers and giving head teachers the authority to hire and negotiate the pay of teachers sometimes makes sense. But you don't need to create academies to do this and it is hardly surprising that the House of Commons Education Committee has found little evidence that converting to academy status leads to improved standards.[75] Converting (read bribing) schools to acquire academy status is also extremely expensive. Between 2010 and 2012 alone, the Department for Education spent £8.3bn on the Academies Programme. Of this, £338m was 'one-off transitional funding' which did not relate to the actual costs of running academies.[76] It also seems to me quite bizarre that, having promoted academies because they are a way of cutting through LEA bureaucracies, academies are now free to create chains of Multi-Academy Trusts in which the authority of individual head teachers within that chain is highly circumscribed and in which there are ample opportunities to divert funds to new layers of management.[77]

Are academies an expression of neoliberalism? As with the use of targets, it is possible to identify points of similarity between the case being made for academies and those parts of the neoliberal ideology which eulogize managerialism, private sector involvement, and a strong state. But as a neoliberal reform agenda goes, academization is thin fare. Rather than questioning the need or value for the state to run schools, the debate about academies boils down to an argument about which bit of the state should run schools. I think that the Conservatives are on the wrong side of this argument and are pursuing a tired and dated agenda when it comes to their vendetta against local education authorities. But academization is not a form of privatization and is not a smoking gun of a piece of evidence for political miserabilism.

What of grammar schools? For Theresa May, academies are old hat and the 1950s grammar schools are the future. My own reading of the evidence is that there is almost no evidence that grammar schools can act as an effective driver of social mobility. Quite the opposite in fact. The writer who I most trust on this issue is Rebecca Allen, who is Director of the Education Datalab. In 2016, she wrote a short piece which made four simple points (all backed by careful data analysis). First, academic selection creates winners and losers. Children who attend grammar schools make more progress than they otherwise would. Children who attend non-selective schools in selective areas make less progress than they otherwise would. This is a big deal because in areas where there are grammar schools, most pupils do not attend a grammar school. Second, resources flow to grammar schools. Grammar schools attract the most experienced and effective teachers (see the previous point). Third, poor children are less likely to get into grammar schools and it will be very hard to change this. There are two factors at play here. First, pupils from relatively poor backgrounds are likely to have markedly lower academic attainment at age 11. Second, even children from deprived backgrounds (who, for example, are eligible for free school meals) who have equivalent Key Stage 2 results to a pupil from a richer background are still less likely to attend a grammar school. Fourth, academic selection increases inequalities in outcomes.

In areas where there are selective schools, there is a greater disparity in education performance between children from poor neighbourhoods and children from wealthier neighbourhoods.[78] Grammar schools would significantly boost the income of the private tutors who would be paid by middle-class parents to do whatever it took to get their child into a grammar school. But I don't see who else benefits. If you want to do something about social mobility, it would make far more sense to pump more money into University Technical Colleges: around fifty of which now teach around 11,000 pupils in conjunction with universities and local employers.[79]

Is the promotion of grammar schools an expression of neoliberalism? Put grammar schools and neoliberalism into Google and you can find plenty of people who say they are. But, once again, I don't think the connections are that strong. Yes, neoliberalism is about competition and yes, grammar schools certainly promote competition, elitism, and a winner-takes-all mentality. But the case for grammar schools takes for granted precisely what neoliberals would want to challenge: the idea that the state ought to be providing schooling free at the point of delivery. Grammar schools, along with immigration fears and, no doubt, a forthcoming campaign about young people not respecting traditional values, look more like a back-to-the-future 1950s Conservatism. This is not a brave new world. In the end, the Conservative's post-election wafer-thin majority means that plans to significantly expand the number of grammar schools are likely to be parked. But this is an issue which is, sooner or later, likely to return.

VIII

More and better public services has always been a policy theme uniting the left and right of the Labour Party. In the 1950s, Crosland, from the social democratic right of the party, provided a powerful defence of how and why good public services promote greater social equality:

> If the state provides schools and hospitals, teachers and doctors, on a generous scale and of a really high quality, comparable with the best available for private purchase, then the result will be, not indeed a greater equality of real incomes, but certainly a greater equality in manners and the texture of social life...The right way, in the field of social expenditure, is a generous, imaginative, long-term programme of social investment which will make our state schools and hospitals, and all the services that go with them, the equal in quality of the best which private wealth can buy.[80]

Are we there yet? Are public-sector education and health services equal in quality to the best which private wealth can buy? No. There are some clear success stories. Private health companies will usually transfer critically ill patients to NHS hospitals for treatment. There are five private universities in the UK: The University of Buckingham, BPP University, Regent's University London, the University of Law, and Arden University. The government is currently trying to encourage more private bodies to offer degrees.[81] It is, however, going to face an uphill battle. Public universities which receive direct funding from funding councils and are state-regulated dominate the market. On the other hand, in the education sector, attendance at an elite fee-paying private school is still advantageous. In 2014, the Social Mobility and Child Poverty Commission found that 71 per cent of senior judges, 62 per cent of senior armed forces officers, 55 per cent of permanent secretaries, and 12 per cent of the *Sunday Times Rich List* had been to private fee-paying schools. That said, to judge by the numbers voting with their feet to pay for their family's health care or their children's education, the gap between the quality of the public and private sectors has narrowed.

Amid stories about funding cuts, hospital closures, plummeting staff morale, abuse and neglect within NHS hospitals, longer waiting lists, more complaints, fewer local GP surgeries, and inadequate schools and teachers it is easy to jump to the conclusion that our schools and hospitals are falling apart. Yet, looked at over the longer term, New Labour's sustained investment in schools and hospitals—between 2004 and 2014, the number of doctors employed by the NHS increased by an average of 2.5 per cent a year, whilst there were 48,000 more teachers and 130,000 more teaching assistants in England and Wales in 2010 than there had been in 1998—has raised standards and, quite rightly, raised expectations of what future governments must do.[82]

All in all, the debate about the state of the public health-care and education systems demands and repays considerable caution. Screaming that everything is going to hell and that public provision is being privatized is not only not true, it does not make much political sense in a situation where overall levels of satisfaction with the NHS remain high and where waiting times are much lower than they were in the 1990s. What the left needs to do here is to advance the entirely plausible argument that public investment in education and health pays off and is not wasted; that, by most international measures, the NHS is actually a remarkably efficient health-care system;[83] that specific services (mental health care and special education needs and disabilities would be at the top of my list) are significantly under-funded; and that with an ageing population, low levels of social mobility, and a high economic premium on skilled labour, there is a strong case for significantly increasing what we spend on health care and education and that standing still in spending terms is not good enough.

6

More and less

Equality and inequality in Britain

I

This is the chapter in which I discuss inequality and in which things get a bit more complicated. One reason they get complicated is that it is very difficult to talk about inequality without using a lot of numbers and graphs. I have relegated some of these to either the endnotes or to various on-line appendices as we go. There are, however, more than enough numbers and graphs left over and I recognize that in places this risks making the overall argument harder to follow. Things also get complicated because inequality is itself a complicated concept. There is no single way of measuring inequality and there are lots of different things we can analyse to see how equal or unequal their distribution is. I am going to look at the distribution of market income, final income, and final income after housing costs, and at regional variations in income, the distribution of income by gender and ethnicity, wealth, and social mobility. I am also going to suggest that we need to look not only at how equal or unequal Britain is today but how much more equal or unequal it has become over the last few decades. This makes for sixteen sections, which is, I appreciate, a lot to digest.

A third reason things get complicated is that I don't have any single and simple story about how unequal Britain is or how much more unequal it has become. The miserabilist argument is, in this respect, quite clear-cut and admirably uncomplicated. Britain is, Jeremy Corbyn argues, 'grotesquely' unequal.[1] It has become far more unequal over the last few decades and it is likely to become much more unequal in the future. There is also a simple one-word explanation as to why inequality has risen. Neoliberalism.

To quote Jeremy Corbyn again, the rise in inequality is not 'unique to Britain' but has occurred 'across Europe, North America and elsewhere' because people are 'fed up with a so-called free market system'.[2] Neoliberals like Boris Johnson view inequality as a 'valuable spur to economic activity'.[3] Margaret Thatcher was the first Prime Minister to pursue a deliberate strategy of creating inequality.[4] New Labour bears a heavy responsibility for turning a blind eye to ever greater levels of inequality and, as a group of social scientists argued in the 1990s, 'erasing the intellectual case for redistribution from the map'.[5]

I want to suggest that things are not quite that simple. In some ways, Britain is an extraordinarily unequal country which has become more unequal over the last few decades. The miserabilist is right about several things when it comes to inequality, including the growth in the income of the richest 1 per cent and the overall distribution of wealth. On the other hand, in the case of final income, the regional distribution of income, and, possibly, social mobility (although social mobility is . . . complicated) overall levels of inequality appear to have stabilized. For a period in the 1980s, Britain became a much more unequal place. In the late 1990s and 2000s, inequality stopped growing. In some cases, it even began to fall. The distribution of market income has become significantly less unequal over the last fifteen or so years.

II

I'm going to start by looking at some of the available evidence on how unequal Britain is today. Let's start with the distribution of market income: the money people get in wages and work-based perks such as free work accommodation or company cars, as well as the money they derive from their wealth through interest payments or dividends. Figure 6.1 shows the annual market income of UK households by different deciles in 2015/16 (the most recent available data). The left-hand side of this chart shows the average income of the poorest 10 per cent of households. It then runs through 10 per cent groupings of the population, ending with the richest 10 per cent of households on the right-hand side. The data itself is taken from the Office for National Statistics.[6]

Judged in terms of market income, the UK is a starkly unequal country. In 2015/16, the average market income of the richest 10 per cent of

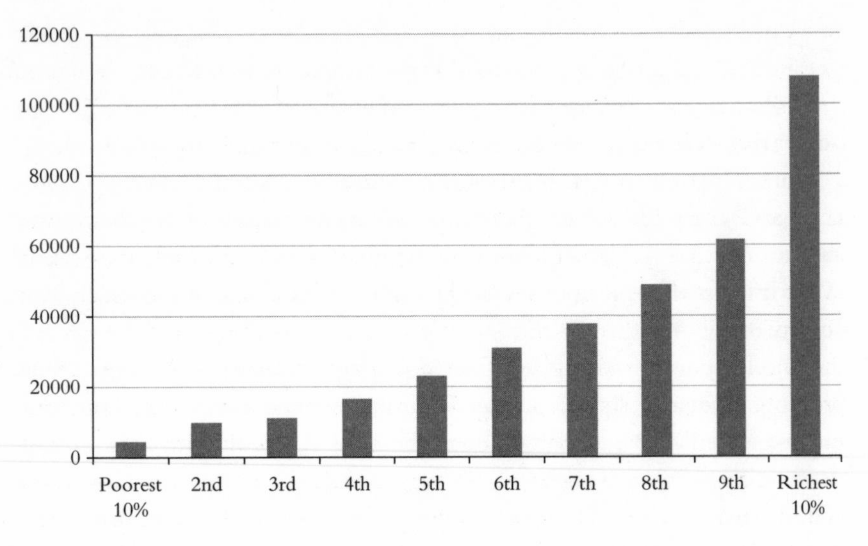

Figure 6.1. Annual household equivalized market income (in £) by decile, 2015/16.[1]

households was just over three times greater than that of the median household (£35,204). This is not too dramatic. The average market income of the richest 10 per cent of households was, however, twenty-four times greater than that of the poorest 10 per cent of households. Indeed, the market income of the richest 20 per cent of households was only slightly less than the income of the other 80 per cent of households combined.

If we want to look beyond the very top and bottom of the income scale, one overall measure of inequality is the Gini coefficient, named after the Italian statistician and sociologist Corrado Gini. The Gini coefficient measures the degree to which the overall distribution of income deviates from perfect equality. The measure ranges from 0 (completely equal) to 1 (completely unequal). Using the most recent available OECD figures, the UK has the most unequal distribution of market income of any of the G10 economies—including the United States—with a Gini coefficient of 0.52 in 2015. By comparison, the coefficient for the other G10 countries was: Switzerland 0.382 (2014), the Netherlands 0.457 (2015, provisional), Sweden 0.429 (2014), Canada 0.427 (2014), Belgium 0.495 (2014), Japan 0.488 (2012), Germany 0.45 (2015), Italy 0.512 (2014), the United States 0.506 (2015), and France 0.512 (2014).[7]

III

So far, this all looks to be consistent with the miserabilist story.

Market income is not, however, the end of the story. Market income is taxed and is then lifted through the provision of free transport, free health care, and free education. Market income is also boosted through welfare payments. What is left at the end of this is final income and final income is much more equally distributed than market income. Anyone who thinks that the UK is in the unrelenting iron-clad grip of neoliberal governments who celebrate and promote inequality should ponder Figure 6.2, which shows final household income alongside the market income of each decile of the population.

What does this chart show? Let's start in the middle. The market income and the final income of the households in the sixth decile of the population is roughly similar. For all the other deciles, they are very different. The *final* income of the poorest 10 per cent of households is 3.06 times greater than that of their market income. The *final* income of the poorest 10–20 per cent of households is 2.1 times greater than that of their market income. The *final* income of the richest 10 per cent of households is 72 per cent of that of their market income.

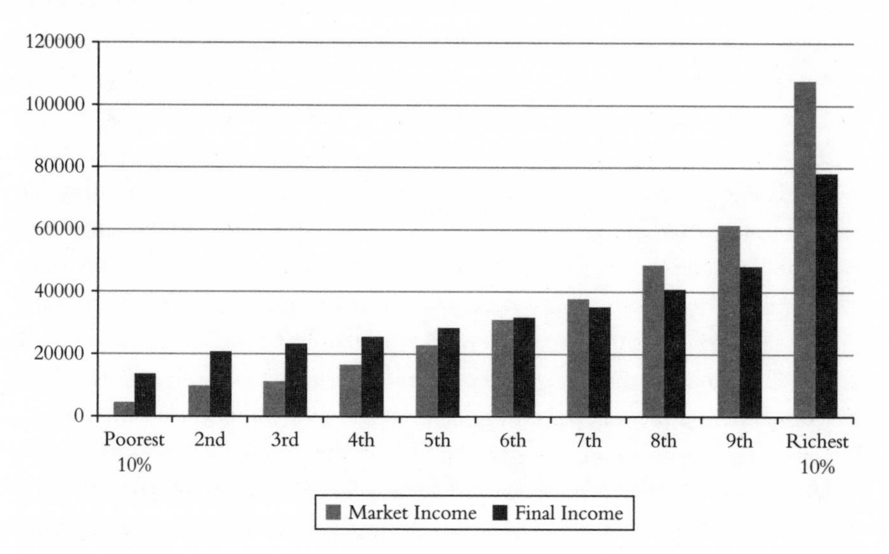

Figure 6.2. Household equivalized market income and final income (in £) by decile, 2015/16.[2]

What difference does this make to overall levels of inequality? The *final* income of the richest 10 per cent of households is now only 2.25 times greater than the final income of the median household (compared with being three times greater in the case of market income). The *final* income of the richest 10 per cent of households is now only 5.74 times greater than that of the poorest 10 per cent of households (compared with being twenty-four times greater in the case of market income). The *final* income of the poorest 80 per cent of the population is significantly higher than that of the *combined* final income of the richest 20 per cent of households. The Gini coefficient for market income is 0.52. The coefficient for final income is 0.36.[8]

One early lesson to draw from this is that the UK is a country in which a significant redistribution of income still occurs. This is not what we might expect from a country in which neoliberalism has become 'part of the air we breathe, elements of our most fundamental assumptions about how the world works'.[9] This is not to say that redistribution is an unalloyed good thing. I can see good reasons to value a relatively equal distribution of *market* income over a relatively equal distribution of *final* income. Relying upon the state puts poorer households in a position of dependency and potential uncertainty. For this reason, 'predistribution' which attempts to reduce market income inequalities may be preferable to redistribution.[10] Yet given how unequal market income is, it is still notable how much redistribution still occurs.

How does this redistribution take place? Taxation plays a part. Figure 6.3(a) shows the average total amount of tax (direct and indirect tax) paid by each decile of the population in 2015/16. What we see here is (as we might hope) that the richest households pay a lot more in tax than the poorest households. To be more precise, the richest 10 per cent of households paid £37,897 in tax in 2015/16, whilst the poorest 10 per cent paid £4,622 (Figure 6.2 shows that the market income of the poorest 10 per cent is less than the amount that group paid in tax, which looks odd, but remember, tax here includes tax paid on goods and services and not just on income). Figure 6.3(b) then shows the amount of tax paid by each of these groups as a percentage of that group's *final* income (i.e. their income after all taxes and welfare cash payments). There is still some redistribution going on here. The richest households pay a larger amount of tax relative to their final income than the poorest households. But notice here just how small this difference is. The richest 10 per cent of households paid an amount in tax

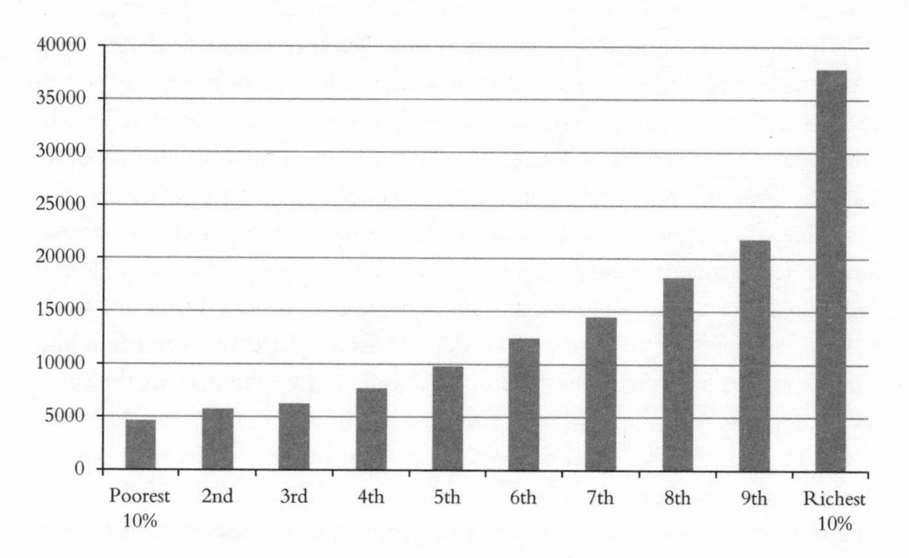

Figure 6.3(a) Total tax paid (in £) by decile, 2015/16 (£).[3]

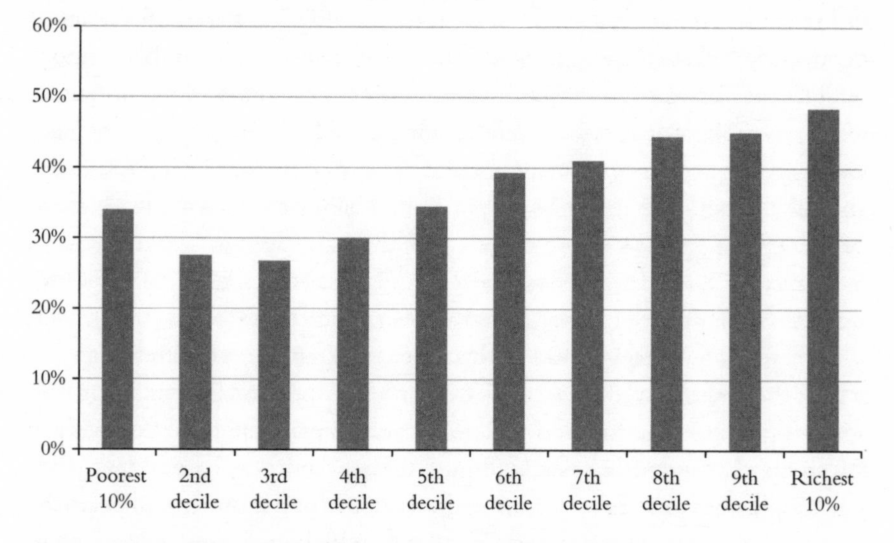

Figure 6.3(b) Total tax paid as a percentage of final income.

that was the equivalent of 48 per cent of their final income. The poorest 10 per cent paid an amount that was equivalent to 34 per cent of their income. This, it should be recalled, is in a context in which the market income of the richest 10 per cent of households is twenty-four times larger than that of the poorest 10 per cent of households.

The welfare system plays a much more significant role in redistributing income. Figure 6.4(a) shows the value of the cash benefits received by each decile of the population. This includes jobseeker's allowance, employment allowance, incapacity benefit, income support, maternity allowance, child benefit, tax credits, housing benefit, the state pension, widows' benefit, war pensions, carer's allowance, attendance allowance, disability living allowance, and other forms of welfare support. What we see here is that the poorest households receive a lot more in cash benefits than the richest households. The poorest 10 per cent of households received £6,556 in benefits, whilst the richest 10 per cent received £2,706. Figure 6.4(b) then shows the value of those cash benefits relative to the final income of each group. Here we see some significant redistributive effects. For the poorest 10 per cent of households, cash benefits were the equivalent of 48 per cent of their final income. For the richest 10 per cent, cash benefits were the equivalent of just 3 per cent of final income.

Welfare expenditure has a significant equalizing effect on final income. On the most recent available figures from the OECD, cash benefits reduced the overall Gini coefficient in the UK by 27 per cent. How does this compare with the performance of welfare systems in other countries? In comparative terms, the UK is at the lower end of the table. In Belgium (44 per cent), Germany (31 per cent), Japan and France (42 per cent), Sweden (35 per cent), and the Netherlands and Italy (33 per cent), welfare cash payments do more to reduce inequality. On the other hand, the UK's welfare system reduces inequality by more than the welfare systems in the Netherlands (21 per cent), Canada (19 per cent), or the United States (16 per cent).[11]

If there is an obvious cloud to this silver lining, it comes with the way in which the tax and welfare systems treat the very poorest households. Look again at the charts in this section. The poorest 10 per cent of households pay less in tax than any other decile (Figure 6.3(a)). But as a share of their final income, the poorest 10 per cent of households pay more in tax than the second, third, or fourth deciles (Figure 6.3(b)). Perhaps more significantly, in the case of the welfare system, the poorest 10 per cent of households receive less in cash benefits in absolute terms than the second, third, fourth, or fifth deciles (Figure 6.4(a)).

More than thirty years after the start of the neoliberal onslaught, there is still a great deal of income redistribution in the UK. This is even though, as we have seen, only 42 per cent of people apparently agree that the government should redistribute income from the better off to the less

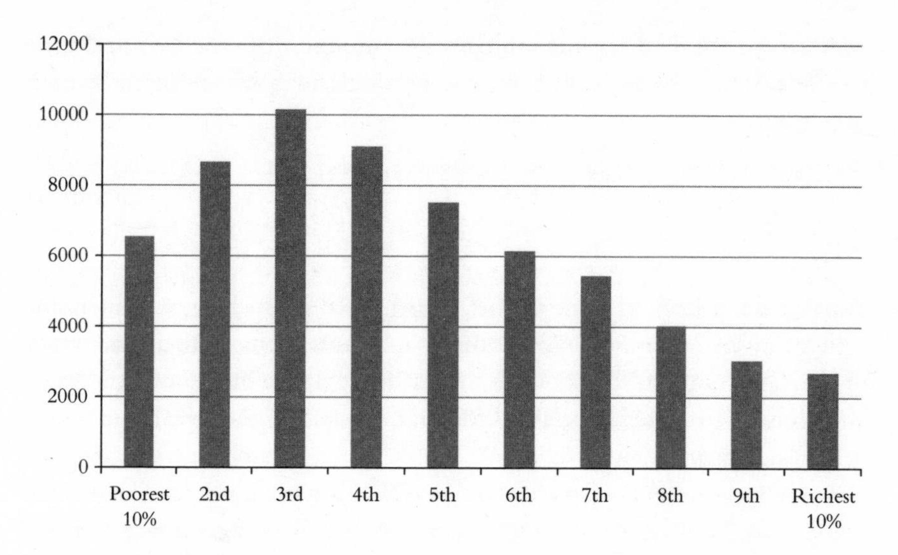

Figure 6.4(a) Total cash benefits (in £) received by decile, 2015/16 (£).[4]

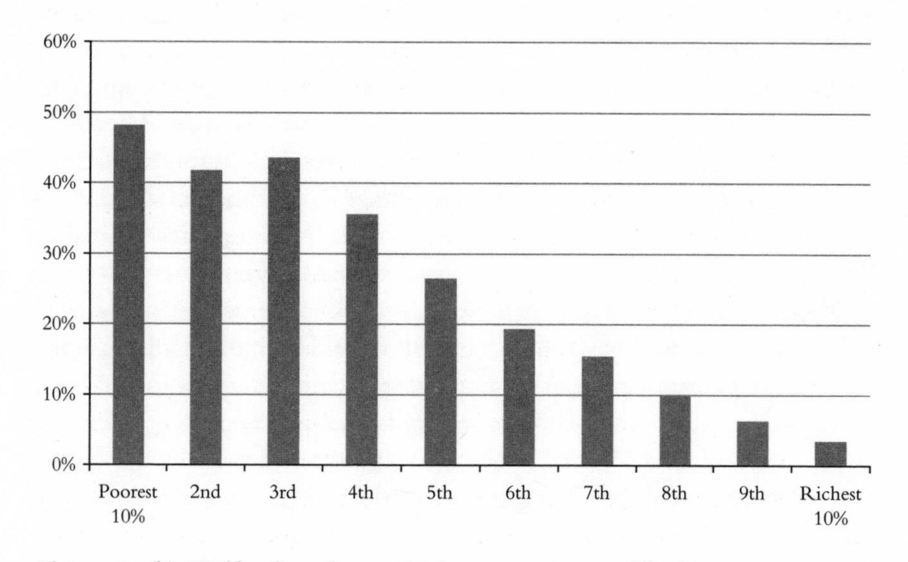

Figure 6.4(b) Welfare benefits received as a percentage of final income.

well off (p. 50). The tax and welfare systems take from the rich and give to the poor. They are not, however, particularly good at giving to the very poor.

IV

When I think back to some of the issues I cared most about when I was a student in the late 1980s, a lot of them no longer seem quite as important or as relevant now as they once did. Apartheid is gone. The Poll Tax is gone. 'Coal not dole' started to seem a little bit uncomfortable in the 1990s when it became apparent just how much of a threat climate change was. If there was one issue I feel passionate about today and which, if I could, I would wave a wand at to make it go away, it is housing. Housing is a key cause of poverty and a key driver of inequality. The basic problem with housing is not so much that the richest households live in nicer houses and nicer suburbs than the poorest households. The real problem is that the richest households spend less of their income on housing and still get to live in nicer houses and nicer suburbs.

Figure 6.5 shows how much money different income groups spent on average on housing each week in 2015/16. There are two main differences to the way in which this data (which is taken from the Institute of Fiscal Studies) is presented when compared with that I have used so far. First, it is presented in terms of ventiles (5 per cent blocks) of the population rather than deciles. Second, it is presented on a weekly rather than annual basis. Putting this aside, what we see here is, I think, quite jaw-dropping. The richest and poorest households spend very similar amounts on housing. Indeed, the poorest 5 per cent of households spent £12.40 less on housing (£84.50) than the richest 5-10 per cent of households (£72.13).

So, what difference do housing costs make to overall household income? The simple answer is that they obviously make a huge difference. Figure 6.6 shows the proportion of the *before* housing cost income each group of households spent on housing in 2015/16. The *before* final housing cost income of the poorest 5 per cent of households was £192.09. They spent an average of £84.50 on housing... which amounts to 44 per cent of their *before* housing cost income. The poorest 5–10 per cent of households spent 31 per cent of their before housing cost income on housing. As we move

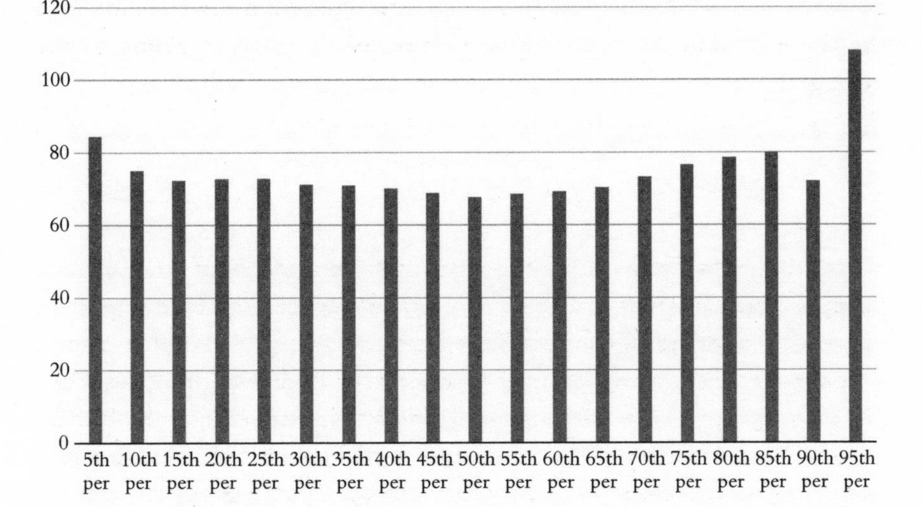

Figure 6.5. Total average weekly housing costs (amount spent in £) by ventile, 2015/16.[5]

from left to right across Figure 6.6, the amount each ventile spends on housing steadily decreases. The richest 5 per cent of households spent just 9 per cent of their before housing cost income on housing. This is a huge difference. The poor are not simply poor because they have a lower income. They are poor because they spend much more of their income on housing than the rich.

Final income is, as we have already seen, a lot more equal than market income. What difference does housing make? Final income *after* housing costs is more equal than market income but significantly less equal than final income *before* housing costs. The tax and welfare systems redistribute money from the rich to the poor. Housing redistributes it back again. The final income of the richest 5 per cent of households *before* housing costs is 2.53 times greater than that of the median household. *After* housing costs, it is 2.68 times greater. The final income of the median household is 2.5 times greater than that of the poorest 5 per cent of households *before* housing costs. After housing costs, it is 3.84 times greater. Finally, the final income of the richest 5 per cent of households *before* housing costs is 6.3 times greater than that of the poorest 5 per cent of households. *After* housing costs, it is 10.3 times greater.

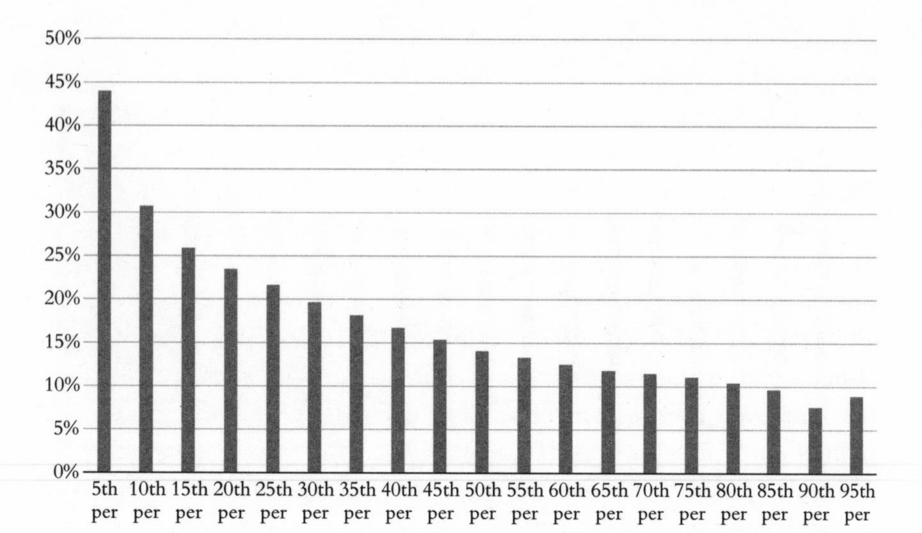

Figure 6.6. Housing expenditure by ventile as a percentage of before housing cost final income, 2015/16.[6]

V

We have so far looked at inequality on a household basis. I now want to cast the net slightly wider.

How does average income vary across the UK? Figure 6.7 shows median full-time gross weekly earnings by region as of October 2016.[12] What is immediately striking here is the extent to which London has become decoupled from the rest of the economy. Average earnings across the UK in 2016 were £538.70. London's average earnings were 124 per cent of the UK average. This may sound attractive, but to go back to housing for just one second, it is also worth noting that the average London property now costs thirteen times more than average income.[13] Average earnings in Wales, on the other hand, are just 91 per cent of the UK average. There are 'islands of affluence' in the North—such as York and Cheshire—and pockets of poverty in the South—most notably parts of the East End of London, Portsmouth, and Plymouth.[14] These figures do, however, confirm the existence of a broad North of England/Midlands–South divide. Average earnings in London, the South-East, the South-West, and the East were £567 a week in 2016.[15] Average earnings in Yorkshire and Humberside, the North-East, and the North-West were just £498. Average earnings in the East and West Midlands were £496. Shorn of London and the South-East, the rest of Britain, if it were a country, would be about as rich as Spain, with a GDP per person below the European Union average.[16] As John Lanchester observes, 'what strikes you if you travel to different parts of the country, though, is that the primary reality of modern Britain is not so much class as geography. Geography is destiny. And for much of the country, not a happy destiny.'[17]

At the local authority level, earnings, as the Office of National Statistics observes, vary significantly. In April 2016, full-time employees working in the City of London had the highest median gross weekly earnings (£958) and those working in Rossendale (North-West) had the lowest (£391). When looking at earnings by place of residence, that is, the place where the employee lives, employees living in the City of London also had highest median gross weekly earnings (£1,034), while those living in Craven (Yorkshire and The Humber) had the lowest (£413).[18] There are also significant inequalities within cities. In 2015, average gross weekly pay in Manchester Central was £481 and in Manchester Withington £394; in Birmingham Erdington it was £523 and in Birmingham Northfield £321; in Edinburgh South-West it was £533 and Edinburgh East £442; and, finally, in Bermondsey in London it was £670 and in Barking £431. In the Royal Borough of Kensington and Chelsea, the location of Grenfell Tower, *The Economist* reports that the average (mean) salary is £123,000, among the highest in Britain but that the median salary (the point which half the population is above and half below) is just £32,700. The huge gap here reflects the huge disparities in income within the area.[19]

	Median full-time gross weekly earnings (£)
UK	538.7
North East	494.0
North West	503.2
Yorkshire and The Humber	498.3
East Midlands	483.2
West Midlands	510.2
East	528.8
London	670.8
South East	566.0
South West	505.0
Wales	492.4
Scotland	535.0
Northern Ireland	495.2
UK	538.7

Figure 6.7. Median full-time gross weekly earnings by region, April 2015.[7]

VI

The next categories I want to discuss relate to gender and ethnicity.

Some of the figures here are startling and can speak for themselves. As of April 2016, the gender pay gap (for median earnings) for full-time employees was 9.6 per cent. When part-time employees are included, the gap is 18.1 per cent.[20] The pay gap consistently widens for more than a decade after a first child is born. After twelve years, women receive 33 per cent less pay an hour than men.[21] 68 per cent of women work, compared with 78 per cent of men. 63 per cent of men who work work full-time and 27 per cent work part-time. For women, the equivalent figures are 57.5 per cent and 42.5 per cent. When women are asked why they are working part-time, the most frequent reply is to 'accommodate family responsibilities'. Of the largest FTSE 100 companies, 95 per cent have male chief executives and 97 per cent have male chairmen.[22] 29 per cent of MPs are women. Women report spending an average of thirteen hours on housework and twenty-three hours on caring for family members each week; the equivalent figures for men are eight hours and ten hours.[23] The LSE Commission on Gender, Inequality and Power reports that around one in twenty women between the ages of 16 and 59 report having been the victim of rape or sexual assault, rising to one in five if we include less serious forms of sexual assault. The Leveson Inquiry into the culture, practices, and ethics of the British press following the News International phone hacking scandal has described the British tabloid press as a 'demeaning and sexualising lens' that reduces 'even the most accomplished and professional women [...] to the sum of their body parts'.[24]

Turning now to ethnicity, the Equality and Human Rights Commission has recently reported that unemployment is significantly higher for ethnic minorities (12.9 per cent) than it is for White people (6.3 per cent); that Black workers with a degree earn 21 per cent less on average than White workers; that just 6 per cent of Black school leavers attended a Russell Group university, compared with 12 per cent of Mixed and Asian school leavers and 11 per cent of White school leavers; that the homicide rate for Black people was 30.5 per million, compared with 14.1 for Asian people and 8.9 for White people; and that 31 per cent of Pakistani/Bangladeshi people live in overcrowded accommodation, while for Black people the figure is 27 per cent and for White people 8 per cent.[25] In 2016, the Casey Review into integration and opportunity in isolated and deprived communities reported that 19 per cent of households headed by someone who was White were living on a low income, compared with 41–51 per cent of households of Black, Pakistani, Chinese, and Bangladeshi ethnicity. The Review also found that in 2015–16, there were 62,518 hate crimes (based on race, sexual orientation, religion, disability, and transgender) recorded by the police—up 19 per cent on the previous year. Finally, the Report found that compared to other minority faith groups, Muslims tend to live in higher residential concentrations at ward level and that, on the most recent available census data, Blackburn, Birmingham, Burnley, and Bradford included wards with between 70 per cent and 85 per cent Muslim populations. The review went on to argue that this can limit labour market opportunities; reduce opportunities for social ties between minority and White British communities; and lead to lower identification with Britain and lower levels of trust between ethnic groups, compared to minorities living in more diverse areas.[26]

VII

Globally, 1 per cent of people own nearly half of all wealth.[27] The distribution of wealth within the UK is more equal . . . but it is a long way from being anything approaching egalitarian. Between 2012 and 2014 (the most recent data available), the wealthiest 10 per cent of households in the UK owned 45 per cent of total aggregate wealth. Figure 6.8 shows the distributions of different kinds of wealth—property wealth, financial wealth, physical wealth (defined as the value of the contents of a person's main residence, the contents of any other property which the household owns, and collectables, valuables, and vehicles), and private pension wealth—by decile of the population. The wealthiest 10 per cent of households have a total property wealth of £1,550,866 million. The poorest 10 per cent of households have a total property wealth of minus £2,276 million. The wealthiest 10 per cent of households have a total financial wealth of £103,200 million. The poorest 10 per cent have a total financial pension wealth of minus £11,766 million. The Gini coefficient for market income in Britain is around 0.52 and the coefficient for final income 0.36. By comparison, the coefficient for property is 0.66; for financial wealth 0.91; for physical wealth 0.45; for private pension wealth 0.73; and for total wealth 0.63.[28]

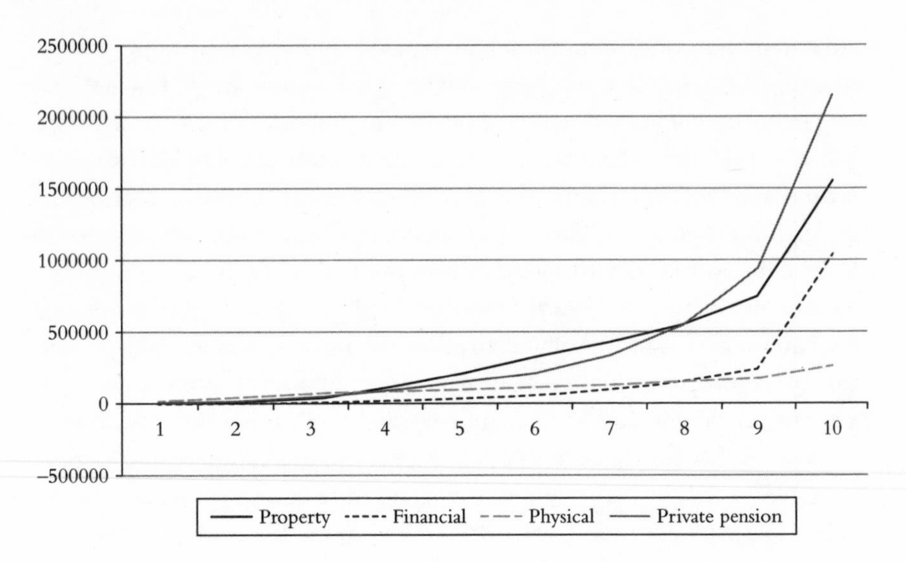

Figure 6.8. Aggregate total wealth (in £ million) by deciles and components (£), 2012–14.[8]

VIII

Neoliberals are generally quite relaxed about equality: partly because they think it does not make any sense to argue that particular distributions of income or wealth can be described as just or unjust if they are the result of millions of voluntary market-based transactions; partly because they think that inequality is a spur to economic growth and that a society in which there is more inequality is also likely to be one in which the poor have a higher absolute income; and, finally, because they think that what really matters in terms of right and wrong is not equality of outcome but equality of opportunity. Give people genuine opportunities and they will exercise those opportunities by becoming more unequal. Impose on people a levelling equality of outcome and you deny them opportunities.

It turns out, however, that this is not actually the case. Far from being mutually exclusive alternatives, equality of opportunity and equality of outcome appear to complement each other quite neatly. In a speech in January 2012, President Obama's Chairman of the Council of Economic Advisors, Alan Krueger, pointed to the inverse relationship between inequality and generational earnings mobility. This became known as the 'Gatsby curve', after F. Scott Fitzgerald's eponymous hero in *The Great Gatsby*.[29] Figure 6.9

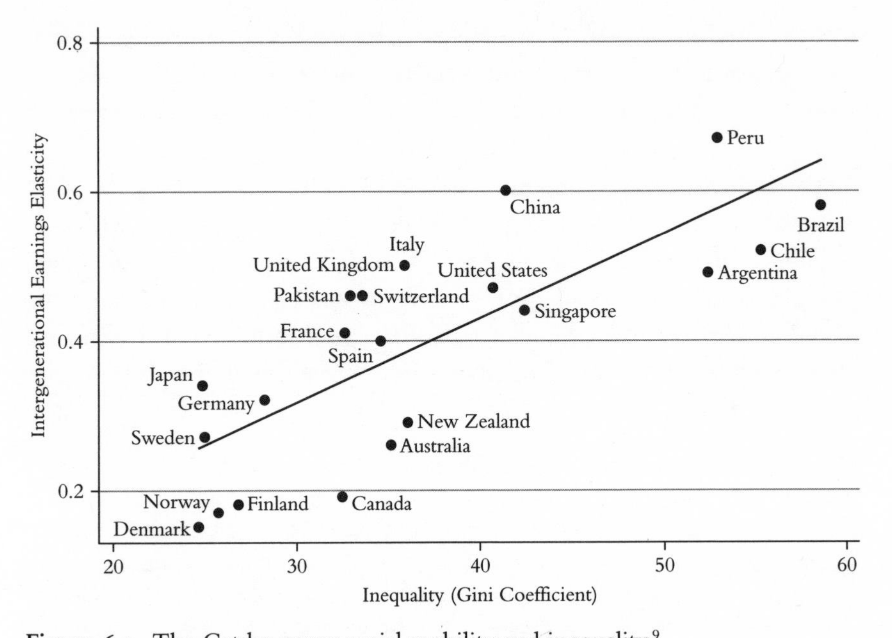

Figure 6.9. The Gatsby curve: social mobility and inequality.[9]
Courtesy of: Miles Corak, *Economics for Public Policy* blog, 'Here is the source for the "Great Gatsby Curve" in the Alan Krueger speech at the Center for American Progress on January 12'.

shows a version of the Gatsby curve. The horizontal axis here shows the overall level of income inequality as measured through the Gini coefficient (the further to the right, the more unequal the distribution of income). The vertical axis measures intergenerational earnings elasticity, i.e. the extent to which somebody's income as an adult matches that of their parents (the higher the point, the higher the degree of correlation). The solid black line running from the bottom-left to the top-right shows the best fit regression mapping the relationship between these variables. What we see here is that countries like Brazil and Peru with high levels of income inequality also have high levels of social immobility, whilst the Scandinavian countries with low levels of income inequality also have high social mobility. The UK, it should be noted, on this data has a relatively middling level of inequality and a low level of social mobility.

The OECD has examined the strength of the statistical relationship between a father's income and their son's income. It finds that in Denmark a father's income can explain 15 per cent of the variance in the son's income. In Australia, it can explain 17 per cent of the variance. In the United States, this figure is 47 per cent. In Britain, it is a staggering 50 per cent.[30] In its

2016 *State of the Nation* report, the Social Mobility Commission reports that whereas in a perfectly mobile society you would expect 4 per cent of those born into the poorest 20 per cent of households to themselves end up in one of the poorest 20 per cent of households, the actual figure is 6.3 per cent. Some of its other key findings were that, in terms of childcare provision, double the percentage of children from the poorest 20 per cent of households are in childcare provision that has been rated as not good enough, compared with the most prosperous areas, and that while a private school student has a 1 in 20 chance of entering Oxbridge, a student from a poor background has odds closer to 1 in 1,500. Overall, the Commission concludes that:

> Our country has reached an inflection point. The rungs on the social mobility ladder are growing further apart. It is becoming harder for this generation of struggling families to move up. Across our country's local economies, education system, and labour and housing markets there are major market failures. New forms of government action are needed to address them. Employers and educators will need to act differently too. The approaches of the past, although they have brought some progress, are no longer fit for purpose. We are in a different world.[31]

IX

I have now come to the end of the first part and it is worth pausing for breath. Imagine a scale running from nought to ten measuring the overall level of equality (figure 6.10). We start with zero (impressively very equal—a social democratic paradise: Norway but with warmer weather); then run through from 3 (Canada—they seem to have some problems but compared with the United States seem quite sane); 7 (Germany—a bit OTT when it comes to Greek Austerity but they have strong trade unions, a strong welfare system, and have not recently lost to Iceland at a major football tournament); and 10 (Texas—a neoliberal dystopia but with Katie Hopkins as lifelong President). Where would we place the UK in each of the categories we have looked at so far? This is (obviously) a subjective judgement. But my own sense here is that, in the order of their initial appearance, I would rank them in something like the pattern shown below. There are particularly sharp inequalities in market income, wealth, and social mobility. Inequalities in final income and by region are not nearly as pronounced. Housing costs

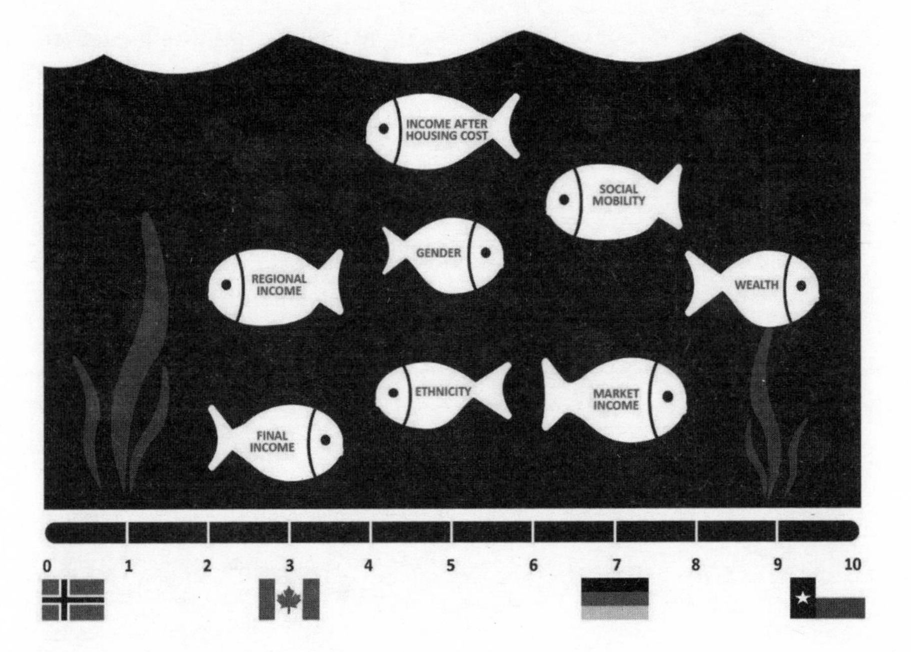

Figure 6.10. Inequality: a first cut.

exacerbate inequality, whilst there are also significant inequalities in gender and ethnicity.

I now want to turn to the second part of the analysis. How have levels of inequality changed over time? The miserabilist history is that Britain is becoming ever more unequal. What Margaret Thatcher started, New Labour continued, and the Coalition and the Conservatives have, under the guise of cutting the deficit, accelerated. To what extent is this argument about changing patterns of inequality justified?

X

Let's start, once again, with market income. In 2015/16, the market income of the richest 10 per cent of households was three times greater than that of the income of the median household and twenty-four times greater than that of the poorest 10 per cent of households. Figure 6.11 shows how these ratios have changed over the last few decades.[32]

In 1977 (the period to which this data set goes back), the market income of the richest 10 per cent of households was 17.6 times greater than that of

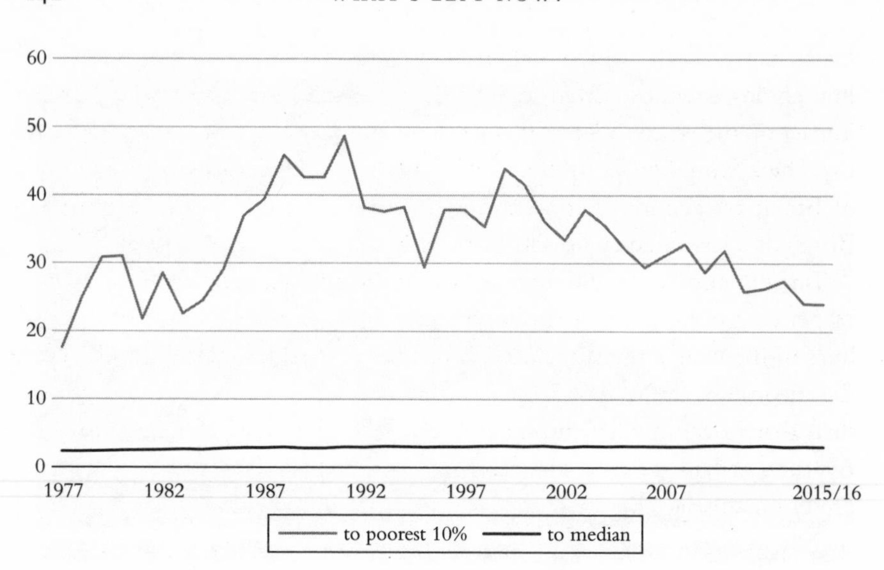

Figure 6.11. Market income, 1977–2015/16 (ratio of richest 10% of households to poorest 10% of households and median household).[10]

the poorest 10 per cent of households. A great deal then changed in a short amount of time. By 1979, the market income of the richest households was 30.8 times greater than that of the poorest 10 per cent of households. Inequality continued to rise in the 1980s. By 1991, the income of the richest 10 per cent of households was 48 times greater than that of the poorest 10 per cent of households. In the 1990s, inequality initially fell and then rose again. By 1995, the income of the richest 10 per cent of households was 29 times greater than that of the poorest 10 per cent of households. By 1999, (two years after New Labour entered office) it was 44 times greater. Since that time, inequality has however fallen steadily. By 2010, the income of the richest 10 per cent of households was 29 times greater than that of the poorest 10 per cent of households. By 2014/15, it had fallen again to just over 24 times. In total, and by this measure, inequality is now 22 per cent *lower* than it was in 1979 and 45 per cent *lower* than it was in 1999. This is not what I think the miserabilist story might lead us to expect. After a slow start, New Labour was in office during a time in which there was a dramatic fall in inequality. Far from reversing that trend, the Coalition has, if anything, maintained it. It is possible that inequality will begin to accelerate prior to and following Brexit. The significant 15–20 per cent devaluation of sterling has boosted exports but will lead to higher import prices for basic goods (particularly food), which will have the most impact on lower-income households. Any post-Brexit reduction in immigration may have a positive impact on the wages of unskilled workers. But it is likely that any such positive effect would be more than offset by the wider negative consequences of Brexit on economic growth and taxation.[33] At the moment, however, Britain is a less unequal country than it has been for some time.

Turning now to the difference between the market income of the richest 10 per cent of households and the median household (the lower of the two lines in the chart), the story takes a similar but less dramatic form. In 1977, the income of the richest 10 per cent of households was 2.3 times greater than that of the median household. By 1979, this ratio had risen to 2.38. By 1989, it had risen to 2.84 and by 1999, it had risen to 3.21. There it pretty much stops. By 2009, the ratio was 3.23 and by 2015/16, it had fallen slightly to 3.09.

Why did market income inequality rise to such an extent in the 1980s? The OECD has published a detailed review of the extent of growth in and the causes of inequality.[34] It finds, above all else, that a shortfall in skills training and education has driven the increase in inequality. Relatedly, it finds that globalization—which, as we saw previously, is often associated on the left with a levelling-down effect—was indeed one factor driving increases in inequality. During the 1980s, British firms were exposed to more international competition, which led, in places, to stagnating wages among unskilled workers. At the same time, rising demand for highly skilled workers in fast-growing, high-value, and globalized industries like banking, the media, and pharmaceuticals also pushed up wage inequalities. The OECD also argues that a decline in the size and bargaining power of trade unions resulted in higher wage inequality. Countries with higher rates of union membership generally have lower levels of market income inequality.[35] In the UK in the 1980s, the unions were excluded from any involvement in government decision-making and were battered with legislation mandating ballots prior to strike action and outlawing secondary picketing. The unions lost several set-piece battles with Margaret Thatcher and their overall membership plummeted from 13.2 million in 1979 to 7.8 million by 1997.[36] Lower union membership (combined with higher rates of unemployment, particularly among low-skilled and semi-skilled workers in the early 1980s) led to higher wage inequality.

New Labour did not seek to reverse the Conservatives' industrial relations reforms and between 1997 and 2010 union membership fell further from

7.8 million to 7.2 million (or from 30 per cent to 26 per cent of the workforce).[37] So why did market income inequality start to fall in the 2000s? One part of the answer is that New Labour introduced a minimum wage in 1999. This was initially set at a rate of £3.60 an hour but has since risen by 76 per cent in real (that is, inflation-adjusted) terms: a rate of growth similar to that of GDP and *higher* than that of the growth in average earnings.[38] To see what difference the minimum wage (together with lower overall rates of unemployment in the 2000s) made to market income inequality, consider the following numbers. Between 1980 and 1999/2000, the average market income of the poorest 10 per cent of households rose 3.15-fold, whilst that of the richest 10 per cent of households rose nearly 4.5-fold. Between 1999/2000 and 2009/10—a much shorter period following the introduction of the minimum wage—the average market income of the poorest 10 per cent of households rose 2.1-fold, whilst that of the richest 10 per cent rose 1.41-fold.[39]

Over the last decade, low wages have, however, once again become a major policy issue. The Social Mobility and Child Poverty Commission found that less than half of the children living in poverty in Britain in 1997 lived in a household in which at least one person worked but that by 2012 this had risen to two-thirds (poverty is defined here as having a household income less than 60 per cent of the national median).[40] What has gone wrong here? One problem is that the number of people being paid the minimum wage has increased from something like 1.8 per cent to 4 per cent of workers.[41] A second problem comes with the growth of zero hour contracts (that is, contracts which do not guarantee a minimum number of hours). The number of people employed on zero hour contracts rose from 166,000 in 2007 (0.6 per cent of people in employment) to 801,000 in 2015 (2 per cent of people in employment) before falling to 705,000 by the end of 2016.[42] It is clear that zero hour contracts suit many people. But 34 per cent of people on zero hour contracts would like to work more hours, compared with 13 per cent of people on other forms of contract.[43] A further problem is that increases in the minimum wage have not kept pace with increases in the cost of living and, in particular, the cost of housing. Hence, more working families have found themselves trapped in poverty.

One notable response to the growing problem of working poverty has been the campaign to pay a living wage. In 2016, the Living Wage Commission (an independent group promoting the cause of a living wage) estimated that there was a 21 per cent gap between the minimum wage and a living wage and that over five million people in Britain were being paid less than the living wage.[44] The Labour Party entered the 2015 election promising to raise the minimum wage to £8 an hour and to promote the living wage via tax rebates for businesses. For their part, the Conservatives warned that the introduction of a living wage would lead to a loss of competitiveness, unemployment, plague, and famine. Yet just a few months later, the newly elected Conservative majority government—under pressure to cut expenditure on tax credits designed to boost low wages—announced it was going to introduce a 'national living wage'. There is some devil in the associated detail. The national living wage is only going to be paid to those aged over 25. There is to be no higher separate allowance for London—a key recommendation of the Living Wage Commission. The national living wage will be set at a level equivalent to 60 per cent of median earnings, whereas the Living Wage Commission estimated the living wage in relation to the cost of living. But it is still worth pausing for breath here. The proposal to pay a national living wage was made despite the very public opposition of many business leaders.[45] For all its limitations, it is a welcome policy development which is a long way from embodying the free-market spirit.

I have so far focused upon the richest 10 per cent of households. In an article in *Vanity Fair* in May 2011, however, Joseph Stiglitz spoke of government of the 1 per cent, by the 1 per cent, and for the 1 per cent.[46] 'We are the 99%' subsequently became a rallying slogan of the Occupy movement. In the 1960s, the richest 1 per cent of people in Britain accounted for around 3.8 per cent of total income. By the late 1970s, their share had fallen to just 3 per cent. Inequality then rose. By the end of the 1980s, the richest 1 per cent accounted for 6 per cent of total income. Whereas overall levels of market income inequality fell under New Labour, the income share of the richest 1 per cent continued to grow, reaching 8.8 per cent immediately prior to the financial crisis. It then fell to just 7 per cent in 2011 but has since grown again to 8.3 per cent.[47]

XI

In 2015/16, the *final* income of the richest 10 per cent of households was 5.74 times greater than that of the poorest 10 per cent of households and 2.25 times greater than that of the income of the median household. Figure 6.12 shows how these ratios have evolved over previous decades. Overall, the story here is pretty similar to that of market income. In the 1970s, overall levels of inequality in the UK were relatively low. In 1979, the final income of the richest 10 per cent of households was 4.3 times greater than that of the poorest 10 per cent of households and 1.83 times greater than that of the median household. In the 1980s, inequality rose significantly. By 1991, the final income of the richest 10 per cent of households was 6.6 times greater than that of the poorest 10 per cent of households and 2.4 times greater than the final income of the median household. Overall levels of inequality have, however, stabilized since then, fluctuating between a high of 6.5 in 2008 and a low of 5.2 in 2011.[48] The same is true of overall levels of inequality as measured through the Gini coefficient. The Institute for Fiscal Studies estimates that the Gini coefficient for final incomes before housing costs was 0.261 in 1961 and 0.25 in 1980. By 1990, the Gini coefficient had risen to 0.33. Since then it has, however, remained relatively stable, rising to 0.35 in 2000 before falling to 0.34 in 2006. In 2015/16, the Gini coefficient was 0.346.[49]

There is one further piece of data I want to briefly look at. The Department for Work and Pensions has collected individual-level data which allows us to see how likely it is that people with the lowest incomes at one point in time are still trapped with the lowest incomes at a later point in time.[50] The most interesting figure here relates to the number of people whose income is amongst the lowest 10 per cent of incomes nationally. Let's start in the 1990s. Of the people with the lowest 10 per cent of incomes in 1990, 14 per cent

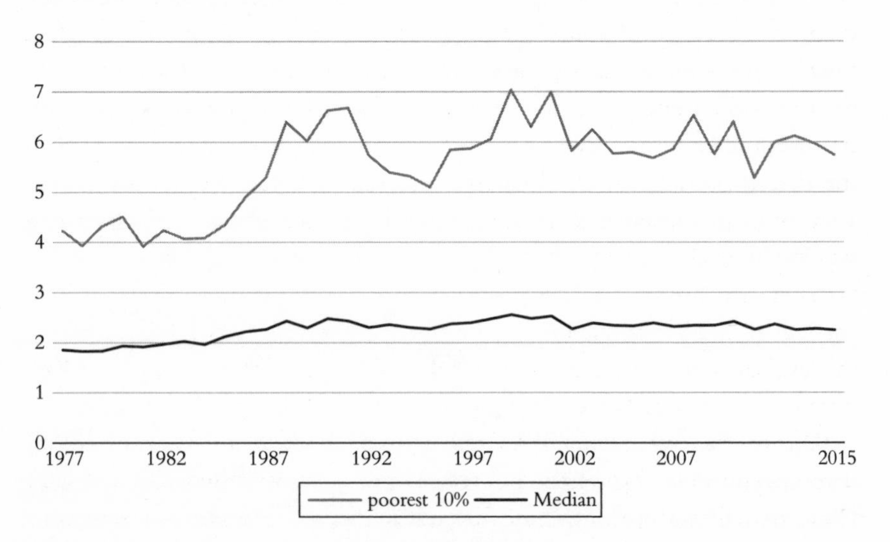

Figure 6.12. Final income, 1977–2015/16 (ratio of richest 10% of households to poorest 10% of households and median household).[11]

had incomes which were still amongst the lowest 10 per cent of incomes over *each* of the following nine years. A further 43 per cent had amongst the lowest 10 per cent of incomes in a majority of the following nine years. During the long boom of the 2000s, 10 per cent of people with incomes amongst the lowest 10 per cent of incomes in 2000 still had amongst the lowest 10 per cent of incomes in each of the following eight years. A further 40 per cent had incomes which were amongst the lowest 10 per cent of incomes in a majority of the following eight years. In other words, and despite overall levels of market income inequality falling in the 2000s and final income inequality stabilizing, there was only a slight increase in *intra*generational income mobility.

I previously showed that the tax system works to redistribute some income from the richest households to the poorest households and that the welfare system works to redistribute much more money from the richest to the poorest households. How much more or less redistributive have the tax and welfare systems become over the last few decades?

Figure 6.13 shows the amount the poorest 10 per cent and richest 10 per cent of households have paid in tax as a percentage of their final income between 1977 and 2015/16. The simplest way of thinking about the redistributiveness of the tax system is in terms of the size of the gap between these two lines. The larger the gap, the more redistributive the system is. In 1978, the richest 10 per cent of households paid 52 per cent of their final income in tax and the poorest 10 per cent of households 28 per cent of their final income in tax: a 24 per cent gap. In the 1980s, the share of tax paid by the richest households fell and that paid by the poorest households rose, and by 1988, the gap was only just over 5 per cent. In the 1990s, the tax paid by the richest households rose slightly and the gap widened to 15 per cent in 1997. By 2005, the gap had widened again to 19 per cent. By 2015/16, the gap was just 10 per cent. Overall, the conclusion I draw from this is that the UK tax system is not particularly redistributive today but that it has not been particularly redistributive in the past either. That said, New Labour reduced the level of tax paid by the poorest households and in doing so made the tax system more redistributive than it once was.

What of the welfare system? The Conservatives have, on many occasions, demonized welfare claimants. Benefits have been capped and tax credits cut. Child benefit and housing benefit have been frozen and a spare-bedroom tax imposed. Over the last decade, benefit sanctions have evolved into a central part of the UK's welfare system, with the number of sanctions

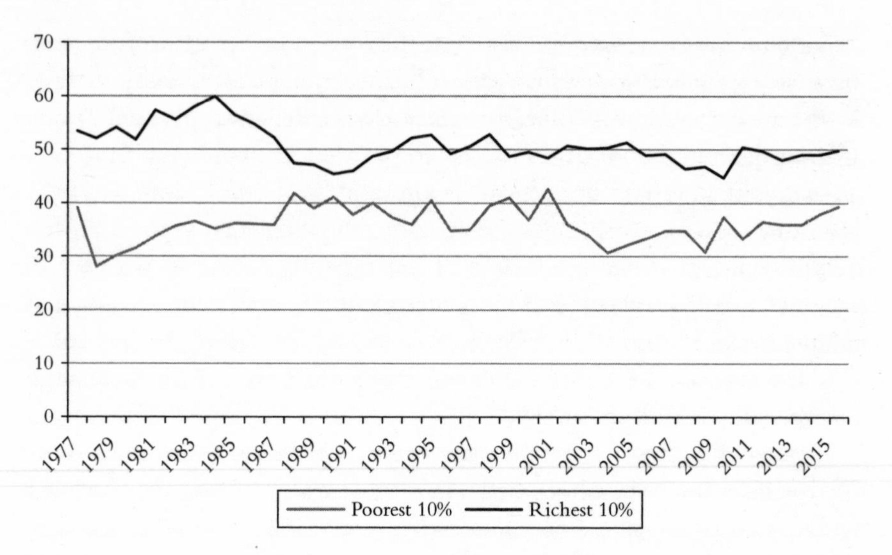

Figure 6.13. Total taxation as a percentage of final income (richest and poorest 10%), 1977–2015/16.[12]

being applied doubling between 2010 and 2015.[51] But the welfare state has not been downsized. Welfare spending was 11.5 per cent of GDP in 1983. It was 11 per cent of GDP in 2006 before the financial crisis and then rose to 12.8 per cent of GDP in 2012. By 2015/16, welfare spending had fallen to 11.8 per cent of GDP. It is currently forecast to fall further to 11 per cent of GDP in 2019/20 (back, in other words, to the level it was prior to the financial crisis).[52] In real (inflation-adjusted) terms (using 2016/17 prices), government expenditure on social protection—which, using the standard OECD definition, includes cash benefits, in-kind benefits, and tax breaks with social purposes—rose from £161.8bn in 1998/9 to £249bn in 2009/10 and £264bn by 2016/17.[53] What is more, governments broadly spend money on broadly the same kind of things as they used to, with state pensions remaining the single most expensive welfare item.[54] The benefits cap is a politically potent but largely symbolic measure which will save perhaps £350m a year.[55] The welfare cap—which requires a subset of welfare spending to be held below a fixed cash limit set in July 2015—is now forecast to overshoot by 7 per cent.[56]

All of this looks quite reassuring. There is, however, a catch. The welfare system has become less redistributive over time. In 1977, the cash benefits received by the poorest 10 per cent of households were the equivalent of 60 per cent of their final income. The cash benefits received by the richest

10 per cent of households amounted to just over 3 per cent of their final income: a 57 per cent gap. By 1990, this gap had risen to 63 per cent. By the year 2000, it had fallen to 54 per cent and by 2007, on the eve of the financial crisis, it had fallen to 43 per cent. The gap then rose again to 49.5 per cent in 2010 before falling to 44.6 per cent in 2015/16. The welfare state is not about to disappear. Indeed, the welfare state has, over a thirty-or-more-year period, proven stubbornly resistant to retrenchment.[57] It would, however, appear that it is becoming a less effective engine of redistribution.[58]

XII

Market income inequality has fallen and final income inequality has stabilized. Housing, however, has lurched from crisis to disaster.

I previously showed how the poorest households spent nearly as much on housing in absolute terms as the richest households (Figure 6.5) and much more on housing as a proportion of their final income (Figure 6.6). The key point to note here is that this is a relatively recent phenomenon. Figure 6.14 shows the share of their final income the poorest 5 per cent, the poorest 5–10 per cent, the median household, and the richest 5 per cent spent on housing between 1961 and 2015/16. If the lines here were taken from an ECG machine, somebody would have pressed an emergency button about thirty years ago. From around 1961 through to 1981, the richest and poorest households spent a roughly similar share of their final income on housing. Things then go haywire. The lines for the median household and the richest 5 per cent of households at the bottom of the chart start to fall. Those for the poorest households start to climb. By 1994, the poorest 5 per cent of households spent 40 per cent of their final income and the poorest 5–10 per cent of households 27 per cent of their income on housing. From the mid-1990s through to the early 2000s, things get a little better. This is, however, the calm before the storm. The lines for the poorest households start to climb again as the economy booms in the early 2000s and they don't stop climbing even when the economy crashes in 2009. By 2015/16, the richest 5 per cent of households spent just 9 per cent of their income on housing; the median household 15 per cent (pretty much what it was spending in the 1960s and 1970s); the poorest 5–10 per cent of households 31 per cent; and the poorest 5 per cent of households spent 44 per cent of their final income

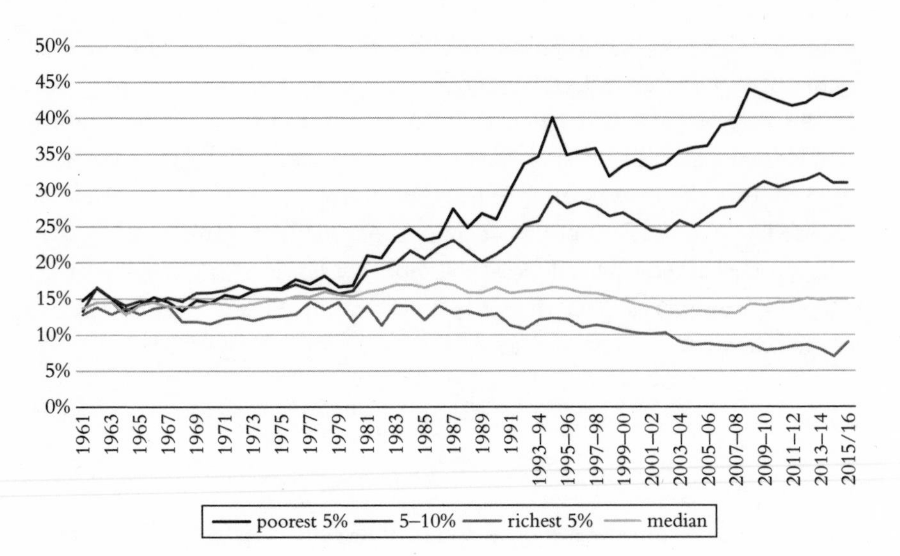

Figure 6.14. Spending on housing as a percentage of final income, 1961–2015/16.[13]

on housing. There are a lot of figures in this chapter. This is, however, one which I think tells an important story about something that has gone horribly wrong in the UK. Housing is a mess.

Housing costs have been a key driver of growing inequality.

The easiest way to show how and why is, I am afraid, with yet another chart. Figure 6.15 shows the ratio of the income of the richest 5 per cent of households compared with the income of the poorest 5 per cent of households *before* housing costs and *after* housing costs since 1961. This is, once again, a pretty simple diagram with a pretty stark message. In the 1960s and 1970s, there is almost no difference between the before and after housing cost ratios. Either way, the income of the richest 5 per cent of households was around four or five times greater than that of the poorest 5 per cent of households. In the 1980s, the ratios start to simultaneously increase and diverge. By 1990, the income of the richest 5 per cent of households was 6.6 times greater than that of the poorest 5 per cent of households *before* housing costs and 7.7 times greater *after* housing costs. From the mid-1990s onwards, the *before* housing cost ratio then stabilizes at around 6.5. The line wobbles back and forth in the 2000s but does not really move by that much, ending up at 6.3 in 2015/16. The *after* housing cost ratio, however, continues to grow. By 2009, the household income of the richest 5 per cent of households is 11.5 times greater than that of the poorest 5 per cent of households

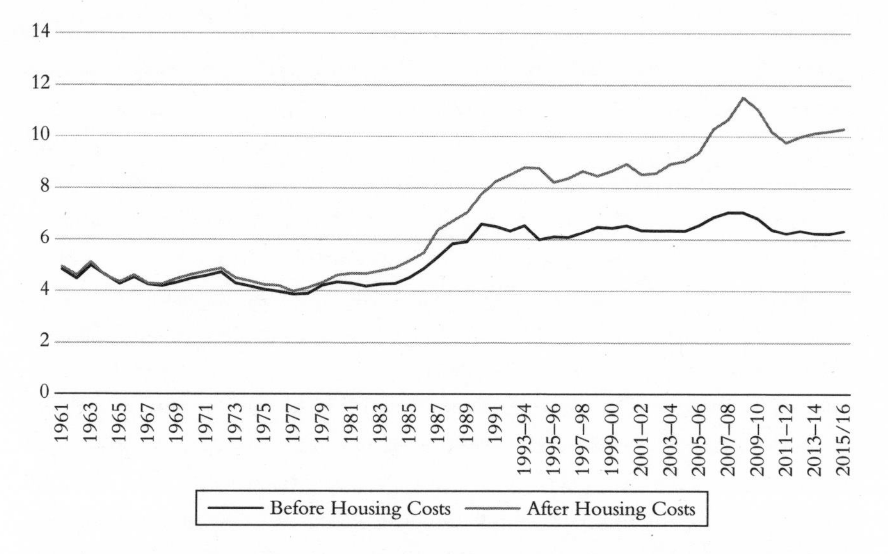

Figure 6.15. Final income of the richest 5% of households as a ratio of the final income of the poorest 5%—before and after housing costs, 1961–2015/16.[14]

after housing costs. When the recession hits, this ratio falls, but by 2015/16, the *after* housing cost income of the richest 5 per cent of households is still ten times greater than that of the poorest 5 per cent of households.

Judged in terms of the ratio of the difference between the incomes of the very richest and the very poorest households, Britain started to become a much more unequal country in the 1980s. Since the early 1990s, *before* housing cost income inequality has stabilized, whilst *after* housing cost inequality has continued to grow. Indeed, we have now got to the point where fully 40 per cent of after housing cost final income inequality in the UK is due to the cost of housing.

What has gone wrong here? The short answer is that not enough houses have been built and this has pushed up the cost of housing and, in particular, rented housing, and this has, in turn, had a disproportionate impact on the incomes of the poorest households because they are far more likely to rent.

Let's run through the stages of this argument in more detail. First, demand for housing has risen as the UK's total population has grown from 52 million people in the early 1960s to 65 million today, at the same time as the average number of people living in each household has fallen from 3 to 2.3. Second, the supply of new houses has fallen. Figure 6.16 shows the number of new private sector, housing association, and local authority houses completed each year in the UK between 1949 and 2015. The total number of new houses being built fell from a peak of 425,000 houses in 1968 to 242,000 houses in 1980 and just 170,000 houses in 2015. The number of new private-sector houses being built fell from 226,000 in 1968 to 198,000 in 2007 before falling off a cliff during the recession and slumping to 114,000 in 2014 before climbing slightly to 133,000 in 2015.[59] The number of new housing association completions increased from around 13,000 in the late 1980s to 34,000 in 2015. This is a welcome development, but the number of local authority home completions has fallen from 196,000 in 1968 (at which point they constituted 46 per cent of all new homes being built) to just 2,730 in 2015 (1.6 per cent of the total).

As the demand for housing has gone up and the supply of new houses has fallen, the price of housing has risen. That is not likely to come as a great surprise to anyone. But in terms of understanding the relationship between housing and inequality, the real issue here relates to the costs of *different* kinds of housing. Between 1969 and 2012/13, the average cost of owning a home with a mortgage rose fourfold from £20 a week in 1969 to £80 a week in 2013 (having peaked at £122 in 2008). It has doubled since 1980. The average cost of social housing has also risen fourfold from £21 in 1969 to £83 in 2013 and has also doubled since 1980. But the average cost of renting a house has risen nearly sevenfold since 1969, from £22 to £150 a week, and has risen 3.5-fold since 1980.[60] In 2015 alone, average rents in

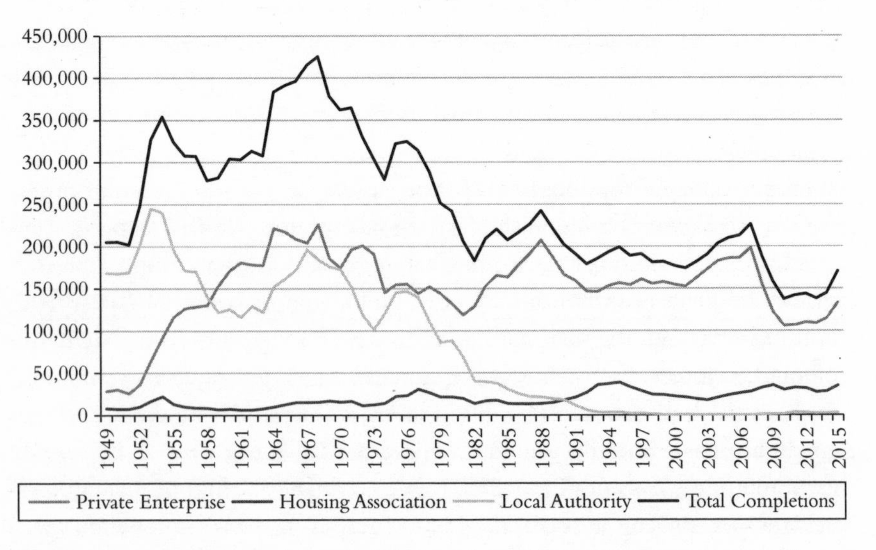

Figure 6.16. Completed house builds (number of houses), UK, 1949–2015.[15]

England and Wales rose by 3.4 per cent.[61] Why is there such a difference? Over the last few decades, the sale of council homes, combined with a dramatic fall in the construction of new local authority houses, has pushed people into the privately rented sector. To be more precise, the numbers living in social housing in England and Wales have fallen from 31 per cent in 1981 to just 17.5 per cent in 2014/15, whilst the numbers renting privately have increased from 11 per cent to 19 per cent over the same period.[62] As more people have been pushed into the private sector, the cost of renting has gone up. At the same time, the cost of owning a home has fallen dramatically as interest rates have fallen.[63]

If most of the people renting were wealthy young 20-somethings living in major cities who work in marketing, own expensive coffee machines, and expect one day to buy a small place in the country, we could probably all sleep comfortably at night. But most of the people who rent are renting because their incomes are too low or too unstable to buy. In 2014/15, 84 per cent of households with a gross annual income of more than £50,000 owned their own home or were paying a mortgage. 15 per cent were renting privately and 1 per cent were renting socially. Of those households earning between £20,000 and £30,000 a year, 58 per cent owned their own home or were paying a mortgage, 18 per cent were renting privately, and 24 per cent were renting socially. Of those households earning between £5,000 and £10,000, 35 per cent owned, 42 per cent rented privately, and 23 per cent rented socially.[64] Furthermore, renting seems to be both a cause and effect of poverty. The Institute for Fiscal Studies reports that private renters with incomes *above* the poverty line are as likely to be materially deprived as owner-occupiers with incomes *below* the poverty line and that private renters in income poverty are more than twice as likely to be materially deprived as owner-occupiers in income poverty.[65]

Can we blame neoliberalism for this policy disaster? The answer to this question must be, in part, yes. The sale of council houses and the failure to invest the proceeds of those sales in new social housing has fuelled the housing crisis. But the state has not simply abandoned housing to the whim of market forces. Successive governments have in fact intervened massively in the housing market to subsidize the cost of private rentals. Overall expenditure on housing benefit has increased from £2.1bn a year in the early 1980s to £23.5bn in 2016/17.[66] This is a huge sum of money and more evidence of irritable intervention syndrome. In the 1980s, the state rolled back on the provision of social housing. The predictable result was a housing crisis. To try to compensate for that failure, government has rolled forward the payment of housing benefit. This has not proven entirely effective. In the short term, housing benefit makes housing more affordable for more people. In the long term, however, it simply contributes to increases in the cost of renting. Landlords know that they can charge more because the state is meeting a part of the cost of renting. The problem with housing in Britain is not so much that government has stopped spending but that successive governments spend large amounts of money on the wrong things. Only 5 per cent of government spending on housing now goes on investments in new buildings.[67]

When it comes to the blame to be attributed to neoliberalism, it is also worth noting that, despite plenty of talk about a 'bonfire of planning regulations', the British housing market is still heavily regulated.[68] Crucially, the British planning system requires developers to lodge individual applications to build on particular sites, which can be opposed by local residents or vetoed by local authorities, rather than—as in Germany, the Netherlands, and the US—zoning particular areas as being suitable for development.[69] Green belt regulations also remain a significant block upon housing development. Critics argue that the green belt is being steadily sacrificed to urban sprawl. I am not so sure. The total amount of green belt land in England fell by less than 1 per cent between 1997 and 2014.[70] Should we seek to preserve the green belt at all costs? I think it probably depends on what green belt land consists of and how much public access there is to it. As things stand, the green belt is not, by and large, a near-urban substitute for national parks. Most green belt land has limited or zero public access and is used for farming. As Paul Cheshire of the London School of Economics suggests, 'green belts really seem to be a very British form of discriminatory zoning' which provides 'a public subsidy for golf and horse-riding and generally already-wealthy homeowners who live on the edges of cities and have seen the value of their homes rocket'.[71] Is the green belt all that stands between civilization and endless urban sprawl? We tend to think that the UK is already a very small and crowded island. During the EU referendum campaign, Nigel Farage kept making this point. Yet, in fact, only 7 per cent of the land in Britain is urban and around two-thirds of this consists of green space—parks, allotments, sports pitches, and private gardens. Perhaps only 2.5 per cent of land in the UK is built on.[72] If you want to do something about inequality, a good place to start would be with building more new homes.

XIII

One of the best things about the 1980s (other than receiving a student grant) was Channel 4 and one of the best things about Channel 4 was *Saturday Live* (which, at the time, I had no idea was a slightly pale imitation of *Saturday Night Live* in the United States). *Saturday Live* helped launch the careers of Stephen Fry and Hugh Laurie, Craig Charles, Tracey Ullman, Ben Elton (who could be usually relied upon to provide a non-ironic twenty-minute rant about Thatcher), and Harry Enfield. Harry Enfield's star turns were sketches featuring a slightly hapless Greek kebab shop owner, Stavros (I'm not sure this one passes the test of time particularly well), and the cashed-up, loudmouth, brash, Thatcherite, offensive, Loadsamoney (from, of course, Essex). 'You!! Shut your mouth and look at my wad!' Loadsamoney became an anti-hero of the Thatcherite economic boom and a living symbol of the North–South divide. At Sheffield United home games in the late 1980s, opposition fans from London could predictably be relied upon to wave notes and shout 'Look at my wad!'[73] The North, so it seemed, was poor and getting poorer and the South, and London in particular, was rich and getting richer.

What has happened since then? George Osborne argues that, under New Labour, the economy became further unbalanced, with too much economic activity in banking and finance and not enough in manufacturing and, relatedly, too much wealth and employment in the South and not enough in the North. Robust data on regional variations in gross earnings only goes back as far as 1997 (which does not allow us to see how far the North–South divide opened up in the 1980s) and ends in 2014.[74] On the whole, what this data shows, however, is that—with one massively notable exception—regional inequalities have *not* grown. Across the UK, full-time employees' real (inflation-adjusted) pay rose 1.61-fold between 1997 and 2013. In eleven of the thirteen UK regions listed in Figure 6.7, pay increased by between 1.55-fold and 1.60-fold. In London, it increased 1.64-fold. In Scotland, it increased 1.68-fold. Scotland has gone from having an average wage that is 95 per cent of the UK average to one that is equal to the UK average.[75] Furthermore, and since 2009, hourly, weekly, and annual pay in areas of the UK other than London and the South-East corner has grown faster than pay in London and the South-East. Inequality has also grown more rapidly in London. Since

2009, someone living in London who has amongst the lowest 10 per cent of incomes of people living in London has seen their real pay fall by over 20 per cent.[76]

XIV

I think one of the things the left conveniently forgets when it comes to the post-war consensus is just how frequently and casually sexist and racist it was and how infrequently politicians challenged lines of social inclusion and exclusion. We previously saw that, in general, people have become much more tolerant when it comes to gender and race differences. The question here is whether this has been reflected in substantive changes in behaviour and society.

Let's start again with gender. Since 1997, the gender pay gap has fallen from 27 per cent to 18 per cent.[77] The employment gap between men and women has fallen from 31 per cent in 1971 to 10 per cent today. Over this time, male employment rates have fallen from 92 per cent to 78 per cent, whilst female employment has increased from 52 per cent to 68 per cent.[78] The number of female MPs has increased from a risible 4 per cent in 1970 and 3 per cent in 1979 to a third in 2017. As recently as 2008, less than 12 per cent of the directors of the largest FTSE100 companies were women. By 2015, that number had risen to 26 per cent.[79] There is some evidence that there has been some very limited change in the division of domestic labour. A research paper by the Institute for Public Policy Research found that while 85 per cent of women born in 1958 said that they do more laundry and ironing than their partner, only 75 per cent of those born in 1970 said the same.[80] That said, a 2013 *YouGov* poll reported that 61 per cent of women say that they do most of the cleaning and tidying in their household and 57 per cent say that they do most of the cooking. Only 5 per cent say that their male partner does most of the cleaning.[81] A 2010 report by the Scottish Government found that 63 per cent of women but only 37 per cent of men provided care to someone not living with them.[82]

The available data we have on racial discrimination is very patchy. On the most recent available figures, only 17 per cent of households in which the head of the household was White had an income which was amongst the lowest 25 per cent of incomes nationally. The equivalent figure for Asian/Asian British households was 32 per cent and for those classified as Black/African/

Caribbean/Black British it was 28 per cent.[83] In 2000, we know that 17 per cent of White households, 25 per cent of Black Caribbean, 34 per cent of Black non-Caribbean, 31 per cent of Indian, and 64 per cent of Pakistani/Bangladeshi households had an income that was amongst the lowest 20 per cent of incomes nationally.[84] Although the classification categories employed here vary somewhat, these numbers suggest that the racial dimension to poverty is not disappearing. In a book examining the impact of the post-2008 recession, *Hard Times*, Tom Clark also reports on some depressing figures in relation to rates of unemployment. At the height of the early 1980s recession, the gap between the rate of White unemployment and Black unemployment was 13 per cent. Over the next decade, this gap then *increased* to 19 per cent. During the economic boom of the 2000s, it then fell to 4 per cent. Does this show that the economy was becoming increasingly colour-blind? Unfortunately, it does not. When the economy stalled, the gap increased again to 10 per cent in 2010 (at which point White unemployment was 10 per cent and Black unemployment was 17 per cent).[85]

XV

I previously showed that wealth is quite massively unequally distributed. How has this changed over time? The Office for National Statistics has only collected data on the distribution of different kinds of wealth since 2006. Even over this short time, it finds that the distribution of wealth has become slightly more unequal (with the Gini coefficient for the distribution of total wealth rising from 0.61 to 0.63).[86] The Chief Economist of the Bank of England, Andy Haldane, also argues that wealth inequalities are becoming more pronounced. Between 2010 and 2016, those with the lowest 40 per cent of incomes have seen virtually no gains in their wealth. Those in the bottom 20 per cent have seen their wealth fall. By contrast, those in the top 20 per cent have seen their wealth increase by around 20 per cent.[87] In his best-selling book *Capital in the 21st Century*, Thomas Piketty has compiled data on the distribution of wealth going back to the first part of the previous century.[88] He estimates that in 1910 the wealthiest 10 per cent of people in the UK held around 90 per cent of total wealth. By 1960, that share had fallen to around 70 per cent and by 1980, it had fallen to 62 per cent. Since that time, the share of the wealthiest 10 per cent has risen to 65 per cent in 1990, 66 per cent in 2000, and to 70 per cent by 2010. The share of wealth held by the wealthiest 1 per cent rose from 22 per cent in 1970 to 28 per cent in 2010. Overall levels of wealth inequality are lower than they were in the first part of the twentieth century. This is largely because the middle classes have acquired significant property and pension wealth. Yet inequalities in the distribution of wealth have increased significantly since the early 1980s. Furthermore, and as Piketty argues, because the rate of return on capital tends to be higher than the rate of economic growth in capitalist economies, wealth inequalities simply increase over time if left unchecked. When it comes to wealth inequality, the miserabilist is right and getting righter.

XVI

Finally, we come back to social mobility. In the 1940s, George Orwell described England as the 'most class-ridden country under the sun': a land of 'snobbery and privilege, ruled largely by the old and silly'.[89] We know that the UK today is, by pretty much any standards, a socially immobile society. The key question here is whether it has become less mobile in recent decades.

We know that many more people have become middle class. In the 1970s, around 35 per cent of households were classified as belonging to the ABC1 social class (higher managerial, administrative, and professional). For the first time in the year 2000, ABC1s accounted for the majority of households. By 2015, ABC1s constituted 54 per cent of households.[90] But what else do we know about social mobility? The data here is imperfect and its interpretation is subject to dispute (the 'it's complicated' warning klaxon is sounding in the background at this moment). A key study here—which has been widely cited by the Social Mobility and Child Poverty Commission as evidence of declining social mobility—comes from a study by a group of economists at the London School of Economics.[91] Using detailed individual-level data, they traced the fortunes of two cohorts of children: one born in the same week in 1958 who became adults during the mid-1970s and another born in the same week in 1970 who became adults in the late 1980s after a decade of Thatcherism. The economists found that for those born in 1958, family income at the age of 16 explained around 30 per cent of that group's subsequent variance in income. For those born in 1970, on the other hand, family income explained nearly 40 per cent of the variance in subsequent income. In other words, social mobility decreased over this twelve-year period.

These results have, however, been challenged by the Oxford sociologist John Goldthorpe.[92] He argues that the LSE finding is misleading because it looks at income rather than social class and confuses changes in the relative rates of social mobility with structural changes in the economy. Looking at social mobility in terms of social class rather than income, he argues that social mobility was low for those born in 1958 and *equally* low for those born in 1970. His key finding is that 34 per cent of people born in 1958 *and* 34 per cent of people born in 1970 whose parents had a routine non-manual or lower and non-skilled manual job themselves went on to have a routine non-manual or lower and non-skilled manual job. On this reading, there was no great rupture in social mobility in 1979 with the advent of Thatcherism. Social mobility was extremely low in the UK before and it is extremely low today.

I was born in 1969: part of Generation X, which the LSE study shows fared far worse than those born during the tail end of the baby boomer generation years but which Goldthorpe argues did no worse than its predecessors. For anyone aged under 40, however, this is all likely to seem rather dated. In *The Pinch*, the former Minister of State for Universities and Science, David Willetts, argues that the real gap in social mobility has opened up far more recently than this. Through a mixture of good luck and sharp political elbows, the baby boomer generation hit a generational jackpot in the 1960s and 1970s: benefiting from free university tuition, full employment, rising real wages, a sustained increase in the number of middle-class jobs, mortgage subsidies, cheap housing prices, and generous final salary pension schemes.[93] This generation did, it is true, grow up in an era in which serving orange juice and melon balls as a starter was the height of sophistication. But, in other respects, no other generation has had it so good.

The real losers in the generational battle, Willetts argues, are not those born in the 1970s who got to watch *Saturday Live* and go on protest marches against the Poll Tax but members of Generation Y born between 1980 and the mid-1990s. They became adults at a time when defined benefit pension schemes were closing; house prices for first-time buyers were rising; the recession had reduced job opportunities; and university tuition fees had created a new source of debt. In the 1970s, the average worker aged between 25 and 29 earned more than the average worker aged between 60 and 64. This is no longer the case. An average worker in their 60s (who would have been in their 20s in the 1970s) now earns 14 per cent more than the average 25–29 year old.[94] Nominal earnings of those under 30 have risen by a cumulative 6 per cent since 2007, while those over 50 have seen cumulative gains of 22 per cent.[95] In 2013, the average weekly income before housing costs of those aged between 22 and 30 was 13 per cent lower than it had been for those aged between 22 and 30 in 2008.[96] The Council of Mortgage Lenders estimates that 71 per cent of people born in 1970 were home owners by the time they were 40, but that among those born in 1990 the figure is likely to be just 47 per cent.[97] In 1998, more than half of people aged 16–34 living in households with incomes between 10 per cent and 50 per cent of the national average bought their own homes. This had dropped to just 25 per cent by 2014 and is forecast to fall to 10 per cent by 2025.[98] In 1977, one in four 25-year-olds were renters. By 2014, that fraction had risen to two-thirds.[99] A quarter of people aged between 20 and 34 now live with their parents.[100]

The policy debate on pensioner income has started to move. In their 2017 manifesto, the Conservatives promised to retain the 'triple lock' on pensions (increasing it in line with the rate of inflation, the rate of earnings, or 2.5 per cent a year) until 2020 but to then replace it with a new double lock (meaning that pensions will rise in line with the earnings that pay for them, or in line with inflation—whichever is highest). They also pledged to means-test the winter fuel allowance and to set a capital floor of £100,000 for the payment of social care (the dementia tax). The Labour Party pledged to retain the triple lock for the duration of the Parliament and to retain the winter fuel allowance and free bus passes.[101] This came in a situation in which the average weekly income of pensioners was *higher* than that of working-age people; in which the number of pensioner households living on less than 60 per cent of the median income had fallen from 29 per cent in 1998/9 to 14 per cent in 2014/15; and in which the number of pensioner households living in absolute poverty (defined here as less than 60 per cent of the *2011* median income) had fallen from 39 per cent to 13 per cent over the same period. In its 2016 report on *Living Standards, Poverty and Inequality in the UK*, the Institute for Fiscal Studies reports that, before housing costs, the median income of individuals aged 60 or above is 11 per cent higher now (in real terms) than it was in 2007/8. By contrast, the median income of those aged 31–59 is largely unchanged. The median income of those aged 22–30 is still 7 per cent below its 2007/8 level.[102]

XVII

At the end of the first part of this chapter, I ranked the extent of different kinds of equality on a scale running from social democratic paradise to neoliberal dystopia. I want to conclude by summarizing whether the different kinds of inequality I have been examining have grown, stabilized, or fallen.

Wealth inequality is growing. Although the evidence on changes in social mobility is mixed, there is reason to think that the millennial generation, who we have seen wrongly labelled as 'Generation Right', is losing ground relative to the baby boomers and Generation X. On the other hand, the evidence I have presented here suggests that, after growing dramatically in the 1980s, final income inequality has stabilized since the mid-1990s (although the same is not true of final income after housing costs). Inequalities in the geographic distribution of income also appear relatively stable, as do inequalities in the distribution of income between ethnic groups. Finally, market income inequality has fallen significantly since the early 1990s and shows no sign yet of increasing again, whilst gender income inequalities have also narrowed.

I have no doubt that inequality poses significant policy challenges. There is robust evidence that inequality retards economic growth.[103] There is robust evidence that countries in which there are high levels of inequality also tend to have higher rates of crime, depression, and obesity.[104] There is very little (if any) evidence that high levels of pay—particularly the pay of the richest 1 per cent of employees—boosts economic growth or that it accurately reflects the actual difference these employees make to the profitability of the firms they work for.[105]

What I am not so sure about is whether the miserabilists are right about inequality. When it comes to the two issues I have looked at previously, the state of public opinion and the role of the state, I think their case is manifestly and massively wrong. When it comes to the two issues I am going to look at next, changes in absolute income levels and the state of British democracy, I also think that the argument leaves a lot to be desired. When it comes to inequality, I think that the miserabilist case has more going for it (figure 6.17). Inequality did rise significantly in the 1980s. Wealth inequality is growing. Social mobility is poor. I do nevertheless think that the argument about inequality is too simple (if you have survived through the numbers and graphs I hope you can agree that, if nothing else, equality is indeed complicated). The miserabilist story fails to recognize that Britain is still a

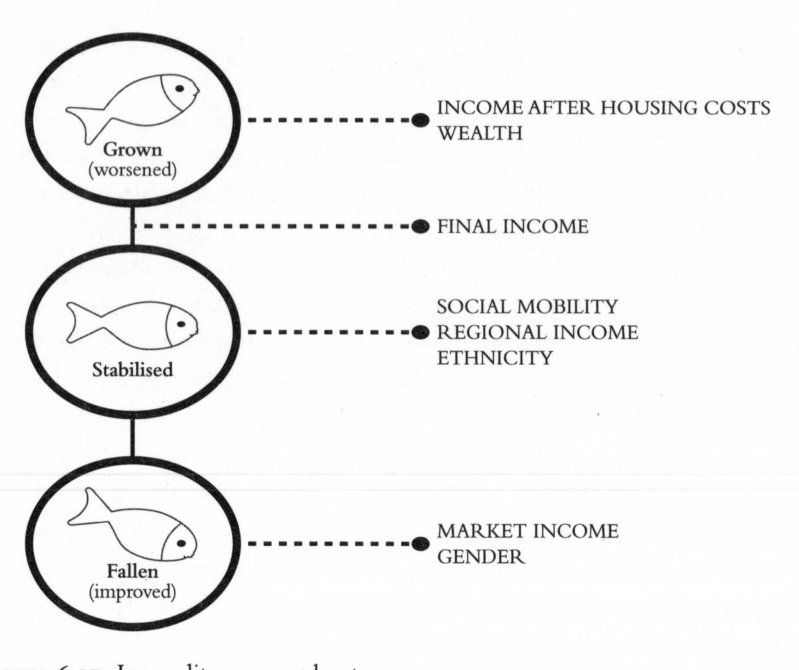

Figure 6.17. Inequality: a second cut.

highly redistributive society in which there is a significant difference in the inequalities between market income and final income. It fails to recognize the degree to which New Labour's record in office was, in many respects, very impressive. In the 2000s, market income inequality fell and final income inequality stabilized. Inequality is not a juggernaut which is running out of political control. New Labour showed that it is possible for a government to address and reduce inequalities.

Here, and finally, we come to perhaps the most significant change when it comes to inequality: its relative political salience. Although market income inequality fell during the 2000s and final income inequality stabilized, New Labour generally preferred to talk about social inclusion and equality of opportunity rather than equality of outcome. In recent years, inequality has, however, become mainstream news. In 2013, President Obama described inequality as the 'defining challenge of our age'.[106] In 2014, the Governor of the Bank of England, Mark Carney, argued the case for an inclusive form of capitalism 'comprised of relative equality of outcome'.[107] In the same year, the Managing Director of the IMF, Christine Lagarde, warned of the economic and social costs of inequality.[108] In the immediate aftermath of the 2015 general election, Tony Blair argued that Ed Miliband had been absolutely right to focus upon inequality during his election campaign and that, in so far as this focus was an implied rebuke to New Labour, it was one he accepted.[109] A few months later, John Major argued that more must be done to address 'shocking' levels of inequality in Britain.[110] In their 2017 manifesto, the Conservative Party stated that the party 'abhors social division, injustice, unfairness and inequality'.[111] The left has not lost the argument about inequality. Indeed, it has gone some way towards neutering arguments about the virtuous benefits of inequality and to pushing inequality further up the political agenda. The left's concern about inequality has not been left behind.

7

Keep calm

On growth, austerity, and happiness

I

On 27 June 2007, Gordon Brown delivered his final Mansion House speech as Chancellor of the Exchequer to an assembled audience from the City of London.[1] Just a few days later, Brown was scheduled to change jobs and become Prime Minister. Mansion House was his valediction speech. It was probably not a difficult one to write. Tony Blair was on the point of being banished after a decade-long feud and the economy was looking good. Unemployment was just over 5 per cent and stable. Inflation was a little over 2 per cent and falling. There had been sixty consecutive quarters of economic growth. The banks were booming.

There had been those who, for the best part of a decade, had been saying that it would all end in tears. Critics on the left argued that the age of affluence was an illusion: that the economy was being propped up by unsustainable and excessive consumption and debt and that the banks were overextended and underinvested in the UK economy. Others argued that the endless pursuit of ever higher growth was itself an economic dead end. More growth simply meant more environmental damage and a poorer quality of life. For a short while in the 2000s, the idea that the developed economies were suffering from an epidemic of affluenza took hold. People, it was argued, were becoming richer but they were also becoming more anxious and less happy.[2] Critics on the right, for their part, also argued that the appearance of prosperity was misleading. The economy in general and the banks in particular were over-regulated. The government was running a budget deficit to sustain public expenditure and this was sure to end badly. In December 2006, the Social Justice Policy Group, which had been commissioned by David Cameron to provide the Conservative Party with social policy recommendations, published an influential report called *Breakdown Britain*.[3] Family breakdown, educational failure, worklessness and economic dependence, addictions, and indebtedness were, it argued, trapping families and communities into cycles of generational poverty which New Labour had failed to deal with. 'Broken Britain' subsequently became a key theme of the Conservatives' 2010 campaign.

With critics to the left of him and critics to the right, Brown, to paraphrase Tennyson's 'Charge of the Light Brigade', rode headlong into the jaws of the financial crisis. In September 2007, the Northern Rock building society failed and had to be rescued by the Bank of England. House prices began to fall and consumer confidence stumbled. In March 2008, the investment bank Bear Stearns ran out of money and had to be rescued by the Federal Reserve.[4] In September of that year, Lehman Brothers failed and the entire global financial system melted.

We now know how the rest of this story goes, with a straight line running from the financial crisis through to the credit crunch, recession, and endless spending cuts. Within the blink of an eye, Britain went from boom to bust and austerity became the new normal. Austerity—the intentional policy of cutting spending and living standards to reduce public debt—has been an economic and social calamity. It has wiped out whatever limited economic gains were made in the 2000s. It has normalized poverty and encouraged social division. A lifetime after the creation of the welfare state, Britain has become a country in which hundreds of thousands of people are left to depend upon charitable foodbanks.[5] The Joseph Rowntree Foundation estimates that poverty costs the UK £78bn a year.[6]

The Conservatives entered office in 2010 assuring anyone who would listen that 'we're all in this together'.[7] The reality has been quite different. The costs of austerity have been loaded on to the poorest and most vulnerable. Meanwhile, the Coalition's promise that we could have the jam of economic growth tomorrow if only we swallowed the bitter medicine of austerity today has been shown to be equally false. The economy has not recovered. Growth remains anaemic. The TUC estimates that, between 2007 and 2015, real wages in the UK fell by more than 10 per cent: the joint lowest in the OECD.[8] The British growth model—built on high debt, high consumption, and rocketing house prices—is broken.[9] In his 2016 Labour Party conference speech, John McDonnell spoke of how 'the Conservative Party built upon the disaster of the 2008 financial crisis by introducing an austerity programme that has made the impact of the economic crisis more prolonged, protected the corporations and the rich, and made the rest of society pay for the mistakes and greed of the speculators that caused the crash', and of how, whilst his generation 'always thought that from here on there would always be a steady improvement in people's living standards', 'successive Tory governments put an end to that'.[10]

It may even be that capitalism itself has entered a new era of never-ending crisis. On the opening pages of *Postcapitalism: A Guide to our Future*, the journalist and commentator Paul Mason says: 'here's a summary of what I've learned since the day Lehman died: the next generation will be poorer than this one; the old economic model is broken and cannot revive growth without reviving financial fragility'.[11] The former Treasury Secretary Larry Summers and Robert Gordon have popularized the notion that the developed economies may be entering an age of 'secular stagnation'.[12]

There is no doubt that the recession which began in 2008 was a severe one. There is no doubt that the recovery which began to finally gather steam in 2012 has been a slow one. There is no doubt that austerity has resulted in genuine hardship. Huge policy mistakes were made before, during, and after the financial crisis. By the early 2000s, Gordon Brown's commitment to 'light-touch' regulation for the banks had degenerated, in the words of his Chancellor, Alistair Darling, into an 'anything goes' philosophy which encouraged a 'culture of lackadaisical supervision [and a] climate where too often regulators and boardrooms alike were happy to look the other way'.[13] Too little was done during the good times to boost manufacturing, raise productivity, and invest in active labour market policies to manage the costs of economic globalization. By 2007, Gordon Brown had abandoned his own self-imposed 'golden rule' that, over the course of an economic cycle, the government would only borrow to invest. The budget deficit the government was running in 2007 did not cause the crisis but it did not help matters once the crisis had started. The Coalition did not always deliver upon the spending cuts it threatened. Those cuts it has made have, however, had the effect—as the chairman of the Office for Budget Responsibility publicly told David Cameron—of undermining growth.

Yet despite all of this, I still want to argue that even when things have been bad, they have not been that bad. During the 2000s, there were substantive increases in real income in both rich, poor, and middle-income households. The economic gains of the 2000s have not been wiped out. The costs of the recession have primarily been experienced in terms of forgone gains rather than absolute losses. The costs of austerity have not been loaded on to the poorest and most vulnerable. Indeed, the available evidence suggests that quite the opposite is true. British society is not broken. Economic growth has not resulted in an epidemic of affluenza. The economy has neither thrived nor dived. Instead, we have in a very British and not always particularly impressive way sort of muddled through. Brexit may change everything: pushing up the prices of imports, cutting inward investment, and undermining long-term growth. For now, at least, the economic news is not all bad.

II

Let's start the ball rolling by looking back to the early 1990s, when John Major was Prime Minister, Britain had just been unceremoniously dumped out of the Exchange Rate Mechanism, and the economy was struggling to recover from recession. For all his subsequent travails, John Major was, in some ways, quite lucky. Britain's forced ejection from the ERM resulted in a significant currency devaluation which boosted exports. Moreover, by the early 1990s, the world economy was entering a new 'platinum age' characterized by high growth rates and rising incomes.[14] In 1990, 43 per cent of the population of developing countries lived in extreme poverty on $1 a day or less. By 2000, the proportion was down to a third. By 2010, it was 21 per cent.[15] In the UK, the economy pulled out of recession in the early 1990s and then boomed. Between the first quarter of 1994 and the fourth quarter of 2007, the economy grew by an average of 2.9 per cent a year (about 0.5 per cent higher than the post-war average).[16] Over the same period, median weekly household income before housing costs (adjusted for inflation and at 2014/15 prices) rose by 36 per cent (from £342 to £464).[17]

In comparative terms, Britain performed quite well during this period. In 1994, UK gross domestic product per head was $27,668 (in constant prices at 2010 purchasing power parity). This was the equivalent of 93 per cent of French GDP per head, 89 per cent of Italy's, 83 per cent of Germany's, and 73 per cent of that of the United States. By 2007, UK GDP per head was $37,929. This was the equivalent of 103 per cent of French GDP, 103 per cent of Italy's, 94 per cent of Germany's, and 76 per cent of that of the United States.[18] These are quite impressive numbers.[19]

To what extent were these gains distributed equally across different income groups? Were the rich simply getting richer at the same time as the poor were left hanging on? Drawing on data from the Institute for Fiscal Studies, Figure 7.1 shows the average weekly final income before housing costs of each ventile of the population in 2007/8 as a percentage of that ventile's income in 1994/5 in real (inflation-adjusted) terms at 2014/15 prices. What we would expect to see here, if the miserabilists were right, is the income gains over this period to be concentrated on the right-hand side of the chart to the benefit of the richest households. What we see is a much more complex wave-like pattern. With one notable exception, which I'll come to in a moment, income gains were quite evenly distributed. In so far as there were clear winners, they were the households toward the bottom and at the very top of the income scale. By 2007/8, the weekly income of the richest 5 per cent of households was 140 per cent of their 1994/5 level. The incomes of the households with the lowest 30–40 per cent of incomes were just under 140 per cent of their 1994/5 level. The percentage of the population living on less than 60 per cent of the 2010/11 median income fell from 37 per cent to 18 per cent over the same period. The one clear exception to this good news story is the poorest 5 per cent of households. By 2007/8, their income was only 119 per cent of the level it had been in 1994/5. We previously saw how the tax and welfare systems struggle to redistribute money effectively to the very poorest households (p. 130). Here, we see one consequence of that failure.

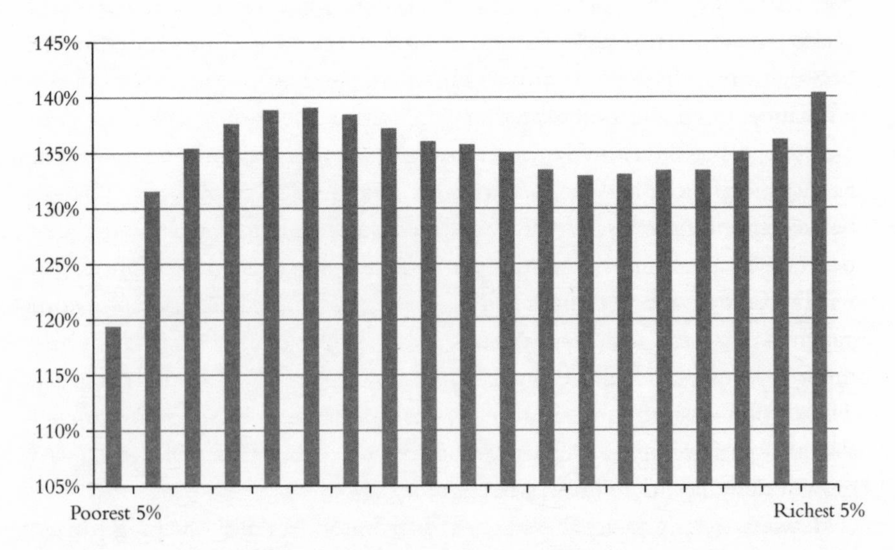

Figure 7.1. 2007/8 weekly median income as a percentage of 1994/5 income.[1]

The figures that we have looked at so far relate to final income. But what about market income? Did that stagnate at the lower end of the income spectrum during the long economic boom, with the difference being topped up through increased welfare payments? No. Using Office for National Statistics data (which distinguishes between market and final income), we can see that whilst the market income of the richest 10 per cent increased by 83 per cent between 1994/5 and 2007/8, that of the poorest 10 per cent of households increased by 125 per cent, and that of the poorest 10–20 per cent, by 154 per cent.[20] The miserabilist is wrong to argue that income gains were unevenly and unfairly distributed in the 2000s. They are, however, right to argue that those at the very bottom of the income scale lost out in relative terms.

III

The fact that income gains during the economic boom of the 2000s were reasonably well distributed is consistent with the evidence showing how market income inequalities fell significantly in the 2000s and final income inequalities stabilized. Most of the people that I have spoken to about this finding are more than a little surprised. Everyone is used to thinking of the last few decades as being a period of accelerating inequality. I think this is in part testimony to the power of the miserabilist narrative on the left. But it is also because it is in the nature of inequality that the *absolute* income gap between the richest and poorest households can continue to grow even in a situation in which their incomes are growing at the same rate.

Imagine a situation in which there are just two households. The first has an income of £100 and the second has an income of £200. The absolute gap between their incomes is £100. Assume that their incomes grow at the identical rate of 2 per cent a year. After twenty years, the first household's income will be £148 and the second household's income £297. The absolute income gap between them will have grown to £149. After fifty years, the income of the first household will be £269 and that of the second household £538. The absolute income gap will have grown to £269. The basic point here is that the passage of time is a key accelerant of inequality. Compounded growth rates have the effect of magnifying initial income differences.

Between 1994 and 2007, the weekly income of most households grew at a pretty similar rate. Figure 7.1 tells us that the poorest 5 per cent of households did relatively badly but that, by and large, the income of most households grew at a similar rate. The absolute gap between the poorest and richest households nevertheless grew dramatically over this period. By 2007/8, the gap between the weekly income of the richest and poorest 5 per cent of households in 2014/15 prices had grown from £727 to £1,051.

The Institute for Fiscal Studies' data set on household income goes back to the early 1960s. How has absolute income inequality grown over this time? Between 1961 and 2007/8, the weekly income of the poorest *5–10 per cent* of households before housing costs grew 2.36-fold and that of the richest *5–10 per cent* of households 3.1-fold. This is a significant inequality in the rate of growth. It pales by comparison, however, to the growth in the size of the differences between their absolute incomes. In 1961, the weekly income of the poorest 5–10 per cent of households was £96 and the weekly income of the richest 5–10 per cent was £306: a £209 difference. By 2007/8, the average weekly income of the poorest 5–10 per cent of households was £226 and that of the richest 5–10 per cent of households £955: a £729 difference.

Where does all of this leave us in terms of our understanding of inequality? The miserabilist's reaction will, I suspect, be to argue that absolute income inequality has grown because of the imposition of neoliberalism. I think this is 25 per cent right but 75 per cent wrong. To see why, assume that the weekly income of these two groups had grown at the same rate. Between 1961 and 2007/8, the income of the median household (again at 2014/15 prices) grew 2.62-fold (from £177 to £465). If the income of the poorest 5–10 per cent of households had grown at an equivalent rate, their income would have risen from £95 to £250 (instead of rising, as it actually did, to £226). If the income of the richest 5–10 per cent of households had grown 2.62-fold, their income would have risen from £306 to £801 (instead of rising, as it did, to £955). In this case, the absolute gap between these groups would have grown from £211 to £551 (instead of growing, as we know it did, to £729). This is a substantive difference. If the incomes of the richest and poorest households had grown at the same rate over the last half decade, absolute income inequality would be 25 per cent lower than it is. But the other way of thinking about these numbers is of course to say that 75 per cent of the growth in the absolute income gap between some of the richest and poorest households was due not to differences in the rate of growth of their initial incomes but the compound effects of growth on a set of incomes which, in 1961, were significantly more equal than they are today but which were still unequal. What causes inequality? There is no simple answer to this question. I previously argued that the spectacular growth in inequality in the 1980s was caused by, amongst other things, globalization, a skills shortage, and a reduction in trade union power. Yet to this list we can now add another factor: time.

None of this is to say that income inequality is either inevitable or unimportant. Indeed, the very opposite lesson might be drawn. If weekly household incomes were to continue to grow at a uniform rate of 2.6-fold over the next fifty years, the absolute weekly income gap between the richest 5–10 per cent and poorest 5–10 per cent of households will grow from £708 in 2014/15 to £1,855 by 2066. Absolute income inequality is a pernicious policy problem because left unchecked it simply grows and grows.

IV

In the summer of 2006, the one-year or eighteen-month low-interest 'teaser' rates which had been offered to hundreds of thousands of people in the United States to encourage them to apply for a new mortgage or extend an existing mortgage expired. The interest payments of these borrowers suddenly jumped and many immediately defaulted on their loans. Taking advantage of 'nonrecourse' mortgage rules which mean borrowers are no longer liable for a mortgage once they have abandoned the house on which that mortgage has been taken, many decided to walk away. Real estate agents suddenly struggled to sell the glut of new properties on the market and for the first time in several decades, house prices in Arizona, California, Florida, and Nevada started to fall.[21] With house prices falling, other households now found that they were caught with negative equity on their loans and also upped sticks. With more vacant houses suddenly available, house prices continued to fall and several real estate firms collapsed.

The first sign that the housing downturn in the United States might morph into a full-scale financial crisis came in the summer of 2007, when it was announced that hedge funds belonging to the investment bank Bear Stearns and the French bank BNP Paribas had sustained significant losses on securitized investments they had made in the US housing market. Significantly, many of these losses were incurred on assets that the credit agencies had rated AAA—that is, supposedly as safe as US Treasury bonds. By October 2008, the IMF estimated that the declared losses in the subprime securities markets exceeded $500bn.[22] This is a significant sum of money. But it ought not to have been enough to have nearly destroyed the financial system. The largest banks have balance sheets measured in the trillions. The kind of losses sustained through subprime ought to have been manageable. In 2013, I interviewed the former chairman of a major UK investment bank. He told me that:

> The balance sheet of [my bank] was £2 trillion. The balance sheet that I was responsible for was £1 trillion. That's one thousand billion pounds, it's a huge number. The subprime part of it, even on the broadest definition, was around £5 billion . . . and almost all of it was rated, quote, 'better than AAA'. So, all the people responsible to me . . . never ever highlighted it or focused on it so as to put it on the dashboard of things to worry about . . . I will go to my grave saying that it is not realistic or fair to expect me to have focused on this tiny apparently very safe part of the overall portfolio. I'd like to say my risk people let me down, that they should have told me about it but I don't think I can even say that. If 'it's better than AAA' one shouldn't have to think about it.[23]

By 2008, the banks were not only too big to fail. They were too large to manage.

Why did relatively small losses on the subprime market eventually lead to a full-blown financial crisis and, in Britain, the collapse of the Royal Bank of Scotland, HBOS, Northern Rock, and Bradford and Bingley? The key problem was that the banks had borrowed too much money and had insufficient equity (shareholder funds) to cover even relatively small losses on the subprime markets. What is more, most of the banks had borrowed much of this money from short-term (often overnight) wholesale lending markets. In the endless pursuit of ever higher profits, RBS had invested heavily in volatile trading markets, whilst HBOS had staked tens of billions of pounds on high-risk commercial business lending. By 2007, the banks, whilst highly profitable, were also extremely fragile. The banking system was a house of cards.[24]

Once house prices had started to fall in the United States and the banks started to incur losses on the loans that they had bought or had insured, the crisis was exacerbated by huge information asymmetries. Bank executives and investors realized that some banks were going to lose significant sums of money and that some might even go to the wall. But because banks had bought and sold each other's securitized mortgage loans, insured each other's loans, and, via market trading floors, had then made bets with each other about whether asset prices would rise or fall (think *The Big Short*), nobody was entirely sure who had lost what money. In this highly uncertain environment, bank executives and investors decided that the best bet was to simply stop lending money to anyone. The result was a funding panic in which banks suddenly found themselves unable to roll over their existing debts. To make matters much worse, bank executives, traders, and outside investors who had seen the value of securitized subprime assets fall began to worry that other kinds of securitized assets on their balance sheets might also be overvalued and so decided to sell them whilst they could still do so. But when everyone decided to do this at the same time, the result was a trading bloodbath.

By the summer of 2008, the financial markets were locked into a vicious cycle from which they could not escape. The value of the assets on their balance sheets was falling. They could not easily sell those assets to cover their losses because nobody was buying and they could no longer borrow money to dig themselves out of a hole because nobody was lending. When the credit rating agencies belatedly realized that there was a problem and downgraded the value of the assets on bank balance sheets, major institutional investors who were legally required to hold AAA rated assets were then obliged to sell their holdings, forcing the market price down further. In the end, everything came to a head in September 2008, when the Federal Reserve, stung by criticism that it had used taxpayer money to bail out Bear Stearns, decided to let another investment bank, Lehman Brothers, declare itself bankrupt. For a short while, it seemed as if no bank was too big to fail and everyone lost confidence in everyone. In October 2008, the Royal Bank of Scotland—which, following its purchase of the Dutch firm ABN Amro, had a balance sheet of over £1,900bn—was offered a £36bn bridging loan by the Bank of England to keep it in business. By November 2009, it had received £45bn in government subsidies and was 84 per cent owned by the taxpayer. Meanwhile, HBOS, which had tried and failed to raise new capital in July 2008, was sold in a shotgun marriage to Lloyds.

V

In 2008, the government responded to the financial crisis by guaranteeing bank liquidity, cutting interest rates, and pump-priming public expenditure. As the banks slashed their business and mortgage lending and consumer confidence evaporated, the banking crisis nevertheless became a credit crunch and the economy slid into recession. Between the second quarter of 2008 and the third quarter of 2009, GDP fell by 6.4 per cent. Between 2009/10 and 2011/12, median household weekly income (again in 2014/15 prices) fell by 3 per cent from £470 to £454.

What has happened since? In 2012, the economy came within a whisker of succumbing to a double-dip recession. In the second quarter of 2012, the economy shrank by 0.2 per cent. In the fourth quarter, it contracted by a further 0.1 per cent.[25] Things then started to get a little bit better. Between the third quarter of 2009 and the third quarter of 2016, the economy grew by an average of nearly 2 per cent a year. Household income has, however, recovered much more slowly. Indeed, it was only in 2014/15 that household median income recovered to its pre-crisis levels.[26] The post-crisis recession has not undone all the gains achieved in the 2000s. In 2015/16, median weekly household income was still 16 per cent higher than it had been in 2000/1 and 32 per cent higher than it had been in 1994/5 at the start of the long boom. The real costs of the recession and of the period of austerity which has followed it ought to be measured in terms of forgone gains. Between 1997/8 and 2007/8, median household weekly income grew by an average of £9.50 in real terms a year. If the recession had not happened and the economy had continued to grow at this rate, then by 2015/16, weekly median household income would have been 11 per cent higher than it was (£539 rather than £480).[27]

What are the prospects for future growth? Throughout 2014 and 2015, the Office for Budget Responsibility was predicting that the economy would continue to grow at a reasonably impressive rate of around 2 to 2.5 per cent a year through to 2020.[28] Critics observed that the actual growth rate was consistently lower than this. In 2015, the Bank of England began to use its biannual *Financial Stability Reports* to warn that the world economy was in danger of slowing down and that a further crisis in the Eurozone or a financial crisis in China might be sufficient to trigger a global crisis. Then, in June 2016, Britain's economic prospects were, to put it mildly, cast into doubt by the European Union referendum result and the prospect of having to renegotiate trade deals with Europe and the rest of the world from scratch. At the time of writing, the early signs are mixed. On the one hand, a series of large businesses have announced new investments in the UK. On the other, higher import prices and inflation and reduced business confidence has led the IMF to downgrade the UK's growth forecast.[29] Yet, over time, economists are still pretty much as one in predicting that lower immigration numbers, reduced investment (caused by uncertainty about future trade access), and higher inflation (caused by the fall in the value of the pound) will cut the long-term growth rate. The Economist Intelligence Unit, to take just one example, predicts a 6 per cent contraction in the British economy by 2020; an 8 per cent decline in investment; and rising unemployment, falling tax revenues, and increasing public debt.[30] The Office for Budget Responsibility, for its part, is adamant that 'any likely Brexit outcome would lead to lower trade flows, lower investment and lower net inward migration than we would have otherwise seen, and hence lower potential output'.[31] Putting a number to this, it forecasts that growth will be 0.6 per cent lower than it would otherwise have been in 2017 and 0.4 per cent lower in 2018. The Institute of Fiscal Studies predicts that Brexit, combined with planned spending cuts, will mean that average real wages in 2021 will be no higher than they were in 2008.[32]

Brexiteers argue that, left to our own devices to negotiate free trade deals with other countries, Britain will prosper. But even if these deals are forthcoming, the bottom line is that any new barriers to entry to the European single market are likely to prove extremely costly. The 'gravity model' of trade tells us that most countries are much more likely to undertake most of their trade with their near neighbours than countries located thousands of miles away. Gaining the option of free trade with India, Australia, and even the United States is not likely to compensate British businesses for losing the option of free trade with Germany, Belgium, and Italy if a 'hard' Brexit is the final outcome of the negotiations to leave the EU. The issue here is not simply of the level of tariffs imposed on trade between the UK and the EU. Economic analysis finds the largest potential costs of Brexit come not from the threat of tariffs, but from higher non-tariff trade barriers due to the imposition of customs procedures and the emergence of regulatory differences between the UK and the EU.[33]

Looking beyond this known unknown, it is true that the British economy enjoys a number of important comparative economic advantages: including strong biotechnology, pharmaceutical, aerospace, and film and media industries;[34] a strong university sector with thirty-four UK universities among the top 200 in the world (and generating around £11bn in export earnings a year—at least up to that point at which new immigration controls make the UK a much less attractive place to study);[35] a great deal of 'soft power' on the world stage (in 2015, the UK was ranked as the most soft-powerful country in the world);[36] the growing use of English as a global language; and an enduring capacity (if it chooses to exercise it) to attract large numbers of skilled migrants.[37]

Against this, it is obvious that the UK faces several connected and serious economic problems which threaten its growth prospects. The most important of these are poor levels of capital investment in the public and private sectors (in 2016, the UK ranked 141st out of 164 countries on a World Bank ranking of gross capital formation—slightly ahead of Burundi but behind Afghanistan and Mali[38]); cripplingly low levels of productivity (in Germany, the United States, and France, output per worker is now 25–30 per cent higher than it is in the UK; in these countries workers could take a three-day weekend and still produce more in a week than the average UK worker[39]); poor vocational training (in 2013, one in ten of new apprenticeships in the UK was at Morrison's supermarket, which enrolled 52,000 staff on a six-month course which included training on how to operate cash tills and other basic operating procedures[40]); a weak manufacturing sector (by 2016, manufacturing output was still 6 per cent below its 2008/9 peak[41]); high levels of household debt (in 2007, household debt was equivalent to 168 per cent of GDP and by 2020, it is forecast to have risen again to 170 per cent of GDP[42]); and a large banking and financial system which generates large tax revenues and hundreds of thousands of jobs but which also makes the UK extremely vulnerable to financial crises and contributes to house price inflation.[43]

It is tempting to see each of these weaknesses as the result of and an indictment upon the diffusion of neoliberal ideas and policies and, therefore, as grist to the miserabilist mill. As the economy has become 'financialized' and more focused upon short-term profits, companies have eschewed long-term investments and training, whilst banks have chased speculative financial deals and property deals.[44] Widening inequality has, in turn, led to an explosion in payday lending and household borrowing. The UK has become a low-productivity economy specializing in cheap labour and light-touch regulation.

Yet, laments about the UK's low levels of investment, productivity, and skills training, small manufacturing sector, and bloated and industry-unfriendly banking sector are long-standing and pre-date the rise of neoliberalism. Debates about Britain's relative economic decline in the late 1950s and early 1960s also highlighted low levels of productivity and investment—attributed at that time to the amateurishness and short-term focus of management practices; the failure of government and industry to work together to fund long-term industrial expansion; and the failure of a tripartite education system in which academic grammar schools received the lion's share of funding at the expense of vocationally orientated technical schools.[45] In the 1970s, amidst tumbling growth, growing unemployment, and social unrest, the right argued that trade unions and an over-generous welfare system were destroying the country.[46] The left, for its part, argued that the focus of the City of London upon speculative trading, predatory lending, and overseas investment at the expense of the development of long-term collaborative partnerships with industry was to blame for decades of low growth.[47] There is little that is new under the sun when it comes to arguments about Britain's economic travails. Neoliberalism may have added a new layer of language to arguments about our economic woes but it has not fundamentally altered the analysis of what our economic weaknesses are.

VI

Who has borne the costs of austerity? The left is in no doubt. Far from us all being in it together, the poorest households have been left to carry the can for a crisis that was caused by millionaire bankers and billionaire hedge-fund owners. Even Iain Duncan-Smith, when resigning from the Cabinet over proposed cuts to disability benefits, was prompted to chide his former colleagues for their failures to act fairly.[48]

In many ways, I entirely agree. Despite the vastly unequal distribution of wealth, capital gains tax has been cut. HMRC has been stripped of the resources it needs to pursue tax avoidance. Benefits have been frozen and housing benefit cut. Yet the claim that the costs of austerity have been loaded on to the poorest and most vulnerable needs to be critically examined.

Figure 7.2 shows the weekly final income before housing costs of the poorest 5 per cent, poorest 5–10 per cent, median, richest 5–10 per cent, and richest 5 per cent of households between 2007/8 and 2015/16 as a percentage of that group's income in 2007/8. Once again, the figures are in real (inflation-adjusted) prices. What do we see? The income of the median household continues to grow until 2009/10 but then falls to 98 per cent of its 2007/8 level in 2011/12 before just about recovering to its 2007/8 level in 2013/14. By 2015/16, median income is 103 per cent of its 2007/8 level. The income of the poorest 5 per cent of households continues to grow until 2011/12 before then falling in 2012/13. By 2015/16, however, the income of the poorest 5 per cent of households is 110 per cent that of the level it had been in 2007/8. Similarly, by 2015/16, the income of the poorest 5–10 per cent of households is 107 per cent that of their 2007/8 level. By comparison, the income of the richest 5 and 5–10 per cent of households falls sharply in 2010/11 and continues to fall in 2011/12. By 2015/16, the income of the richest 5 per cent of households is 100 per cent that of their 2007/8 level and that of the richest 5–10 per cent 99 per cent of their 2007/8 level.[49]

What happened here? The Institute for Fiscal Studies argues that three things happened.[50] First, pensioners toward the bottom of the income scale benefited from increases in benefits and state pensions and were unaffected by falling real wages. Second, among non-pensioners, 'workless' households again benefited from increases in benefits which either matched or narrowly outpaced inflation at a time when real wages were falling for middle-income and high-income households. Between 2007/8 and 2011/12, median income in workless households rose from 50 per cent to 56 per cent of that in working households. Third, and within working households, wages increased at a faster rate in lower-income households than they did in high-income households. In the median-income household, real earnings grew by 1.3 per cent between 2011/12 and 2014/15. Within those households with the highest 10 per cent of incomes, real earnings fell by 1.2 per cent in in real terms. Within households with the lowest 10 per cent of incomes, real earnings grew by 4.4 per cent.

All of this looks quite positive. There is, however, a kicker. The fall in the inequality in real earnings was not driven by falling inequality in hourly wages. Rather, it was a result of an increase in the total number of hours worked in lower-income households. The number of people working in each household increased at a faster rate in lower-income households. Beyond this, the average number of hours people worked increased at a faster rate in lower-income households.

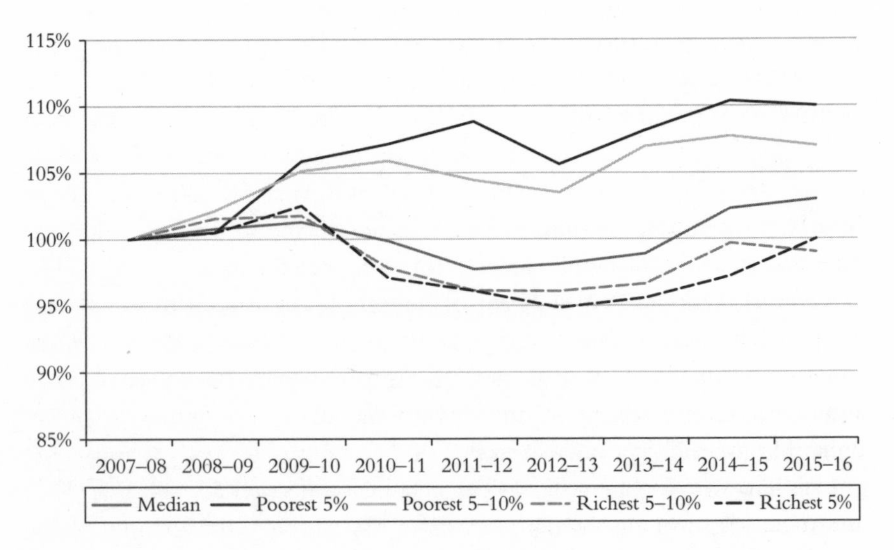

Figure 7.2. The distribution of the costs of austerity.[2]

VII

I have so far focused largely upon economic growth and income. There is, however, an argument that what is wrong with the UK (and much of the rest of the world) is an unrelenting focus upon the ideology of growth and of increases in GDP at the expense of a sustainable quality of life. Arguments of this sort have echoes on the political right, where, as we have seen, they were packaged together by the Centre for Social Justice under the moniker of 'Broken Britain'. It is, however, economists on the left who have led the charge in arguing that GDP is a dreadful measure of economic performance which fails to take account of the numerous external costs of economic growth, including climate change, environmental degradation, unpaid domestic labour, longer working and commuting hours, family breakdown, the fragmentation of communities, and addiction.[51] Meanwhile, and drawing on a separate social science literature which shows that overall levels of happiness have not increased in line with economic growth and increases in income, a number of psychologists have argued that the economic boom of the 2000s simply accelerated the growth of affluenza.[52] Summarizing this line of research in the *Financial Times*, Andrew Oswald suggested that

> Politicians mistakenly believe that economic growth makes a nation happier... Western politicians think this way because they were taught to do so. But today there is much statistical and laboratory evidence in favour of a heresy: once a country has filled its larders there is no point in that nation becoming richer. The hippies, the Greens, the road protesters, the down-shifters, the slow-food movement—all are having their quiet revenge. Routinely derided, the ideas of these down-to-earth philosophers are being confirmed by new statistical work by psychologists and economists.[53]

Money, it transpires, can't buy happiness (although, as Spike Milligan once observed, it can buy a better class of misery).

There is no doubt that the pursuit of economic growth for its own sake is a pretty hopeless policy objective and that the benefits of growth ought to be set against its costs. But I am going to conclude by suggesting that arguments about the costs of growth and the degree to which Britain is broken have been overstated.

Let's start with the literature on happiness. It is true that economic growth and increases in living standards over the last half-century have not been matched by equivalent increases in average levels of measured happiness.

Gross domestic product per head (at current prices) has risen from £1,449 in 1973 to £29,580 in 2016.[54] Median household weekly income (adjusted for inflation) has increased from £240 in 1973 to £482 in 2015/16.[55] Yet average self-reported levels of happiness—conventionally measured along a 1–10 scale—have only increased by around 10 per cent from an average of 6.9 to 7.6.[56] What does this tell us about the relationship between growth and happiness? The miserabilist argument is that it tells us that growth and increases in income have nothing to do with personal happiness. On the other hand, I'm not sure that it tells us very much at all. The simple problem here from a data perspective is that income and happiness are being measured in different ways along very different kinds of scales. GDP per head and median income are being measured along an unbounded scale. There is no mathematical limit to how much GDP or income can grow by and to. Happiness, on the other hand, is being measured along a fixed scale. So, given the starting-point of an average level of happiness of 6.9 in the 1970s, it is simply impossible for average levels of happiness to have grown at the same rate as median income.

Between 2014 and 2016, the countries in the world with the highest levels of self-reported happiness—a list headed by Norway (with an average level of happiness of 7.53 out of 10), Denmark (7.52), Iceland (7.52), and Switzerland (7.494)—were all exceptionally wealthy, whilst the countries with the lowest levels of self-reported happiness and life satisfaction—the Central African Republic (2.093), Burundi (2.905), Tanzania (3.349), Syria (3.462) and Rwanda (3.471)—were generally poor.[57] Differences in national income clearly do not explain all the variations in happiness. Syria is not an unhappy country simply because it is relatively poor. Costa Rica (the 12th happiest country), Mexico (the 14th), and Venezuela (the 23rd) have high levels of average self-reported happiness even though they do not have particularly high levels of average median income or GDP per head. But income is one factor—along with levels of social support, health, life expectancy at birth, freedom to make important life choices, and levels of perceived corruption—which the authors of the World Happiness Report suggest can best explain variations in self-reported levels of happiness.[58]

The UK, for the record, was the 19th happiest country in the world between 2014–16 (slightly behind Belgium and Luxembourg). What is also notable, however, is that in terms of the distribution of happiness within the UK, the richest region in the country, London, had the lowest average levels of happiness, whilst the poorest region, Northern Ireland, had the highest average levels of happiness. What perhaps seems even odder is that during a period of austerity in which, as we have seen, many households have experienced falling real income, average levels of happiness across the UK have risen consistently.[59] The lesson is, I think, that we ought to be quite circumspect about thinking of growth as being either an unalloyed good or bad thing.

VIII

What do other social indicators tell us about the state of British society? I have already reported on a few pieces of data of relevance to this question in previous chapters. In the third chapter, I argued that there has been no obvious fall in overall levels of social capital or social trust. In the fourth chapter, I noted that there has been a significant increase in the UK prison population over the last few decades. In the fifth chapter, I highlighted falling mortality rates. In the sixth chapter, I noted that there has been a significant increase in the number of people being paid the minimum wage and the number working on zero hour contracts.

There is clearly a danger of statistical overload here in trying to say too many more things when I have already loaded up on data and graphs. Yet, at the same time, I think that numbers offer the easiest way of effectively challenging often quite pernicious claims about broken Britain.

Let's start with a tabloid favourite: teenage pregnancies. In the 1990s, teenage girls getting pregnant and jumping to the front of the queue for council houses became a national problem to rank alongside yobbish teenagers, too many repeats on the telly, and overpaid footballers who get injured all the time and, if they are foreign, probably dive-to-the ground-when-tackled-and-roll-around-like-they-have-been-shot. Following the launch of a much-derided national plan to reduce teenage pregnancies in 1998, the conception rate per 1,000 women aged 15 to 17 has fallen from 47.1 in 1998 to 21 in 2015.[60] Close behind teenage pregnancies in the roll call of the horrors of a permissive society gone mad is divorce. Once upon a time, wedding vows meant something and couples stuck together through thick and thin. But now, commitment is a thing of the past. However, the divorce rate (measured in terms of the number of divorces per year per thousand opposite-sex marriages), which rose from 8.4 in 1973 to a peak of 14.3 in 1993, has since steadily fallen to 8.5 in 2015.[61]

In July 2017, the Office for National Statistics reported that there had been a 10 per cent increase in police-recorded crime: the largest for over a decade. This included an 18 per cent rise in violent crime. Yet, over the long-term, the story here looks quite different. In the 1970s and 1980s, there were rapid rises in crime and the fear of crime. One of the most remarkable social developments of the last few decades is the equally spectacular fall in crime which has happened since. The Crime Survey for England and Wales suggests that there was a 60 per cent fall in overall crime between 1999 and March 2017 and that, over the same period, violent crime has fallen by 58 per cent; robbery by 68 per cent; and domestic burglary has fallen by 53 per cent.[62] The OECD's 2015 better life index records that 1.9 per cent of people in the UK had been assaulted or mugged in the previous year, compared with 6.6 per cent in Belgium, 3.6 per cent in Germany, 4.9 per cent in the Netherlands, and 5 per cent in France.[63] The most notable exception to this general pattern is sexual offences. Between 2002.3 and 2017. there was a 234 per cent increase in the total recorded number of sexual offences.

There has been a slight increase in the number of adults who say that they do not drink at all (from 19 per cent in 2005 to 21 per cent in 2016) and a significant increase in the number of young adults (aged 16 to 24) who do not drink from 19 per cent to 26 per cent. The number of adults who binge drink has fallen slightly, whilst the number of young adults who binge drink has fallen by two-thirds.[64] The number of adults who have taken drugs during the previous year has fallen from 11 per cent in 1990 to 8.8 per cent in 2014/15 (although there has been a slight rise in the number taking Class A drugs, from 2.5 per cent to 3.2 per cent).[65]

Longer working hours (compounded by work cultures which encourage employees to respond to email traffic at weekends and on holidays) are a significant social cost to be set against measures of GDP growth. The number of people working over forty-five hours a week has, however, fallen from 24 per cent in 1992 and 20.5 per cent in 2006 to 19 per cent in 2016.[66] The number of workers who have a 'good job' (defined as having at least four positive attributes such as being interesting, helping others or society, and offering chances of advancement) has increased from 57 per cent in 1989 and 62 per cent in 2005 to 71 per cent.[67] On the other hand, the number of workers who commute for more than two hours each day has risen by a third since 2010, from one in nine to one in seven workers.[68] 37 per cent of workers now say that they are always or often stressed at work, compared with 28 per cent in 1989.[69] 54 per cent of workers say that they have no control over their working hours. 35 per cent say that they have some control over their working hours within limits. Only 9 per cent have complete freedom to determine their starting and finishing times. These numbers have not changed a great deal over the last decade.[70] Unemployment—which climbed to 11.8 per cent in the early 1980s and 10.7 per cent in the early 1990s—rose from 5.2 per cent at the start of 2008 to 8.5 per cent in September 2011. It has since fallen to around 4.5 per cent.[71] The unemployment rate of those aged between 15 and 24 is 13 per cent in the UK. In Germany, it is just 7 per cent. In France, it is 23.6 per cent and in Spain, it is 42 per cent.[72] Two and a half million new jobs have been created since 2010. Nearly two-thirds of these job are full-time and employed (rather than part-time or self-employed).[73] In the longer term, the Bank of England estimates that up to 15 million jobs in Britain are at risk of being lost due to automation. At the moment, however, employment is at a record high.[74]

In the early 1980s, homelessness became a very visible symbol of growing inequality. The number of people declared to be statutorily homeless by local authorities declined from 25,000 a year in 1998 to 10,000 a year in 2010, although it has since risen to 14,600 in 2017.[75] During the first snapshot count in 1998, an estimated 1,850 people were sleeping rough in England. This number fell to around 500 in the early 2000s and remained stable through to 2009. Progress has since been reversed. In February 2016, it was reported that over 3,500 people were sleeping rough in England and that this number had increased by 30 per cent in just one year.[76] Given just how often I have said that the miserabilists are wrong about things, I should say loud and clear that this is one issue on which they are right. The rise in the number of people sleeping rough deserves to be described as a national disgrace.

Arguments about affluenza often draw upon statistics relating to mental health. The argument here is that the cost of a highly competitive and socially isolating society in which people do not trust each other and do not interact with each other is a steady rise in the incidence of depression. It is true, in this regard, that the number of prescriptions issued for antidepressants has increased from around 15m in 1998 to 40m in 2012 and 53m in 2014.[77] It is also true that the number of young people reporting frequent feelings of anxiety or depression has doubled since the mid-1980s from 1 in 30 to 2 in 30 for boys and 1 in 10 to 2 in 10 for girls.[78] Yet whilst it is clear that more people are being treated for depression and anxiety, it is not clear that more people are suffering from depression. Since 1996, the incidence of recorded depression in UK general practice has fallen, whilst the overall incidence of recorded depression within the population has remained broadly stable.[79]

Finally, and turning to some indicators of environmental quality, there is a mixed picture. Total net greenhouse gas emissions in the UK have fallen from 800m metric tonnes of carbon dioxide equivalent in 1990 to 570m tonnes in 2014.[80] There has been a 1 per cent decline in the amount of green belt land in England and Wales. Four new national parks have, however, been established in recent years.[81] The number of days of moderate or high air pollution in urban areas has fallen from 53 in 1992 and 15.4 in 2010 to 10.8 in 2015. Yet, over the same period, the number of days of moderate or higher air pollution in rural areas has risen from 10.2 in 2010 to 11.6 in 2015.[82] There has also been a significant fall of around 12 per cent in the UK's bird population and a 50 per cent fall in the farmland bird population since the early 1970s.[83] In the late 1980s, around two-thirds of UK bathing waters met minimum regulatory standards. This has increased to over 95 per cent.[84] The number of UK beaches reaching the more stringent standards set for Blue Flag status has increased from 37 per cent in 1994 to 76 per cent.[85]

Is Britain broken? Are things getting steadily worse? Half of those who voted Labour in 2015 believe that life is worse now than it was thirty years ago.[86] It is of course impossible to say whether they are right or wrong. There is no measuring machine available into which we can throw numbers and wait for an answer to *Life, The Universe and Everything*. But these numbers do not suggest to me that everything is going to the dogs.

IX

Over the last decade, Keep Calm and Carry On has become a design icon (figure 7.3).

Keep Calm and Spend Money
Keep Calm and Believe in Yourself
Keep Calm and Save the NHS
Keep Calm and Watch Top Gear
Keep Calm and Fight ISIS
Keep Calm and Be British
Keep Calm and Boogie On

The original Keep Calm poster was designed in 1939 as one of a series aimed at stiffening the nation's resolve in the event of a German invasion.

Figure 7.3. 'Keep Calm and Carry On.'

It was never actually published and languished lost for several decades. One of the few surviving test printings of the poster was then found in a consignment of second-hand books bought at an auction by a bookshop in Northumberland. It was picked up by and first sold at the Victoria and Albert Museum before being catapulted to prominence at the start of the financial crisis.

Keep Calm and Carry On invokes the spirit of the Blitz and privations collectively endured. It reminds us of and celebrates a sort of quiet stiff-upper-lip stoicism that is the flip side of the low-octane moaning which is also part of our national character. I've always found it to be generally inoffensive. Some people on the left do, however, get quite worked up about Keep Calm. This is in part because of the way in which the slogan has been ruthlessly commercialized (the Keep Calm examples listed above are taken from the officially licensed Keep Calm and Carry On on-line store, where you can buy mugs, coasters, T-shirts, bags, aprons, mobile phone cases, biscuits, posters, and cushions). Keep Calm also implies a kind of very British 'mustn't grumble, things could be worse' acceptance of the political status quo which the left finds infuriating. Faced with the onslaught of austerity, the French and Greek organized protest marches and rioted. The British middle class, on the other hand, bought into the basic idea that there were not enough resources to go around and that there was no alternative to austerity and bought brightly coloured mugs to ruefully acknowledge this fact.

Yet Keep Calm may be quite a useful piece of guidance when confronted with hyperbolic statements about austerity. Is the UK a shining light of social justice and economic prosperity? It is absolutely not. Has austerity destroyed 'society as we know it' (Richard Murphy, Tax Research UK)?[87] Has it 'ripped the soul out of Britain' (*Labour List*)?[88] Does the rise and rise of the Keep Calm motif need to be viewed in the context of a 'sadomasochistic Toryism imposed by the Coalition government of 2010–2015, and its presentation of austerity in a manner so brutal and moralistic that it almost seemed to luxuriate in its own parsimony' (Owen Hatherley)?[89] I'd have to say probably not.

Hatherley—from whom the last of these quotes is taken and who has written extensively and often insightfully on this subject—recognizes that Keep Calm is often meant to signal quiet irony and a self-aware recognition that things are maybe not really *that* bad. He wants to challenge this view and assert that things really are bad and getting worse and that keeping calm is not the appropriate way to respond:

> [Keep Calm] evokes a sense of loss over the decline of an idea of Britain and the British, it is both reassuring and flattering, implying a virtuous (if highly self-aware) consumer stoicism. Of course, in the end, it is a bit of a joke: you don't really think your pay cut or your children's inability to buy a house, or the fact that someone somewhere else has been made homeless because of the bedroom tax, or lost their benefit, or worked on a zero-hours contract, is really comparable to life during the blitz—but it's all a bit of fun, isn't it?'[90]

Framing things in this way is discomforting. Who wants to suggest that being made homeless or losing your benefit is a trivial thing? But I still think that we can say that being made homeless and losing your benefit is a personal tragedy which results from political failings whilst also saying that there is a slight area of unreality hanging over a lot of the statements made about the extent, distribution, and impact of austerity. Keep Calm and Look at the Numbers.

8

The unspectacular world of a reasonably well-functioning democracy

I

In its 2017 'Audit of Political Engagement', the Hansard Society found that 3 per cent of people think that Britain's democratic works extremely well and cannot be improved upon and that a further 29 per cent think that it works well and can only be improved upon in small ways.[1] This group must feel like an embattled minority. If there is anything the British enjoy moaning about more than the weather, it is politicians, political parties, and elections.

If voting changed anything, they'd abolish it. The parties are all the same. Election campaigns go on for too long and yet fail to debate any of the serious issues. Politicians will say or do anything to get elected. They never keep their promises. Most of them are only in it for what they can get out of it. Politicians are out of touch and have no idea about the real world. Only 21 per cent of people trust politicians to tell them the truth (compared to 89 per cent for doctors and even 69 per cent for hairdressers).[2] To this common or garden low-level carping, the left can add new layers of contempt. It does not matter which party is in power because all they offer are different shades of the same political colour. Parties and politicians kowtow to big business. The parties depend upon them for their campaign funds and politicians depend upon them for backhanders and the promise of future employment. Democracy has been privatized. Real power is exercised by multinational corporations and unelected technocrats working in quangos.

Jeremy Corbyn has made the case for a 'new politics' to mobilize a generation of voters who have tired of politics but, for his pains, has been ridiculed by newspapers, the political establishment, and the ghosts of New Labour past. Meanwhile, the EU referendum campaign showed, once and for all, just how disenchanted the public are with the political status quo. When the great and the good of the Labour Party (David and Ed Miliband, Tony Blair, and Gordon Brown), the Conservatives (David Cameron, John Major, and Kenneth Clarke), and the Lib Dems, the Governor of the Bank of England, Barack Obama, David Beckham, and even James Bond said that they supported remaining, the vote to leave increased.[3]

Politics is unambiguously broken and something has to be done to fix it. Or should it? What if the problem here is not so much with politicians and parties but rather with voters' understanding of what politicians and parties do and of how democracy works? What if the 26 per cent are more right than those who argue that voting is a waste of time, that the parties are all the same, and that none of it makes any difference anyway because giant corporations rule the world?

After a series of popular uprisings in East Germany in 1953 which had been violently crushed by the Red Army, the Communist-supporting playwright Bertolt Brecht made the ironic comment that the Communist regime, having tried as hard as it could to create a socialist paradise, ought to dismiss the people and appoint another.[4] It sounds like I am saying something quite similar here. The people don't like the politicians and the people are to blame. This is not quite right. I don't for a second think that politicians are selfless geniuses who never tire in pursuit of the public interest and that election campaigns offer nothing but dazzling displays of forensic analysis and high wit. I don't believe parties always keep their promises come what may. I don't think British democracy constitutes a high point of political evolution which cannot be improved upon (indeed, at a later point in this chapter, I list some necessary reforms to it) But I do think that our political system basically kind of works reasonably well. Politicians are generally responsive to public opinion. Political parties are not all the same. By and large, they keep their election promises. Corruption is not endemic. Behind all the platitudes and evasions, politicians generally go to great lengths to avoid telling lies. Business is an important voice within the policy process. But business does not always get what it wants.

This is a good news story because the left needs to believe that democracy works. There is a debilitating nihilism to arguments that all politicians are the same and that elections don't change anything. Politics is a grubby and often disappointing business. But it does sometimes work. Political parties are sometimes able to offer voters a compelling account of who we are, where we have gone wrong, and what we can do about it. Democracy does offer an alternative to the impersonal logic of the market. Elections do change things.

II

Are political parties all the same? In the third chapter, I argued that the two parties with the strongest chance of forming a government have an incentive to move toward and occupy the centre-ground of politics.[5] The obvious corollary of this is that parties often end up agreeing on a lot of things. In the 2015 general election, for example, Labour and the Conservatives promised to cut the deficit and return the budget to a surplus by 2020; to restrict the right of EU migrants to claim benefits; to integrate health and social care (without really saying very much about what this would entail or how much it would cost); to not raise VAT or National Insurance contributions; and to retain tuition fees and the welfare cap. If you happen to be on the far left of the political spectrum and disagree with these policies, the two parties are going to appear pretty similar in many respects. Is this an affront to democracy and sure-fire evidence that voting does not make any difference? I am not sure. The other point to remember here is that most voters see themselves as being at or around the centre-ground of politics. The fact that the two largest parties often end-up chasing that centre-ground and saying similar things could therefore be seen as quite reassuring. Would we think that democracy was working well if the major parties were saying things most of the electorate did not agree with? Besides, even when parties do agree on a lot of things, this still leaves plenty of room for argument. During the 2017 general election, the parties were obviously very different. But even during the 2015 campaign, when Labour and the Conservatives were routinely derided as saying the same things, they actually had substantively different policies. Labour fought that election promising to introduce a new and higher minimum wage; to repeal the Health and Social Care Act and cap the amount of profit private firms could make from the NHS; to reintroduce a 50 per cent top rate of tax; to abolish the spare bedroom tax; to freeze energy bills; to cut tuition fees to a maximum £6,000 a year; and to impose new regulations on zero hour contracts.

Should these differences be regarded as significant? I can, once again, see that if you are on the far left, they may not seem that important. But the idea that the parties are all the same nevertheless seems a bit glib. There is something approaching a contradiction in the argument on this issue. On the one hand, the miserabilist wants to say that the parties are all the same and that elections don't change anything. On the other hand, they want to argue that the election of the neoliberal Conservatives in 1979 was a national disaster which changed the country beyond recognition and that the Conservatives are going to use their mandate from the 2015 election to destroy what is left of the welfare state. Elections, like Schrödinger's cat, are simultaneously both alive and dead and this does not make sense.

The major parties are not all the same but they are not that different. Let's try to be a bit more precise about this. Over the last few decades, a consortium of European political scientists has set itself the task of estimating the left–right position of European political parties over the last sixty years. To understand how this has been done, recall how I previously argued that left and right have come to be associated with a set of policy positions such as higher tax and public expenditure and a commitment to reducing inequalities on the left or lower taxes and stable inflation on the right. By and large, these links between policies and spatial position have remained reasonably stable over time and across countries. Issues and personalities may change but being on the left in France in the 1950s and being on the left in Britain in the 2000s means believing in similar kinds of things. What this means is that if you have enough patience and a lot of researchers to do the hard work, party manifestos can be coded for left–right position using a common set of criteria. This is what the Manifestos Project has done. The result is a 'Rile' score for each party in each election in Europe running from 100 (entirely right-wing) to −100 (entirely left-wing).[6]

Figure 8.1 shows the Rile scores for the Conservative and Labour parties between 1955 and 2015 (the 2017 election has not been coded at the time of writing). What it shows is that the Conservative Party moved to the right between 1955 (when its Rile score was +30) and 1987 (+27) before then drifting slowly back toward the centre by 2010 (+16) and then, surprisingly, moving to the left in 2015 (−2). Labour, for its part, moved toward the centre between 1955 (−38) and 1970 (−10) before then shifting quite dramatically toward the left between October 1974 (−27) and 1983 (−40). In the late 1980s and 1990s, Labour then moved just as dramatically back toward the centre (+8 by 1997) before then inching back to the left in 2010 (−2) before moving quite dramatically to the left in 2015 (−18). In many ways, this data fits with the miserabilist history that I outlined in the second chapter. There was once a left-of-centre consensus in Britain, which began to fall apart in the 1970s as the Conservatives lurched to the right, only to be followed, twenty years later, by New Labour. But in the 2015 election both parties moved to the left. This data is, however, difficult to reconcile with any simple claim that the two largest parties are essentially the same. Rather, the distance between Labour and the Conservatives waxes and wanes. In the 1955 and 1959 elections, the distance between the two parties was less than 10 points. By 1979, there was a 51-point difference. In 1983, there was a whopping 66-point difference and in 1992, there was a 55-point difference. The parties then moved back together as Labour moved to the right and centre. By 1997, there was a 16-point difference and by 2001, only a 9-point difference between them. In 2010, the parties moved further apart (an 18-point difference) and in 2015 they were 16-points apart. In the 2017 election, Labour and the Conservatives will, I suspect, have been as far apart as they have been since the early 1980s. The fact that, in this context, the 2016 NatCen British Social Attitude Survey reported that only 27 per cent of voters thought that there was a 'great difference' between the parties seems perplexing.[7]

The Rile Scores tell us something about how the parties have positioned themselves. But how are their moves to the left and right related to changes in public opinion? Have parties responded to and tracked changes in public opinion? Does it matter what voters think? The sceptic will argue that it does not: that parties do what they want (or, failing that, what business or other sectional interests want them to do). One of the most impressive academic

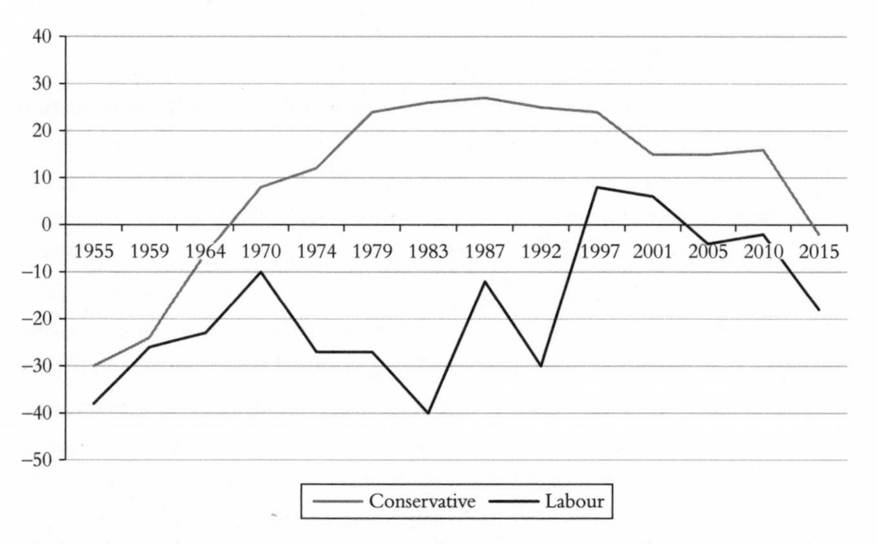

Figure 8.1. Labour and Conservative Rile scores, 1955–2015.[1]

studies that I have come across which attempts to answer this question is by Michael McDonald, Silvia Mendes, and Ian Budge.[8] They set out to calculate the gap between average public opinion on a large range of issues and the average views of elected politicians in twenty European countries between the 1950s and 1995. What they found is interesting. If you look at the average views of *all* the elected representatives in national parliaments, then Britain fares badly. The gap between what, on average, the public thinks and what its elected representatives think is six times larger in Britain than it is in countries such as Belgium and the Netherlands where there are proportional voting systems. As we all know, in the 'first-past-the-post' British system, the smaller parties can accumulate large number of votes without winning many seats. In 2015, UKIP got over 12 per cent of the vote and won one seat. The Greens got nearly 4 per cent of the vote and achieved the same result. So, large numbers of people end up finding that their views are not being represented and a gap opens up between voters and their elected representatives.

This all sounds like the trailer for an election broadcast about the virtues of proportional representation. And up to a point it is. I probably do now think that some form of proportional representation is needed to ensure a greater measure of representativeness in a country in which, in 2017, the Conservatives gained an overall majority with the support of just 29 per cent of the electorate. Yet, at the same time, there is no getting away from the fact that, in the 2011 referendum on the use of the Alternative Vote, only 32 per cent of the 40 per cent of people who voted wanted to change the electoral system and that, as of 2016, support for coalition government in preference to single-party government is down from 40 per cent in 2010 to 33 per cent (although support for changing the electoral system has risen from just 27 per cent in 2011 to 45 per cent).[9]

There is, however, another side to this argument because the same study by Michael McDonald and colleagues also finds that the gap between what the public thinks and what the elected representatives in its *governing* party think is significantly lower in Britain than it is in any other European country. What is going on here? In Britain, the two largest parties have a strong incentive to anticipate and respond to changes in public opinion in an effort to acquire an overall majority. When a governing party fails to do this, it tends to lose the subsequent election. In countries with a proportional voting system where no party is likely to acquire an overall majority, the larger parties get to form coalitions with smaller parties. So even if the junior coalition party only gets a handful of seats in the Cabinet, coalition-building can push the government away from average public opinion. Basically, when it comes to democratic systems, you pays your money and you takes your choice. You can have proportional representation and a parliament which tracks public opinion or you can have first-past-the-post and a government which tracks public opinion or gets kicked out. But it is not an easy thing to get both.

There is one further part to this story. McDonald's work shows that, one way or another, the public broadly gets what the public wants. Does this happen by accident? Do parties adopt positions and then leave it to voters to choose between them? In a celebrated academic paper published in 1995, James Stimson argued that representation in US politics is 'dynamic'.[10] Parties don't simply adopt positions and wait to see what happens. Rather, they are pretty good at changing their positions in response to changes in public opinion. When the electorate shifts to the left, parties tend to shift to the left, and so on. More recently, Armen Kahuendan has shown that a similar thing has happened in British elections since the late 1970s.[11] Labour and the Conservatives have done a good job of tracking changes in public opinion. Kahuendan's article is a tough read. But the overall argument is as straightforward as it is important:

> Government policy on the left–right scale shifts as public preferences change ('rational anticipation'). Secondly, a public with right-wing preferences elects the Conservatives, who pursue right-wing policies in office ('electoral turnover') . . . the Westminster system is criticized for its weak link between the rules and the ruled, but dynamic representation on the left–right scale in the United Kingdom seems to have functioned admirably in this period.

I previously quoted George Osborne's maxim that 'in opposition you move to the centre. In government, you move the centre.'[12] Kahuendan's work suggests that this is not right. Parties follow voters rather than voters following parties.

So far, all things look like sunshine, lollipops, rainbows, and everything that's wonderful. There is, however, an important sense in which democracy is malfunctioning and in which the major parties are indeed all very similar. 68 per cent of the MPs elected in 2017 were male. 92 per cent were white (as against 82 per cent of the British population). 86 per cent had been to university. 23 per cent went to Oxford or Cambridge. 29 per cent went to one of the other elite 'Russell Group' universities. 29 per cent had been educated privately. In the 2015 Parliament, 2 per cent had worked in a blue-collar manual job before becoming an MP (25 per cent of Conservative MPs had worked in finance or banking). Fully 25 per cent of MPs had had a job in politics before becoming an MP. The average age of an MP was 50.[13] You could, at a pinch, argue that things are, in this respect, changing for the better. In 1979 just 3 per cent of MPs were women. In 1987, there were just four non-white MPs. In 1979, 73 per cent of MPs went to a fee-paying private school and 64 per cent studied at Oxbridge. The pace of change has, however, hardly been breathtaking. What's more, the number of MPs who have not been to university and who have done a manual job has fallen.

How much of a problem is it that MPs look and sound so different from so many of the constituents that they represent? There is credible evidence that working-class voters are more likely to vote Labour when given the option of voting for a candidate with a working-class background and that a decline in the number of working-class candidates has undercut Labour's vote.[14] I don't, however, think that a simple causal line can be drawn between the un-representativeness of MPs, distrust in politicians, and a lack of interest in politics. In the 1950s, the public did, by and large, trust MPs at a time when politicians were, if anything, even less representative than they are today. But background does matter. A lot of the debates in politics are, at least in part, about identity: about race, religion, gender, nationality, and belonging. Political argument is often strengthened by claims of personal experience. We generally want some of the politicians who talk about austerity to know what it feels like not to have any money. We want at least some of the politicians who send us to war to have had some experience of fighting. Background matters. This is why representativeness matters. Politics is not simply about what politicians say. It is about how they say it and the accent and experiences they say it with.

III

The major political parties are different and they make different promises to the electorate. But this is unlikely to persuade any sceptic who is convinced that the parties simply cannot be trusted to keep their promises. Recall here a figure I cited earlier. In 2015, 63 per cent of people thought that Labour and the Conservatives would promise anything to get elected but only 24 per cent of Labour supporters and 23 per cent of Conservative supporters believed that they would keep their promises.[15]

It is certainly not hard to think of examples of politicians breaking their promises. In 2010, the Conservatives promised no top–down reorganization of the NHS. Within a few months of winning, they had unveiled health reforms which the then chief executive of the NHS, David Nicholson, described as being 'so large you can see them from outer space'.[16] In 2015, David Cameron promised that tax credits would not be cut after the election, only to announce plans to do just that a few months later. He was, however, then forced to abandon those plans a few months later in the face of strong public opposition. In March 2016, Philip Hammond used his budget to announce a raise in National Insurance Contributions for the self-employed. Once again, the proposals were withdrawn when the Conservatives were held to be breaking an election promise. A particular accountability problem arises when a party changes its leader. Theresa May has put an increase in the number of grammar schools somewhere near the top of her domestic policy agenda. This was, to put it mildly, not a top-drawer policy during the 2015 campaign. Long before the *Oxford English Dictionary* declared post-truth to be its word of the year, the journalist Peter Oborne argued that

> Britain now lives in a post-truth environment. Public statements are no longer based, but operational. Realities and political narratives are constructed to serve a purpose, dismantled and the show moves on... This is new. All governments have contained liars, and most politicians deceive each other as well as the public from time to time. But in recent years mendacity and deception have ceased to be abnormal and become an entrenched feature of the British system.[17]

I doubt that very many people would want to disagree.

It may, however, be that cases in which politicians brazenly mislead us about what they are going to do are memorable not simply because they are an affront to the democratic process but in part because they are relatively unusual. The academic literature here is quite thin but nevertheless interesting. The first point to make is that it is quite difficult to measure whether and when parties have kept their election promises. During election campaigns, politicians may give dozens of interviews in which they appear to make certain commitments. Promises made in election manifestos have a more formal standing but they are sometimes worded quite vaguely. Furthermore, it is not always straightforward to judge whether a party has subsequently kept its manifesto commitment. Gerry Stoker, who has written an excellent book about how and why so many people hate politics, observes that 'one problem with much of the debate in this area is that it neglects the gradations between lying at one end of the spectrum, and full truth at the other'.[18] Parties may sometimes want to do what they said they wanted to do but then find themselves unable to do it. This is likely to be the case with a large part of the contents of the Conservative's 2017 election manifesto. But with these caveats in mind, the most detailed study that I have found estimates that parties do 90 per cent or more of what they say they are going to do in their manifestos.[19]

It might be objected that even if they eventually keep their manifesto promises, politicians routinely and knowingly tell barefaced lies when campaigning and that this brings politics into disrepute. In July 2017, a year on from the publication of his major inquiry into the conduct of the Iraq War, Sir John Chilcot suggested that whilst Blair had been 'emotionally truthful' with the public he had not been 'straight with the nation'.[20] Yet, once again, there is evidence here to suggest otherwise. During the 2015 election, the independent watchdog organization *Full Fact* asked a series of policy experts to assess the claims being made by the major political parties in relation to a series of policy issues (the 2017 election has not, at the time of writing, been subject to a similar audit).[21] They found that the parties were often guilty of cherry-picking statistics which best suited their claims; misinterpreting results; ignoring baseline trends (claiming that something had improved or deteriorated by a certain amount during the previous five years whilst ignoring the fact that the rate of improvement or deterioration had not changed); and making unfair statistical comparisons on the basis of different kinds of data. But *Full Fact* also concluded that the publication of misleading information was more often the result of a cock-up than a conspiracy and that erroneous claims were not generally repeated once they had been shown to be false. Overall, *Full Fact* found that most of what the parties said in 2015 was 'reliable' and that whilst public scepticism about the honesty of politicians was 'understandable', it was not 'well founded'.[22] Throughout his Presidential campaign, Donald Trump did a good job of showing what post-truth politics really looks like: attributing quotes to his opponents that they had not made and denying that he had said things which he had said on camera. By comparison, British politicians appear as paragons of virtue.

The 2016 referendum campaign was, in many respects, the exception which proves this rule. One of the many problems with the referendum was that with a stark 'in or out' alternative, there was little space for politicians to carve out a centre-ground position with which most of the electorate could live. A second problem came with the campaign itself, with politicians on both sides of the debate making increasingly wild claims about the likely consequences of staying or pulling out. Probably the most egregious was the double-barrelled claim that Britain sends £350m to the European Union each week and that this money could, post-Brexit, be spent on the

NHS (a 'mistake' Nigel Farage said, a few hours after the result had been declared).[23] The referendum campaign was, however, a one-off event. During normal election campaigns, political parties generally have a strong incentive to do what they say they are going to do and appear reliable because acquiring a reputation for breaking promises is, in the longer term, likely to prove exceptionally costly. The prospect of having to fight future elections does not always cast a long enough shadow to keep parties honest. But, by and large, elections reward some measure of honesty because they are repeated. During the referendum campaign, in contrast, the politicians from different parties who were thrown together to lead the campaign knew that, if they won, they would not have to form a government and make policy decisions for which they could then be held accountable. Theresa May did appoint the 'three Brexiteers', Boris Johnson, David Davis, and Liam Fox, to key Brexit-related positions, but sixteen members of the Cabinet first appointed by Theresa May in July 2016 campaigned to remain in the EU (as, of course, the Prime Minister herself did).[24] Add to this the largely uncoordinated nature of the referendum itself, with the politicians involved being apparently free to say and unsay things independently of the official and unofficial leave and exit campaign organizations, and it is perhaps not surprising that the referendum generated so much heat and so little light.

Party politicians generally keep their promises. And they generally avoid deliberately lying. But they do sometimes go to extraordinary lengths to avoid giving straight answers to simple questions. In this respect, it is tempting to say that politicians are simply human. We all sometimes go to great lengths to present our own actions in the best possible light and to avoid clearly answering difficult questions. But politicians also face the additional constraint of having to defend a party position with which they may personally disagree or having to answer questions in a situation in which no formal party line has been settled. Politicians would no doubt appear more human and trustworthy if they were prepared to say that they disagree with the agreed line or to say what their own views are in a situation in which no agreed line had been settled. But in such situations, politicians risk being damned no matter what they do. If they dissent from an agreed party line, the story becomes one of splits and divisions. If they say that they and their party have not decided what to think about some issue, they are going to be accused of being indecisive and incompetent. If they go on *Newsnight* and try to anticipate a policy but get it wrong, the story becomes one of leadership struggles and U-turns. There is a certain measure of self-righteous deceit involved when journalists lambast politicians for not answering a question honestly when those questions are often asked in the hope of being able to ridicule a politician who gives an honest answer to them.

IV

Has British politics been infected by the neoliberal spirit of entrepreneurial self-interest? Are most politicians only in it for what they can get out of it personally? Have political parties been fundamentally corrupted by the pursuit of campaign funds from large businesses and other sectional interests?[25] Many people certainly seem to believe so. 46 per cent agree that politicians are only in it for themselves.[26] 62 per cent believe that corruption is a major or widespread problem in our public life.[27] The anarchist and activist David Graeber suggests that Jeremy Corbyn's landslide victory in the Labour leadership contest should be understood as a reaction to corruption in political life:

> On one level, the pundits were probably right: Corbynmania was just a way of giving the finger to the establishment. The man's appeal rests largely on a complete absence of conventional charisma. He has no rhetorical flair whatsoever. He simply tells you what he thinks. In a political field so corrupt that it often seems the moral spectrum for public figures runs roughly from calculating cynic to actual child molester, the idea that a genuinely honest man could successfully run for public office was a kind of revelation.[28]

There is no doubt that Corbyn's personal integrity was an electoral asset for Labour in 2017. The televised sight of Corbyn emerging from his modest North Islington home every morning during the campaign was a constant reminder of his personal integrity. But, putting Corbyn aside, is it right to think that many or even most politicians are corrupt? Well, I guess a lot depends on what you mean by corruption. Let's start with a basic definition that corruption is what happens when somebody in public office takes a decision or does something to benefit themselves or their party. It is not hard to see why so many people believe that politicians are corrupt. Successive cash-for-questions, cash-for-access, and expenses scandals have done huge damage to politicians' reputations. But it is difficult to square the perception that corruption is a major problem in public life with Transparency International's finding that Britain is perceived as being one of the least corrupt countries in the world.[29] It is also difficult to square with the finding that no more than 5 per cent of people say that they personally have been asked to pay a bribe to receive a public service.[30] In their day-to-day dealings, people don't, on the whole, act as if they believe people working in the public sector are corrupt. People don't offer to make a cash payment to their MP in return for dealing with a constituency problem. They don't try to bribe a head teacher to get their child into a particular state school and they don't expect the police to charge them to investigate a crime.

It is also difficult to reconcile the idea that politicians are only in it for what they can get out of it with the fact that MPs' pay is not particularly high. MPs were, controversially, awarded a 10 per cent pay rise by the Independent Parliamentary Standards Authority in 2015 (and a further 1.4 per cent rise in late 2016) at a time when public sector pay increases were capped at 1 per cent. MPs are paid around two-thirds of the amount of a GP or secondary school head teacher and less than half of that of a typical local authority chief executive. Elected politicians in Australia, Italy, and the United States are paid around twice as much.[31] The expenses scandal cast MPs in the worst possible light. But a generous and, in the end, corrupt expenses culture had developed in Parliament in part because MPs were not willing to vote for a higher basic rate of pay and so, in a rather spineless fashion, decided to use expenses as an alternative source of income (whilst also making liberal use of taxpayer-subsidized bars within the Houses of Parliament).[32] They deserve our derision for the cowardly and dishonest way in which they behaved but the idea that MPs are riding a collective gravy train does not stack up.

What of campaign donations? These have provided another seemingly never-ending source of political scandal. Yet the first point to make here is that the sums of money at stake in British elections are quite small. Parties must declare individual donations of over £7,500 to the Electoral Commission. In the general election campaign between the 3 May and the 8 June 2017, the Conservatives received £12m in donations, Labour £4.5m, the Lib Dems £1.1m, UKIP £99,300 and the SNP £63,000.[33] This pales by comparison with the cost of US elections. The 2016 Congressional and Presidential elections in the United States consumed around $7bn.[34] How do we explain this difference?

I previously namechecked public choice theory as providing one of the intellectual foundations of neoliberalism.[35] Public choice theory starts from the assumption that people—whether they are politicians seeking elected office, regulators, or business executives—are consistently self-interested. As applied to the study of campaign finance, public choice theorists predict that businesses and other interest groups will donate money to political parties in return for policy favours and that this will be an efficient market in which price reflects the balance of demand and supply. How much companies donate will depend upon the value of the political rents they expect to receive. If they think that their preferred party is unlikely to win, they may be reluctant to invest too much. If they think that their preferred party is going to be unable to deliver much in the way of political favours if it is elected, they will also reduce their investment. But the general expectation within the literature on what gets called 'rent-seeking' is that the post-war growth in the public sector and regulation provides plenty of opportunities for governments to dispense policy favours (indeed, public choice theorists argue that this is precisely why governments have inflated the state and promoted new regulations).[36] Businesses don't just donate money to political parties because they get a warm glow from participating in the democratic process. In the United States, the level of campaign contributions suggests that businesses expect to benefit significantly from government largesse. The small size of the British rent-seeking industry suggests that firms have made a very different calculation.

The issue here is not simply the relatively small size of campaign donations. It is also their genesis. Only around a quarter of donations to the Conservative Party come from businesses (for Labour, it is, in most years, closer to 5–10 per cent).[37] The biggest donor by far is JCB Research, which donated £1.4m between 2010 and 2013. The mobile phone company Lycamobile and city investment group Flowidea have also made sizeable donations.[38] But the largest FTSE100 companies have generally avoided making donations to the political parties. In Britain, the size of campaign donations suggests that the policymaking process is not systematically corrupt. Business leaders may believe that campaign contributions can secure them access to a meeting with a senior minister. They may even believe that a donation will help their chances of a knighthood. But they do not seem to believe that they can be used to buy policy favours.

I can see a strong case for state funding of parties, combined with stricter limits on campaign expenditure. I can also see that, sooner or later, another major Grade 1 funding scandal is going to erupt. Political parties and campaign donations are, in the end, a combination which makes as much sense as cross-Channel swimming and heavy alcohol consumption. If a party needs money, somebody who is tasked with getting that money is eventually going to step over some ethical or legal line to get it. What I don't buy is the idea that the search for campaign donations has fundamentally corrupted the democratic process and that parties, when elected, spend the next few years paying off their campaign debts.

So, do we need a broader definition of corruption here? Many on the left will want to argue that the problem with Britain is not the number of things which are done that are illegal but the number of things which are done that are perfectly legal.[39] On this reading, corruption is about tax rules which allow wealthy individuals and corporations to store their money in offshore tax havens. Corruption is about a regulatory culture in the City of London which allows market traders to exploit information asymmetries to the advantage of their supposed clients. Corruption is about allowing wealthy business leaders to pay to sit next to a government minister at lunch and those ministers then being offered a position on the board of directors. Corruption is about giving knighthoods to business executives who sell arms and peerages to MPs who don't rock the boat.

One important point to make, however, is that a democratic reform agenda is possible. The political system as it stands is not so fundamentally corrupt that any efforts at reform are futile. Here I want to come back to a point that I made right at the start of the book. Miserabilism is dangerous because the left needs to convince itself and others that politics can work and that governments can and do sometimes change things for the better. If enough people genuinely come to believe that voting never changes anything and that all parties are the same, then, short of the revolution Russell Brand has called for, a lot of people are going to conclude that there is nothing to be gained by caring about what happens.[40] The left needs to strike a sometimes difficult balance between arguing that reforms to the current system are needed and that reform is possible within the current system.

It has been one of the recurring themes in this book that New Labour does not deserve the vitriol now routinely poured upon it. New Labour rolled forward the frontiers of the state. It oversaw a massive and, in many respects, successful programme of investment in the state health and education systems. It halted and in some cases reversed the growth in income inequality. It is also worth saying that New Labour showed that it is possible to reform and improve the democratic system. After several decades of political argument, New Labour established a Scottish Parliament and Welsh Assembly; it established a Human Rights Bill and a Supreme Court with the power to strike down primary legislation; it reformed the House of Lords (removing most of the hereditary peers); it created an elected mayor for London and for a handful of other cities; it reformed the system of party funding by establishing the Electoral Commission and banning anonymous donations; and it passed freedom of information legislation.

New Labour's record was—understatement alert—obviously imperfect. House of Lords reform was left incomplete. Freedom of information legislation was hedged in with exemptions and exceptions and was largely disowned by Tony Blair.[41] Donations to parties were regulated but soft loans to parties were left largely untouched.[42] Rupert Murdoch's position as someone who, at times, and according to the former media advisor Lance Price, 'seemed like the 24th member of the Cabinet' went largely unchallenged.[43] The Serious Fraud Office was ordered to abandon an inquiry into corrupt arms sales.[44] New Labour talked about using citizens' juries and other deliberative democratic forums to revitalize local democracy but largely failed to follow through.[45] New Labour's record was a messy one, with some steps forward and some steps back.

There is a pretty clear democratic reform agenda for any future left-of-centre government to modernize the British state. Top of my own to-do list here would be reform of the House of Lords (with peers being appointed to the upper house to correct for a shortfall in the representativeness of the House of Commons);[46] new freedom of information rules to prevent a catch-all blanket of commercial confidentiality being thrown over contracting-out arrangements; tighter controls on the jobs former ministers can take whilst also receiving a public pension; a review of and an explicit government statement of and limitations upon Royal prerogative powers which can be exercised by the Prime Minister independently of Parliament (think Article 50 and the High Court and Supreme Court judgment); an increase in the resources and powers given to select committees; state funding for parties; the publication of minutes of meetings between ministers and civil servants on the one hand and lobbyists and interest groups (including business) on the other (more on this in a moment); and, perhaps above all, a significant devolution of tax-raising and tax-spending powers to local and regional government. In the aftermath of the announcement, in March 2017, that the former Chancellor, George Osborne, had accepted an invitation to edit the *London Evening Standard* whilst still being an MP, a further overhaul of the rules relating to MPs extra-Parliamentary work would also seem entirely appropriate (Osborne, it should be noted, stepped-down as an MP in April 2017). This is a long but entirely plausible list. New Labour showed that political reforms can be messy and provoke strong opposition but also that they are entirely do-able.

V

What of the power of business more generally? Do we live in a post-democratic state in which the sound and fury of party politics signifies little and in which politics is really shaped in private by globalized business interests?[47] Jeremy Corbyn's one-time Head of Policy, Andrew Fisher, argues that 'over the last thirty-five years, politicians of all parties in government ceded power over fundamental sectors of our economy to a new oligarchy of corporations'.[48]

I know some perfectly sane and very clever people who interpret British politics as if it were a Bond movie in which, behind the scenes, an evil megalomaniac is pulling all the strings. I also know some people who view major corporations like Apple as harbingers of world peace and who think that Britain would be much better governed if we dispensed with elections and just appointed a bunch of business leaders with a proven track record of turning failed businesses around. It is not going to come as a great surprise to learn that I think that each of these positions leaves something to be desired.

Business often gets what it wants. Business has a great deal of what sometimes gets called instrumental power.[49] It can afford to invest significant funds not only in campaign contributions but in lobbying government and preparing briefing papers. It can afford to hire former ministers as consultants and can pay for the best corporate hospitality boxes at Wimbledon and Twickenham. In a capitalist system in which business leaders get to make decision about how much to invest and where, business also has a great deal of 'structural' power.[50] It can threaten—or even simply imply—that unless it gets what it wants by way of lower taxes and preferential regulation, it will cancel investment projects or move them to another country. Finally, businesses can benefit from an ideological climate in which policymakers and voters are sometimes predisposed to believe that what is good for business is good for Britain.

It is not hard to think of cases in which business has appeared to get what it wants from the political process. Prior to the 2008 crisis, the banks successfully lobbied for even lighter light-touch regulation.[51] The food and drinks industry has been credited with blocking stricter controls on the advertising of junk food.[52] Newspaper editors directly intervened in the post-Leveson debate about press regulation.[53] Businesses on both sides of the Atlantic have pressed for a Trade and Investment Partnership which includes provisions for an investor–state dispute settlement allowing businesses to sue governments in closed court hearings.[54]

It would, however, be a mistake to think that the power of business is a limitless and fixed part of the political firmament. Since 2010, the government has pursued the introduction of a living wage, reductions in immigration, and tougher bank regulation despite sustained opposition from business interests.[55] The government also persistently delayed making a final decision on the location of an additional runway in London despite howls of protest from business, before finally plumping for Heathrow in November 2016. In 2013, David Cameron pledged a referendum on British membership of the EU despite opposition from the business sector. During the referendum campaign itself, a clear majority of business leaders argued the case for staying. We know what happened next.[56] Once the referendum campaign had concluded and the new Prime Minister had confirmed that 'Brexit means Brexit', business leaders sought assurances about free trade. Some banks even threatened to leave the UK.[57] Yet, in a speech to the CBI in November 2016, Theresa May, whilst promising to redouble her efforts to secure a transitional trade deal to avoid a 'cliff-edge' Brexit, made it clear that she did not intend to delay triggering Brexit to appease business concerns. Indeed, it was only after the Conservtive's disastrous 2017 election result that business re-entered the Brexit battleground in a significant way.[58]

There are a significant number of limitations on the power of business. First, business is itself often divided about what it wants. The power of the National Farmers' Union is, for example, increasingly limited by the influence of large supermarket chains which have resisted calls for minimum prices on, for example, the price of milk.[59] Second, the power of business is limited by electoral considerations. Business exercises structural power in so far as higher investment means more growth and higher incomes, which tends to mean more votes for the incumbent party. But precisely because the government cares about votes, it also has good reason to avoid giving business what it wants when what it wants is unpopular with voters. The Confederation of British Industry and the Institute of Directors have, for example, consistently opposed tighter controls on immigration.[60] This has not, however, proven decisive in a political situation in which there is strong public opposition to high levels of net immigration. Third, and relatedly, the power of business is limited by prior political and sometimes moral convictions about the rights and wrongs of certain kinds of business activity. Governments may sometimes be predisposed to talk about UK PLC and to conflate the interests of British business with the public interest, but particular businesses can and do fall foul of politicians. The power of the tobacco industry is limited by a view that no matter how many jobs it creates, smoking destroys lives. In the aftermath of the financial crisis, banks have suddenly had to learn to operate in a political environment in which politicians have been outraged not only by the bank bail-outs but by the assorted scandals which have since engulfed the industry.[61] Although the regulatory landscape has only just started to move, the ability of firms like Google, Facebook, and Starbucks to minimize their tax liabilities through financial engineering is also increasingly viewed by ministers as being politically unpalatable, economically damaging, and morally unacceptable.[62]

Finally, the power of business is limited by the presence of dissenting voices within policy debates. I don't think that even those who buy the Bond-villain view of British politics believe that business leaders can simply tell politicians to do certain things because it will increase their profits. Business must argue that what it wants is in the public interest—that government should do something because it will create jobs or boost exports. Sceptics on the left may think that this is all quite hypocritical and that all business really cares about is the bottom line. But the pressure upon business to argue a public interest case is nevertheless important because it creates an opportunity for other groups to question some of the claims made by business leaders and to stake out alternative positions.

Those who want to argue that business is overly powerful argue that political debate does not take place on a level playing field. The journalist Greg Palast warns that 'when government gives special access to business interests, the rest of the public is left outside the door'.[63] This can indeed sometimes happen. In 2001, I was living in Exeter during the foot and mouth crisis which resulted in the closure of farmland and Dartmoor national park. One of the things which infuriated me at the time was the way in which the National Farmers' Union was allowed to argue the case for closing land and culling animals, whilst the tourist industry and the Ramblers' Association were largely ignored.[64]

It is, however, dangerous to generalize from a small number of cases. In 2010, the newly elected Coalition agreed to publish details of the meetings ministers (and some senior civil servants) had with outside individuals and organizations (along with details of ministerial visits and gifts). Along with two colleagues, Kate Dommett and Matt Wood, I have collected and started to code this material to assess differences in levels of access. The headline story is that business attended 45 per cent of the 6,300 recorded meetings between May 2010 and April 2015 held by either the Prime Minister, Deputy Prime Minister, or Secretaries of State across eighteen government departments. In the Treasury and the Department for Business Innovation and Skills, business was present at something like 60 per cent of meetings. By comparison, representatives from charities attended around 14 per cent of meetings, whilst trade unions were present at around 5 per cent of meetings. This suggests that whilst government meets with and listens to a range of different kinds of organizations, business has by far the loudest and most frequently heard voice.

In some policy debates, business has too much influence. I think that when it comes to understanding the likely practical impacts of a proposed piece of legislation, government departments are far too ready to acquiesce to business concerns. I also think that the whole world of business lobbying is unnecessarily opaque. Too much business influence is exercised in closed networks out of sight of the media and voters.[65] Requiring ministers to list meetings that they have had with outside interests is a step forward but it is not enough. Meetings between ministers and those seeking to influence them ought to be recorded and those recordings eventually made public. But to argue that business invariably gets what it wants and that, behind the scenes, politics is really shaped by business interests is a significant exaggeration. Business has power but that power is limited.

VI

In the fourth chapter, I argued that whilst the state has in some respects been rolled back, it has, in other ways, been rolled forward. The last few decades have seen the rise and rise of the 'regulatory state' and, with this, the creation of a range of new regulatory bodies which operate at arm's length from the government, like the Monetary Policy Committee and Financial Policy Committee within the Bank of England, the Food Standards Agency, the Charity Commission, and the Human Fertilisation and Embryology Authority. This has prompted Frank Vibert to talk about the Orwellian-like *Rise of the*

Unelected.[66] It is easy to exaggerate the extent to which these bodies are truly independent of party politics. Ministers retain a power to appoint the chair and sometimes board members of these bodies and they often appoint supporters of their own party.[67] It is also important to note that the mandates and powers of these bodies are set (and can be revised) by politicians and that they must account for their actions to ministers and to Parliament. OFSTED is meant to operate independently of the Department for Education and Skills but its former head, Sir David Bell, has nevertheless gone on record to complain that efforts to reform schools are being undermined by 'ridiculous' political interference driven by 'ministerial whims'.[68] In many cases, these quangos (as they are often known) only have the authority to make recommendations, which ministers must then decide whether to follow. At the same time, the quango-ization of British politics has resulted in a kind of 'depoliticization' of decision-making, in so far as these bodies operate independently of the fray of day-to-day politics.[69]

David Harvey argues that the establishment of an ever-larger number of quangos is an essential part of the neoliberal programme of neutering democracy.[70] Neoliberalism's first preference is to put the policymaking process beyond the reach of the ballot box by privatizing parts of the state apparatus. Where this is not possible, Harvey argues that the creation of quangos is an attractive democracy-busting second-best. An alternative explanation for the growth of quangos is that they offer a useful form of blame-insulation for politicians.[71] Politics takes place in a low-trust but high-blame environment in which successes are rarely acknowledged but failures and controversies are amplified. Politicians realize that their decisions are going to be criticized come what may. So, they try to offload responsibility for taking those decisions on to an independent body (who, in turn, they may be able to blame when things go wrong).

A third and slightly more heart-warming explanation of the rise of the quangos is that politicians have come to recognize that they cannot and should not be trusted to make decisions where there is a conflict of interest between their own party's short-term electoral interest and the public interest. Here, we are, once again, back on the terrain of public choice theory. In the 1970s, economists discerned what they called a 'political business cycle' in democracies. The basic idea of Keynesian economics is that governments ought to intervene to pump-prime the economy when a recession is looming and calm things down by raising taxes or interest rates when a boom is getting out of control. What public choice theorists argued was that regardless of the actual state of the economy, elected politicians were cutting interest rates and taxes and increasing government expenditure in the run-up to an election to maximize their chances of re-election.[72] Any tough decisions were being postponed and the end result of all of this was steadily accelerating inflation and lower growth.

The answer to this problem, public choice theorists went on to argue, was to hand over responsibility for setting interest rates to an independent central bank free from the pressures of day-to-day politics. This was, of course, precisely the justification given by New Labour for making the Bank of England independent in 1997. Governments have since used similar arguments when establishing bodies like the Office for Budget Responsibility (which provides independent economic forecasts), the Office for National Statistics, the Infrastructure Commission, and the Committee on Climate Change (which advises government on the carbon reductions needed to meet its overall targets of reducing greenhouse gas emissions).

The creation of independent bodies might, then, be viewed as part of an effort by politicians to shore up faith in the political process. My colleague Colin Hay argues that, regardless of whether that was the intention, the creation of so many new unelected bodies has had the very opposite effect.[73] By handing over their powers to unelected technocrats, politicians have simply sent a signal to voters that they cannot be trusted and that they will, if given the opportunity, take decisions to further their own party political interests. Furthermore, the net effect of handing over powers in this way is, he argues, to narrow the reach of democratic decision-making, which risks convincing ever more people that voting does not make any difference.[74] Whilst depoliticization was meant to restore faith in democracy and politics, it has, for these reasons, had the very opposite effect. Similarly, William Davies argues that the rise of technocratic bodies like the Financial Policy Committee and the Office for Budget Responsibility, in whose organizational DNA are imprinted neoliberal assumptions about the value of competition and the overriding importance of efficiency, has hollowed out democratic debate and made it extremely difficult to carve out alternative political positions.[75]

This is an ingenious argument but I don't find it entirely convincing. Assume that politicians had not delegated their powers to a set of semi-autonomous bodies. How would this have been interpreted by voters? I suspect that it would have been construed as a sure sign that politicians cannot be trusted and that policymaking was being gamed for partisan advantage. In other words, politicians cannot win. Now, in the case of the political business cycle, the evidence that elected politicians really did systematically make interest-rate and tax cuts to maximize their chances of re-election is decidedly mixed.[76] But it would be quite heroic to claim that politicians never take policy decisions with one eye on their own electoral interests. At the very height of his *Strictly* fame, the former Shadow Chancellor, Ed Balls, published an academic paper arguing that the body responsible for monitoring and limiting systemic risk in the financial system (since 2011, the Financial Policy Committee within the Bank of England) ought to be chaired by a government minister with the power to set the agenda and veto proposals. I may well have missed something here but I don't remember politicians from either party exactly covering themselves in glory when it came to anticipating and managing down the kinds of systemic risk which led to the 2007/8 financial crisis. Indeed, in June 2006, the then Economic Secretary to the Treasury, Ed Balls, told an audience of bankers that 'we must keep the UK's regulatory system at the cutting-edge—the best in the world . . . at all times we will apply a principled system of risk-regulation, without unnecessary administrative burden'.[77] Arguments of this sort are corrosive of public support for politicians and democracy. Hay argues that the medicine of depoliticization has significant and unfortunate side-effects. Nevertheless, my sense is that, in this situation, the costs of doing nothing would have been higher. Far from seeing a proliferation in the numbers of quangos as part of an effort to neuter democracy, they may be an attempt—however imperfect—to protect it. Nearly 40 per cent of people agree that 'Britain would be better governed if our politicians got out of the way, and instead our ministers were non-political experts who knew how to run large organisations'.[78] In this environment, handing over some powers to independent bodies so as to forestall a further erosion of support for politicians and democracy might be the lesser of two evils.

Has the rise of technocratic quangos hollowed out political debate? I am not sure. It is true, as Davies argues, that these bodies often operate with a particular and economistic view of the world. But I do not recognize his argument that the rise of these kind of organizations is associated with a hollowing out of political debate. There has, in recent years, been a sometimes vigorous political debate about quantitative easing and financial stability, food standards, fertility treatment, and infrastructure investment, even though these are policy areas in which policy decisions have been devolved to technocratic bodies. It is also worth remembering, in this context, that the Office for Budget Responsibility—which was once derided as the

Chancellor's 'poodle'—emerged as a trenchant critic of the Coalition's austerity policies (p. 91).[79]

VII

I have so far spent most of my time here looking at some of the specifics of the British democratic system. I want to finish, however, by talking about politics as an activity.

The three-minute trailer for *Politics: The Movie* would look pretty impressive: the collective setting of inspiring goals; exposing corruption; safeguarding people's lives through the provision of new opportunities and the extension of legal safeguards; all interspersed with cut-away shots of Nelson Mandela walking to freedom and Nye Bevan talking about the creation of the NHS. At the very start of the book, I said that our understanding of history shapes how we think about who we are. Politics is the activity through which we collectively talk and decide about who we want to be.[80]

The reality of day-to-day politics is of course a lot less lovely: car crash television interviews which make you to want shout out loud; tactical alliances with lifelong enemies; petty arguments and long-running feuds. Politics involves numerous dead ends and retreats punctuated by only occasional moments of progress and achievement. Politics is, as I have already quoted Max Weber as saying right at the start of the book, 'the slow boring of hard boards'. It takes time and is not always very pleasant to do. No wonder parties and politicians are held in such contempt. The yawning chasm between what we hope politics can be about and what it actually involves should not, however, be taken as conclusive evidence that the political system is not working; that the wrong kind of politicians are being elected; or that we have the wrong kind of voting system or the wrong kind of Parliament and that there is an alternative kind of 'new politics' out there just waiting to be grasped, in which all the things that we don't like about politics will disappear and all we will be left with is the good stuff.[81] There may well be good reasons to vote for different kinds of politicians and for changing the way we go about taking decisions, but the gap between what we expect of politics and what it is capable of delivering is not going to disappear because it is an unavoidable part of what it means to live in a democratic country in which people disagree about who we are and what we ought to be doing and in which, as a result, making decisions that everyone can live with is going to involve messy compromises, trade-offs, and disappointments.[82] I think in this respect the former Home Secretary, David Blunkett, who is now Professor of Politics at the University of Sheffield, has it about right:

> [To] adhere to the belief that there is some day zero, in which a magic wand is waved, the ills of the world are abolished and an individual government within one parliament sets right the inequities of history [may be tempting]... but understanding the nature of compromise, making progress through the morass of contradictions of both human frailty and public bureaucracy, is an essential feature of ensuring that those crucial differences can be made.[83]

Think back to one of the great achievements of British politics in recent decades: the Northern Ireland peace process. The search for a political solution to what had become a military stalemate began in the mid-1980s when, in the face of ferocious opposition from the Unionist parties, Margaret Thatcher and the Irish Taoiseach Garrett Fitzgerald negotiated the Anglo-Irish Agreement. The political process gained momentum with the Downing Street Declaration in 1993, which asserted the right of the people of Ireland to self-determination and confirmed that Northern Ireland would be returned to the Republic of Ireland if a majority of its people so wished. The Downing Street Declaration led to an IRA ceasefire and then, through various twists and turns, to the 1998 Good Friday Agreement and the establishment of a power-sharing executive.

The peace process involved an endless series of compromises, setbacks, and accusations of betrayal. The decision to negotiate with the IRA via Sinn Féin was a hugely controversial one which ran against the wishes of the Conservative Party and public opinion. The Unionist parties—with some justification—repeatedly accused the government of ignoring clear violations of the ceasefire by the IRA. During the negotiation of the Good Friday Agreement, Blair gave certain assurances to Sinn Féin about the release of terrorists and a *de facto* amnesty which were not made public for fear of prompting a walk-out by the Unionists.[84] Since the official end of the Troubles, there have been numerous terrorist attacks in Northern Ireland, whilst the power-sharing executive has been suspended and come close to collapse on several occasions. More than a decade on, most schools in Northern Ireland and most of the political parties are still separated along denominational lines and Brexit poses an acute challenge in a political environment in which the status of the border between Northern Ireland and the Republic is so important.

Yet, whatever the obvious shortfalls, Northern Ireland has come a long way. The basic principle of power-sharing has been accepted by all of the mainstream parties in a way that would once have been unthinkable. The IRA and the major loyalist terrorist groups have disbanded and disarmed.[85] The Protestant-dominated Royal Ulster Constabulary has been replaced by the non-sectarian Police Service of Northern Ireland. After the deaths of over three and a half thousand people between 1969 and 2000, Northern Ireland is now largely peaceful. The jaw-jaw of politics is indeed better than war-war.

There are some good news stories when it comes to public attitudes toward the political system. People basically support the idea of democracy. 66 per cent of people think that everyone has a duty to vote (up from 56 per cent in 2008). 36 per cent of people say that they have a great deal or quite a lot of interest in politics (up from 30 per cent in 1997). A further 33 per cent say that they have some interest in politics.[86] The number of people who think that 'people like me don't have any say about what the government does' has fallen from 71 per cent in 1986 to just 44 per cent in 2014.[87] Membership of political parties has risen from a low of 0.8 per cent of people in 2013 to 1.6 per cent in 2016.[88] People are also more likely than they once were to go on a march, write to their MP, or attend the meetings of a campaign group.[89] Putting to one side some of the bile about immigration and the misty-eyed nostalgia for Britain's great days as a world power, the EU referendum also showed that many people care deeply about democracy. One of the problems with the European Union is that it suffers from a clear 'democratic deficit' in which policies emerge from a sausage factory of consultations and negotiations between the European Council, the European Commission, the European Parliament, and a set of other interested parties.[90] Nick Clegg—no Brexiteer he—is quite clear about the limitations of European-level democracy, describing it as a 'fearfully opaque arrangement' in which 'national administrative elites congregate and take decisions well beyond the reach of their domestic constituencies'.[91] In the end, the best argument for staying in Europe was that in a world of interdependencies and complex trade-offs, remaining was better than throwing the dice and hoping that free-trade deals would materialize at a time when the rest of the world shows every sign of turning away from free trade. As it happens, I think that this argument is a pretty good one. Politics is, as

I have argued, always about muddling through. As the French philosopher Raymond Aron put it, within a democratic system, the choice is never between good and evil, it is always between the preferable and the detestable.[92] Yet it is not hard to see why it was so difficult to rally the electorate around this particular standard when the alternative was an argument about taking back democratic control.

British democracy may have won the beauty contest with European Union democracy but this is setting the bar pretty low. There is no getting away from the basic fact here that many people—perhaps most people—think that British politicians can't be trusted, that politics is a pointless and grubby business, and that general elections don't change anything. The fact that so many people are convinced that parties are all the same, do not keep their promises, and are in the pockets of big business and that politicians are only in it for what they can get out of it is deeply troubling. It is also, I have argued, mistaken. Why do so many people get it so wrong? The print media is culpable for assuming the worst possible interpretation of the motives for any decision and for presenting any policy failures as being entirely predictable and avoidable. Politicians dig their own graves when they exaggerate the failings of their opponents and suggest that long-standing problems could easily be resolved if only they rather than their venal and incompetent rivals were in power. But I also think we get it wrong in so far as we think that politics is something that would be easy to do if only it were possible to get rid of the politicians.

VIII

A lot of people will recall Winston Churchill's famous dictum that democracy is the worst form of government except for all of those other forms that have been tried from time to time. In Britain, there is a great deal of criticism of politicians and of elections. But there is little if any appetite for any alternative to representative democracy. The question, in Britain at least, is not whether democracy itself is a good or bad thing but whether our particular democratic arrangements are good or bad and how they might be improved upon. I certainly think that our democracy can and should be reformed. Yet, at the same time, I think that a lot of the criticisms of our electoral system which have acquired the status of conventional wisdom are misplaced or exaggerated and that this is bad for the left and the cause of

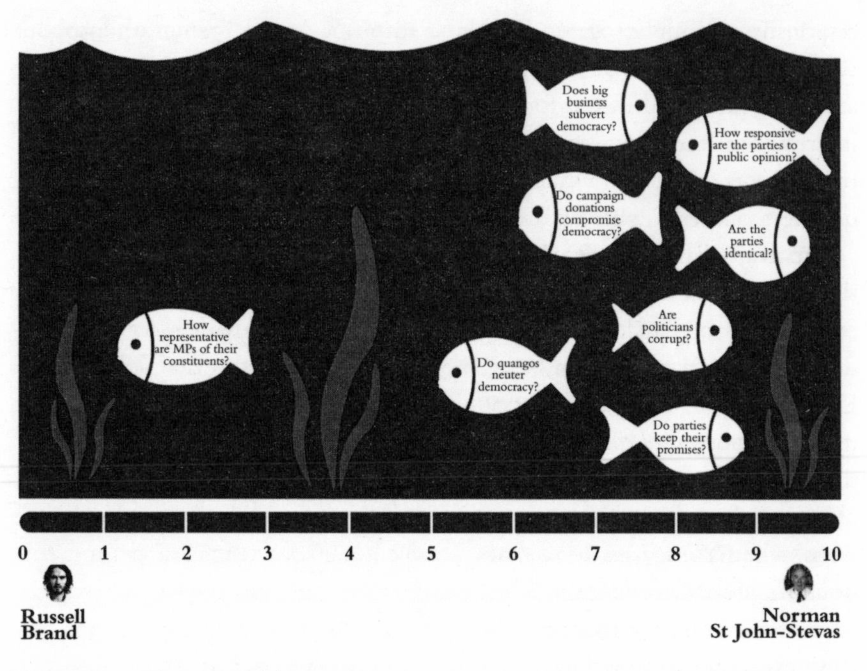

Figure 8.2. The state of democracy.

social democracy because it sustains a conviction that nothing changes and that nothing can change. So, for one last time, and to summarize the arguments in this chapter, I want to use a simple scale in Figure 8.2, running from nought to ten, to assess the health of British democracy. On the one side of this scale, in terms of the positions they espouse about the democratic status quo, we can put Russell Brand, looking devilishly handsome and telling anyone who will listen that 'governments are corrupt and the opposition parties pointlessly similar'.[93] At the other end, we can put the kind of old-school Conservative like the late Norman St John-Stevas, who used to regularly appear on Radio 4 to argue that even thinking about changing even one part of the glorious British democratic system was not only entirely unnecessary but sure to end with a rerun of the French Revolution.

The lack of representativeness of MPs is a self-evident failing of our democracy. It is also one that the major political parties could, if they wanted, fix quite quickly. Are the parties identical? Up to a point, they are similar. That is what we would expect in a democratic system in which party leaders have a strong incentive to go looking for votes. But the parties are not identical. Quite how similar and different they are varies over time. Are the parties responsive to public opinion? The answer to this question depends on whether we look at MPs as a whole or MPs in the governing party. If we are more interested in the former, the answer is not really. If we are more interested in the latter, the answer is yes. Do parties keep their promises once they are elected? I would really like to see a more detailed study of this question, but from what we know, the answer to this question is a clear yes.

Are politicians corrupt? Well, it depends on what you mean by corruption. But the view that politicians are simply in it for what they can get out of it is horribly wide of the mark. Do campaign donations compromise democracy? Up to a point but to nothing like the same extent as in the United States. There is a perception in Britain that politicians are corrupt and use the opportunity of elected office to feather their own nest. I don't think that this perception is accurate but this is an area in which the democratic chain is only as strong as its weakest link. The fact that there have been occasions when campaign donations do appear to have been bartered for honours means that there is a problem which needs fixing either through more state funding or more regulation. Is big business a threat to democracy? Business is one voice influencing policy decisions and I know that some on the left consider this to be in and of itself a bad thing. I don't think it is plausible, however, to argue that business routinely gets what it wants from the political process. Are quangos bad for democracy? In an ideal world, I would want elected politicians to make all the key decisions and to only ever make them for the right reasons. Given that we don't live in that world, I see them as an imperfect solution to a difficult problem. This is pretty much what we might also say about democracy itself.

9

Conclusion

I

At the end of the first chapter, I said, somewhat indulgently, that I was writing this book to settle an argument in my head about the state of British politics. One way of describing that argument is as a set of questions. How far down a neoliberal road has Britain travelled in recent decades? Was New Labour an alternative expression of or an alternative to neoliberalism and Thatcherism? Has the centre of public opinion shifted to the right? How far have the frontiers of the post-war state been rolled back? Have public services been run down and privatized? In what ways and to what extent has Britain become a massively unequal society? Has austerity been used as a tool of political warfare to further punish the poor and most vulnerable? Does voting make a difference? Is Corbynism a welcome antidote to political timidity? Sitting behind these questions is a slightly more personal question which I also alluded to in the first chapter. Does the fact that I consider these questions worth asking simply show that my own once left-of-centre politics have changed and that I have become a Radio 2-listening and slipper-wearing Tory who no longer feels a sense of outrage at self-evident social injustices?

One thing I have come to realize is that challenging a one-sided and selective miserabilist viewpoint creates a new problem: that of pulling too far in the other direction and constructing an equally one-sided Panglossian alternative reality in which the glass is not simply half-full but perfectly full. In Voltaire's novel *Candide*, Professor Pangloss was the Royal educator who was the greatest philosopher of his age and mentor to Candide: the illegitimate son of the sister of the local Baron. At the start of the novel, Candide is living a sheltered life and being taught by Professor Pangloss a philosophy of Leibnizian optimism. As the novel progresses, Candide is cast out into the world and experiences a painful sense of disillusionment as he and those around him endure a set of ever greater hardships. As a result, Candide comes to reject his former mentor's view that 'all is for the best' in this, the 'best possible of all worlds'.

So, it is probably worth saying, just for the record, that I don't think that all is for the best in Britain or that Britain is the best of all possible worlds. Looking back at the previous chapters, I have documented a series of policy failures and challenges which ought to try the sunny optimism of any Panglossians. Housing is an absolute mess which fuels inequality and drives poverty. There has been a dizzying rise in wealth inequality and a startling rise in the absolute gap between the income of the richest and poorest households. Social mobility in Britain has always been poor and is not getting any better. Our elected representatives are, when judged in terms of their social background, completely unrepresentative. Public health and education expenditure rose in the 2000s and will need to rise further in the future but has been left in a holding pattern for the last half-decade. Mortality rates from a range of diseases are still much higher in Britain than they are in most of the rest of Europe. Homelessness has grown significantly since 2010. Business investment and productivity are laughably low. There are other issues—the fracturing of mental health services, health inequality, a backlash of hate-filled misogyny on the internet and beyond—which I could add to this list. And then on top of all of this, as of June 2016, is the European referendum result: a spectacular political earthquake which has revealed a country that is crossly and painfully divided by age, geographic location, and income.

Yet despite all of this, I think the left's miserabilist account of Britain, in which we are going (or have probably already gone) to hell in a handcart, is not simply an exaggeration but simply wrong.

Long lists can make for uncomfortable reading, but to look back at some of the previous arguments: public opinion has not shifted dramatically to the right; indeed, on many issues it is positively left-wing. The frontiers of the state have not been rolled back and the state itself has not been re-engineered to meet nefarious neoliberal demand for ever more police, prisons, and a stronger army. Public spending increases have ground to a halt but spending has not been slashed and burned. Between 2000/1 and 2009/10, public sector current expenditure measured in real (inflation-adjusted) terms at 2016/17 prices rose from £477bn to £680bn (a 42 per cent increase). Between 2009/10 and 2016/17, real public sector current expenditure rose from £680bn to £691bn (a 1.6 per cent increase). Health and education funding increased dramatically in the 2000s and this investment paid off. The health service has not been privatized. Judged in terms of the difference between the richest and poorest 10 per cent of households, market income inequality is now 22 per cent *lower* than it was in 1979 and 45 per cent lower than it was in 1999. Final income inequality has been stable since the mid-1990s. The costs of austerity have not been loaded on to the poorest and most vulnerable households. By 2015/16, the real weekly income of the poorest 5 per cent of households was 110 per cent of the level it had been in 2007/8. The income of the richest 5 per cent of households was, in real terms, the same as it had been in 2007/8. Voting does make a difference (the 2016 EU referendum and the 2017 general election each showed just what a difference a 2 per cent difference can make). Political parties are responsive to changes in public opinion and they do, by and large, keep their manifesto promises.

In the summer of 1992, I wrote my postgraduate thesis on the political significance of Britain joining the Exchange Rate Mechanism. I can't remember the details of the argument but I do remember arguing that joining the ERM constituted a fundamental and irrevocable turning point in the conduct of British politics and economic policymaking. I went on holiday and one week later (and before the thesis had been assessed) Britain had been ejected from the ERM. One lesson here is that Europe has been a fault line in British politics for a long time. A second lesson is that things can change quickly in politics. A final lesson is that I am not very good at predictions (and neither, as a rule, are very many political scientists[1]). By the time this book has been published, Theresa May may or may not have been invited to step aside by the rest of the Cabinet; the terms of the United Kingdom's withdrawal from the EU may be a little bit clearer; Northern Ireland's peace process may be in tatters; Jeremy Corbyn's political momentum may have dissipated; the SNP may be back to seeking a second referendum; and President Trump may or may not have started a nuclear war to avenge an insult on Twitter. But right now, and nearly thirty years after Margaret Thatcher was first elected, Britain is a long way from looking like an exemplar of neoliberalism.

Neoliberal ideas are a long way from being anything approaching 'hegemonic'. For neoliberalism to really qualify as hegemonic it would have to be the case that ideas about the virtues of markets and the inequities of government are considered such obvious common sense that they are effectively beyond dispute and so are not disputed. Yet, all the time, neoliberal ideas are being relentlessly disputed not only by socialists but by one-nation conservatives, liberals, social democrats, statists, nationalists, libertarians, feminists, socialists, environmentalists, and sundry others. Just try typing 'what's wrong with neoliberalism' into Google. As things stand, the philosophy and ideals of neoliberalism have been repudiated by every single leader of a British political party, including Theresa May. I have heard it argued that neoliberalism exercises an intellectual dominance in so far as it is the ideology about which every ideology must have something to say. There is, perhaps, something to this. The intellectual left has certainly devoted huge amounts of time and effort to knocking down often paper-thin caricatures of neoliberal arguments. But this would seem to say more about the flight from reality on the intellectual left than it does about what is actually happening in Britain. People don't simply spend a lot of time talking about neoliberalism on the left: they probably spend too much time talking about neoliberalism (and I'm aware of the irony in saying this).

There is a fallback position here. This is to argue that no matter what political leaders might say and no matter what intellectual hits it has taken, neoliberalism has nevertheless been remorselessly rolled forward. Neoliberalism is like the T-1000 at the end of *Terminator 2*: it just keeps going of its own accord. I do not want to be thought to be claiming, in response to this argument, that neoliberalism is a fairy tale invented by parents to scare their children. The imprint of neoliberal ideas can clearly be discerned in privatization, the creation of internal markets within public services, contracting out, deregulation, and the creation of new markets in, for example, carbon emissions. Yet Britain falls far short of being a neoliberal policy dystopia. For if neoliberal ideas and arguments have proven influential in some policy contexts, on other occasions they have been ignored, abandoned, or marginalized in day-to-day policy practice. The Conservatives have spoken about the moral and economic imperative of cutting public debt. Yet debt has grown. They have spoken about the need to trim costs to compete in global markets. Yet they have introduced a living wage. They have attacked welfare claimants and introduced a welfare cap but have 'triple-locked' the state pension. Above all, and since 2010, the Conservatives have pursued the distinctly non-neoliberal policy of seeking to restrict immigration. It is not enough here to simply say in reply that neoliberalism is a utopian project and that, in practice, it was always going to fall short and that what really counts is our overall direction of travel. It is not enough because such an argument actually assumes precisely what I think ought to be at stake: whether there *has* been a significant shift in a neoliberal direction. I am not sure that there has.

II

If, as I have argued, left miserabilism is wrong, why is it so pervasive? Why do so many people on the left think that everything which could have gone wrong has gone wrong (and in contra-Panglossian fashion believe that anything that looks like a potential good news story is almost certainly going to turn out to be a neoliberal disaster)? Why does Jeremy Corbyn's argument that New Labour was an unmitigated disaster attract so much support within the Labour Party? Why did so many natural Labour supporters vote to leave the EU in June 2016 as a howl of protest against the political status quo? I don't have any single answer to this question but I do want to make a number of observations.

At the risk of turning my back upon some of the arguments in the previous chapter, I think there is undoubtedly something in the nature of political campaigning and party politics which fuels disillusionment with politics and the state of the country. Political parties may, on the whole, be quite good at delivering upon their manifesto promises but politicians are also pretty good at raising public expectations of what they can do once elected and, simultaneously, at portraying their opponents as hopeless know-nothings who are pushing the country closer to its eventual and certain destruction. Politics is all about trade-offs and compromises. But political campaigning is all about telling voters that they can have their cake and eat it: that it is possible to cut taxes without cutting public expenditure (after all, there is always a steady supply of waste and inefficiency to take the slack); that it is possible to cut welfare expenditure dramatically and punish 'scroungers' without also hurting hard-working families; and that it is possible to leave the European Union and cut migration whilst getting access to the single market on the same terms as other countries. Companies have to answer to the Advertising Standards Authority for the claims that they make when advertising their wares or denigrating their rivals. Politicians may, in the longer term, pay a heavy price if they raise expectations which they cannot then deliver upon. But a week is, as we all know, a long time in politics.

Second, I think that miserabilism on the left tells us a great deal about the way in which New Labour ended. It is of course the case that—as Enoch

Powell observed and as David Cameron reportedly said at the moment he learnt of the EU referendum result—all political careers end in failure.[2] But some end as greater failures than others. When he assumed office in 2008, Gordon Brown not only dropped the New Labour label but set about actively trashing Tony Blair's record as leader. Today, Tony Blair is remembered as the Prime Minister who promised that things could only get better but who lied about weapons of mass destruction; refused to apologize for the botched invasion of Iraq; and deregulated the City of London. I am not going to argue that New Labour is deeply misunderstood or that the invasion of Iraq will one day be judged as a great military and strategic success story. But I do think it is unfortunate that New Labour's legacy—which includes significant public expenditure increases, the introduction of tax credits, a minimum wage, devolution, and freedom of information—has been reduced to its foreign policy failures and the 2007/8 financial crisis.

Third, and whilst recognizing that this is a soft target, political miserabilism is also hardened by those parts of the press and print media which have decided that the best way to cope with the demands of a 24-hour news cycle and falling circulation is to turn any drama into a crisis and any mistakes into sure-fire evidence of incompetence and dishonesty. Journalists (like academics) are in the great position of writing about the obvious and heinous mistakes others have made without, by and large, having any experience of having to make policy decisions which involve difficult trade-offs and a great deal of uncertainty. The British tradition of political satire—which, in the television age, runs from *That Was the Week That Was* and *The Frost Report* through to *Yes Minister*, *Spitting Image*, *Saturday Live*, *Bremner and Fortune*, *The Thick of It*, and *Charlie Brooker's Screen Wipe*—also bolsters a view that politicians are dim, shallow, self-serving, and cowardly.[3]

Politics is an expressive form of human activity. It gives us the opportunity to think about who we are and what we want to be and how we want other people to view us. In the 1980s, being on the left and hating Margaret Thatcher came as part of a package with listening to certain kinds of music, going to certain pubs, and dressing in a certain way. This has not changed. Today, drinking Fair Trade coffee, deploring the Brexit referendum result, and pronouncing Tony Blair to be a war criminal are not simply political positions but social signals that you belong within a certain kind of group. I don't want to sound too snide here. Social signalling is something we all do. Saying that you don't believe in social workers and bemoaning welfare scroungers is another equally performative way of asserting your social identity.

The fact that we use our political identities to carve out a social space in which we feel we belong is, however, politically costly in so far as it means that people often find themselves talking to people who they basically already agree with, reducing political debate to an echo chamber. Enclave politics is dangerous because it can leave people who are on the left out of touch with what many other people are thinking. I also think it is dangerous in so far as it can trap people who are on the left into a rhetorical arms race in which, when you are discussing politics with other people who are also on the left, seeing two sides of the story or saying that a Tory minister may be trying (however ineffectively) to do the right thing is socially risky because it risks being interpreted as a sign of political naivety or even bad faith. Miserabilism can become a reflexive habit on the left because it is a safe social bet when the alternative is saying things which your peers may view as, at best, hopelessly naive or, at worst, showing that, deep down, you are a Tory.

III

What are the implications of my argument for British politics as things stand?

One thing I want to say is that whilst I have spent a great deal of time in this book criticizing the way the left often thinks, I am in no doubt about the continuing relevance of the left. In the opening chapter, I argued that the left can be distinguished in part in terms of its resolutely miserabilist outlook. In the third chapter, however, I defined the left, more conventionally, in terms of a set of policies and values: including, first and foremost, a commitment to using government to correct and control the outcome of market forces. These definitions are not exclusive of each other. The latter is, however, the more enduring of the two and this matters because I don't think that the problems I have spoken about in this book (problems which, by and large, many Conservative politicians also accept are a problem) can be resolved via the invisible hand of the market. The housing crisis, low levels of productivity and investment, and the social unrepresentativeness of MPs are all things that we can fix but fixing them is going to require the involvement of government. This does not mean that we need mass nationalization and profit controls. In the case of housing, for example, central government needs to take the lead in allowing local government to borrow against its considerable assets to fund house-building. But this does not mean that housing associations or private developers can or should be excluded. The key here is that housing needs to be re-established as a 'managed market' in which government gets to set the rules of the game.

The good news here is that the left in Britain remains an important political force. It is true that the Labour Party's traditional strongholds in the post-industrial North are shrinking. It is also true that no matter what happened during the 2017 election, the Labour Party is in an effective state of civil war. Finally, and stating the obvious, it is also true that Labour has lost the last three general elections. In 2017 Labour secured 10 per cent more of the vote than it had managed in 2015. But it is also worth remembering that Labour only secured four more seats than it had managed in 2010. But there is another side to this coin. Labour lost four successive elections in the 1980s and 1990s before going on to comfortably win the next three general elections. Far from being a political community of zealous free-market neoliberals, Britain is still a country in which there is broad support for the basic notion that government has a responsibility to look after its citizens by providing things like health care and housing and reducing inequality. The fact that so many people no longer identify with any particular party and so are much more willing than they once were to switch their vote means that the decline in Labour's traditional bases of support does not necessarily mean that the party is doomed to a slow and painful political death.[4] Furthermore, with the link between class and voting having loosened further, Labour is now routinely able to appeal to swathes of middle-class voters. In 2017 Labour increased its share of ABC1 voters by 12 points compared with 2015 (the Conservatives, that said, also increased their share of C2DE voters by the same amount).

The 'New' Labour brand is dead. But this does not mean that there is no future for a left-of-centre party which, whilst accepting parts of the political status quo and, up to a point, accommodating itself to the views of the electorate, is nevertheless able to offer innovative policy solutions premised upon a more active role for government in correcting market failures. The former Labour MP turned academic David Marquand used to write about the 'progressive dilemma' in British politics. The left, he argued, was at its strongest when Labour and Liberals worked together. The tragedy not just of the 1980s but of post-1914 politics in general was, he argued, that these two progressive forces have, by and large, failed to work together, allowing the Conservatives to cling to power on a minority of the vote.[5] The logic of the progressive dilemma still holds. Nowadays, however, the issue is not simply one of making the case for either formal or informal cooperation between Labour and the Liberal Democrats. It is also about forging coalitions with the SNP, the Greens, and disaffected parts of the Conservative Party and reaching-out to centre-ground voters who struggled to support any party in 2017.

One of the key arguments in the last chapter was that compromise is an inevitable and attractive feature of politics as it is of human relationships in general. Compromise means, however, that a certain level of disappointment and frustration with the results of the political process is inevitable. The baseline for judging whether a miserabilist stance is warranted is not whether you get everything you want from the political process but whether you get some of the things you want and can at least live with the bits that you do not. Compromise does not mean selling out and achieving nothing. Indeed, I would argue that, whatever its record on Iraq and whatever part its promotion of a culture of light-touch regulation may have played in planting the seeds of the financial crisis, New Labour showed that it is possible, from a left-of-centre position, to compromise on a great deal whilst also achieving a great deal. In the future, Labour is going to have to not only strike compromise positions within the party but between the parties and between the party and the electorate.

All of this is going to take policy ideas. The left is going to have to demonstrate that it has new things to say about how the state can and should intervene to fix problems in the housing market; with productivity; with low investment; with stretched public services in areas of high immigration; with social care; wealth inequality; and in our democratic system. It is then going to need great dollops of 'statecraft' to sell those policies to the electorate and forge cross-party coalitions to refine and implement them.[6] At the heart of a part of the modern campaigning left lies a faith in a form of 'horizontal' politics which rejects the state and other formal institutions because it believes that they lead, inevitably, to domination and an abuse of power. In its place, the campaigning left privileges society as a place of protest and resistance. This is a form of politics which celebrates the local, the spontaneous, and the participatory and lives in fear of being co-opted and having to make tangible policy demands.[7] Yet it is by achieving power and passing laws and regulations that the world gets changed. I am conscious in saying this that I have not, by and large, offered much in the way of concrete policy suggestions in this book. In my defence, what I can say is that I wanted to use this book to show that all is not lost for the left and that neoliberalism has not swept all before it, and to then use my next book to, very specifically, pull together an agenda for a new left.

What of Corbynism? Right up until 9.59 pm on the 8th of June, it still appeared likely that Labour would crash and burn. At the start of the election campaign, Corbyn's personal ratings were awful. The party had done dreadfully in local elections a month before and was trailing badly in the opinion polls. The election campaign changed everything and it is no longer credible to argue that Corbyn is simply and obviously unelectable. In 2017, Labour mobilized young voters, increased its share of the vote by 10 per cent and gained a majority of the vote of those in work. In the aftermath of the election, John McDonnell suggested that, if the campaign had lasted another week, Labour would have won. At a rally in Bournemouth, in July 2017, Corbyn felt sufficiently confident to call upon Theresa May to step aside for a Labour government in-waiting and told his audience that there were 'no no-go areas anywhere in the country' for his party. But, as I have argued, there is, nevertheless a reasonable question to ask about whether the 2017 election was a one-off and whether Labour, under Corbyn, can keep adding enough voters to win an election without poaching current Conservative voters. 2017 was a very unusual election because Theresa May had promised not to call an election; because she was widely expected to win by a landslide; because she focused the campaign upon leadership rather than upon the tried-and-tested Conservative favourites of immigration and the economy; and because she ran a truly, monumentally, awful campaign. 2017 was a success. Labour defied expectations and mobilized young voters and appealed to those tired of austerity. But Labour still ended up with 56 seats fewer than the Conservatives, having struggled to persuade those who had voted Conservative in 2015 to vote for them in 2017. 'Corbynmania' is real enough but so too was 'Cleggmania' in 2010. But the issue here, now, is not simply whether Corbyn's Labour is electable. It is also about the veracity of the story Jeremy Corbyn and his supporters tell about Britain. And I think this story is wrong. Corbynism gets it wrong about New Labour and what happened to Britain in the 2000s and, thereby, about the possibilities of a left-of-centre party which can appeal to voters at the political centre-ground winning elections and achieving tangible political results in relation to political reform, public spending, and labour market regulation.

The final implication of my argument is that, when it comes to political argument, caution is a virtue. I have already said that I am aware of the need to exercise caution to avoid appearing Panglossian. I have also accepted that I am very bad at political predictions. Like most people, I thought that Britain would vote to remain in the European Union in 2016. Like most British people, I thought Trump was bound to fail. I also now think that Corbyn cannot do as well in the next election as he did in the previous one. But then again, I was very wrong about how well Corbyn would do in 2017. But, finally, my argument is that we need to exercise a great deal of caution when it comes to understanding our own recent history and that we need to resist the temptation to reduce everything to black or white, good or bad, pre-Thatcher or post-Thatcher, neoliberalism or social democracy. The 2013 film *American Hustle* is about two con artists who are forced by an FBI agent to set up an elaborate sting operation to snare some local corrupt politicians. It is loosely based on an FBI operation from the 1970s. Christian Bale plays the part of the con artist Irving Rosenfeld and Bradley Cooper plays the role of FBI agent Richard 'Richie' DiMaso. Rosenfeld is, it appears, being backed into a corner by Richie but is eventually able to turn the tables by exploiting Richie's naivety and lack of caution. At one point, Irving and Richie are in an art museum along with a fake sheikh admiring a Rembrandt painting.

IRVING: I want show you something. This Rembrandt here? People come from all over the world to see this.

RICHIE: Yeah, he's good. Yeah.

IRVING: It's a fake.

RICHIE: Wait, what're you talking about? That's impossible.

IRVING: People believe what they want to believe. 'Cause the guy who made this was so good that it's real to everybody. Now who's the master—the painter or the forger?

RICHIE: That's a fake?

IRVING: That's the way the world works. Not black and white, like you say. Extremely grey.

The lesson—which Richie does not heed—is that sometimes it pays to be cautious.

Notes

CHAPTER 1. INTRODUCTION

Most of the articles and reports listed in these notes can be accessed by simply using the title as a search term. Where things are not as obvious, I have included a full website address. I have tried—as far as possible—to avoid references to academic articles which cannot easily be accessed online.

1. Writing in the London Review of Books in July 2017, Will Davies wrote that: 'the coincidence of the Corbyn surge with the horror of Grenfell Tower has created the conditions—and the demand—for a kind of truth and reconciliation commission on forty years of neoliberalism. It is too simple to cast Corbyn as a throwback, but it is undeniable that his appeal and his authority derive partly from his willingness to cast a different, less forgiving light on recent history, so that we don't have to carry on repeating it,' Will Davies, 'Reasons for Corbyn', *London Review of Books*, 13 July 2017.
2. Andrew Marr, 'Teaching History', BBC Start the Week, 30th December 2013.
3. Available via: http://www.presidency.ucsb.edu/ws/?pid=43130
4. Joseph Stiglitz uses the term 'market fundamentalism' in *Globalisation and its Discontents* (New York: W. W. Norton and Norton, 2002). Michael Sandel talks about 'market imperialism' in *What Money Can't Buy: The Moral Limits of Markets* (New York: Farrar, Straus and Giroux, 2012).
5. In February 2015, the Church of England's bishops released a joint letter in which they warned that Britain has become 'a society of strangers' and that 'individualism has tended to estrange people from one another'. Esther Addley, 'Church of England calls for "Fresh Moral Vision" in British Politics', *Guardian*, 17 February 2015.
6. Department of Health, *Annual Reports and Accounts, 2015–16* (London: Stationery Office), 40. For the 2014/15 figure, see p. 47 of the previous year's report.
7. Gunter Grass, *From the Diary of a Snail* (London: Vintage, 1972). I first came across this reference in a piece by the BBC's Andrew Marr on John Smith's leadership of the Labour Party. 'Look Closely and You Will See the Snail Moving', *Independent*, 12 March 1993.
8. On the evening of 1 April 1992, the Labour Party held a giant rally for 10,000 members at the Sheffield Arena. Amidst much sound, fury, and celebrity endorsements, Shadow Cabinet ministers were introduced one-by-one to the audience. Neil Kinnock arrived by helicopter and walking on to the stage proclaimed,

'We're all right'. The Conservative press took this as an unmistakable sign of overconfidence and poor judgement and the Sheffield rally was subsequently described by some commentators as a turning point in the campaign. Truth be told, the rally barely made the news headlines at the time. The Conservative press would have pretty much taken anything Kinnock said as a sign of over-confidence and poor judgement. The polls had got it wrong. The Conservatives were, by this stage, already comfortably ahead. There was no turning point and Sheffield was not to blame.

9. Brian Barry, *Why Social Justice Matters* (Cambridge: Polity, 2005), p. ix.
10. The *Newsnight* interview was broadcast on 23 October 2013 and is available via: https://www.youtube.com/watch?v=3YR4CseY9pk
11. Matthew Weaver, 'David Cameron: Brexit Vote Part of "Movement of Unhappiness"', *Guardian*, 9 December 2016.
12. Nick Clegg, *Politics Between the Extremes* (London: Penguin, 2016), 224.
13. This list is adapted from one prepared by Polly Toynbee in 'Death to the Tribal War', *Guardian*, 18 November 1998.
14. Ryan Barrell, 'Tony Blair Insists He's Not "Super-Rich" Despite Earning Millions Every Year', *Huffington Post*, 9 April 2015.
15. Rhiannon Cosslett, 'I May Have Kissed a Tory, But I (Probably) Wouldn't Marry One', *Guardian*, 10 February 2016. Upping the stakes somewhat, 28% of Labour supporters say that they would be unhappy if their son or daughter married a Tory (compared with just 19% of Tory parents who would feel the same about their child marrying a leftie). Nadia Khomami, 'Parents Disapprove of Offspring Marrying Someone of Different Political Persuasion', *Guardian*, 10 February 2016.
16. Kate Fox, *Watching the English: The Hidden Rules of English Behaviour*, rev. edn (London: Hodder and Stoughton, 2014), 267.
17. Nadia Khomami, 'Over One Third of Oxford Students Want Cecil Rhodes Statue Removed', *Guardian*, 15 January 2016.
18. Jemma Buckley and Tamara Cohen, 'Luvvie Emma Sneers at Britain: I'm European She Claims in Bizarre Tirade Against Us Quitting Brussels', *Daily Mail*, 16 February 2016.
19. Polly Toynbee and David Walker, *Cameron's Coup: How the Tories Took Britain to the Brink* (London: Faber & Faber, 2015), 63.
20. This remark appears to have been addressed by Trotsky to the Marxist theorist Karl Kautsky and was popularized by the German philosopher Carl Schmitt in 1923 in *The Crisis of Parliamentary Democracy*.
21. The first Professor of Politics at the University of Sheffield, Bernard Crick, offers a classic assessment of the nature, requirements, achievements, and disappointments of politics in *In Defence of Politics* (London: Penguin, 1962). His argument is extended and defended by my colleague Matthew Flinders in *Defending Politics* (Oxford: Oxford University Press, 2012), which became the basis for a three-part BBC Radio 4 series of the same name.

22. The quote appears in a lecture Weber gave in 1919, subsequently reprinted as 'Politics as a Vocation'. Available via: http://anthropos-lab.net/wp/wp-content/uploads/2011/12/Weber-Politics-as-a-Vocation.pdf
23 For examples and a (critical) discussion, see Nick Srnicek and Alex Williams, *Inventing the Future: Postcapitalism and a World without Work* (London:Verso, 2016), chapters 1 and 2.
24. Jonathan Freedland, 'The Corbyn Tribe Cares about Identity Not Power', *Guardian*, 24 July 2015.
25. Adam Payne, 'Poll: Corbyn Supporters Admit the Labour Leader isn't Electable but are Voting for him Anyway', *Business Insider UK*, 31 August 2016.

CHAPTER 2. ENTER NEOLIBERALISM . . . AND IT ALL WENT HORRIBLY WRONG

1. For an overview, see Nicholas Wapshott, *Keynes Hayek: The Clash That Defined Modern Economics* (New York: W. W. Norton, 2011).
2. Friedrich von Hayek, *The Road to Serfdom* (London: Routledge, 1944).
3. This statement of the aims of the Mont Pelerin Society is still carried on the Society's website, along with a potted history of its organization and membership. See: https://www.montpelerin.org/
4. In Hayek's account, competitive markets are 'superior not only because [they] are in most circumstances the most efficient method known but even more because it is the only method by which our activities can be adjusted to each other without coercive or arbitrary intervention of authority. Indeed, one of the main arguments in favour of competition is that it dispenses with the need for "conscious" social control' (von Hayek, *The Road to Serfdom*, 38).
5. Friedrich von Hayek, *Law, Legislation and Liberty*. Volume II: *The Mirage of Social Justice* (London: Routledge, 1978).
6. Margaret Thatcher Foundation, House of Commons Speech, November 1990. Available via: http://www.margaretthatcher.org/document/108256
7. In an on-line appendix to this chapter (2a), I say a bit more about the logic of public choice theory and its important connections to neoliberalism.
8. Joseph Stiglitz uses the term 'market fundamentalism' in *Globalisation and its Discontents* (New York: W. W. Norton and Norton, 2002). Michael Sandel talks about 'market imperialism' in *What Money Can't Buy: The Moral Limits of Markets* (New York: Farrar, Straus and Giroux, 2012).
9. Colin Crouch, *The Strange Non-Death of Neoliberalism* (Cambridge: Polity, 2011), 7.
10. David Harvey, *A Brief History of Neoliberalism* (Oxford: Oxford University Press, 2005), 3.
11. Pierre Bourdieu (1998), 'The Essence of Neoliberalism', *Le Monde Diplomatique*. Available via: http://mondediplo.com/1998/12/08bourdieu

In a second on-line appendix to this chapter (2b), I say a bit more about how neoliberalism has been defined. In the final part of this chapter, I look at the connection between neoliberalism and state authoritarianism.

12. On Hayek's doubts about the link between merit and reward, see his essay on 'The Principles of a Liberal Social Order', in *Studies in Philosophy, Politics and Economics* (London: Touchstone, 1967), 172.
13. In a 1932 speech, the German sociologist Alexander Rüstow complained of the 'failure of economic liberalism'. What was needed, he argued, was 'a strong state, a state above the economy, above the interest groups where it belongs'. Rüstow was concerned that misguided state intervention and 'crony capitalism' were damaging the economy and that what was needed was for the state to set clear and strict rules about how markets should work. Rüstow also called for a ban on excessive advertising, the introduction of progressive corporation tax rates, and the nationalization of all utilities and corporations with natural monopolies. See Oliver Hartwhich, *Neoliberalism: The Genesis of a Political Swearword*, Centre for Independent Studies, 2009. Available via: http://www.cis.org.au/app/uploads/2015/07/op114.pdf
14. 'Of Rules and Order: German Ordoliberalism has had a Big Influence on Policy During the Euro Crisis', *The Economist*, 9 May 2015.
15. Murray Rothbard, 'Do You Hate the State?', Mises Institute, 27 July 2012. Available via: https://mises.org/library/do-you-hate-state
16. James Buchanan, 'Man and the State', Mont Pelerin Society Presidential Talk, August 1986. Cited, Vivien Schmidt and Cornelia Woll, 'The State: The Bete Noire of Neoliberalism or its Greatest Conquest?', in Vivien Schmidt and Mark Thatcher (eds), *Resilient Liberalism in Europe's Political Economy* (Cambridge: Cambridge University Press, 2013), 118.
17. In June 1945, Churchill warned that 'no Socialist Government conducting the entire life and industry of the country could afford to allow free, sharp, or violently-worded expressions of public discontent. They would have to fall back on some form of Gestapo, no doubt very humanely directed in the first instance. And this would nip opinion in the bud; it would stop criticism as it reared its head, and it would gather all the power to the supreme party and the party leaders, rising like stately pinnacles above their vast bureaucracies of Civil servants, no longer servants and no longer civil.'
18. One-nation conservatism is a brand of Conservatism which, whilst recognizing the salience of different classes, argues that, as the expression has it, 'we are all in it together', and that it is the responsibility of the upper and middle classes and those in power to protect and advance the interests of the poor as well as the rich and the North as well as the South. In recent times, David Cameron and Theresa May have claimed the mantle of being one-nation Conservatives, whilst Ed Miliband has also spoken about Labour's brand of one-nation politics.

In terms of domestic policy, the post-war consensus is held to have consisted of a basic acceptance of Keynesian economics and state planning, the welfare state (including, crucially, the NHS and state schools), and a close working relationship with the trade union movement. I return to and question the extent to which some of these rhetorical principles were reflected in the policy process in the fourth chapter. In terms of foreign and defence policy, the post-war consensus also included membership of NATO, the special relationship with the United States, withdrawal from the empire, and the possession of an independent nuclear deterrent. The existence of a consensus did not mean that Labour and the Conservatives adopted identical policies on these issues and said the same things. Rather, consensus implied the existence of a broad agreement on some broad policy areas. This consensus was always stronger amongst the frontbench leadership of the two main parties than it was amongst the backbenchers. Indeed, in 1954, *The Economist* described the consensus as 'Butskellism', after the Conservative Chancellor Rab Butler and the former Labour Chancellor Hugh Gaitskell. Backbenchers always tended to prefer the red meat of further nationalization and the elimination of private schools on the one side and trade union reform and public expenditure cuts on the other.

19. Tony Crosland, *The Future of Socialism* (London: Constable, 2006), 31.
20. This line is taken from the Conservatives' 1970 election manifesto. Available via: http://www.conservativemanifesto.com/1970/1970-conservative-manifesto.shtml
21. Ryan Bourne, 'Lady Thatcher's Relationship with Friedrich Hayek and Milton Friedman', *Pieria*, 10 April 2013. Available via: http://www.pieria.co.uk/articles/lady_thatchers_relationship_with_friedrich_hayek_and_milton_friedman
22. Available via: http://www.margaretthatcher.org/document/110858
23. Bourne, 'Lady Thatcher's Relationship with Friedrich Hayek and Milton Friedman'.
24. Ipsos MORI, Social and Political Trends, 'Voting Intentions in Great Britain, 1976–87'. Available via: https://www.ipsos-mori.com/researchspecialisms/socialresearch/specareas/politics/trends.aspx#vii
25. See Charles Moore, *Margaret Thatcher: The Authorized Biography*. Volume 1 (London: Penguin, 2013), 651.
26. Polly Toynbee, 'Thatcher's Reckless Acolytes Don't Know When to Stop', *Guardian*, 9 April 2013.
27. 'Margaret Thatcher is Dead—Alexei Sayle and Louise Mensch Give Their Views', *Channel 4 News*, 8 April 2013.
28. Margaret Thatcher, 'Speech to the College of Europe', Bruges, 20 September 1988. Available via: http://www.margaretthatcher.org/document/107332
29. In his 2001 speech to the Labour Party Conference, Blair said: 'the journey hasn't ended. It never ends. The next stage for New Labour is not backwards; it is renewing ourselves again. Just after the election, an old colleague of mine said: "Come on Tony, now we've won again, can't we drop all this New Labour and do what we believe in?" I said: "It's worse than you think. I really do believe in it".' Quoted, Simon Jenkins, *Thatcher and Sons: A Revolution in Three Acts* (London: Allen Lane, 2006), 205.
30. Tony Blair, *The Journey* (London: Hutchinson, 2010), 94.

31. John Rentoul, 'Intensely Relaxed about People Getting Filthy Rich', *Independent*, 14 February 2013. The second part of Mandelson's sentence rarely gets cited: 'So long as they pay their taxes.'
32. Blair, *The Journey*, 116.
33. In 2002, twelve years after she left Downing Street for the last time, Margaret Thatcher was asked what she thought was her greatest achievement. According to one person at the dinner that night, she replied: 'Tony Blair and New Labour. We forced our opponents to change their minds' (Kiran Stacey, 'Opposition Moves to Damp Down Triumphalism', *Financial Times*, 9 April 2013). In his excellent history of the 1990s, Alwyn Turner quotes Margaret Thatcher as saying: 'I am very strongly in favour of the current government. I don't regard it as left-wing' (*A Classless Society: Britain in the 1990s* (London: Aurum, 2013), 418).
34. Bob Jessop, 'From Thatcherism to New Labour: Neoliberalism, Workfarism and Labour Market Regulation', in Henk Overbeek (ed.), *The Political Economy of European Employment* (London: Routledge, 2003), 137.
35. Danny Dorling, 'Mapping the Thatcherite Legacy', in Colin Hay and Stephen Farrall (eds), *The Legacy of Thatcherism* (Oxford: Oxford University Press, 2014), 253.
36. Robert Taylor, 'New Labour, New Capitalism', in Anthony Seldon (ed.), *Blair's Britain* (Cambridge: Cambridge University Press, 2007), 216.
37. Jenkins, *Thatcher and Sons*, 3.
38. Will Hutton, *Them and Us: Changing Britain—Why We Need a Fair Society* (London: Little Brown, 2010), 282.
39. Quoted, Turner, *A Classless Society*, 326.
40. See Rosie Swash, 'Jarvis Cocker: I'm no Tory Boy', *Guardian*, 28 April 2009.
41. Joseph Stiglitz, *Freefall: America, Free Markets and the Sinking of the World Economy* (New York: W.W. Norton, 2010), 219. For a similar prediction, see George Soros, *The New Paradigm for Financial Markets* (New York: Barnes and Noble, 2009), 95.
42. Boris Johnson, 'The Annual Margaret Thatcher Lecture', 27 November 2013. Available via: http://www.cps.org.uk/events/q/date/2013/11/27/the-2013-margaret-thatcher-lecture-boris-johnson/
43. Patrick Kingsley, 'Maggie's Nightclub—The Ultimate Tribute to Thatcher', *Guardian*, 22 November 2010.
44. Phillip Blond, *Red Tory: How Left and Right have Broken Britain and how we Can Fix it* (London: Faber, 2010).
45. David Cameron, 'Speech to the Conservative Party Conference', 8 October 2009.
46. Polly Toynbee and David Walker, 'Cameron's Five-Year Legacy: Has he Finished what Thatcher Started?', *Guardian*, 28 January 2015.
47. Suzanne Moore, 'Labour's Child Benefit Stance Maintains the Momentum of Tory Cruelty', *Guardian*, 22 September 2014.
48. In 2011, the Archbishop of Canterbury, Rowan Williams, spoke of the 'quiet resurgence' of the 'seductive language of deserving and undeserving poor' (George Eaton, 'Archbishop of Canterbury: "No One Voted" for the Coalition's

Policies', *New Statesman*, 8 June 2011). A year later, in his speech to the Conservative Party conference in October 2012, George Osborne bemoaned the plight of the 'shift-worker, leaving home in the dark hours of the early morning, who looks up at the closed blinds of their next-door neighbour sleeping off a life on benefits'.

49. Owen Jones, *The Establishment: And How They Get Away with It* (London: Allen Lane, 2014), 45.
50. Kailash Chand, 'The NHS is on the Brink of Extinction—We Need to Shout About It', *Guardian*, 8 January 2014.
51. 'Measuring Poverty—Below the Line', *The Economist*, 5 December 2015.
52. *BBC News*, 'In Full: Iain Duncan Smith Resignation Letter', 18 March 2016. Once out of office, Nick Clegg claimed that George Osborne had cut at the welfare budget for purely political reasons. Anushka Asthanan and Simon Hattenstone, 'Clegg: Osborne Casually Cut Welfare for Poorest to Boost Tory Popularity', *Guardian*, 2 September 2016.
53. Michael Portillo, 'Cameron's Blunder and the Conservative Party Leadership', Portland, 8 July 2016. Available via: http://portland-communications.com/2016/07/08/camerons-blunder-and-the-conservative-party-leadership/
54. Guardian Readers and James Walsh, 'Brexit, Austerity and the NHS: Readers on David Cameron's Legacy', *Guardian*, 13 September 2016.
55. 'Theresa May's Keynote Speech at Tory Conference in Full', *Independent*, 5 October 2016.
56. Robert Peston, 'May Appoints Right-Wing Cabinet for Left-Wing Agenda', *ITV News*, 14 July 2016.
57. Polly Toynbee, 'Let's Whoop at the Failure of May's Miserabilism. Optimism Trumped', *Guardian*, 9 June 2017.
58. Katie Allen and Heather Stewart, 'IFS Warns of Biggest Squeeze on Pay for 70 Years Over Brexit', *Guardian*, 24 November 2016.
59. Jonathan Freedland, 'Margaret Thatcher's Britain: We Still Live in the Land Maggie Built', *Guardian*, 8 April 2013.
60. Vivien Schmidt and Mark Thatcher, 'Preface', in Schmidt and Thatcher (eds), *Resilient Liberalism in Europe's Political Economy* (Cambridge: Cambridge University Press, 2013), p. xvi.
61. George Monbiot, 'Neoliberalism—The Ideology at the Root of all our Problems', *Guardian*, 15 April 2016.
62. Andrew Gamble, 'Neoliberalism', *Capital and Class*, 75 (2001), 127–34.
63. Philip Mirowski, *Never Let a Serious Crisis go to Waste: How Neoliberalism Survived the Financial Meltdown* (London: Verso, 2013), 92.
64. David Harvey, *A Brief History of Neoliberalism* (Oxford: Oxford University Press, 2005), 60.
65. Jones, *The Establishment*, 6. In a similar vein, Thomas Palley argues that 'for the last twenty-five years, economic policy and the public's thinking has been dominated by a conservative economic philosophy known as neoliberalism' ('From Keynesianism to Neoliberalism: Shifting Paradigms in Economics', in

Alfredo Saad-Filho and Deborah Johnston (eds), *Neoliberalism: A Critical Reader* (London: Pluto Press, 2005)). In her history and defence of social democracy, Sheri Berman suggests that neoliberalism has acquired an 'almost Gramscian hegemony over mainstream public debate' (*The Primacy of Politics: Social Democracy and the Making of Europe's Twentieth Century* (Cambridge: Cambridge University Press, 2006), 209). In *Inventing the Future: Postcapitalism and a World Without Work,* Nick Srnicek and Alex Williams also describe neoliberalism as 'hegemonic' (London: Verso, 2016), 51. Peter Hall and Michele Lamont describe the age in which we now live as the 'the neoliberal era' (*Social Resilience in the Neoliberal Era* (Cambridge: Cambridge University Press, 2013), 3).

66. Larry Elliot, 'Austerity Policies do More Harm than Good, IMF Study Concludes', *Guardian*, 27 May 2016. The IMF report in question argued that the global diffusion of neoliberal policies lifted large numbers of people out of absolute poverty but that austerity policies have reduced growth and increased income and wealth inequalities. Jonathan Ostry, Prakash Loungani, and Davide Furceri, 'Neoliberalism: Oversold?', *Finance and Development*, 53 (2016), 38–41. Available via: https://www.imf.org/external/pubs/ft/fandd/2016/06/pdf/ostry.pdf
67. Jodi Dean, *Democracy and Other Neoliberal Fantasies: Communicative Capitalism and Left Politics* (Durham, NC: Duke University Press, 2009), 73.
68. Martin Jacques, 'The Death of Neoliberalism and the Crisis in Western Politics', *Guardian*, 21 August 2016.
69. Mirowski, *Never Let a Serious Crisis go to Waste*, 130.
70. Office for Budget Responsibility, *Economic and Fiscal Outlook*, July 2015, pp. 88–9.
71. Jamie Peck, Nick Theodore, and Neil Brenner, 'Neoliberalism Interrupted', in Damien Cahill, Lindy Edwards, and Frank Stilwell (eds), *Neoliberalism: Beyond the Free Market* (Cheltenham: Edward Elgar, 2012), 15.
72. Ibid. 20.
73. Harvey, *A Brief History of Neoliberalism*, 19.
74. Vivien Schmidt and Mark Thatcher, 'Theorising Ideational Continuity: The Resilience of Neoliberal Ideas in Europe', in Schmidt and Thatcher (eds), *Resilient Liberalism in Europe's Political Economy* (Cambridge: Cambridge University Press, 2013), 29–31.
75. In the United States, regulators intervened to rescue the savings and loan industry in the late 1980s and then, in 1984, the seventh largest bank, Continental Illinois, when it ran into trouble. During a subsequent Congressional hearing, the comptroller of the currency stated what many observers had previously only suspected: that the government would not allow the eleven largest 'money center' banks to fail. One congressman responded by suggesting that 'we [now] have a new kind of bank. It is called "too big to fail".' In Britain, there was no formally stated 'too big to fail' guarantee. Nevertheless, many banks' executives and investors believed that they *were* too big to fail. The former Governor of the Bank of England, Mervyn King, suggests that one of the key reasons for the

crisis occurring was that 'the incentives to manage risk and to increase leverage were distorted by the implicit support or guarantee provided by government to creditors of banks that were seen as "too important to fail"' (Stephen Bell and Andrew Hindmoor, *Masters of the Universe but Slaves of the Market* (Cambridge, MA: Harvard University Press, 2015), 42 (on the United States) and 188–9 (on Britain)).

76. Peck, Theodore, and Brenner, 'Neoliberalism Interrupted', 25–6.
77. For a particularly searing indictment, see the High Pay Commission, *Winners and Losers: The Great Privatisation Game* (High Pay Commission, 2014).
78. Department for Business Innovation and Skills, 'Trade Union Membership 2015: Statistical Bulletin', May 2017.
79. 'The Guardian View on Sports Direct: A Bad Business', *Guardian*, 10 December 2015.
80. Committee of Public Accounts, *Contracting Out Public Services to the Private Sector*, House of Commons, HC777, 26 February 2014.
81. Elizabeth Thurbon, 'Ideas and Industrial Governance: Has the Influence of Neoliberalism Been Overstated', in Damien Cahill, Lindy Edwards, and Frank Stilwell (eds), *Neoliberalism: Beyond the Free Market* (Cheltenham: Edward Elgar, 2012), 182.
82. William Davies, who has written most powerfully about the imperialistic nature of neoliberalism and the ways in which competition has become a mantra of the age, quotes Michel Foucault as saying that neoliberalism 'is not a question of freeing an empty space, but of taking the formal principles of a market economy and referring them and relating them to, of projecting them on to a general art of government'. William Davies, *The Limits of Neoliberalism* (London: Sage, 2014), 21. Even when people are not actually operating in a competitive market, neoliberalism treats them as if they ought to be.
83. Patrick Wintour, 'George Osborne Aims at Tax Credits and Benefits in New Squeeze on Working Poor', *Guardian*, 30 September, 2014.
84. The CityUK, *Key Facts about UK Financial and Related Professional Services*, April 2017.
85. Jim Cuthbert, 'How Serious a Threat is the UK's Financialised Economy?', *The Resolution Foundation*, June 2014.
86. 'Pay-as-you-go Government', *The Economist*, 29 August 2015.
87. 'Britain's university system is being reorganised in a neoliberal direction. This is precisely the opposite of headline news: it is a slow-burning process that has been going on for over thirty years. But one aspect of the coalition's austerity project is the radicalisation of this programme. By raising tuition fees and introducing competition and "marketisation" across the system, they are accelerating the rate at which university administrations convert their campuses into "enterprises".' Richard Seymour, 'Neoliberalism and Solidarity in Universities: The Case of Sanaz Raji', *New Left Project*, 9 April 2014.
88. 'Runway Robbery', *The Economist*, 22 August 2015.
89. 'Smells Like Middle Aged Spirit', *The Economist*, 27 June 2015.

90. Jeevan Vasagar, 'Privately Owned Public Space: Where are they and Who Owns them?', *Guardian*, 11 June 2012. This article links to a data base listing privately owned public developments. Also see Mark Townsend, 'Will Self Joins London Mass Trespass over Privatisation of Public Space', *Guardian*, 13 February 2016.
91. Hutton, *Them and Us*, 32.
92. Josh Halliday and Haroon Siddique, 'Boris Johnson Calls for Removal of Anti-Homeless Spikes', *Guardian*, 9 June 2014.
93. *BBC News*, 'Profile: John Prescott', 27 August 2007.
94. Henry A. Giroux, 'The Age of Neoliberal Terrorism', interview, *truthdig.com*, December 2010. This argument about the social consequences of capitalism is a long-standing one. In the 1840s, Karl Marx described a process of commodification in which human values were being reduced to the pursuit of profit and in which the ties binding people to each other were being dissolved. During the same era, the English poet and social critic Matthew Arnold decried the way in which the commercial mentality of the new capitalist middle class was corrupting culture and encouraging philistinism (see Jerry Zuller, *The Mind and the Market: Capitalism in Modern European Thought* (London: Alfred Knopf, 2002)).
95. John Harris, 'Does the Left Have a Future?', *Guardian*, 6 September 2016.
96. Robert Putnam, *Bowling Alone: The Collapse and Revival of American Community* (New York: Simon & Schuster, 2000).
97. Colin Hay, *Why we Hate Politics* (Cambridge: Polity, 2007), 43.
98. Diane Abbott, 'The Dispossessed Voted for Brexit. Jeremy Corbyn Offers Real Change', *Guardian*, 24 June 2016.
99. The figure of £2bn is taken from Tasmin Cover and Andy Rowell, *A Quiet Word: Lobbying, Crony Capitalism and Broken Politics in Britain* (London: Random House, 2014).
100. Jacob Rowbottom, *Democracy Distorted: Wealth, Influence and Democratic Politics* (Cambridge: Cambridge University Press, 2010), 117–24.
101. Jones, *The Establishment*, 71. Democracy, he concludes, 'has been managed and rendered safe'.
102. Colin Crouch, *Post-Democracy* (Cambridge: Polity, 2004), 4.
103. The details of the case and of the Cabinet Secretary's report are discussed by Anthony Seldon and Peter Snowdon, *Cameron at 10: The Inside Story, 2010–15* (London: Harper Collins), 99.
104. Hutton, *Them and Us*, 178.
105. Ian Bruff, 'The Rise of Authoritarian Neoliberalism', *Rethinking Marxism*, 26 (2014), 113–29.
106. Quoted, Andrew Rawnsley, *The End of the Party* (London: Penguin, 2010), 371.
107. Rebecca Lefort, 'Four Labour MPs Implicated in "Cash for Influence" Scandal', *Daily Telegraph*, 21 March 2010.
108. Rowena Mason, 'Tories Charge £2,500 a Head for Access to Ministers at Party Conference', *Guardian*, 17 September 2014.

109. Rowena Mason, 'Cameron's "Cronies" Honours List Leads to Calls for Overhaul of System', *Guardian*, 1 August 2016.
110. Ipsos MORI, 'Politicians Trusted Less Than Estate Agents, Bankers and Journalists', January 2015. Available via: https://www.ipsos-mori.com/researchpublications/researcharchive/3504/Politicians-trusted-less-than-estate-agents-bankers-and-journalists.aspx
111. John Curtice and Rachel Ormston (eds), *British Social Attitudes Survey: The 32nd Report* (2015), London: NatCen Social Research, 136.
112. Committee on Standards in Public Life, 'Public Perceptions of Standards in Public Life in the UK and Europe' (2014), 6.
113. Rose Troup Buchanan, 'TUC leader Claims Conservative Party is Sliding Britain back to "Downton-Abbey Style Society"', *Independent*, 8 September 2014.
114. Will Hutton, *How Good Can We Be?* (London: Little Brown, 2015), 92.
115. Jeremy Corbyn, 'Speech to the 2016 Labour Party Conference'. Available via: http://press.labour.org.uk/post/151053788194/jeremy-corbyn-leader-of-the-labour-party-speech
116. For those perplexed by the reference, 'to handbag'—meaning 'to subject to a forthright verbal assault or to strident criticism'—was a term often associated with Margaret Thatcher's style of leadership. The *Oxford English Dictionary* reports that the first recorded use of the term came in 1982, when *The Economist* reported that the Treasury had been required to bend its views to those of the Prime Minister. See: http://blog.oxforddictionaries.com/2013/04/margaretthatcher/. *Handbagged* was, eventually, the title of a play by Moira Buffini examining the relationship between Margaret Thatcher and Queen Elizabeth.
117. David Marquand, 'The Paradoxes of Thatcherism', in Robert Skidelsky (ed.), *Thatcherism* (Oxford: Blackwell, 1988).
118. Andrew Gamble, *The Free Economy and the Strong State*, 2nd edn (London: Palgrave Macmillan, 1988).
119. Peregrine Worsthorne, 'Who now Speaks for the People?', *Sunday Telegraph*, 12 June 1983.
120. Nigel Morris, 'More than 3,600 New Offences Under New Labour', *Independent*, 4 September 2008.
121. David Barrett, 'One Surveillance Camera for Every 11 People in Britain, Says CCTV Survey', *Daily Telegraph*, 10 July 2013.
122. Nicholas Watt and Frances Perraudin, 'Cameron's Government has 'Worrying Authoritarian Streak'—ex Civil Service Boss', *Guardian*, 11 January 2016.
123. Vivien Schmidt and Cornelia Woll put the point particularly starkly: 'The more the state has put neo-liberal ideas into practice, by transforming itself as it liberalizes the markets, the state has—if anything—grown in size and scope, thereby violating neo-liberal principles' (Vivien Schmidt and Cornelia Woll, 'The State: The Bete Noire of Neoliberalism or its Greatest Conquest?', in Schmidt and Thatcher (eds), *Resilient Liberalism in Europe's Political Economy* (Cambridge: Cambridge University Press, 2013), 113). Martijn Konings

similarly argues that neoliberalism was 'a return to classical liberalism only on an ideological level; neoliberal practices were never about institutional retreat or the subordination of public and private actors to the discipline of disembedded markets, but precisely involved the creation, legitimation and consolidation of... new mechanisms of control' (Martijn Konings, 'Neoliberalism and the State', in Damien Cahill, Lindy Edwards, and Frank Stilwell (eds), *Neoliberalism: Beyond the Free Market* (Cheltenham: Edward Elgar, 2012), 54–5).

124. Mirowski, *Never Let a Serious Crisis go to Waste*, 41.
125. Paul Mason, *Postcapitalism* (London: Allen Lane, 2015), p. xi.
126. Loic Wacquant, *Punishing the Poor: The Neoliberal Government of Social Insecurity* (Durham, NC: Duke University Press, 2009).
127. William Davies, 'The New Neoliberalism', *The New Left Review*, 101 (September–October 2016).

CHAPTER 3. BAD ATTITUDE? PUBLIC OPINION, THE LEFT, AND NEOLIBERALISM

1. In an election marked by surprises and upheaval, Labour and the Conservatives both held on to around 90 per cent of their voters. Hardly any Labour voters defected to the Liberal Democrats, UKIP, or the Greens. But very few Conservatives defected to Labour. Only around half of those who had voted Liberal Democrat in 2015 voted Liberal Democrat in 2017 as well. Around 30 per cent of those who had voted Liberal Democrat in 2015 voted Labour in 2017 and 15 per cent voted Conservative. The big story of the 2017 election was the collapse of UKIP. It was widely expected that most of those who had voted UKIP in 2015 would vote Conservative in 2017. This did not happen. Nearly 60 per cent of those who had voted UKIP in 2015 but did not vote UKIP in 2017 voted Conservative. Around 40 per cent voted Labour.
2. See the YouGov 'Political Trackers' archive available via: https://yougov.co.uk/publicopinion/archive/?category=political-trackers.
3. John Curtice, 'Labour's Strategy Delivered—Up to a Point', *Guardian*, 9 June 2017.
4. Rebecca Mead, 'Thatcher's Children', *New Yorker*, 12 April 2013. 'The Boris Generation', *The Economist*, 1 June 2013. 'Is This Generation Right?', *BBC Magazine*, 17 June 2014.
5. Andrew Hindmoor, *New Labour at the Centre: Constructing Political Space* (Oxford: Oxford University Press, 2004), 3–4.
6. The language of left, right, and centre might be pervasive but I should also acknowledge that a lot of people do not feel comfortable using these terms. 28 per cent of people said, 'don't know' when asked by YouGov to describe their political position in spatial terms. When the British Election Survey asked people in 2010 whether they used the terms left and right to describe political parties, ideas, and leaders, less than 10% said 'yes, very often'; 33% said 'yes, sometimes'; and 53% said 'no, never'. During some of the preliminary work for

the 2015 British Election Study, researchers found that around 17% could not place themselves on a left–right scale, 19% struggled to place Labour and the Conservatives, 21% could not place the Liberal Democrats, and 22% could not place UKIP. Philip Cowley, 'Left, Right and Centre', British Election Study News (December 2015). Available via: http://www.britishelectionstudy.com/bes-impact/left-right-and-centre-by-professor-phil-cowley/#.VqCq4_mLTIU

I have also lightly brushed over some of the difficulties here involved in reducing political ideologies to spatial locations. It is true that we might equate socialism and social democracy with the left and neoliberalism with the right. But where does this leave conservatism, understood as an ideology valuing order, tradition, and stability? We could simply put conservatism next to neoliberalism on the right. But it would be a mistake to imply that conservative and neoliberal thought is one and the same thing. Indeed, in so far as it venerates individualism and the market over society and hierarchy, there are good reasons for small-c conservatives to oppose neoliberalism. This takes us back to the discussion of Thatcherism in the previous chapter. Should we view Thatcherism as an uncomfortable ideological hybrid of neoliberalism and conservatism, the faultlines of which were exposed by issues like Europe, where neoliberal (free-trade) instincts pulled in a different direction from conservative ones? Or should we say that neoliberals, like conservatives, recognize the need for a strong state as well as a free economy and that Thatcherism was a project to put this into practice?

7. Toby Helm, 'Blair Tells Labour: Return to the Centre Ground to Win Again', *Guardian*, 10 May 2015. Patrick Hennessy, 'David Cameron: Conservatives will Never Vacate the Centre Ground', *Daily Telegraph*, 6 October 2012. 'Theresa May's Keynote Speech at Tory Conference in Full', *Independent*, 5 October 2016.

   In an on-line appendix (3a), I describe the 'median voter theorem', which seeks to establish the conditions under which parties will find it in their interests to move toward and occupy the centre-ground.
8. George Osborne was once reported as saying that 'in opposition you move to the centre. In government, you move the centre.' James Forsyth, 'The Political Centre Just Moved, to the Right', *Spectator*, Coffee House Blog, 5 June 2013.
9. Walt Borges, Harold D. Clarke, Marianne C. Stewart, David Sanders, and Paul Whiteley, 'The Politics of Austerity: Modelling British Attitudes Towards Public Spending Cuts' (on-line published working paper, 2012), 29. Available via: http://www.bes2009-10.org/papers/austeritypolitics.pdf
10. Peter Moore, 'Austerity: The New Normal', YouGov, 24 April 2013.
11. Lord Ashcroft, General Election Day Poll, 5–7 May 2015. Available via: http://lordashcroftpolls.com/wp-content/uploads/2015/05/Post-vote-poll-GE-2015-150507-Full-tables.pdf. People's views on austerity were, unsurprisingly, closely linked to party support.

    - 46% agreed that 'the national economy is not yet fully fixed, so we will need to continue with austerity and cuts in government spending over the next five years'. But whereas 84% of Conservative voters agreed with this proposition, only 17% of Labour voters did so.

- 30% agreed that 'while a period of austerity was needed to fix the national economy, we don't need another five years of cuts in government spending'. But whereas only 14% of Conservative voters agreed with this, 43% of Labour voters did so.
- Finally, 24% agreed that 'austerity and cuts in government spending were never really needed to fix the national economy, it was just used as an excuse to cut public services'. 40% of Labour voters agreed but only 2% of Conservative voters.

12. http://www.besis.org/Home. These options are not posited as mutually exclusive alternatives to each other. Hence, the numbers sum to more than 100%.
13. Christopher Wlezien, 'The Public as Thermostat: Dynamics of Preferences for Spending', *American Journal of Political Science*, 39 (1995), 981–1000.
14. Bryan Caplan, *The Myth of the Rational Voters: Why Democracies Choose Bad Policies* (Princeton: Princeton University Press, 2007).
15. *BBC News*, 'Three Quarters of People Cannot Name their Local MP', 16 May 2013.
16. David Harvey, *A Brief History of Neoliberalism* (Oxford: Oxford University Press, 2005), 2.
17. Elizabeth Clery, John Curtice, and Roger Harding (eds), *British Social Attitudes: The 34th Report* (2017), London: NatCen Social Research, 71.
18. In 1986, 43% agreed that the government should redistribute income. This rose to 54% in 1994 before falling steadily to 32% in 2003 and 2004.
19. Karen Rowlingson, Michael Orton, and Eleanor Taylor, 'Do We Still Care about Inequality?', University of Birmingham, School of Social Policy, Working Paper (2011). Available via: http://www.birmingham.ac.uk/Documents/college-social-sciences/social-policy/CHASM/do-we-still-care-about-inequality.pdf
20. Jonathan Freedland, 'Summoning the L-Word', *Guardian*, 20 December 2000.
21. Elizabeth Clery, Lucy Lee, and Sarah Kunz, *Public Attitudes to Poverty and Welfare, 1983–2011* (London: Joseph Rowntree Foundation, 2013), 8. Available via: https://www.natcen.ac.uk/media/137637/poverty-and-welfare.pdf
22. John Lanchester, 'There's Poverty in the UK, But We Are Better Off Calling It Inequality', *Guardian*, 5 September 2014.
23. *BBC News*, 'Tories Claim Big Change on Poor', 24 November 2006.
24. John Bartle, 'The Policy Mood and the Moving Centre' (2015) (Available via: http://www.bsa.natcen.ac.uk/media/38862/the-policy-mood-and-the-moving-centre.pdf). Also see John Bartle et al., 'The Moving Centre: Preferences for Government Activity in Britain, 1950–2005', *British Journal of Political Science*, 41 (2010), 259–85.
25. Cleary et al. (eds), *British Social Attitudes: The 34th Report* (2017), 116.
26. John Curtice and Rachel Ormston (eds), *British Social Attitudes: The 32nd Report* (2015), London: NatCen Social Research, 23.
27. Park et al. (eds), *British Social Attitudes: The 30th Report* (2013), p. ix.
28. British Future, *The Melting Pot Generation: How Britain Became More Relaxed on Race* (2012), 2.

29. Park et al. (eds), *British Social Attitudes: The 30th Report* (2013), 122.
30. Cleary et al. (eds), *British Social Attitudes: The 34th Report* (2017), 119.
31. British Future, *The Melting Pot Generation: How Britain Became More Relaxed on Race* (2012), 2.
32. Anthony Crosland, *The Future of Socialism* (London: Jonathan Cape, 1956), 403.
33. Nick Clegg, *Politics Between the Extremes* (London: Penguin, 2016), 185.
34. Sascha O. Becker, Thiemo Fetzer, and Dennis Novy, 'Who Voted for Brexit? A Comprehensive District-Level Analysis', University of Warwick, Centre for Competitive Advantage in the Global Economy, Working Paper (October 2016). Available via: http://ukandeu.ac.uk/research-papers/who-voted-for-brexit-a-comprehensive-district-level-analysis/
35. John Harris, 'Does the Left Have a Future?', *Guardian*, 6 September 2016.
36. http://www.besis.org/Home
37. Robert Ford and Anthony Heath, 'Immigration: A Nation Divided?', in Alison Park, Caroline Bryson, and John Curtice (eds), *British Social Attitudes: The 31st Report* (2014), London: NatCen Social Research, 79.
38. YouGov/*Sunday Times* poll, 13–14 December 2012, p. 4 (available via: https://d25d2506sfb94s.cloudfront.net/cumulus_uploads/document/wohvkihpjg/YG-Archive-Pol-Sunday-Times-results-14-161212.pdf)
39. In May 2015—immediately prior to the general election—Ipsos MORI found that 17% regarded poverty as one of the most important issues facing the country, 19% unemployment, 21% education, 36% the economy, 40% immigration, and 44% the NHS.
40. Will Dahlgreen, 'No Increase in Syrian Refugee Numbers—Public', YouGov, 6 September 2015.
41. http://www.besis.org/Home
42. YouGov/Prospect Survey Results, 29–30 January 2012, p. 3 (available via: https://d25d2506sfb94s.cloudfront.net/cumulus_uploads/document/x3d4a39z0a/YG-Archives-Prospect-Results-welfareReform-120130.pdf)
43. Peter Kellner, 'Welfare Reform: Who, Whom?', YouGov, January 2013.
44. Curtice and Ormston (eds), *British Social Attitudes: The 32nd Report*, 91.
45. See: http://www.besis.org/Home and Cleary et al. (eds), *British Social Attitudes: The 34th Report* (2017), p. 48, p. 96, and p. 39.
46. I previously suggested that, when politics is defined in terms of left and right, politicians have a strong incentive to move to and be seen to move to the centre-ground. In the on-line appendix on the 'median voter theorem' (3a), I show that things get a lot more complicated when there are two dimensions across which parties compete.
47. For an overview of post-war public opinion, see Rob Ford, Will Jennings, and Will Sommerville, 'Public Opinion, Responsiveness and Constraint: Britain's Three Immigration Policy Regimes', *Journal of Ethnic and Migration Studies*, 41 (2015), 1391–411.
48. Paul Whiteley, 'Public Opinion and the Demand for Social Welfare in Britain', *Journal of Social Policy*, 10 (1981), 453–75, p. 460.

49. Brian Harrison, *Seeking a Role: The United Kingdom 1951–70* (Oxford: Oxford University Press, 2009), 269.
50. Dominic Sandbrook, *Seasons in the Sun: The Britain for Britain*, 1974–9 (London: Allen Lane, 2012), 372. Stories of this sort often had a racial dimension: welfare scroungers were black and were sponging off the system. As Sandbrook says, 'in pubs and clubs across the country, people exchanged urban legends about "sponging" immigrants, almost always passed on via some mysteriously untraceable "mate" or "friend of a friend"'.
51. Peter Golding and Sue Middleton, *Images of Welfare* (Oxford: Blackwells, 1982), 162.
52. Cleary et al. (eds), *British Social Attitudes: The 34th Report* (2017), p. 128, p. 131, and p. 138.
53. *BBC News*, 'EU Referendum: The Result in Maps and Charts', 24 June 2016.
54. Cleary et al. (eds), *British Social Attitudes: The 34th Report* (2017), p. 13 and http://www.besis.org/Home.
55. Philip Mirowski, *Never Let a Serious Crisis go to Waste: How Neoliberalism Survived the Financial Meltdown* (London: Verso, 2013), 130.
56. In a 2008 survey, Hills and colleagues found that, within Britain, there was 46% support for a progressive tax system; 41% for a proportional tax system (where all pay at the same rate); and 12% support for a regressive tax system (in which the rich pay a lower rate of tax). There was 59% support for the payment of flat-rate universal benefits; 21% support for earnings-related benefits; and 19% support for means-tested benefits. Across an average of eleven other European countries, there was 47% support for earnings-related benefits and only 36% support for flat-rate benefits. John Hills, *Good Times, Bad Times: The Welfare Myth of Them and Us* (Bristol: Policy Press, 2015), 36–7.
57. A summary of this research has been prepared by Bobby Duffy, 'Perceptions are not Reality', Ipsos MORI, July 2013. Available via: https://www.ipsos-mori.com/researchpublications/researcharchive/3466/Perceptions-are-not-reality-Things-the-world-gets-wrong.aspx
58. For a review of and references to each of these claims, see Iain Begg, 'Brexit: Why, What Next and How, the UK in a Changing Europe'. Available via: http://ukandeu.ac.uk/wp-content/uploads/2016/08/Brexit-why-what-next-and-how.pdf, pp. 32–3.
59. Department for Work and Pensions, *Fraud and Error in the Benefit System*, (19 May 2016). Available via: https://www.gov.uk/government/collections/fraud-and-error-in-the-benefit-system. This figure refers to the share of spending that is fraudulent. Cutting the numbers in a different way, the share of claims that are fraudulent is estimated to be between 2 and 10 per cent depending on the benefit in question.
60. Hills, *Good Times, Bad Times*, 47–74.
61. In 2015 the Bank of England issued a report which suggested that a 10 per cent increase in the proportion of unskilled immigrant workers was associated with a 2 per cent reduction in the pay of semi-skilled and unskilled non-immigrant workers in service industries. Peter Dominiczak and Peter Spence, 'Mass

Migration Driving Down Wages Offered to British Jobseekers', *Daily Telegraph*, 21 December 2015. By far the best summary I have read of the economic effects of migration concludes that 'Immigration makes countries neither rich nor poor, but it does change them. The largest effects of migration are distributional in nature. The chief economic benefit of immigration is wage depression, so when immigrants' skill sets overlap with those of natives, unskilled migration will reduce the wages of the unskilled native workers (thus increasing inequality). Skilled migration, on the other hand, will reduce the wages of skilled workers (thus increasing equality). Thus, immigration to the UK from 1997 to 2005 depressed wages for the bottom twentieth percentile, increased them slightly for the top fortieth percentile and produced a modestly positive overall wage effect.' Randall Hansen, 'Making Immigration Work: How Britain and Europe Can Cope with their Immigration Crises' (The Government and Opposition/Leonard Schapiro Lecture, 2015), *Government and Opposition*, 51/2, 183–208. This is one of the few occasions in the book where I can't provide a hyperlink but he has written an LSE 'policy and politics' blog containing a lot of the same data which is available via: http://blogs.lse.ac.uk/politicsandpolicy/how-to-make-immigration-work/ The other point to make here, however, is that even if a more restrictive immigration policy has some (probably quite small) positive impact on wages for low-skilled workers, this is likely to be more than offset by the wider negative economic and fiscal impacts of lower immigration and, in particular, lower tax revenues. See the discussion by Jonathan Portes, 'Immigration After Brexit', *National Institute Economic Review*, 238 (November 2016).

62. In the year ending December 2012, total immigration to the UK was 158,000 by EU citizens and 284,000 by non-EU citizens. In the year ending 2016 it was 284,000 by EU citizens and 289,000 by non-EU citizens. Office for National Statistics, 'Migration Statistics Quarterly Report', 25 May 2017, 12. On attitudes toward migration see Cleary et al. (eds), *British Social Attitudes: The 34th Report* (2017), p. 135.
63. On the shortfall in EU nurses see Daniel Boffey, 'Record Number of EU Nurses Quit NHS', *Guardian*, 18 March 2017.
64. For those who had not worked and had not paid national insurance and so were not eligible for these flat-rate payments, Beveridge supported the introduction of a means-tested safety net of national assistance to be paid at such a low level as to 'leave the person assisted with an effective motive to avoid the need for assistance and to rely on earnings and insurance'. David Kynaston, *Austerity Britain, 1945–51* (London: Bloomsbury, 2007), 26.
65. Kayte Lawton, Graeme Cooke, and Nick Pearce, *The Condition of Britain: Strategies for Social Renewal* (London: Institute for Public Policy Research, 2014), 55.
66. *BBC News*, 'Swiss Voters Reject Basic Income Plan', 16 June 2016.
67. Howard Reed and Stewart Lansley, *Universal Basic Income: An Idea Whose Time has Come?* (London: Compass, 2016). Available via: https://www.compassonline.org.uk/wp-content/uploads/2016/05/UniversalBasicIncomeByCompass-Spreads.pdf

68. Friedrich von Hayek, *Law, Legislation and Liberty*. Volume 3: *The Political Order of a Free People* (London: Routledge, 1993), 55. It is also worth recalling that, no matter how politically radical it may appear, Presidents Nixon and Carter attempted to pass legislation to introduce a basic income in the United States in the 1970s and that, more recently, the *Financial Times* and the *Economist* have expressed qualified support for a basic income. Nick Srnicek and Alex Williams, *Inventing the Future: Postcapitalism and a World Without Work* (London: Verso, 2016), 118–20.
69. Park et al. (eds.), *British Social Attitudes: The 30th Report*, 51.
70. Patrick Butler, 'Profile: Robert Putnam', *Guardian*, 30 March 2001.
71. Peter Hall, 'Social Capital in Britain', *British Journal of Political Science*, 29 (1999), 417–61.
72. European Social Survey data can be accessed via: http://www.europeansocialsurvey.org/. Britain, it transpires, is a relatively high-trust society. In 2012, 34% of people gave high-trust answers in Britain, compared with an impressive 50% in the Netherlands, 34% in Italy, 27% in Germany, and 16% in France.
73. Curtice and Ormston (eds), *British Social Attitudes: The 32nd Report* (2015), 126.
74. Rich Bengamin, 'The Gated Community Mentality', *New York Times*, 29 March 2012.
75. Paul Kelbie, 'Rise in Gated Communities Could Pose a Threat to Public Services', *Independent*, 27 September 2003.
76. Graham Norwood, 'London Leads Move Away from Gated Housing Schemes', *Financial Times*, 31 May 2013.
77. National Council for Voluntary Organisations, *Participation: Trends, Facts and Figures* (March 2011).
78. See the discussion of Labour's failings and electoral weaknesses in David Kynaston, *Modernity Britain*. Book 2: *A Shake of the Dice, 1959–62* (London: Bloomsbury, 2014), 61.
79. Anthony Heath, Roger Jowell, and John Curtice (eds), *Labour's Last Chance? The 1992 Election and Beyond* (Aldershot: Dartmouth, 1994).
80. Peter Kellner, 'Could Jeremy Corbyn Even Win?', *Prospect*, 15 October 2015.
81. http://www.besis.org/Home
82. NatCent's British Social Attitudes Survey, 2013. Accessed via: UK Data Service. Available via: http://nesstar.ukdataservice.ac.uk/webview/index.jsp?v=2&mode=documentation&submode=abstract&study=http://nesstar.ukdataservice.ac.uk:80/obj/fStudy/7500&top=yes (link to data on education).
83. NatCen's British Social Attitudes Survey, 2013. Accessed via: UK Data Service. Available via: http://nesstar.ukdataservice.ac.uk/webview/index.jsp?v=2&mode=documentation&submode=abstract&study=http://nesstar.ukdataservice.ac.uk:80/obj/fStudy/7500&top=yes (link to data on health).
84. Simon Walters, 'Ed Ball's Plan to Raise Top Rate of Tax is Populist—But Tories Are More Trusted', *Mail on Sunday*, 26 January 2014.
85. Will Dahlgreen, 'Voters Dismiss Trickle-Down Economics', YouGov, 21 January 2015.

86. Peter Moore, 'Unlike Americans, Brits Think Taxation is Moral', YouGov, 6 November 2014.
87. 'Theresa May's Keynote Speech at Tory Conference in Full', *Independent*, 5 October 2016.
88. Steven Hopkins, 'Labour Missed an "Open Goal" against Theresa May Says MP Chris Leslie', *Huffington Post*, 10 June 2017.
89. Anthony McDonnell, 'Could Corbyn Win an Election by Mobilising Non-Voters? Not if He Doesn't Win over Conservative Supporters Too', *Democratic Audit UK*, 12 April 2016. Available via: http://www.democraticaudit.com/?p=
90. Vivien Schmidt and Mark Thatcher, 'Preface', in Schmidt and Thatcher (eds), *Resilient Liberalism in Europe's Political Economy* (Cambridge: Cambridge University Press, 2013), p. xvi.
91. At the start of a recession, when confidence is low, growth is falling, and jobs are being lost, consumers and businesses have an incentive to rethink their spending plans. Fearing for their own jobs, consumers may well shelve plans to buy a new and safer car in favour of saving more money for a rainy day. Fearing that consumers are going to save rather than spend, business managers might then cancel proposed investments. From an individual perspective, such behaviour makes perfect sense. It would be pretty foolish not to adjust your behaviour when the world around you is changing. But as John Maynard Keynes argued in *The General Theory of Employment, Interest and Money*, published in the midst of the Great Depression in 1936, if everyone behaves in this way, it will simply result in lower consumption, more job losses, and a vicious circle of economic contraction. Skip forward a few generations and critics of austerity argue that Keynes's paradox of thrift, as it is known, tells us why it was a mistake for so many governments to cut public expenditure when the global economy was faltering in the aftermath of the 2008 financial crisis. In a recession, government needs to spend more to compensate for lower spending in the private sector and to boost confidence.
92. A report by the Media Standards Trust found that press coverage of Ed Miliband in 2015 was more hostile than that of Neil Kinnock in 1992. See John Plunkett and Ami Sedghi, 'The Sun has Torn into Ed Miliband Even More Viciously than it Hit Neil Kinnock', *Guardian*, 6 May 2015.
93. Bob Jessop, 'From Thatcherism to New Labour: Neoliberalism, Workfarism and Labour Market Regulation', in Henk Overbeek (ed.), *The Political Economy of European Employment* (London: Routledge, 2003), 137.

Notes to figure captions

1. See YouGov Survey Results, 14–15 February 2017. Available via: https://d25d2506sfb94s.cloudfront.net/cumulus_uploads/document/n34shyp79t/InternalResults_170215_Left-RightScale_ExtraCB_W. Have voters changed their positions over time? The answer is: not hugely. In 2015 the British Election Study found that, measured along a ten-point scale, nearly 40% of people located themselves at the centre (position 5) and a further 22% just to the left

of centre (position 4) or just to the right of centre (position 6). In 1997, 52% placed themselves at either the centre or just to the left or right of centre (positions 4, 5, and 6 along this 10-point scale) and 3.6% placed themselves on the left (positions 0 and 1). By 2010, only 37% positioned themselves at the centre (positions 4, 5, and 6) and just 1.7% on the left (positions 0 and 1).

2. This data is taken from Elizabeth Clery, Professor John Curtice, and Roger Harding (eds), *British Social Attitudes: The 34th Report* (2017), London: NatCen Social Research, 77. The British Social Attitude Survey data we have here only goes back as far as 1983. Could it plausibly be argued that, by this stage, the damage had already been done and the electorate had shifted to a neoliberal position? I don't think it can. It is true that, on a range of issues, the electorate did start to shift to the right during the 1970s and that this underpinned the Conservatives' 1979 victory. In 1964, after thirteen years of Conservative government, 79% favoured increasing taxes to 'spend more on pensions and social services'. But by 1966, this had fallen to 55%. By 1970, it had fallen again to 41% and by October 1974, only 28% believed 'more social services and benefits' were needed. But, at the same time, a claim that the electorate had already been converted to the neoliberal cause is difficult to reconcile with 66% support for raising taxes and spending in the early 1990s. If anything, the evidence here is that the electorate actually became less Thatcherite once Margaret Thatcher had been elected. See, for example, Ivor Crewe, 'Has the Electorate Become Thatcherite?', in Robert Skidelsky (ed.), *Thatcherism* (London: Chatto & Windus, 1988).
3. This data has been downloaded from the NatCen British Social Attitudes Survey dataset via the UK Data Service (https://discover.ukdataservice.ac.uk/series/?sn=200006).
4. This data is taken from an Ipsos MORI research archive available via: https://www.ipsos-mori.com/researchpublications/researcharchive/101/How-Britain-Voted-Since-October-1974.aspx.

CHAPTER 4. ALIVE AND KICKING: WHAT THE STATE DOES AND WHY IT HAS NOT BEEN ROLLED BACK

1. Margaret Thatcher, 'Speech to the College of Europe', Bruges, 20 September 1988. Available via: http://www.margaretthatcher.org/document/107332
2. Michael Sandel, *What Money Can't Buy: The Moral Limits of Markets* (New York: Farrar, Straus and Giroux, 2012), 5.
3. Paul Mason, *Postcapitalism* (London: Allen Lane, 2015), p. xi.
4. The socialist theoretician (and father of Ed and David) Ralph Miliband observed of the nationalized industries that 'though ultimate control was vested in the Minister and provision made for a measure of Parliamentary accountability more formal than real, the Government's conception of public ownership ensured the predominance on the boards of the nationalised corporations of men who had been, or who still were, closely associated with private finance and industry, and

who could hardly be expected to regard the nationalised industries as designed to achieve any purpose other than the more efficient servicing of the private sector'. Ralph Miliband, *Parliamentary Socialism: A Study in the Politics of Labour* (London: Merlin, 1961), 288 (quoted, Peter Hennessy, *Never Again: Britain 1945–51* (London: Penguin, 1992), 201).

5. See Samuel Brittan, *The Role and Limits of Government: Essays in Political Economy* (London: Temple Smith, 1983), 93. The historian Kenneth O. Morgan says of Labour's efforts to plan industry that they were 'half-hearted, indirect and in many ways unsuccessful' (Quoted, David Kynaston, *Austerity Britain, 1945–51* (London: Bloomsbury, 2007), 137). The limited impact of Keynesianism on the British state in general and on the Treasury in particular is analysed by Ben Clift and Jim Tomlinson, 'Credible Keynesianism? New Labour Macroeconomic Policy and the Political Economy of Coarse Tuning', *British Journal of Political Science*, 37 (2007), 47–69. A prepublication version of this paper can be accessed via: www2.warwick.ac.uk/fac/soc/pais/people/clift/.../keynesianism.doc
6. Kynaston, *Austerity Britain*, 139.
7. Nicholas Shaxson, *Treasure Islands: Tax Havens and the Men Who Stole the World* (London: Vintage Books, 2012), chapters 5 and 6.
8. Dominic Sandbrook, *White Heat: A History of Britain in the Swinging Sixties* (London: Little Brown, 2006), 171–6.
9. Michael Moran, *The British Regulatory State: High Modernism and Hyper-Innovation* (Oxford: Oxford University Press, 2003).
10. Jamie Peck, Nick Theodore, and Neil Brenner, 'Neoliberalism Interrupted', in Damien Cahill, Lindy Edwards, and Frank Stilwell (eds), *Neoliberalism: Beyond the Free Market* (Cheltenham: Edward Elgar, 2012), 20.
11. James Meek, 'The Great Train Robbery', *London Review of Books*, 38/9, 5 May 2016.
12. Office of Rail and Road, 'UK Rail Industry Financial Information 2015–16', 22 February 2017, p. 13. Available via: http://www.orr.gov.uk/__data/assets/pdf_file/0020/24149/uk-rail-industry-financial-information-2015-16.pdf. At the time of its privatization, British Rail received the lowest subsidy of any nationalized railway in Europe. Tony Judt, *Postwar* (London: Heineman, 2005), 543.
13. Chris Ames, 'Grayling Accused of "Piecemeal Privatisation" Over Rail Plans', *The Transport Network*, 6 December 2016.
14. Anthony King and Ivor Crewe, *The Blunders of Our Governments* (London: Oneworld, 2013), 221.
15. *BBC News*, 'Pensions Scandal Costs £11.8bn', 27 June 2002.
16. Djuna Thurley, *The New Single Tier State Pension* (House of Commons Library Briefing Paper, SN06525, 30 October 2015).
17. Public Spending UK. Available via: http://www.ukpublicspending.co.uk/. Antoine Bozio, Rowena Crawford, and Gemma Tetlow, 'The History of State Pensions in the UK: 1948 to 2010', IFS Briefing Note BN105 (London: Institute for Fiscal Studies, 2010), 64, cite a figure of 5.5% of GDP.

18. Peter Gowan, 'Crisis in the Heartland', *New Left Review*, 55 (2009), 5–30.
19. Gordon Brown, 'Speech by the Chancellor of the Exchequer to Mansion House', London, 20 June 2007. David Cameron's comments on excessive regulation can be found in a speech, 'The New Global Economy', delivered to the Euromoney Conference on 22 June 2006.
20. To be more precise, RBS was nationalized; Lloyds was encouraged by the government to take over HBOS in return for a promise to waive the usual application of competition rules; whilst the viable parts of Bradford and Bingley were sold to Santander, with the toxic assets being dumped into public ownership.
21. HM Treasury, *Budget 2015* (Red Book), HC1093 (London: HMSO, 18 March 2015), 18.
22. The Bank of England also intervened aggressively to stabilize the economy in the aftermath of the referendum result. It cut the Bank Rate to 0.25% and announced further purchases of government bonds, corporate bonds, and a scheme to provide cheap funding to banks to ensure that interest rate cuts are fed through to consumers.
23. Office for National Statistics, *Wealth in Great Britain: Wave 4, 2012–14* (18 December 2015). (Article: Main results from the Wealth and Assets Survey: July 2012 to June 2014.)
24. The basic economic idea of using quantitative easing in this way was developed by Richard Murphy, the Director of Tax Research UK. See 'How Green Infrastructure Quantitative Easing Would Work', March 2015 blog. Available via: http://www.taxresearch.org.uk/Blog/2015/03/12/how-green-infrastructure-quantitative-easing-would-work/
25. See Liz Peek, 'Tea Party Rallying Cry: Abolish the Federal Reserve', *Fiscal Times*, 10 November 2010.
26. Karen Yeung, 'The Regulatory State', in Robert Baldwin, Martin Cave, and Martin Lodge (eds), *The Oxford Handbook of Regulation* (Oxford: Oxford University Press, 2010) and references therein.
27. David Osborne and Tom Gaebler, *Reinventing Government: How the Entrepreneurial Spirit is Transforming the Public Sector* (Reading, MA: Addison-Wesley, 1992).
28. Rosie Campbell and Sarah Childs, 'What the Coalition did for Women: A New Gender Consensus, Coalition Division and Gendered Austerity', in Anthony Seldon and Mike Finn (eds), *The Coalition Effect 2010–2015* (Cambridge: Cambridge University Press, 2015).
29. *BBC News*, 'Bill-by-Bill Summary: Queen's Speech At-a-Glance', 18 May 2016.
30. 'Theresa May's Keynote Speech at Tory Conference in Full', *Independent*, 5 October 2016.
31. *BBC News*, 'Uber Drivers Win Key Employment Case', 28 October 2016.
32. Philip Stephens, 'Three Years on and the Markets are the Masters Again', *Financial Times*, 29 July 2010. The argument that very little has changed since the financial crisis is a staple of much of the academic literature on post-crisis financial reform. See Eric Helleiner, *The Status Quo Crisis: Global Financial Governance after the 2008 Meltdown* (Oxford: Oxford University Press, 2014);

Martin Wolf, *The Shifts and the Shocks: What We've Learned—And Have Still to Learn from the Financial Crisis* (London: Penguin, 2014); and Philip Mirowski, *Never Let a Serious Crisis go to Waste: How Neoliberalism Survived the Financial Meltdown* (London:Verso, 2013).

33. Timothy Edwards, *The Independent Commission on Banking—The Vickers Report* (House of Commons Library Briefing Paper, SNBT 6171, 30 December 2013).
34. Richard Sharp, 'The Financial Policy Committee of the Bank of England: An Experiment in Macroprudential Regulation—The View of an External Member', speech given at the LSE, 4 June 2014.
35. Mark Carney, 'Building Real Markets for the Good of the People', Mansion House speech, 10 June 2015.
36. Stephen Bell and Andrew Hindmoor, *Masters of the Universe but Slaves of the Market* (Cambridge, MA: Harvard University Press, 2015), chapter 9.
37. Karl Marx, *Grundrisse* (London: Penguin, 1973), 56.
38. Barnaby Fedder, 'Theodore Levitt, 81, Who Termed the Term "Globalization" is Dead', *New York Times*, 6 July 2006.
39. Thomas Friedman, *The Lexus and the Olive Tree: Understanding Globalization* (New York: Farrar, Straus and Giroux, 1999), 87.
40. Naomi Klein, *The Shock Doctrine: The Rise of Disaster Capitalism* (London: Penguin, 2007); Naomi Klein, 'Outflanking the Rich and Powerful', *Guardian*, 26 January 2001; Joseph Stiglitz, *Globalisation and its Discontents* (New York: W. W. Norton, 2002); George Monbiot, 'This Transatlantic Trade Deal is a Frontal Assault on Democracy', *Guardian*, 4 November 2013.
41. Rupert Neate, 'World Bank and IMF Chiefs: Tax Dodging is Grave Concern for Global Economy', *Guardian*, 14 April 2016.
42. A key early moment in the campaign for greater tax transparency came in 1998, when the OECD launched the Harmful Tax Competition Initiative. This included a formal recognition that 'tax schemes aimed at attracting financial and other geographically mobile activities can create harmful tax competition between States, carrying risks of distorting trade and investment and could lead to the erosion of national tax bases'. The United States has aided financial disclosure in so far as the Foreign Account Tax Compliance Act of 2010 requires banks and other financial institutions based outside of the US to disclose information about US customers who have deposited money with them: often in the attempt to avoid tax. No equivalent requirements have been imposed on non-US citizens who have deposited money in the United States. Laura Saunders, 'Offshore Accounts: What do we do Now?', *Wall Street Journal*, 20 June 2014.
43. Rupert Neate and Simon Bowers, 'UK and European Allies Plan to Deal Hammer Blow to Tax Evasion', *Guardian*, 15 April 2016.
44. Stephen Bell and Andrew Hindmoor, *Rethinking Governance* (Cambridge: Cambridge University Press, 2009), 39–43.
45. The notion of there being a 'competition state' was developed by the Anglo-American political economist Phil Cerny. The most easily accessible on-line

account of his argument can be found in Phil Cerny and Mark Evans, 'New Labour, Globalisation and the Competition State' (University of York Centre for European Studies: Working Paper 70, 2000). For an interesting discussion of how neoliberal precepts on the importance and value of competition have driven the growth of the competition state via the construction of league tables measuring the competitiveness of national state economies and the ease of doing business in them, see William Davies, *The Limits of Neoliberalism* (London: Sage, 2014), 108–47.

46. Mariana Mazzucato, *The Entrepreneurial State: Debunking Public vs Private Sector Myths* (London: Anthem Press, 2011).
47. David Cameron, 'Speech to the CBI', 19 November 2012.
48. HM Government, *Industrial Strategy: Government and Industry in Partnership. Progress Report*, April 2014.
49. 'Theresa May's Keynote Speech at Tory Conference in Full', *Independent*, 5 October 2016.
50. For an overview, see 'Coming and Going: Truth and Myths about the Effects of Openness to Trade', *The Economist*, 1 October 2016.
51. 'Policies to Help Britons Who Lose Out from Free Trade are Woefully Inadequate', *The Economist*, 29 October 2016.
52. Jessica Elgot, 'Brexit will be Titanic Success Says Boris Johnson', *Guardian*, 3 November 2016.
53. Will Martin, 'The Government is Denying that it gave a "Sweetheart Deal" to Nissan to Boost its UK Production', *Business Insider UK*, 28 October 2016.
54. Peter Dominiczak, 'Brexit Plan is "Months Away" as Civil Service Needs 30,000 Extra Staff to Cope with Workload, According to Leaked Memo', *Daily Telegraph*, 15 November 2016.
55. Joseph Schumpeter, *The Crisis of the Tax State* (Leipzig: Leuschner and Lubensky, 1918), 42.
56. OECD General Government Expenditure Series (Available via: https://data.oecd.org/gga/general-government-spending.htm)
57. OECD, Fiscal Decentralisation Database (Section C, spending and revenue shares of state and local government). Available via: https://www.oecd.org/ctp/federalism/oecdfiscaldecentralisationdatabase.htm.
58. Ministry of Justice, National Offender Management Service, and HM Prison Service, Prison Population Figures: 2017, 7 July 2017.
59. *BBC News*, 'Western Europe Prison Populations' and 'World Prison Populations' (undated).
60. HM Treasury, *Budget 2017* (Red Book), HC1025, (London: HMSO, 8 March 2017), 4.
61. Public Spending UK, available via: http://www.ukpublicspending.co.uk/
62. Gavin Berman and Tom Rutherford, *Defence Personnel Statistics* (London: House of Commons Standard Briefing Note, SN02183), 27 March 2017.
63. Graham Allen and Elise Uberoi, *Police Service Strength* (London: House of Commons Library Briefing Paper, 00634, 14 June 2017.
64. Home Office, 'Police Use of Firearms: Statistics', England and Wales', 28 July 2016.

65. In the United States, an average of 3.1 people are killed each day by the police. Ian Swaine and Oliver Langhard, 'Number of People Killed by US Police in 2015 at 1,000 After Oakland Shooting', *Guardian*, 16 November 2015.
66. HM Government, *The Coalition: Our Program for Government* (2010). Available via: https://www.gov.uk/government/uploads/system/uploads/attachment_data/file/78977/coalition_programme_for_government.pdf
67. The economic case for austerity was also driven by the findings of two prominent economists, Carmen Reinhart and Kenneth Rogoff, concerning the long-term historical relationship between public debt and economic growth. This purported to identify a level of public debt (90% of GDP) at which an economy's growth stagnates. The key policy implication taken by the Coalition was that in order to avoid a 'Greek-style' fiscal meltdown, Britain needed to cut its debt and cut it quickly. Rogoff's data analysis was, to put it charitably, subsequently found to be open to debate. See Ruth Alexander, 'Reinhart, Rogoff... and Herndon: The Student Who Caught out the Profs', *BBC Magazine*, 20 April 2014. For a more general account (and critique) of the logic of austerity, see Mark Blyth, *Austerity: The History of a Dangerous Idea* (Oxford: Oxford University Press, 2013).
68. Polly Toynbee, 'Nothing Will Stop David Cameron's Race to the Weightless State?', *Guardian*, 20 May 2014.
69. Liam Byrne, 'I'm Sorry There is no Money: The Letter I will Regret for Ever', *Guardian*, 9 May 2015.
70. 'Budget 2014: All Osborne's Budgets so far in Five Charts', *Guardian*, 19 March 2014. Totals for each budget are achieved by adding up the cumulative estimated effect of the policy decisions over the five financial years after the budget.
71. Anthony Seldon and Peter Snowdon, *Cameron at 10: The Inside Story, 2010–15* (London: William Collins), 252–4.
72. Office for Budget Responsibility, *Economic and Fiscal Outlook*, Cm. 9098 (July 2015), 17.
73. Paul Krugman, 'The Austerity Delusion', *Guardian*, 28 April 2015. For a largely equivalent and equally damning assessment, see Simon Wren-Lewis, 'The Austerity Con', *London Review of Books*, 37, February 2015.
74. Philip Inman, 'OBR Chief Writes to Cameron Disputing his Austerity Claims', *Guardian*, 8 March 2013.
75. Office for Budget Responsibility, *Economic and Fiscal Outlook*, Cm. 9098 (July 2015), 17.
76. Jonathan Freedland, 'Budget 2016: Magical Thinking from Charmed World of Chancellor', *Guardian*, 16 March 2016.
77. Office for Budget Responsibility, *Economic and Fiscal Outlook*, Cm. 9346 (October 2016), 7.
78. HM Treasury, *Public Expenditure, Statistical Analyses*, 2017, 65. Available via: https://www.gov.uk/government/uploads/system/uploads/attachment_data/file/630570/60243_PESA_Accessible.pdf
79. See the on-line appendix on public sector expenditure (4a) for more details.

80. This data is taken from the Office for National Statistics figures on Public Sector Finance (May 2017 figures). Available via: https://www.ons.gov.uk/economy/governmentpublicsectorandtaxes/publicsectorfinance/bulletins/publicsectorfinances/may2017
81. Office for Budget Responsibility, *Economic and Fiscal Outlook*, Cm. 9212 (March 2016), 17.
82. Office for Budget Responsibility, *Economic and Fiscal Outlook*, Cm. 9346 (October 2016), 20.
83. Between 2010 and 2013, there were huge cuts to the prison service which resulted in something like a 20% fall in the number of serving prison officers (as well has huge cuts to education and drug counselling services). See 'The Parlous State of Prisons in England and Wales has Echoes of the Past', *The Economist*, 26 November 2016.
84. Press Association, 'Elderly Britons Bearing Brunt of Cuts to Social Care, Report Says', *Guardian*, 15 September 2016.
85. HM Treasury, *Public Expenditure, Statistical Analyses*, 2017.
86. Jonathan Portes, 'Immigration After Brexit', *National Institute Economic Review*, 238 (November 2016).
87. Office for Budget Responsibility, *Fiscal Risks Report*, July 2017, 3.
88. House of Commons Committee of Public Accounts, *Contracting Out Public Services to the Private Sector*, HC777 (London: HMSO, 2014), 3.
89. National Audit Office, *The Role of Major Contractors in the Delivery of Public Services*, HC810 (London: Stationery Office, 2013), 5.
90. National Audit Office, *Central Government's Use of Consultants and Interims*, HC488 (London: Stationery Office, 2010).
91. Johal Sukhdev, Michael Moran, and Karel Williams, 'Breaking the Constitutional Silence: The Public Services Industry and Government', *Political Quarterly*, 2016.
92. Rob Davies, 'Complex Chain of Companies that Worked on Grenfell Tower Raises Oversight Concerns', *Guardian*, 16 June.
93. See Home Office (2014), 'An Introduction to the Drugs Intervention Program for Prisons and Probation Services', available via: http://www.ohrn.nhs.uk/resource/policy/DIPProbation.pdf
94. Gabrielle Garton Grimwood et al., *Delivering Public Services: The Growing Use of Payment by Results*, SN/HA/6621 (London: House of Commons Library, April 2013), 17–18. On the stumbling fortunes of the payment for results programme, see: 'Pay Up', *The Economist*, 4 June 2016.
95. Alan Travis, 'Two Companies to Run more than Half of Privatised Probation Services', *Guardian*, 29 October 2014.
96. The following stories all relate to proposals to contract out government services: Caroline Mortimer, 'Government Quietly Announces Plan to Privatise Land Registry on Night Before Easter Holidays', *Independent*, 25 March 2016; Alan Travis and Zoe Williams, 'Revealed: Government Plans for Police Privatisation', *Guardian*, 2 March 2012; Matthew Taylor, 'Surge in Privatization Threatening Free NHS Treatment, Unions Say', *Guardian*, 8 February 2016;

Ray Jones, 'Plans to Privatize Child Protection are Moving at Pace', *Guardian*, 12 January 2015.

97. The Smith Institute, *Outsourcing the Cuts: Pay and Employment Effects of Contracting Out* (London: The Smith Institute, 2014). Andrew Bowman et al., *What a Waste: Outsourcing and How it Goes Wrong* (Manchester: Manchester University Press, 2015).
98. On the concept of managed markets, see Michael Keating, *Who Rules? How Government Retains Control of a Privatised Economy* (Sydney: Federation Press, 2004).
99. Jonathan Stanley, 'Narey Report Gives Children's Homes the Status They Deserve', *Guardian*, 11 July 2016. Around 30% of children in care now live in homes provided by local authorities. Around 5% live in homes provided by the voluntary sector. Nearly 70% live in privately provided homes. Sir Martin Narey, *Residential Care in England*, July 2016, p. 9.
100. John Morrison, 'Defining the Social Licence', *Guardian*, 29 September 2014. Rowena Mason, Matthew Weaver, and Stephanie Kirchgaessner, 'George Osborne Insists Google's UK Tax Deal is a Major Success', *Guardian*, 28 January 2016.
101. On Sports Direct, see: *BBC News*, 'Sports Direct Founder Mike Ashley Admits Errors', 7 June 2016. On Wonga, see Miles Brignall, 'Wonga Tells MPs it is Halfway Through Culture Turnaround', *Guardian*, 18 November 2014. On the sorry saga of BHS, see: Ashley Armstrong, 'Sir Phillip Green to be Grilled amid Calls he be Stripped of Knighthood', *Daily Telegraph*, 9 June 2016. Finally, on the transformation of Boots' corporate culture, see Aditya Chakraborty, 'How Boots Went Rogue', *Guardian*, 13 April 2016.
102. Sean Coughlin, 'Labour Challenges Final End of Student Grants', *BBC News*, 19 January 2016. http://www.bbc.co.uk/news/education-35347598
103. In December 2016, the advertising industry announced that it would ban on-line adverts for food and drinks high in fat, salt, or sugar aimed at children and would apply that ban on all other media where under-16s constitute a quarter of the audience. Critics argue that the ban does not go far enough and that, in the absence of effective monitoring, it will not be properly implemented. *BBC News*, 'Children's Online Junk Food Ads Banned by Industry', 8 December 2016.
104. Office for National Statistics, 'Public Sector Employment: UK December 2015', 16 March 2016.
105. Dawn Foster, 'Who Lives in the 4.1m Social Homes in England and Wales?', *Guardian*, 18 November 2015.
106. There are toll road or bridge charges on four motorways, nine A-roads, and eight minor roads. London and the City of Durham levy congestion charges. See https://www.gov.uk/uk-toll-roads

Note to figure caption

1. Office for Budget Responsibility, *Economic and Fiscal Outlook*, Cm. 9212 (March 2016), 182.

CHAPTER 5. PUBLIC SERVICES: HEALTH AND EDUCATION

1. For recent examples of the genre, see: Richard Wellings, *How to Abolish the NHS* (Adam Smith Institute, 23 January 2012); James Stanfield, *Freedom is the Missing Ingredient in Education* (Adam Smith Institute, 19 July 2012); Kristian Niemietz, *Health Check: The NHS and Market Reforms* (IEA Discussion Paper, 54, 2014); and Gabriel Sahlgren, *Schooling for Money: Swedish Education Reform and the Role of the Profit Motive* (IEA Discussion Paper, 33, 2010).
2. Andrew Rawnsley, 'Kenneth Clarke: I had Lots of Views but they Didn't Coincide with No. 10's', *Observer*, 19 July 2014. Recently released Cabinet archives suggest that, behind the scenes, and following a Cabinet revolt in 1982, Margaret Thatcher in fact commissioned a report by a Treasury Official on secondment to the Central Policy Review Staff which included proposals to charge for state schooling and to introduce private health insurance. The point remains, however, that these proposals were, eventually, shelved. Alan Travis, 'Thatcher Pushed for Breakup of Welfare State Despite NHS Pledge', *Guardian*, 25 November 2016.
3. Dennis Campbell, 'NHS Group Considers Charges for Crutches and Neck Braces', *Guardian*, 16 April 2014; Javier Espinoza, 'Primary Schools to Charge Parents to use Car Parks', *Daily Telegraph*, 15 June 2015; and Javier Espinoza, 'State Schools Charge Parents to Let Children Eat their Own Packed Lunches', *Daily Telegraph*, 28 March 2016.
4. Dr Youssef El-Gingihy, 'The NHS is on a One-Way Road to Privatisation', *Guardian*, 2 October 2015.
5. Matthew Taylor, 'Surge in Privatisation Threatening Free NHS Treatment, Unions Say', *Guardian*, 8 February 2016. The journalist Anne Perkins observes that 'many Conservatives truly believe that the state is incapable of doing anything better than the private sector'. Anne Perkins, 'We Must Fight Plans to Privatise the NHS', *Guardian*, 3 July 2014.
6. Quoted, Jackie Davis and Raymond Tallis, *NHS SOS: How the NHS Was Betrayed—and How we Can Save it* (London: One World Books, 2013), 5.
7. Jamie Doward, 'Thousands of New Doctors Opt for a Better Life Abroad', *Guardian*, 23 August 2015; Sally Weale, 'UK Schools Suffering as Newly Qualified Teachers Flock Abroad', *Guardian*, 26 February 2016.
8. Dennis Campbell, '300,000 More Patients on NHS Waiting List Under Coalition', *Guardian*, 13 February 2014; Sarah Cassidy, 'Growing Crisis Over Shortage of School Places Could Lead to "Titan" Secondary Schools to Cope with Thousands of Extra Pupils', *Independent*, 11 September 2015.
9. Dawn Foster, 'Austerity is Making People Physically Sick', *Guardian*, 22 March 2016.
10. Rebecca Smith, 'Target Culture that Led to Mid Staffs Still Exists in NHS', *Daily Telegraph*, 25 January 2013.
11. Jacky Davis, 'What Were You Doing While the NHS was being Destroyed?', *Guardian*, 13 November 2013.

12. John Curtice and Rachel Ormston (eds), *British Social Attitudes: The 32nd Report* (2015), London: NatCen Social Research, 112.
13. Ibid., 114.
14. The NHS has developed into a world-class illness service but still struggles to function effectively as a health service. One huge problem here is the lack of integration between health and social care services. In 2014, a commission of inquiry chaired by Kate Barker described the health and social care systems as rubbing up against each other like bones on an open fracture (Commission on the Future of Health and Social Care in England, *A New Settlement for Health and Social Care*, Interim Report, 2014, p. x). Health and social care services are commissioned separately by different organizations using different pots of government money in ways that threaten both efficiency and equity. Despite being a medical illness with devastating health consequences, dementia is, for example, treated primarily as a social care issue (this is not simply an age-related issue: a chronic lack of integration also affects children with long-term care needs, many physically disabled people, and those with mental health problems and drug and alcohol addictions).

    The failure to integrate health and social care is not a new problem, the origins of which we can trace back to Thatcherism or the growing influence of neoliberalism. The social care system has always been organized separately from the NHS and has always been relatively poorly funded. Social care services have, for a long time, also been subject to a means-test which cuts right against the grain of universal provision. The Coalition has made some progress in supporting social care by legislating for a maximum cap of £72,000 on social care costs (in response to the recommendations of the Dilnot Commission). At the same time, the Health Foundation estimates that between 2010 and 2014, public expenditure on home and day care services was cut by £539m (23%); spending on nursing placements by £160m (15%); and spending on residential care by £330m (12%) (Sharif Ismail, Ruth Thorlby, and Holly Holder, *Quality Watch: Focus on Social Care for Elderly People: Reductions in Adult Social Services for Older People in England*, March 2014, 6).
15. Rowena Mason, 'Andrew Lansley Chides Chancellor Over Lack of NHS and Social Care Funding', *Guardian*, 24 November 2016. A few weeks later, the Secretary of State for Communities and Local Government promised £900m for local authorities to fund social care by bringing forward council tax rises.
16. Between 2009/10 and 2013/14, accident and emergency admissions rose by 6%. See Howard Glennester, 'Health and Long-Term Care', in Anthony Seldon and Mike Finn (eds), *The Coalition Effect* (Cambridge: Cambridge University Press, 2015), 305–7.
17. HM Treasury, *Public Expenditure, Statistical Analyses*, 2017. Available via: https://www.gov.uk/government/uploads/system/uploads/attachment_data/file/630570/60243_PESA_Accessible.pdf
18. Dennis Campbell, 'NHS is Cash-Strapped and Fraying at the Edges Warns BMA Chairman', *Guardian*, 30 June 2014.

19. HM Treasury, *Public Expenditure, Statistical Analyses*, 2016. Available via: https://www.gov.uk/government/uploads/system/uploads/attachment_data/file/630570/60243_PESA_Accessible.pdf
20. The Conservative and Unionist Party Manifesto, *Forward Together*, p. 66. Available via: https://s3.eu-west-2.amazonaws.com/manifesto2017/Manifesto2017.pdf
21. Office for National Statistics, *United Kingdom Population: Mid-Year Estimate* (June 2017).
22. Office for National Statistics, *Estimates of the Very Old (including Centenarians), UK: 2002 to 2015* (29 September 2016).
23. John Bingham, 'Queen's Birthday Card Team Expands to Cope with Surge of 100-Year-Olds', *Daily Telegraph*, 25 September 2014.
24. See Glennester, 'Health and Long-Term Care', 305–7.
25. Theresa May has also provoked the disquiet of the Chief Executive of NHS England, Simon Stevens, in relation to the accuracy of her claim to have increased NHS funding by £10bn. Dennis Campbell, 'Government Scolded by Watchdog Over NHS Funding Claims', *Guardian*, 23 November 2016.
26. HM Treasury, *Public Expenditure, Statistical Analyses*, 2016. Available via: https://www.gov.uk/government/statistics/public-expenditure-statistical-analyses-2016
27. Chris Belfield et al., *Living Standards, Poverty and Inequality in the UK: 2016* (London: Institute for Fiscal Studies, 2016), 40.
28. Haroon Chowdry and Luke Sibieta, *Trends in Education and Schools Spending* (London: Institute for Fiscal Studies, Briefing Note BN121, 2011), 1.
29. During the Coalition's time in office, real expenditure increased. The balance of funding has, however, switched away from government and to students following the decision to allow universities to charge up to £9,000 in tuition fees. Institute for Fiscal Studies, *Education Spending* (29 September 2015). Available via: http://www.ifs.org.uk/tools_and_resources/fiscal_facts/public_spending_survey/education
30. Ruth Lupton and Stephanie Thomson, *The Coalition's Record on Schools: Policy, Spending and Outcomes 2010–2015* (LSE: Centre for the Analysis of Social Exclusion, 2015), 25.
31. Ibid. 28. In their 2015 manifesto, the Conservatives promised to 'continue to provide the pupil premium, protected at current rates'. Tim Jarrett, Robert Long, and David Foster, *School Funding Pupil Premium* (House of Commons Library Briefing Paper, 06700, 26 November 2015), 7.
32. Richard Adams, 'Secondary Schools Face Sharpest Cuts to Funding Since 1970s, Says Thinktank', *Guardian*, 15 April 2016.
33. In an on-line appendix to this chapter (5a), I look at the historical trends here in more detail.
34. Ruth Thorlby and Jo Maybin (eds), *A High-Performing NHS? A Review of Progress, 1997–2010* (London: The King's Fund, 2010), 15.
35. OECD Data, Health Status. Available via: https://data.oecd.org/healthstat/infant-mortality-rates.htm#indicator-chart. In 2016, Macmillan Cancer Support published a report in which it estimated that people are twice as likely to live at

least ten years after being diagnosed with cancer than they were at the start of the 1970s. Press Association, 'Thousands of Cancer Sufferers Surviving Decades After Diagnosis', *Guardian*, 1 August 2016.

36. OECD Data, Health Status. Available via: https://data.oecd.org/healthstat/infant-mortality-rates.htm#indicator-chart
37. Lupton and Thomson, *The Coalition's Record on Schools*, 7.
38. The OECD's PISA test is taken by 15-year-olds in maths, science, and reading every three years.

    - In 2006, the UK mean test scores for reading were 495 (the UK was ranked 17th); for mathematics 498 (ranked 28th); and for science 513 (ranked 14th).
    - Skip forward nearly a decade and in 2015 the UK mean test scores for reading were 498 (ranked 22nd); for mathematics 492 (ranked 27th); and for science 509 (ranked 15th).

    For a more detailed analysis of the UK's performance in the most recent round of results, see the OECD summary, available via: http://www.oecd.org/pisa/PISA-2015-United-Kingdom.pdf. Some educationalists argue that because the tests are undertaken in different ways in different countries, the rankings derived from them are meaningless (*Times Education Supplement*, 'Is PISA Fundamentally Flawed?', Comment, 27 September 2014).
39. For a detailed analysis see Ruth Robertson, 'Public Satisfaction with the NHS in 2016', The King's Fund, 30 March 2017.
40. OECD. Stat. Health Expenditure and Financing. Available via: http://stats.oecd.org/index.aspx?DataSetCode=SHA#
41. Sandeepa Arora, Anita Charlesworth, Elaine Kelly, and George Stoye, *Public Payment and Private Provision: The Changing Landscape of Health Care in the 2000s* (London: Institute for Fiscal Studies, 2013), 26.
42. Ibid., 11.
43. Paul Bolton, *Education: Historical Statistics* (House of Commons Library Paper, SN/SG/4252, 27 November 2012).
44. 'Why Private Schooling is on the Decline in England', *The Economist*, 1 December 2015.
45. Richard Adams, 'Private Schools in UK Attracting Record Numbers of Students', *Guardian*, 1 May 2015.
46. Richard Adams, 'Massively Improved State Schools Threaten Private Sector', *Guardian*, 5 February 2016. In December 2016, the Independent Schools Council—under pressure from Theresa May to justify their charitable status—offered to provide 10,000 places to children from low-income families if the government, in return, paid them the amount it costs to educate a child within the state sector (around £5,500 a year). Effectively, this would amount to a reincarnation of the Assisted Places Scheme abolished by New Labour.
47. The data used here is taken from the Institute for Fiscal Studies, 'Incomes in the UK', available via: http://www.ifs.org.uk/tools_and_resources/incomes_in_uk (hyperlink to the 'spreadsheet' under data).

48. Gwyn Bevan and Christopher Hood, 'What's Measured is What Matters: Targets and Gaming in the English Public Health Care System', *Public Administration*, 84/3 (2006), 517–38.
49. Alison Little, 'Overhaul of Targets Frees up NHS', *Daily Express*, 22 June 2010.
50. Chris Ham, Beccy Baird, Sarah Gregory, Joni Jabbal, and Hugh Alderwick, *The NHS Under the Coalition Government. Part One: NHS Reform* (London: The King's Fund, 2015), 41.
51. In March 2016, it was reported that hospitals were collectively being fined more than £600m a year for breaches of this target. Dennis Campbell, 'NHS Trust Bosses Slam £600m Hospital Fines over Patient Targets', *Guardian*, 29 March 2016.
52. Lupton and Thomson, *The Coalition's Record on Schools*, 16–17.
53. As long ago as 2003, there were reports that hospitals were requiring patients to wait in queues of ambulances outside the front entrance of accident and emergency departments during busy periods in order to help meet targets relating to admission waiting times. Nicholas Timmins, 'Blair Bemused over GP Waiting Times', *Financial Times*, 30 April 2005. Sarah Boseley, 'Ambulance Queues Highlight A and E Crisis', *Guardian*, 16 September 2003.
54. *BBC News*, 'Lincolnshire 999 Call Staff Suspended Over Data Manipulation Claims', 23 May 2016.
55. Michael Barber, *Instruction to Deliver: Fighting to Transform Britain's Public Services* (London: Methuen, 2008).
56. The Mid Staffordshire NHS Foundation Trust Public Inquiry, *Report of the Mid Staffordshire NHS Foundation Trust Public Inquiry Executive Summary* (London: The Stationery Office, 2013).
57. Bevan and Hood, 'What's Measured is What Matters', 517–38. Simon Burgess, Deborah Wilson, and Jack Worth of the University of Bristol have examined the impact of publishing school league tables by tracing the outcome of the devolved Welsh government's decision to abolish publishing these tables in 2001. They argue that, following this decision, school performance in Wales and England began to diverge and that by the late 2000s, the grades of pupils in Wales were around 2 GSCE grades lower than they would otherwise have been. Simon Burgess, Deborah Wilson, and Jack Worth, *A Natural Experiment in School Accountability: The Impact of School Performance Information on Pupil Progress and Sorting* (Bristol: Centre for Market and Public Organisation, 2010).
58. Within the study of public administration, academics often refer to the doctrine of the *New Public Management* (NPM). According to Christopher Hood, NPM was a term coined in the 1980s to 'denote a new (or renewed) stress on the importance of management and "production engineering" in public service delivery'. The emphasis within NPM was 'firmly managerial in the sense that it stressed the difference management could and should make to the quality and efficiency of public services' (Christopher Hood, 'New Public Management' (undated). Available via: http://christopherhood.net/pdfs/npm_encyclopedia_entry.pdf). In practice and as it was applied in the UK and beyond, NPM was associated with: (i) an

attention to lessons from private-sector management; (ii) the growth of hands-on 'management', in its own right and not as an offshoot of professionalism; (iii) the establishment of 'arm's-length' organizations where policy implementation is organizationally distanced from the policymakers; (iv) a focus upon entrepreneurial leadership within public service organizations; (v) an emphasis on input and output control and evaluation and on performance management and audit; (vi) the disaggregation of public services to their most basic units and a focus on their cost management; and (vii) the growth of use of markets, competition, and contracts for resource allocation and service delivery within public services (Stephen Osborne, 'The New Public Governance?', *Public Management Review*, 8/3 (2006), 377–88). As the fifth and sixth items on this list most clearly indicate, there is a strong intellectual association between neoliberalism and NPM.

59. John Grey, 'The Neoliberal State', *New Statesman*, 7 January 2010.
60. Bevan and Hood, 'What's Measured is What Matters', 517–38.
61. Elaine Kelly and Gemma Tetlow, *Choosing the Place of Care: The Effect of Patient Choice on Treatment Location in England, 2003–2011* (London: Institute of Fiscal Studies, 2013), 17.
62. David Cameron, 'Speech on Open Public Services', 11 July 2011.
63. *BBC News*, 'Hinchingbrooke Hospital: Circle to Withdraw from Contract', 9 January 2015.
64. Neil Roberts, 'Cornish GPs Take Back Out-of-Hours from Serco', *GP Magazine Online*, 13 February 2015.
65. Will Smith, 'What Circle Has Learned from its Bedford MSK Contract', *Heath Service Journal*, 7 October 2015.
66. Nick Triggle, 'NHS Privatisation: Why the Fuss?', *BBC News*, 20 February 2015.
67. Taylor, 'Surge in Privatisation Threatening Free NHS Treatment, Unions Say'.
68. Chris Smyth, Rachel Sylvester, and Alice Thomson, 'NHS Reforms our Worst Mistake, Tories admit', *The Times*, 13 October 2014. On Cameron's failure to engage with the details of the legislation in time, see Anthony Seldon and Peter Snowdon, *Cameron at 10: The Inside Story, 2010–15* (London: William Collins, 2015), 181–3.
69. Michelle Roberts, 'A Third of NHS Contracts Awarded to Private Firms—Report', *BBC News*, 10 December 2014.
70. Department of Health, *Annual Reports and Accounts, 2015–16* (London: Stationery Office), 40. For the 2014/15 figure, see p. 47 of the previous report.
71. See Policy Agendas UK, Acts of UK Parliament. Available via: http://www.policyagendas.org.uk/
72. *BBC News*, 'Government U-Turn on English Schools to Academies Plan', 7 May 2016.
73. Any decision by that trust to sell school buildings or playing fields or to dissolve the Academy must, however, be approved by the Secretary of State for Education.
74. The Department of Education advice is that charges can only be issued for materials, books, instruments, or equipment a child's parent wishes them to own; optional extras such as board and lodging on residential visits; some music and vocal tuition; certain kinds of early years provision; and community facilities such

as sports halls. Department for Education, *Charging for School Activities: Departmental Advice for Governing Bodies, School Leaders, School Staff and Local Authorities* (October 2014). Available via: https://www.gov.uk/government/uploads/system/uploads/attachment_data/file/514619/Charging_for_school_activities.pdf

75. House of Commons Education Committee, *Academies and Free Schools*, HC258 (London: Stationery Office, 2015), 4.
76. Lupton and Thomson, *The Coalition's Record on Schools*, 29.
77. Toby Helm, 'Tory Backbench Rebellion Threat over George Osborne's Academies Plan', *Guardian*, 2 April 2016. On claims about the diversion of funds, see Daniel Boffey, 'Taxpayers Fund Large Wages and Lavish Perks of Academic School Chiefs', *Guardian*, 24 July 2016.
78. Rebecca Allen, 'Grammar Schools: Four Key Research Points', 24 September 2016. Available via: http://educationdatalab.org.uk/2016/09/grammar-schools-four-key-research-points/. Also see the post 'Grammar Schools Contaminate Comprehensive Schooling Areas' by the same author: http://educationdatalab.org.uk/2016/08/grammar-schools-contaminate-comprehensive-schooling-areas/
79. 'The New Three R's', *The Economist*, 29 October 2016.
80. Anthony Crosland, *The Future of Socialism* (London: Jonathan Cape, 1956), 99 and 102.
81. Richard Adams, 'Government May Give Start-Up Universities Degree Awarding Powers', *Guardian*, 16 May 2016.
82. NHS Confederation, Key Statistics on the NHS (12 May 2016) and Ruth Lupton and Polina Obolenskaya, *Labour's Record on Education: Policy, Spending and Outcomes 1997–2010* (LSE: Centre for the Analysis of Social Exclusion, 2013), 26.
83. In recent years, the Commonwealth Fund (a private foundation) has compared and ranked the Australian, Canadian, French, German, Dutch, New Zealand, Norwegian, Swedish, Swiss, UK, and US health-care systems. In the most recent exercise, the UK was ranked first for quality of care, access, and efficiency, second for equity of treatment, and first overall. Karen Davis, Kristof Stremikis, David Squires, and Cathy Schoen, *Mirror, Mirror on the Wall: How the Performance of the US Health Care System Compares Internationally* (New York: The Commonwealth Fund, 2014). Available via: http://www.commonwealthfund.org/~/media/files/publications/fund-report/2014/jun/1755_davis_mirror_mirror_2014.pdf

Notes to figure captions

1. This data has been taken from UK Public Spending (http://www.ukpublicspending.co.uk/).
2. This data has been taken from UK Public Spending (http://www.ukpublicspending.co.uk/).
3. Office for National Statistics, *The Effects of Taxes and Benefits on Household Income, Historical Datasets* (25 April 2017). Available via: https://www.ons.gov.uk/peoplepopulationandcommunity/personalandhouseholdfinances/incomeandwealth/datasets/theeffectsoftaxesandbenefitsonhouseholdincomehistoricaldatasets

4. Office for National Statistics, *The Effects of Taxes and Benefits on Household Income, Historical Datasets* (25 April 2017).
5. NatCen's British Social Attitudes Survey, 32 (2015), 18.

CHAPTER 6. MORE AND LESS: EQUALITY AND INEQUALITY IN BRITAIN

1. Chris Johnston, 'Jeremy Corbyn Calls for New Economics to Tackle "Grotesque Inequality"', *Guardian*, 21 May 2016.
2. 'Jeremy Corbyn's Full Speech to the 2016 Labour Party Conference', *New Statesman*, 28 September 2016.
3. Boris Johnson, 'The Annual Margaret Thatcher Lecture', 27 November 2013. Available via: http://www.cps.org.uk/events/q/date/2013/11/27/the-2013-margaret-thatcher-lecture-boris-johnson/
4. Carol Walker, 'Don't Cut Down the Tall Poppies: Thatcherism and the Strategy of Inequality', in Colin Hay and Stephen Farrall (eds), *The Legacy of Thatcherism* (Oxford: Oxford University Press, 2014).
5. Rodney Lowe, *History of the Welfare State in Britain since 1945* (Basingstoke: Palgrave Macmillan, 2004), 378.
6. The data I use from the Office for National Statistics and the Institute for Fiscal Studies is compiled on a UK-wide basis.
7. OECD data on income inequality can be accessed via: http://stats.oecd.org/Index.aspx?DataSetCode=IDD
8. These figures are also taken from the OECD dataset on income equality, which can be accessed via: http://stats.oecd.org/Index.aspx?DataSetCode=IDD
9. Jodi Dean, *Democracy and Other Neoliberal Fantasies: Communicative Capitalism and Left Politics* (Durham, NC: Duke University Press, 2009), 73.
10. The concept of predistribution was coined by the American political scientist Jacob Hacker. See Jacob Hacker, 'Miliband's not Talking about Predistribution but he has Embraced my Big Idea', *New Statesman*, 29 April 2015. For a more detailed discussion, see Claudia Chwalisz and Patrick Diamond, 'Predistribution: A New Governing Prospectus for the Centre Left', *Policy Network*, 17 November 2015.
11. The data I have used to calculate these figures come from the OECD website on income inequality and use the most recently available numbers for each country (see http://stats.oecd.org/Index.aspx?DataSetCode=IDD). In each case, I have simply calculated the % difference between the market income Gini coefficient and the gross income Gini coefficient after all cash welfare payments but before taxes.
12. Office for National Statistics, *Annual Survey of Hours and Earnings: 2016 Provisional Results*, 25 October 2016 (Section 7, Regional Earnings). This section has been quoted directly.
13. John Lanchester, 'Capital Gains: John Lanchester's Satire of London's Boom Years is Adapted for TV', *Guardian*, 21 November 2015.

14. 'The North of England: The Great Divide', *The Economist*, 15 September 2015.
15. The 'East' here is composed of Norfolk, Suffolk, Essex, Hertfordshire, and Cambridgeshire. In calculating North–South earnings, I have *not* adjusted for the size of the respective populations in different regions.
16. 'How the Other Three Quarters Lives', *The Economist*, 17 September 2016.
17. John Lanchester, 'Brexit Blues', *London Review of Books*, 28 July 2016.
18. Office for National Statistics, *Annual Survey of Hours and Earnings: 2016 Provisional Results*, 25 October 2016.
19. Ibid. (Table 9.1a). 'Kensington and Chelsea: A Wealthy but Deeply Divided Borough', *The Economist*, 24 June 2017.
20. Ibid., 25 October 2016.
21. Katie Allen, 'UK Women Still Far Adrift on Salary and Promotion as Gender Pay Gap Remains a Gulf', *Guardian*, 23 August 2016.
22. LSE Knowledge Exchange, *Confronting Gender Inequality: Findings from the LSE Commission on Gender, Inequality and Power* (London: LSE, 2015), 13.
23. Alison Park, Caroline Bryson, Elizabeth Clery, John Curtice, and Miranda Phillips (eds), *British Social Attitudes: The 30th Report* (2013), London: NatCen Social Research, 115.
24. LSE Knowledge Exchange, *Confronting Gender Inequality*, 49–50.
25. Equality and Human Rights Commission, Race Report Statistics, 16 September 2016. Available via: https://www.equalityhumanrights.com/en/latest-projects/race-report-statistics
26. The Casey Review, *A Review into Opportunity and Integration*, December 2016, p. 11.
27. Jill Treanor, 'Richest 1% of People Own Nearly Half of Global Wealth, Says Report', *Guardian*, 14 October 2014.
28. Office for National Statistics, *Wealth in Great Britain: Wave 4, 2012–14* (18 December 2015), Table 2.5.
29. Alan Krueger, Speech, 'The Rise and Consequences of Inequality in the United States', January 2012. Available via: https://www.whitehouse.gov/sites/default/files/krueger_cap_speech_final_remarks.pdf
30. OECD, *Going for Growth* (Paris: OECD, 2010), 186.
31. Social Mobility Commission, *State of the Nation 2016: Social Mobility in Great Britain*, November 2016, p. iv.
32. In an on-line appendix (6a), I show how the incomes of the richest 10–20% of households have changed relative to that of the poorest 10–20% of households over the same period.
33. Jonathan Portes, 'Immigration After Brexit', *National Institute of Economic and Social Research*, 238 (November 2016), R. 20 and references therein.
34. OECD, *Divided We Stand? Why Inequality Keeps Rising* (Paris: OECD, 2011).
35. Ibid., 301. For a review of the literature on the impact of trade unions on wages and equality, see Anthony Atkinson, *Inequality: What Can Be Done?* (Cambridge, MA: Harvard University Press, 2015), 93–5.
36. Department for Business, Innovation and Skills, *Trade Union Statistics 2015* (3 June 2015).

37. New Labour did introduce statutory procedures for trade union recognition in firms with more than 20 employees where a majority of the relevant workforce wanted it. For an overview of Conservative and then New Labour industrial relations reforms, see Vincent Keter, *Trade Union Legislation: Labour's Changes to Conservative Reforms* (House of Commons Library Briefing Note, 7 October 2010).
38. Low Pay Commission, *The Future Path of the National Minimum Wage* (2014), 6.
39. Office for National Statistics, *The Effects of Taxes and Benefits on Household Income, Historical Datasets* (24 May 2016).
40. Social Mobility and Child Poverty Commission, *State of the Nation 2013: Social Mobility and Child Poverty in Great Britain*, 14.
41. Low Pay Commission, *The National Minimum Wage Report, 2015*, 129.
42. Office for National Statistics, 'Contracts that do not Guarantee a Minimum Number of Hours', 11 May 2017.
43. Andrew Walker, 'Who Uses Zero-Hour Contracts and Why?', *BBC News*, 1 April 2015.
44. Living Wage Commission, *Final Report of the Living Wage Commission* (2014), 10.
45. On business opposition to the living wage proposal, see: 'Cleaning Up', *The Economist*, 1 August 2015, and James Quinn, 'A Living Wage is all Very Well, But Lower Pay is Better than None', *Daily Telegraph*, 15 July 2015.
46. Joseph Stiglitiz, 'Of the 1%, By the 1%, For the 1%', *Vanity Fair*, 30 April 2011.
47. Chris Belfield et al., *Living Standards, Poverty and Inequality in the UK* (London: Institute for Fiscal Studies, 2015), 33.
48. See on-line appendix (6a) for an extended analysis.
49. Institute for Fiscal Studies, 'Incomes in the UK'.
50. Department for Work and Pensions, *Low Income Dynamics, 1991–2008* (23 September 2010), 33–4.
51. Adam Tinson, *The Rise of Sanctioning in Great Britain* (London: New Policy Institute, June 2015).
52. Office for Budget Responsibility, *Welfare Trends Report, 2015* (June 2015), 8–9.
53. HM Treasury, *Public Expenditure, Statistical Analyses*, 2017. Available via: https://www.gov.uk/government/uploads/system/uploads/attachment_data/file/630570/60243_PESA_Accessible.pdf
54. Office for Budget Responsibility, *Welfare Trends Report, 2014* (October 2014), 47.
55. *BBC News*, 'Life on the Front Line after the Benefits Cap', 10 April 2014.
56. Office for Budget Responsibility, *Economic and Fiscal Outlook*, Cm. 9346 (October 2016), 7.
57. Paul Pierson, *Dismantling the Welfare State? Reagan, Thatcher and the Politics of Retrenchment* (Cambridge: Polity, 1998).
58. There is another side to this story. New Labour did not skew the welfare system to benefit the rich. Indeed, between 1997 and 2010, the benefits received by the richest 10% of households as a share of their final income remained at just over 2%. The redistributive gap fell because the value of the cash benefits going to the poorest households fell from 58% to 45% over the same time. This in part

reflects a slow rate of growth in the real (inflation-adjusted) value of benefits. It also reflects the fact that, during this period, and as we have seen, the market income of the poorest households was increasing because of the introduction of the minimum wage.

59. Developers have been accused of hoarding land to increase the prices of their developments. In 2015, *The Economist* reported that permission was granted for the development of 250,000 new housing units but that only 140,000 commenced. 'Sitting on their Hands', *The Economist*, 26 November 2016.
60. Belfield et al., *Living Standards, Poverty and Inequality in the UK*, 24.
61. Hilary Osborne, 'Average Rents in England and Wales Rose 3.4% in 2015', *Guardian*, 22 January 2016.
62. Department for Communities and Local Government, *Tenure Trends and Cross-Tenure Analysis* (21 July 2016) (Table FT1101). Office for National Statistics, *A Century of Home Ownership and Renting in England and Wales* (19 April 2013).
63. Belfield et al., *Living Standards, Poverty and Inequality in the UK*, 23.
64. Department for Communities and Local Government, *Tenure Trends and Cross-Tenure Analysis* (13 July 2017) (Table S188).
65. Belfield et al., *Living Standards, Poverty and Inequality in the UK*, 74.
66. Department for Work and Pensions, *Benefit Expenditure and Case Load Tables* (17 January 2017).
67. See the discussion on the 'full fact' website—'Are we Spending More on Housing Benefit than Bricks and Mortar' (7 June 2013).
68. Oliver Wainwright, 'What Cameron's Bonfire of the Building Regulations will do to our Homes', *Guardian*, 27 January 2014.
69. For a detailed discussion of planning regulations, see Miguel Castro Coelho and Vigyan Ratnoo, *Housing that Works for All: The Political Economy of Housing in England* (London: Institute for Government, 2013). In June 2015, George Osborne announced that a new 'zonal' planning system will be introduced in London, which will grant automatic planning permission to build on suitable brownfield sites, and that Londoners will be able to add extra storeys onto their houses up to the height of adjoining buildings. *The Economist*, 'Two Birds with One Stone', 18 July 2015.
70. Department for Communities and Local Government, *Green Belt Statistics for England* (8 September 2016), Annex 1, Table 3. Some care needs to be taken with this figure. The Department for Communities advises that, whilst figures go back to 1997, these are only available on a 'consistent basis' from 2006 following the designation of 47,300 hectares of Green Belt land as part of the New Forest National Park in 2005.
71. Paul Cheshire, *Turning Houses into Gold: The Failure of British Planning*, LSE British Politics and Policy Blog, 7 May 2014.
72. Mark Easton, 'The Great Myth of Urban Britain', *BBC News*, June 2012. The urban landscape accounts for 10.6% of England, 1.9% of Scotland, 3.6% of Northern Ireland, and 4.1% of Wales.
73. By the latter part of the 1980s, Loadsamoney's status was such that Margaret Thatcher herself was forced to deny that she had created a 'greed-is-good' culture

by telling reporters: 'We are not a loadsamoney economy'. Simon Hattenstone, 'Harry Enfield: I don't like doing me', *Guardian*, 25 September 2010.

74. Office for National Statistics, *Patterns of Pay 1997 to 2012* (7 January 2016).
75. Office for National Statistics, *Patterns of Pay: Estimates from the Annual Survey of Hours and Earnings, UK, 1997–2013*, Table 11.
76. 'How the Other Three Quarters Lives', *The Economist*, 17 September 2016. A very different perspective on regional inequalities has been offered by the Chief Economist of the Bank of England, Andy Haldane. He notes that, by 2015, GDP per head had only recovered to the levels it had been in two areas: London and the South-East. In Northern Ireland, he reports, it remains 11% below its peak and in Yorkshire and Humberside 6% below. Andy Haldane, 'Whose Recovery?', speech at Port Talbot, 30 June 2016. Available via: http://www.bankofengland.co.uk/publications/Pages/speeches/2016/916.aspx
77. Office for National Statistics, *Annual Survey of Hours and Earnings, 2015 Provisional Results* (18 November 2015), 6.
78. LSE Knowledge Exchange, *Confronting Gender Inequality*, 13.
79. 'On the Up', *The Economist*, 28 May 2016.
80. LSE Knowledge Exchange, *Confronting Gender Inequality*, 11.
81. YouGov, 'Women Still do the Housework' (2 September 2013).
82. Fraser Stuart and Euan Patterson, 'Caring in Scotland: Analysis of Existing Data Sources on Unpaid Carers in Scotland' (Scottish Government: Social Research, 2010), 5.
83. Department for Work and Pensions, *Households Below Average Income: An Analysis of the Income Distribution 1994/5 to 2011/12* (June 2013), 166.
84. Department for Work and Pensions, *Households Below Average Income, 1994/5–2000/1*, 'Individuals—Composition of Various Per Centiles of the Income Distribution Analysed by Economic Status' (Table D2) (14 October 2010).
85. Tom Clark, *Hard Times: Inequality, Recession, Aftermath* (New Haven: Yale University Press, 2014), 63.
86. Office for National Statistics, *Wealth in Great Britain: Wave 4, 2012–14* (18 December 2015), p. 18. Available via: http://webarchive.nationalarchives.gov.uk/20160105160709/http://www.ons.gov.uk/ons/rel/was/wealth-in-great-britain-wave-4/2012-2014/index.html
87. Andy Haldane, 'Whose Recovery?', speech at Port Talbot, 30 June 2016.
88. Thomas Piketty, *Capital in the Twenty First Century* (Cambridge, MA: Harvard University Press, 2014), 344.
89. George Orwell, *The Lion and the Unicorn: Socialism and the English Genius* (London: Secker and Warburg, 1941).
90. George Arnett, 'UK Became More Middle Class than Working Class in 2000 Data Shows', *Guardian*, 26 February 2016. In an on-line appendix (6b), I look at an alternative measure of social class.
91. Jo Blanden and Stephen Machin, *Recent Changes in Intergenerational Mobility in Britain* (Sutton Trust, December 2007). Jo Blanden, Alissa Goodman, Paul Gregg, and Stephen Machin, 'Changes in Intergenerational Mobility in Britain', in Miles Corak (ed.), *Generational Income Mobility in North America and Europe*

(Cambridge: Cambridge University Press, 2004). For a discussion of this work, see the Social Mobility and Child Poverty Commission, *State of the Nation 2013: Social Mobility and Child Poverty in Great Britain*, 126–30.

92. John Goldthorpe, *Understanding—and Misunderstanding—Social Mobility in Britain: The Entry of the Economists, the Confusion of Politicians and the Limits of Educational Policy* (University of Oxford: Department of Social Policy and Intervention, 2012), 13.
93. David Willetts, *The Pinch: How the Baby Boomers Took Their Children's Future—and Why They Should Give It Back* (London: Atlantic Books, 2010).
94. Ibid., 69.
95. Andy Haldane, 'Whose Recovery?', speech at Port Talbot, 30 June 2016.
96. Belfield et al., *Living Standards, Poverty and Inequality in the UK*, 6.
97. Hilary Osborne, 'Generation Rent: The Housing Ladder Starts to Collapse for the Under-40s', *Guardian*, 22 July 2015.
98. Larry Elliot and Hilary Osborne, 'Under-35s in the UK Face Becoming Permanent Renters, Warns Thinktank', *Guardian*, 13 February 2016.
99. Andy Haldane, 'Whose Recovery?', speech at Port Talbot, 30 June 2016.
100. Belfield et al., *Living Standards, Poverty and Inequality in the UK*, 93.
101. The Conservative and Unionist Party Manifesto, *Forward Together*. The Labour Party Manifesto, *For the Many, Not the Few*, pp. 55-6. Available via: http://www.labour.org.uk/page/-/Images/manifesto-2017/Labour%20Manifesto%202017.pdf
102. Belfield et al., *Living Standards, Poverty and Inequality in the UK*, 12.
103. Christine Lagarde, 'A New Global Economy for a New Generation', Speech, Davos, Switzerland, January 2013. Jonathan Ostry, Andrew Berg, and Charalambos G. Tsangarides describe the existence of a 'tentative consensus' within the economics literature that high levels of inequality can undermine economic growth: 'Redistribution, Inequality and Growth', IMF Staff Discussion Paper (Washington: IMF, 2014), 4.
104. Richard Wilkinson and Kate Pickett, *The Spirit Level: Why Equality is Better for Everyone* (London: Penguin, 2009).
105. CEO pay is linked to either share price or salaries paid at equivalent-sized companies, or some mixture of these. The problem with the first of these is that share price is no necessary indicator of long-term profitability (as the banking crisis and, more recently, the manipulation of accounts at Tesco shows). The problem with the second of these is a ratchet effect. To signal their confidence in their CEO, remuneration committees will be tempted to push somebody's pay up, which creates a ripple effect as other companies are forced to respond. Underlying this is a more general incentive failure. Shareholders have little incentive to exercise close control over pay. If they are unhappy with company performance, it is far easier for them to sell their shares and exit than it is to exercise their voice and complain.
106. Jim Kuhnehenn, 'Obama: Income Inequality is "Defining Challenge" of our Time', *Huffington Post*, 12 April 2013.

107. Mark Carney, 'Inclusive Capitalism: Creating a Sense of the Systemic', Speech, May 2014.
108. Christine Lagarde, 'Lifting the Small Boats', Speech, 17 June 2015.
109. Tony Blair, 'Labour Must be the Party of Ambition as Well as Compassion', *Guardian*, 9 May 2015.
110. Ben Quinn, 'Shocking Inequality Levels in Britain Must Be Addressed, Says Major', *Guardian*, 11 November 2015.
111. The Conservative and Unionist Party Manifesto, *Forward Together*.

Notes to figure captions

1. Office for National Statistics, *The Effects of Taxes and Benefits on Household Income, Historical Datasets* (25 April 2017). Available via: https://www.ons.gov.uk/peoplepopulationandcommunity/personalandhouseholdfinances/incomeandwealth/datasets/theeffectsoftaxesandbenefitsonhouseholdincome-historicaldatasets. A lot of the diagrams in this chapter use data which has been 'equivalized'. What does this mean? The income that a household needs to attain a given standard of living will depend on its size and composition. For example, a couple with dependent children will need a higher income than a single person with no children to attain the same material living standards. 'Equivalization' means adjusting a household's income for size and composition so that we can look at the incomes of all households on a comparable basis. See Institute for Fiscal Studies, 'Where do you Fit in?' Available via: http://www.ifs.org.uk/wheredoyoufitin/about.php
2. Office for National Statistics, *The Effects of Taxes and Benefits on Household Income, Historical Datasets* (25 April 2017).
3. Ibid.
4. Ibid.
5. Institute for Fiscal Studies, 'Incomes in the UK', available via: https://www.ifs.org.uk/tools_and_resources/incomes_in_uk (hyperlink to the 'spreadsheet' under data).
6. Institute for Fiscal Studies, 'Incomes in the UK'. To calculate these figures, I have subtracted before housing cost income from after housing cost income and then expressed that figure as a % of before housing cost income.
7. Office for National Statistics, *Annual Survey of Hours and Earnings: 2016 Provisional Results*, 25 October 2016.
8. Office for National Statistics, *Wealth in Great Britain: Wave 4, 2012–14* (18 December 2015), Figure 2.3.
9. Miles Corak, *Economics for Public Policy* blog, 'Here is the source for the "Great Gatsby Curve" in the Alan Krueger speech at the Center for American Progress on January 12' (12 January 2012).
10. Office for National Statistics, *The Effects of Taxes and Benefits on Household Income, Historical Datasets* (25 April 2017).
11. Ibid.
12. Ibid.

13. Institute for Fiscal Studies, 'Incomes in the UK'.
14. Calculated using data from Institute for Fiscal Studies, 'Incomes in the UK'.
15. Department for Communities and Local Government, *Live Tables on House Building*, (25 May 2017), Table 241.

CHAPTER 7. KEEP CALM: ON GROWTH, AUSTERITY, AND HAPPINESS

1. Gordon Brown, 'Mansion House Speech', 20 June 2007. Available via: http://webarchive.nationalarchives.gov.uk/+/http:/www.hm-treasury.gov.uk/2014.htm
2. On affluenza, see John de Graaf, David Wann, and Thomas Naylor, *Affluenza: The All-Consuming Epidemic* (San Francisco: Berrett Koehler, 2001); Clive Hamilton and Richard Denniss, *Affluenza: When Too Much is Never Enough* (London: Allen and Unwin, 2005); Oliver James, *Affluenza* (London: Random House, 2007).
3. Social Justice Policy Group, *Breakdown Britain: Interim Report on the State of the Nation* (London: Centre for Social Justice, 2006).
4. Stephen Bell and Andrew Hindmoor, *Masters of the Universe but Slaves of the Market* (Cambridge, MA: Harvard University Press, 2015), 86–7.
5. Patrick Butler, 'Food Bank Use Tops Million Mark Over the Past Year', *Guardian*, 22 April 2015.
6. Glen Bramley, Donald Hirsch, Mandy Littlewood, and David Watkins, *Counting the Cost of UK Poverty* (Joseph Rowntree Foundation, 2016). Available via: file:///C:/Users/ahind/Downloads/3221_-_counting_the_cost_of_uk_poverty_low_res.pdf
7. David Cameron, 'Speech to the Conservative Party Conference', 7 October 2009. Available via: http://www.theguardian.com/politics/2009/oct/08/david-cameron-speech-in-full
8. Katie Allen and Larry Elliot, 'UK Joins Greece at Bottom of Wage Growth League', *Guardian*, 27 July 2016.
9. For an analysis of the nature and failures of the British growth model, see Colin Hay, *The Failure of Anglo-Liberal Capitalism* (Basingstoke: Palgrave Macmillan, 2013).
10. John McDonnell, 'Labour Party Conference Speech', *Spectator*, 25 October 2016. Available via: http://blogs.spectator.co.uk/2016/09/full-speech-john-mcdonnell-labour-conference/
11. Paul Mason, *Postcapitalism: A Guide to Our Future* (London: Allen Lane, 2015), 5.
12. Larry Summers, 'The Age of Secular Stagnation: What It Is and What to do About It', *Foreign Affairs* (March/April 2016); Robert Gordon, 'The Economics of Secular Stagnation', *American Economic Review*, 105 (2015), 54–9. Available via: http://piketty.pse.ens.fr/files/Gordon2015.pdf. For other examples of economic pessimism about the prospects for capitalism, see Wolfgang Streeck, *Buying Time: The Delayed Crisis of Democratic Capitalism* (London: Verso Books, 2014); Andrew Gamble, *Crisis without End? The Unravelling of Western Prosperity*

(London: Palgrave Macmillan, 2014); and Tyler Cowen, *The Great Stagnation* (New York: Dutton, 2011).

13. Alistair Darling, *Back from the Brink* (London: Atlantic Books, 2011), 318.
14. Ross Garnaut and David Llewellyn-Smith, *The Great Crash of 2008* (Melbourne: Melbourne University Press, 2009).
15. 'Not Always with Us', *The Economist*, 1 June 2013.
16. Office for National Statistics, *Key Economic Time Series Data*, GDP Quarter on Quarter Growth.
17. Institute for Fiscal Studies, 'Incomes in the UK', available via: http://www.ifs.org.uk/tools_and_resources/incomes_in_uk (hyperlink to the 'spreadsheet' under data).
18. OECD, 'GDP per Head of Population'. The data here is expressed in terms of constant purchasing power at 2010 prices in US$. Available via: https://stats.oecd.org/Index.aspx?DataSetCode=PDB_LV
19. In an on-line appendix (7a), I show how, over a much longer period, the ownership of goods has been socialized.
20. Office for National Statistics, *The Effects of Taxes and Benefits on Household Income, Historical Datasets* (24 May 2016).
21. This section of the chapter draws upon Bell and Hindmoor, *Masters of the Universe but Slaves of the Market*, 56–72.
22. Anat Admati and Martin Hellwig, *The Bankers' New Clothes: What's Wrong with Banking and What to Do About It* (Princeton: Princeton University Press, 2013), 60.
23. Bell and Hindmoor, *Masters of the Universe but Slaves of the Market*, 208–9.
24. William Cohan, *House of Cards: A Tale of Hubris and Wretched Excess on Wall Street* (New York: Doubleday, 2009).
25. The technical definition of a recession is two consecutive quarters of negative growth.
26. *BBC News*, 'Average Income Back to Pre-Crisis Levels, Says IFS', 4 March 2015.
27. The figures here are for final income before housing costs. The numbers are taken from Institute for Fiscal Studies, 'Incomes in the UK'.
28. Office for Budget Responsibility, *Economic and Fiscal Outlook* (July 2015), 7.
29. Katie Allen, 'The Brexit Economy: Remarkable Resilience as Spectre of Inflation Looms', *Guardian*, 22 November 2016. As of December 2016, Google, Facebook, Apple, Boeing, and Nissan had all announced significant new investment programmes in the UK following the referendum result. This is not the end of the investment story but it is not the result many who voted to stay expected. *BBC News*, 'McDonald's Move will Test the Type of Post-Brexit Economy Theresa May Wants', 8 December 2016. Gwyn Topham, 'BMW Pledges to Build New e-Mini at UK Car Plant', *Guardian*, 25 July 2017. Larry Elliot, 'IMF Cuts 2017 Growth Forecasts for UK and US', *Guardian*, 24 July 2017. If, on the whole, predictions that major industrial manufacturers would abandon the UK prior to Brexit have not yet been borne out, the situation is less clear in banking and finance. Under EU regulations, any bank or financial firm in any member state can serve customers in any other EU state without

having to establish a local branch or subsidiary. This 'passport' is threatened by Brexit. A free trade deal, if it could be negotiated, will not, in itself, compensate for this loss. Faced with this uncertainty, many financial firms are reviewing their operations. *The Economist* reports that by July 2017 59 of 222 firms tracked by a consultancy firm, EY Services, had said they had started moving staff or operations out of the UK, or were reviewing their domiciles. At least 20 investment banks had also declared that they would move staff. On 3 July Sumitomo Mitsui Financial Group, one of Japan's three giant banks, said it would establish new banking and securities subsidiaries in Frankfurt. 'The City of London Prepares for Brexit', *The Economist*, 6 July 2017.

30. Jonathan Freedland, 'A Warning to Gove and Johnson—We Won't Forget What You Did', *Guardian*, 1 July 2016.
31. Office for Budget Responsibility, *Economic and Fiscal Outlook*, Cm. 9346 (October 2016), 6.
32. Katie Allen and Heather Stewart, 'IFS Warns of Biggest Squeeze on Pay for 70 Years Over Brexit', *Guardian*, 24 November 2016.
33. In 2015, 44% of British exports were to other countries in the European Union. The most plausible discussion of the economic costs and potential benefits of Brexit I have read is by Iain Begg, 'Brexit: Why, What, When and How?'. Available via: http://ukandeu.ac.uk/research-papers/brexit-why-what-next-and-how/. On the importance of non-tariff barriers see Political Studies Association, *EU Referendum: One Year On,* 1 July 2017. Available via: file:///C:/Users./ahind/Downloads/EU-referendum-one-year-on.pdf.
34. Tony Dolphin, *Gathering Strength: Backing Clusters to Boost Britain's Exports* (London: IPPR, 2014).
35. Katherine Sellgren, 'University Rankings: UK a Standout Performer', *BBC News*, 30 September 2015. On the export earnings of UK universities, see: Universities UK, *The Funding Environment for Universities: The Economic Role for UK Universities* (September 2015).
36. Jonathan McClory, *The Soft Power 30: A Global Ranking of Soft Power* (Portland Communications, 2015). Also, see 'Power: Softly Does It', *The Economist*, 18 July 2015. Soft power refers to the ability to achieve influence through attraction and co-option rather than force.
37. In pre-referendum days, the Office for Budget Responsibility argued that if the economy were to grow at the forecast rate of around 2% a year through until 2020, it was essential that net migration remain at its current levels. Alberto Nardelli, 'Osborne Reliant on Rising Immigration to Achieve Budget Surplus', *Guardian*, 1 December 2015. For the original analysis, see Office for Budget Responsibility, *Economic and Fiscal Outlook* (November 2015), 43.
38. Gross capital formation consists of outlays on and additions to the fixed assets of the economy plus net changes in the level of inventories. Fixed assets include land improvements, plant, machinery, and equipment purchases, and the construction of infrastructure (including railways and roads). The data here are taken from the World Bank's statistical database (available via: http://data.

worldbank.org/indicator/NE.GDI.TOTL.ZS/countries/1W?display=default). For a commentary see 'Let's Try to Catch up with Mali', *The Economist*, 6 July 2013.

The Office for Budget Responsibility estimates that business investment has fallen from 15% of GDP in 1990 to less than 11% (Office for Budget Responsibility, *Economic and Fiscal Outlook* (July 2015), 64). These figures are for 'nominal' investment. Because inflation in investment goods has been significantly lower than overall inflation, 'real investment' is estimated to have only fallen from around a peak of 11.7% of GDP in 1999 to 10.8% by 2015.

39. 'Bargain Basement', *The Economist*, 14 March 2015. Between 2007 and 2015, output per worker in the UK fell by 2%. In the rest of the G7 economies, it grew by an average of 5%. The Office for Budget Responsibility concludes that low levels of productivity have been the key drag upon GDP growth and wage growth since 2010. Yet despite confidently predicting 2% productivity growth a year between 2016 and 2020, it also suggests that 'it is difficult to explain the abrupt fall and persistent weakness of productivity ... [and] hard to judge when or if productivity growth will return'. Office for Budget Responsibility, *Economic and Fiscal Outlook* (July 2015), 34.
40. 'Keeping Up with the Schmidts', *The Economist*, 26 April 2014. In the early 1990s, New Labour identified shortfalls in vocational training and, in particular, in the number of high-quality apprenticeship schemes as a key cause of youth unemployment and low productivity. Yet by 2011, the Wolf Report on vocational training found that whereas 60% of German youths completed an apprenticeship by the time they were 25, the equivalent figure in Britain was just 5% (Alison Wolf, *Review of Vocational Education—The Wolf Report* (2011), 25). The Coalition subsequently increased by half the government subsidy for training programmes and offered £1,500 grants to small businesses to employ their first apprentice. In 2015, the Conservative government also announced an apprenticeship levy of 0.5% of payroll to be used to fund apprenticeship training. On the surface, this investment of political attention has already paid off. The number of people starting an apprenticeship each year in England increased from 300,000 in 2009/10 to 500,000 in 2015. Yet the strong evidence here is that most of these training programmes are of a relatively low quality and do not lead to the kind of substantive qualifications and experience for which the German apprenticeship system is lauded. In 2014/15, 60% of apprenticeship starts were at an intermediate level (broadly equivalent to a GCSE qualification), 37% at an advanced level (broadly equivalent to an A-level), and only 4% at a higher level (broadly equivalent to a degree qualification). Jeanne Delebarre, *Apprenticeship Statistics for England: 1996–2015* (London: House of Commons Library Briefing Paper, November 2015), 6.
41. 'Industrial Woes: The Makers Stumble', *The Economist*, 19 December 2015. By 2016, manufacturing output was still 6% below its 2008/9 peak. Manufacturing accounts for around 9% of UK GDP, compared with 20% in Germany, 14% in Italy, 12% in the US, and 10% in France.

42. Office for Budget Responsibility, *Economic and Fiscal Outlook* (July 2015), 63. During the 1990s and 2000s, Britain came to practise a form of 'privatised Keynesianism' in which growing levels of household debt drove higher consumption and GDP growth (Colin Crouch, 'Privatised Keynesianism: An Unacknowledged Policy Regime', *British Journal of Politics and International Relations*, 11 (2009), 382–99). Rapidly increasing house prices allowed wealthier households to withdraw equity to feed consumption. In 2006—as the housing bubble reached its frothy peak—more than £37bn was withdrawn: equivalent to around 5% of household consumption (Craig Berry, *Austerity Politics and UK Economic Policy* (London: Palgrave Macmillan), 21). In July 2017 the Bank of England's Director of Financial Stability, Alex Brazier, warned of a 'spiral of complacency about household debt'. Between July 2016 and July 2017, he warned, household incomes had grown by 1.5 per cent whilst outstanding car loans, credit card balances, and personal loans had risen by 10 per cent. Larry Elliot, 'Bank of England Warns of Complacency over Big Rise in Personal Debt', *Guardian*, 24 July 2017.
43. Britain has a large and generally competitive banking sector, which means that it is capable of sustaining a large loan book at relatively low interest rates. From the perspective of individual borrowers, this is a good thing. People can get access to the loans that they need to put themselves on the property ladder and they can then trade up as their income grows. From the banks' perspective, mortgage lending is a good thing because it is relatively safe. Default rates on mortgage loans tend to be quite low and banks can, if necessary, usually recover their money if things go wrong through repossession. But from a wider social perspective, high levels of mortgage lending in the context of a fixed or at least very inflexible supply of housing simply contributes to house-price inflation. High mortgage lending means that more and more money ends up chasing the same number of houses, which pushes prices and household debt up and means that an ever higher fraction of final income is, as we saw in the previous chapter, being spent on housing. See Adair Turner, *Between Debt and the Devil* (Princeton: Princeton University Press, 2015), 216.
44. Financialization here refers to a general trend within many capitalist economies (including Britain's) for the banking and finance sector to grow in importance and, beyond that, for firms to derive an ever larger share of their profits from financial activities. In the United States, over a third of the profits of non-financial firms and over half of the profits of manufacturing firms now come from financial activities. See Ken-Hou Lin and Donald Tomaskovic-Devey, 'Financialization and U.S. Income Inequality, 1970–2008', *American Journal of Sociology*, 118/5 (2013), 1284.
45. See David Kynaston, *Modernity Britain: A Shake of the Dice, 1959–62* (London: Bloomsbury, 2014), 121–56, and Dominic Sandbrook, *Never Had it so Good: A History of Britain from Suez to the Beatles* (London: Abacus, 2005), 513–46, for an overview of the arguments.
46. Samuel Brittan, 'The Economic Contradictions of Democracy', *British Journal of Political Science*, 5 (1975), 129–59, and Corelli Barnett, *The Audit of War: The Illusion and Reality of Britain as a Great Power* (London: Macmillan, 1986).

47. For an overview of and reflections upon the academic debate, see Andrew Gamble, *Britain in Decline* (London: Macmillan, 1981), and Richard English and Mike Kenny, *Rethinking British Decline* (Basingstoke: Palgrave, 1999).
48. *BBC News*, 'In Full: Iain Duncan Smith Resignation Letter', 18 March 2016.
49. In an on-line appendix (7b), I repeat this analysis for income after housing costs.
50. The analysis in this section it taken from Chris Belfield et al., *Living Standards, Poverty and Inequality in the UK: 2016* (London: Institute for Fiscal Studies, 2016), chapter 3 (inequality), especially pp. 21–4.
51. Joseph Stiglitz, 'The Great GDP Swindle', *Guardian*, 13 September 2009. The entirely reasonable concerns many people on the left have about the inadequacies of GDP as a measure of economic well-being form part of a more general critique of the ideology of 'growthism'. Growthism is defined by Umair Haque as the political mantra that 'growth must be achieved at all costs' and that 'when growth is achieved, societies are said to be successful; when it is not, they are said to be failing'. Umair Haque, 'This isn't Capitalism, its Growthism and it's Bad for Us', *Harvard Business Review* (November 2013). Zoe Williams, 'Fed Up with Growth-Focused Politics? For Real Change, Look Left', *Guardian*, 6 October 2014.
52. On the social science literature on happiness, a good place to start is Richard Layard, *Happiness: Lessons from a New Science* (London: Penguin, 2011).
53. Andrew Oswald, 'The Hippies Were Right All Along About Happiness', *Financial Times*, 18 January 2006.
54. Office for National Statistics, 'Gross Domestic Product (Average) per Head, at Current Market Prices', 25 May 2017.
55. Institute for Fiscal Studies, 'Incomes in the UK'.
56. These data are taken from the World Database of Happiness, available via: http://worlddatabaseofhappiness.eur.nl/hap_nat/nat_fp.php?cntry=16&name=United%20Kingdom&mode=3&subjects=784&publics=108
57. John Helliwell, Richard Layard, and Jeffrey Sachs (eds), *World Happiness Report* (2017), 20–5.
58. John Helliwell, Richard Layard, and Jeffrey Sachs (eds), *World Happiness Report* (2015), 6.
59. The figures on the regional distribution of happiness and the increase in overall levels of happiness are both taken from a speech by Andy Haldane, 'Whose Recovery?', at Port Talbot, 30 June 2016, p. 12.
60. Office for National Statistics, *Conceptions in England and Wales, 2014* (9 March 2016), 6.
61. Office for National Statistics, *Divorces in England and Wales, 2015* (21 June 2017). The fall in the divorce rate may in part reflect a steady rise in the number of couples cohabiting, from 2.9 million in 1990 to 6 million in 2012. Office for National Statistics, *Cohabitation in the UK Since 1996* (1 November 2012).
62. Alan Travis, 'Crime Rise Is Biggest in a Decade, ONS Figures Show', *Guardian*, 20 July 2017. Office for National Statistics, *Crime in England and Wales, Year Ending March 2017* (20 July 2017), Table 1.
63. OECD *Better Life Index*. Data available via: http://stats.oecd.org/Index.aspx?DataSetCode=BLI

64. Office for National Statistics, *Adult Drinking Habits in Great Britain*, 3 May 2017. Men are considered to have binged if they drank more than eight units of alcohol on their heaviest drinking day in the week before being interviewed, and women if they drank more than six units.
65. Home Office, *Drug Misuse: Findings from the 2014/15 Crime Survey* (6 July 2015). Figures on drug misuse do not generally take account of the changing strength of drugs—and, in particular, the prevalence of domestically grown skunk in the place of cannabis resin. See 'Weeded Out', *The Economist*, 6 June 2015.
66. Office for National Statistics, *Labour Market Statistics Dataset* (12 July 2017). On the most recent OECD figures, 12.7% of British employees still work more than 50 hours a week, compared with just 11.3% in the United States, 8% in France, 5% in Germany, and just 1.1% in Sweden.
67. British Social Attitudes Survey, 33 (2016), London: NatCen Social Research, 'Work', 1. Available via: http://www.bsa.natcen.ac.uk/downloads/bsa-33-downloads.aspx
68. Damien Gayle, 'Daily Commute of Two Hours—Reality for 3.7m UK Workers', *Guardian*, 18 November 2016.
69. NatCen's British Social Attitudes Survey, 33 (2016), 'Work', 1.
70. Ibid., 16–17.
71. Office for National Statistics, *Time Series: Unemployment Rate* (12 July 2017).
72. Eurostat News Release, 'Euro Area Unemployment Rate at 9.6%', 2 March 2017.
73. Andy Haldane, 'Whose Recovery?', speech at Port Talbot, 30 June 2016, p. 6.
74. Larry Elliot, 'Robots Threaten 15m UK Jobs, Says Bank of England's Chief Economist', *Guardian*, 12 November 2015.
75. Department for Communities and Local Government, *Homelessness Statistics* (22 June 2017).
76. Amelia Gentleman, 'Number of People Sleeping Rough in England Rises by Almost a Third in a Year', *Guardian*, 25 February 2016.
77. Haroon Sidique, 'Antidepressant Use Soared During Recession in England, Says Survey', *Guardian*, 28 May 2014.
78. Nuffield Foundation, *Changing Adolescence Programme: Social Trends and Mental Health: Introducing the Main Findings* (Oxford: Nuffield Foundation, 2012), 1.
79. G. Rait, K. Walters, M. Griffin, M. Buszewicz, I. Petersen, and I. Nazareth, 'Recent Trends in the Incidence of Recorded Depression in Primary Care', *British Journal of Psychiatry*, 195 (2009), 520–4. Doctors, it would seem, are now more ready to prescribe antidepressants than they once were. This may, in part, reflect a greater medical awareness of the symptoms and personal costs of depression and a greater willingness to prescribe antidepressants to patients suffering from increasingly common conditions such as dementia. Given that NHS guidelines actually caution against issuing antidepressants in less severe cases of anxiety and depression, the prescription boom may be a reflection of the limited consultation time available to GPs and a severe shortfall in publicly funded counselling services.
80. Department of Energy and Climate Change, *2015 UK Greenhouse Gas Emissions: Statistics* (7 February 2017).

81. Cairngorms and Loch Lomond and the Trossachs were established as Scottish National Parks in 2000 and the New Forest and South Downs as National Parks in 2005 and 2010.
82. Department for Environment, Food and Rural Affairs, *Air Quality Statistics in the UK 1987 to 2016* (27 April 2017).
83. Department for Environment, Food and Rural Affairs, *Wild Bird Populations in the UK, 1970 to 2014* (29 October 2015).
84. Department for Environment, Food and Rural Affairs, *Environmental Statistics—Key Facts* (January 2013).
85. Ibid.
86. Allister Heath, 'A Bright New Optimism is Sweeping Britain—and it Hails from the Right', *Daily Telegraph*, 9 September 2015. Among Conservative voters, 71% believed that, overall, life in Britain was better than it had been thirty years ago.
87. Richard Murphy, 'Osborne Is Planning to Destroy Society as We Know It. What Are We Going to Do about It?', *Tax Research UK* (4 December 2014).
88. Sara Hyde, 'Prisons Crisis Shows How Austerity Has Ripped the Soul out of Britain', *Labour List*, 20 May 2016.
89. Owen Hatherley, 'Keep Calm and Carry On—The Sinister Message Behind the Slogan that Seduced the Nation', *Guardian*, 8 January 2016. Also, see Owen Hatherley, *The Ministry of Nostalgia* (London: Verso, 2016).
90. Ibid.

Notes to figure captions

1. The data used here are taken from the Institute for Fiscal Studies, 'Incomes in the UK'.
2. The data used here are taken from the Institute for Fiscal Studies, 'Incomes in the UK'.

CHAPTER 8. THE UNSPECTACULAR WORLD OF A REASONABLY WELL-FUNCTIONING DEMOCRACY

1. Hansard Society, *Audit of Political Engagement, 2017 Report* (London: Hansard Society), 47.
2. Ipsos MORI, 'Politicians are Still Less Trusted than Estate Agents, Journalists and Bankers', 22 January 2016.
3. Marian Breslin, 'EU Referendum 2016 Remain Campaign Gets James Bond's Backing', *Liverpool Echo*, 23 June 2016.
4. Tony Judt, *Postwar* (London: Heineman, 2005), 177.
5. Also see the on-line appendix (2a).
6. The Rile score is calculated by counting the number of right-wing statements in each manifesto as a proportion of the overall number of statements and then subtracting the number of left-wing statements as a proportion of the number of overall statements in the manifesto. For a detailed description and a list of statements coded as being left-wing and right-wing, see the Manifesto Project

website (available via: https://manifestoproject.wzb.eu/) and the detailed coding instructions within it (available via: https://manifestoproject.wzb.eu/information/documents/handbooks).

7. British Social Attitudes Survey, 33 (2016), London: NatCen Social Research, 'Politics', 16.
8. Michael McDonald, Silvia Mendes, and Ian Budge, 'What are Elections For? Conferring the Median Mandate', *British Journal of Political Science*, 34 (2004), 1–26. A version of this paper is available to download via: http://www.binghamton.edu/cdp/docs/whatare-elections.pdf. Also see Michael McDonald and Ian Budge, *Elections, Parties, Democracy: Conferring the Median Mandate* (Oxford: Oxford University Press, 2005).
9. NatCen's British Social Attitudes Survey, 33 (2016), 'Politics', 23.
10. James A. Stimson, Michael B. MacKuen, and Robert Erikson, 'Dynamic Representation', *American Political Science Review*, 89 (1995), 543–65.
11. Armen Kahuendan, 'Political Representation and its Mechanisms: A Dynamic Left–Right Approach for the UK, 1976–2006', *British Journal of Political Science*, 40 (2010), 835–56.
12. James Forsyth, 'The Political Centre Just Moved, to the Right', *Spectator*, Coffee House Blog, 5 June 2013.
13. On the 2017 intake of MPs see The Sutton Trust, *Parliamentary Privilege—the MPs in 2017* (Edition: 18 June 2017) and Julia Rampen, 'How Representative Is Parliament after the General Election 2017?', *New Statesman*, 9 June 2017. On the 2015 intake, see Feargal McGuinness, 'Social Background of MPs' (London: House of Commons Standard Note, 14 December 2010; The Sutton Trust, *Parliamentary Privilege—the MPs 2015* (Edition 4: May 2015); and Paul Hunter and Dan Holden, *Who Governs Britain? A Profile of MPs in the 2015 Parliament* (London: Smith Institute, 2015).
14. Anushka Asthana, 'Lack of Working Class Labour MPs has "Alienated Voters"', *Guardian*, 3 September 2016.
15. Ipsos MORI, 'All Parties Seen to Promise Anything to Get Votes', April 2015.
16. Sue Cameron, 'David Nicholson—The Man Who Believed in Being Ruthless with the NHS', *Daily Telegraph*, 26 March 2014.
17. Peter Oborne, *The Rise of Political Lying* (London: Free Press, 2005). Quoted, Gerry Stoker, *Why Politics Matters: Making Democracy Work* (Basingstoke: Palgrave Macmillan, 2006), 125. In declaring it to be the word of the year, Oxford Dictionaries defined post-truth as an adjective 'relating to or denoting circumstances in which objective facts are less influential in shaping public opinion than appeals to emotion and personal belief'. See https://en.oxforddictionaries.com/word-of-the-year/word-of-the-year-2016
18. Stoker, *Why Politics Matters*, 126.
19. Judith Bara, 'A Question of Trust: Implementing Party Manifestos', *Parliamentary Affairs*, 58 (2005), 585–99. For earlier research on the same subject which reached the same conclusion, see Richard Rose, *Do Parties Make a Difference?* (London: Macmillan, 1984), 65.

20. *Independent*, 'Chilcot: Tony Blair 'Not Straight' with Nation over Iraq', 6 July 2017.
21. Full Fact, *General Election Factcheck 2015: A Guide for Journalists and Voters.*
22. Ibid., 4.
23. Jon Stone, 'Nigel Farage Backtracks on Leave Campaign's "£350m for the NHS Pledge", Hours After Result', *Independent*, 24 June 2016.
24. *BBC News*, 'Theresa May's Cabinet: Who's in and Who's Out?', 14 July 2016.
25. John Curtice and Rachel Ormston (eds), *British Social Attitudes: The 32nd Report* (2015), London: NatCen Social Research, 136.
26. Ibid.
27. Committee on Standards in Public Life, *Public Perceptions of Standards in Public Life in the UK and Europe* (25 March 2014), 6. Around 55% of people believe that national politicians take bribes or abuse their position for personal gain. Around 45% believe the same of local politicians. Around 30% believe that public servants awarding contracts are corrupt. Around the same number believe that the police and the judiciary are corrupt.
28. David Graeber, 'Despair Fatigue: How Hopelessness Grew Boring', *The Baffler*, 30 (2016).
29. Transparency International, *Corruption Perceptions Index, 2016*. Available via: https://www.transparency.org/news/feature/corruption_perceptions_index_2016.
30. Committee of Standards in Public Life, *Public Perceptions of Standards in Public Life in the UK and Europe* (25 March 2014), 8.
31. Independent Parliamentary Standards Authority, *MPs' Pay and Pensions: A New Package* (July 2013), 66.
32. Matt Dathan, 'John Bercow Accused of Covering Up Staff Drinking Problems in Parliament', *Independent*, 1 January 2016.
33. Kate Forrester, 'Tories Frittered away Huge Cash Gifts from Rich Donors during General Election', *Huffington Post*, 20 June 2017.
34. Open Secrets, 'Cost of Election'. Available via: https://www.opensecrets.org/overview/cost.php
35. I discuss the logic of public choice theory in an on-line appendix (2a).
36. Andrew Hindmoor and Brad Taylor, *Rational Choice*, 2nd edn (Basingstoke: Palgrave Macmillan, 2015), 165–78, for an introduction to rent-seeking theory.
37. The Electoral Commission provides a breakdown of the sources of donations to political parties (including public funds) on a quarterly basis. See: http://www.electoralcommission.org.uk/find-information-by-subject/political-parties-campaigning-and-donations/donations-and-loans-to-political-parties/quarterly-donations-and-loans
38. Channel 4, *Factcheck: Party Donors—Who Funds Labour and the Tories?*, 15 July 2013.
39. See George Monbiot, 'Let's Not Fool Ourselves. We May Not Bribe, But Corruption is Rife in Britain', *Guardian*, 18 March 2015, and Jeffrey Sachs, 'To End Corruption, Start with the US and UK. They Allow it in Broad Daylight', *Guardian*, 12 May 2016.
40. Russell Brand, *Revolution* (New York: Random House, 2014).

41. Martin Rosenbaum, 'Why Tony Blair Thinks he was an Idiot', *BBC News Open Secrets*, 1 September 2010.
42. Jacob Rowbottom, *Democracy Distorted: Wealth, Influence and Democratic Politics* (Cambridge: Cambridge University Press, 2010), 122.
43. Lance Price, 'Rupert Murdoch is Effectively a Member of Blair's Cabinet', *Guardian*, 1 July 2006.
44. David Leigh and Rob Evans, 'National Interest Halts Arms Corruption Inquiry', *Guardian*, 15 December 2006.
45. A citizens' jury is a small body of around twenty people who deliberate about an issue before making recommendations. One alternative to it is the Consensus Conference, which involves a small number of deliberating citizens who choose the advocates and experts they wish to question before producing a report. Citizens' assemblies involve a larger number of people and, in some cases, have met over a period of several months to discuss an issue. See Hayley Stevenson and John Dryzek, *Democratizing Global Climate Governance* (Cambridge: Cambridge University Press, 2014), 18–19.
46. The case for a 'secondary mandate' system has been made by Billy Bragg. 'There's no need for further elections. You would go on election day with the same ballot paper, cast your vote for your preferred choice for MP and instead of your vote being discarded if you lose, it would be accumulated at a regional level and lead to representation for your region, for your party of choice in the second chamber.' Press Association, 'Billy Bragg Presents Lords Reform Plans', *Guardian*, 9 February 2004.
47. Colin Crouch, *Post-Democracy* (Cambridge: Polity, 2004), 4.
48. Andrew Fisher, *The Failed Experiment* (London: Comerford and Miller, 2014).
49. Doris and Markus Lederer, 'The Power of Business', *Business and Politics*, 9 (2007), 1–17.
50. The concept of structural power was developed by the American political scientist Charles Lindblom. In a classic contribution to the academic literature on business power, he argued that business is in a uniquely 'privileged' position because within a capitalist system, governments and the wider society depend on a healthy economy and hence on the willingness of business to produce and invest. Government cannot force firms to invest or produce. They will therefore anticipate what it is that business wants. Charles Lindblom, *Politics and Markets* (New York: Basic Books, 1977). I have written about the structural power of business on and off with my colleague Stephen Bell for several years. See 'Taming the City: Power, Structural Ideas and the Evolution of British Banking', *New Political Economy*, 20 (2015), 454–74; 'Rethinking the Structural Power of Business: The Strange Case of the Australian Mining Tax', *New Political Economy*, 19 (2014), 470–86; and 'Structural Power and the Politics of Bank Capital Regulation in the UK', *Political Studies* (forthcoming).
51. Stephen Bell and Andrew Hindmoor, *Masters of the Universe but Slaves of the Market* (Cambridge, MA: Harvard University Press, 2015), 229–30.
52. Felicity Lawrence, 'Industry Lobbying Derailed Junk Food Ban', *Guardian*, 22 April 2006.

53. John Plunkett and Lisa O'Carroll, 'Leveson Inquiry: Blair Says Newspapers Used as Instruments of Political Power', *Guardian*, 28 May 2012.
54. George Monbiot, 'This Transatlantic Deal is a Full-Frontal Assault on Democracy', *Guardian*, 4 November 2013.
55. Bell and Hindmoor, 'Structural Power and the Politics of Bank Capital Regulation in the UK'.
56. George Monbiot reports that the leave campaign collected 54% of the £4.5m raised during the referendum campaign. George Monbiot, 'Billionaires Bought Brexit—They are Controlling our Venal Political System', *Guardian*, 13 July 2016.
57. Daniel Boffey, 'Brexit: Leading Banks Set to Pull Out of UK Early Next Year', *Observer*, 22 October 2016.
58. Steven Swinford, 'Theresa May Seeking Transitional Deal to Avoid Cliff Edge', *Daily Telegraph*, 21 November 2016. 'British Business Seeks a Bare-Knuckle Fight with the Government', *The Economist*, 24 June 2017.
59. *BBC News*, 'Milk Price Row: Farmers and Ministers in "Productive Talks"', 17 August 2015.
60. Helen Warrell, 'Business Groups Criticise Calls for Tougher UK Immigration Curbs', *Financial Times*, 7 January 2014.
61. Robert Winnett, 'David Cameron: We Must Clean Up Shoddy Banks', *Daily Telegraph*, 30 June 2012.
62. Christopher Hope, 'David Cameron: Tax Avoiding Foreign Firms Like Starbucks and Amazon Lack "Moral Scruples"', *Daily Telegraph*, 4 January 2013.
63. Jacob Rowbottom, *Democracy Distorted: Wealth, Influence and Democratic Politics* (Cambridge: Cambridge University Press, 2010), 92.
64. Andrew Hindmoor, 'Explaining Networks through Mechanisms: Vaccination, Priming and the 2001 Foot and Mouth Disease Crisis', *Political Studies*, 57 (2009), 75–94.
65. See Pepper Culpepper, *Quiet Politics and Business Power: Corporate Control in Europe and Japan*. (Cambridge: Cambridge University Press, 2011).
66. Frank Vibert, *The Rise of the Unelected* (Cambridge: Cambridge University Press, 2007).
67. Sue Cameron, 'Of Course Quango Appointments Are Political', *Daily Telegraph*, 5 February 2014. *BBC News*, 'In Graphics: The Politics of Quangos', 3 February 2014.
68. Sean Coughlan, 'Political Interference "Damaging Schools"', *BBC News*, 9 January 2015.
69. Peter Burnham, 'New Labour and the Politics of Depoliticisation', *British Journal of Politics and International Relations*, 3 (2001), 127–49.
70. David Harvey, *A Brief History of Neoliberalism* (Oxford: Oxford University Press, 2005), 66.
71. Christopher Hood, *The Blame Game: Spin, Bureaucracy and Self-Preservation in Government* (Princeton: Princeton University Press, 2013).
72. Andrew Hindmoor, *Rational Choice*, 1st edn (Basingstoke: Palgrave Macmillan, 2005), 46.

73. Colin Hay, *Why we Hate Politics* (Cambridge: Polity, 2007). Also see Nick Clarke, Will Jennings, Jonathan Moss, and Gerry Stoker, 'Is Anti-Politics Explained by Depoliticisation?', *Political Insight*, 12 April 2015.
74. A similar set of concerns appears to have underpinned David Cameron's promise to create a 'bonfire of the quangos'. He argued that too many decisions are now taken by public officials who cannot be voted out of office and who are under no pressure to account for their actions and that this undermines faith in democracy. *BBC News*, 'Tories Pledge to Cut Back Quangos', 6 July 2009.
75. William Davies, *The Limits of Neoliberalism* (London: Sage, 2014), 8.
76. One basic problem with the early versions of the political business cycle is that they tend to portray voters as being basically stupid and easily and repeatedly fooled by politicians. If people are rational (as public choice theory assumes), surely they should *expect* politicians to engineer a boom and if they expect them to do so, why would they then reward them at the polls? In recent years, theorists have sought to reconcile such 'rational expectations' with the existence of a political business cycle. Alberto Alesina argues that because voters cannot be certain which party is going to win the next election, a left-wing party government will, for a short time at least, be able to 'surprise' voters by stimulating the economy and reducing unemployment, and a right-wing party will be able to reduce inflation. There is, on this reading, a political business cycle but it is not one an incumbent politician will necessarily be able to exploit for electoral advantage.
77. In a report into the failure of the Royal Bank of Scotland, the Financial Services Authority pointedly observed that 'it is likely that, if the FSA had proposed before the first signs of the crisis (i.e. before the summer of 2007) the measures that in retrospect appear appropriate, such proposals would have been met by extensive complaints that the FSA was pursuing a heavy-handed, gold-plating and unnecessary approach'. Similarly, the former Governor of the Bank of England, Mervyn King, has suggested that any regulator who had sought to persuade politicians that the banks were under-regulated prior to 2007 would have confronted a 'massively difficult task'. In an interview that I conducted as a part of a study of the banking crisis, a financial journalist observed that 'the banks like to always talk to the Prime Minister, the Chancellor of the Exchequer, anybody else's ear they can get' and that if regulators had raised concerns about a bank's behaviour, they would have been told, 'We don't want these people leaving and going to Frankfurt or New York or Hong Kong'. Bell and Hindmoor, *Masters of the Universe but Slaves of the Market*, 229 (including a reference to the Ed Balls quote).
78. Peter Kellner, '*Democracy on Trial: What Voters Really Think of Parliament and Our Politicians*', YouGov (2012), 9.
79. Helia Ebrahimi and Angela Monaghan, 'Office for Budget Responsibility: Chancellor's Poodle or an Important Institution?', *Daily Telegraph*, 7 July 2010.
80. For a more detailed exposition of this basic insight, see Andrew Gamble, *Politics and Fate* (Cambridge: Polity, 2000).

81. George Packard and Jim Pickard, 'Jeremy Corbyn Faces Birth Pangs of New Politics', *Financial Times*, 15 September 2015.
82. This account of what politics involves is taken from Bernard Crick's seminal *In Defence of Politics* (Chicago: University of Chicago Press, 1962). My colleague Matt Flinders has provided a Crick-inspired defence of politics and politicians. Politics, he writes, 'is about reconciling the irreconcilable, bashing square pegs into round holes, and squaring circles whilst at the same time achieving a degree of consent'. Matthew Flinders, *Defending Politics* (Oxford: Oxford University Press, 2012), 53.
83. David Blunkett, *In Defence of Politics Revisited* (2012), 11–12. Available via: https://gruposhumanidades14.files.wordpress.com/2014/01/david-bucklett-in-defence-of-politics-revisited.pdf
84. Tony Blair, *The Journey* (London: Hutchinson, 2010), 173. *Sky News*, 'Blair Sorry Over IRA Fugitive Letter Blunder', 13 January 2015.
85. In August 2015, the Chief Constable of the Police Service of Northern Ireland stated that whilst much of the structure of the IRA remains in place, it no longer exists as a paramilitary organization and that the group is committed to a peaceful political path. Vincent Kearney, 'NI Paramilitary Report: Does IRA "Army Council" still Exist?', *BBC News*, 20 October 2015.
86. NatCen British Social Attitudes Survey, 33 (2016), 'Politics', 26.
87. Curtice and Ormston (eds), *British Social Attitudes: The 32nd Report*, 131.
88. Richard Keen and Lukas Audickas, 'Membership of UK Political Parties', House of Commons Library Briefing Paper, SN05125 (August 2016), 3.
89. The number of people who say that they have signed a petition in the previous year fell slightly between 2004 and 2014 (despite the proliferation of on-line petitions). The numbers who say that they have donated money or raised funds for a political cause; contacted a politician or a civil servant to express their views; or attended a political meeting or rally have increased. Curtice and Ormston (eds), *British Social Attitudes: The 32nd Report*, 127.
90. Matt Ford, 'Europe's Democratic Deficit is Getting Worse', *The Atlantic*, 23 May 2014.
91. Nick Clegg, *Politics: Between the Extremes* (London: Penguin, 2016), 212.
92. Raymond Aron, *Thinking Politically: A Liberal in the Age of Ideology* (London: Transaction Publishers, 1997), 242.
93. Brand, *Revolution* (from the inside cover of the book).

Note to figure caption

1. These data have been downloaded via the on-line dashboard function of the Manifesto Project Database. Available via: https://visuals.manifesto-project.wzb.eu/mpdb-shiny/cmp_dashboard/

CHAPTER 9. CONCLUSION

1. Philip Tetlock, *Expert Political Judgment: How Good is It?* (Princeton: Princeton University Press, 2005). The difficulties involved in predicting what is going to

happen mean that any claims of expertise need to be treated with caution. This does not, however, mean that expertise itself is of no value. The British people may indeed, as Michael Gove suggested, have had enough of experts. But this is not necessarily a good thing. Henry Mance, 'Britain has had Enough of Experts, Says Gove', *Financial Times*, 3 June 2016.

2. Katie Forster, 'David Cameron's First Words when he Realised he had Lost the EU Referendum', *Independent*, 2 July 2016.
3. Matthew Flinders, 'Dear Russell Brand: On the Politics of Comedy and Disengagement', LSE Blog, 31 October 2013.
4. In 1987, 46% of voters expressed either a 'very' or 'fairly' strong identification with a particular political party. By 2015, this had fallen to 41%. NatCen's British Social Attitudes Survey, 33 (2016), 'Politics', 15.
5. David Marquand, *The Progressive Dilemma: From Lloyd George to Blair* (London: Heinemann, 1991). There is an interesting interview with Marquand about the progressive dilemma and post-2010 politics on the Our Kingdom website. https://www.opendemocracy.net/ourkingdom/david-marquand/david-marquand-on-post-election-progressive-dilemmas.
6. Winning elections and retaining office requires a great deal of what the late James Bulpitt called 'statecraft'. Successful parties need to know when they can manage to change the public's views on an issue; when they can prosper despite their policies being at odds with public opinion; and when they need to compromise with the electorate. They need to be able to ruthlessly expose their opponents' divisions and inconsistencies. They need to be able to push to the very front of the campaign agenda those issues on which they have the largest polling leads. They need to be able to successfully project an image of their leader as caring and in touch with the concerns of ordinary people but decisive and strong. They need to be able to sideline internal opposition. They need to maintain good working relationships with potential coalition partners. They need to be able to acquire valued endorsements. They need to be able to offer some clear policy alternatives to the opposition party whilst not offering too many policy hostages to fortune. Above all—and looking back once again at Figure 3.1 and people's self-placement along the ideological spectrum—parties need to be able to credibly present themselves as moderate and firmly anchored to the political centre-ground and their opponents as crazed ideologues. Jim Bulpitt, 'The Discipline of the New Democracy: Mrs Thatcher's Domestic Statecraft', *Political Studies*, 34 (1986), pp. 19–39.
7. Nick Srnicek and Alex Williams, *Inventing the Future* (London: Verso, 2015). I disagree with a lot of what the authors of this book have to say about neo-liberalism. But I find their analysis of what is wrong with a lot of the left in the first two chapters of their book very convincing.

Index